Complete MathSmart

Grade 4

Consultant: Ann Bobker

Printed in China

Contents

Section I

Section II

Section I

Overview

In Grade 3, students practised the four basic arithmetic operations and were introduced to mixed operations and using brackets with whole numbers. In Grade 4, these skills are further developed and practised.

In Section I, the emphasis is placed on Multiplication and Division. Students are given ample opportunity to learn the multiplication and division facts to 81, and to see the relationship between multiplication and division operations. They learn to multiply 2- and 3-digit numbers by 1-digit numbers, to multiply 2-digit numbers by 2-digit numbers, and to understand the concept of a multiple.

They practise multiplying by 10, 100 and 1000.

They also learn to divide 2-, 3- and 4-digit numbers by 1-digit numbers with or without a remainder.

1 Multiplication Facts to 81

EXAMPLES

1. 5 groups of 2 = 5 twos = 5 times 2 = 5 × 2 = 2 + 2 + 2 + 2 + 2 = 10
2. 2 groups of 5 = 2 fives = 2 times 5 = 2 × 5 = 5 + 5 = 10

HINTS:

- Multiplication is a short way to add groups of the same size.
- "x" means "MULTIPLY".
- Multiplication facts can be written in 2 different ways.

  e.g. 2 × 5 = 10 (2 and 5 ↑ factors; 10 ↑ product) or 5 x 2 = 10 (written vertically)

- Changing the order of multiplication does not affect the product.

  e.g. 2 × 5 = 5 × 2 = 10

Multiply.

① 4 x 3 = 12	② 5 x 6 = 30		
③ 9 x 7 = 63	④ 3 x 8 = 24		
⑤ 2 x 6 = 12	⑥ 7 x 4 = 28		
⑦ 0 x 4 = 0	⑧ 1 x 5 = 5	⑨ 6 x 6 = 36	⑩ 7 x 7 = 49
⑪ 6 x 3 = 18	⑫ 7 x 2 = 14	⑬ 8 x 5 = 40	⑭ 3 x 9 = 27
⑮ 5 x 9 = 45	⑯ 7 x 0 = 0	⑰ 4 x 8 = 32	⑱ 9 x 9 = 81

Write 2 multiplication sentences for each picture.

⑲

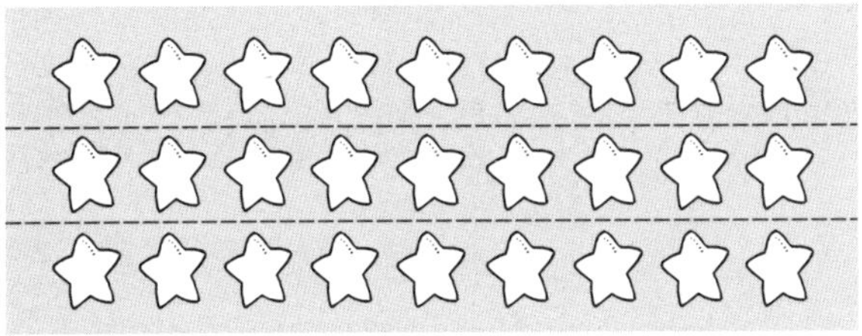

3 x 9 = 27

9 x 3 = 27

⑳

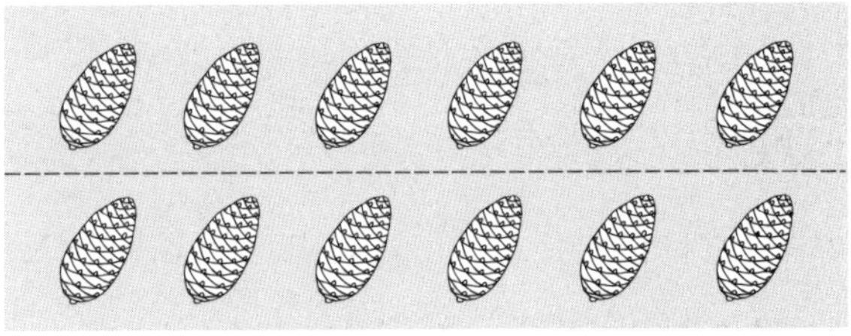

2 x 6 = 12

6 x 2 = 12

㉑

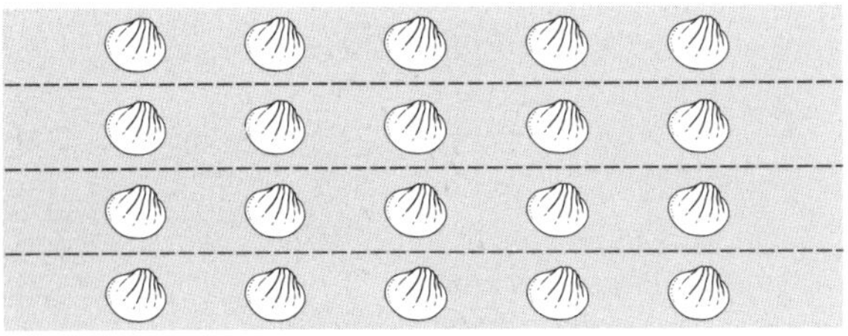

4 x 5 = 20

5 x 4 = 20

㉒

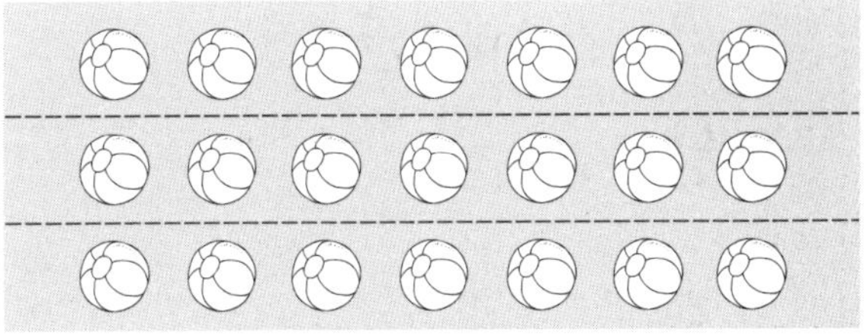

3 x 7 = 21

7 x 3 = 21

Complete the following multiplication sentences.

㉓ 7 x 9 = 63

㉔ 5 x 2 = 10

㉕ 1 x 3 = 3

㉖ 6 x 0 = 0

㉗ 8 x 4 = 32

㉘ 5 x 7 = 35

㉙ 2 x 4 = 8

㉚ 6 x 6 = 36

㉛ 6 x 8 = 48

㉜ 3 x 7 = 21

㉝ 4 x 5 = 20

㉞ 9 x 2 = 18

㉟ 0 x 3 x 6 = 0

㊱ 8 x 1 x 6 = ~~12~~ 15

㊲ 1 x 7 x 8 = 56

㊳ 5 x 4 x 0 = 0

㊴ 4 x 7 = 7 x ______
= ______

㊵ 5 x ______ = ______ x 5
= 40

㊶ 3 x 3 = ______ x 9
= ______

㊷ 8 x ______ = 0 x 4
= ______

In each group, put a ✗ in the ◯ beside the number sentence that is different.

㊸ A. 7 x 6 (X) B. 7 + 6 (X) C. 6 sevens ◯ D. 7 groups of 6 ◯	㊹ A. 5 threes ◯ B. 3 x 5 ◯ C. 5 + 5 + 5 + 5 + 5 (X) D. 3 times 5 ◯
㊺ A. 4 + 4 + 4 + 4 (X) B. 4 ones (X) C. 1 x 4 ◯ D. 1 group of 4 ◯	㊻ A. 5 times 6 ◯ B. 5 + 5 + 5 + 5 + 5 (X) C. 6 groups of 5 ◯ D. 6 x 5 ◯

Fill in the missing numbers.

㊼ 10 15 <u>20</u> <u>25</u> <u>30</u> 35 <u>40</u> <u>45</u>

㊽ 9 ____ 27 ____ ____ 54 ____ ____

㊾ ____ ____ 28 35 ____ ____ 56 ____

Circle the correct answers.

㊿ When a number is multiplied by these numbers, the products are always even numbers.

0 1 2 3 4 5 6 7 8 9

51. When a number is multiplied by 5, these numbers are at the ones place of the product.

0 1 2 3 4 5 6 7 8 9

52. When a number is multiplied by this number, the product is always zero.

0 1 2 3 4 5 6 7 8 9

Solve the problems. Show your work.

53. A dragonfly has 4 wings. How many wings do 7 dragonflies have?

    7 dragonflies have __28__ wings.

54. May plants 8 rows of tulips in the garden. There are 9 tulips in a row. How many tulips does May plant?

    May plants __72__ tulips.

55. There are 3 hands on a clock. How many hands are there on 6 clocks?

    There are __18__ hands on 6 clocks.

56. The teacher has 7 boxes of crayons. Each box contains 8 crayons. How many crayons does the teacher have?

    The teacher has ______ crayons.

57. A bag of cookies contains 4 different shapes. There are 6 cookies for each shape. How many cookies are there in the bag?

    There are ______ cookies in the bag.

Complete the puzzles.

Put 1, 2, 3, 4 or 5 in each of the five boxes in each diagram, so that adding the numbers either vertically or horizontally will give the sum indicated for each diagram.

① sum = 8 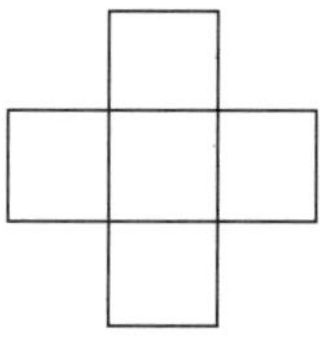

② sum = 9 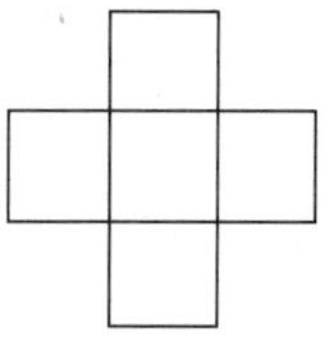

③ sum = 10 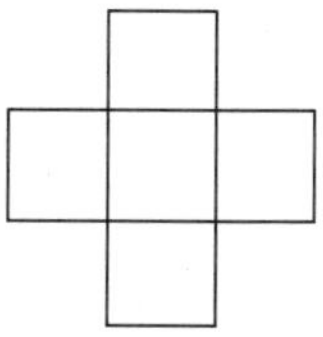

2 Multiplication and Division Fact Families

EXAMPLES

1. 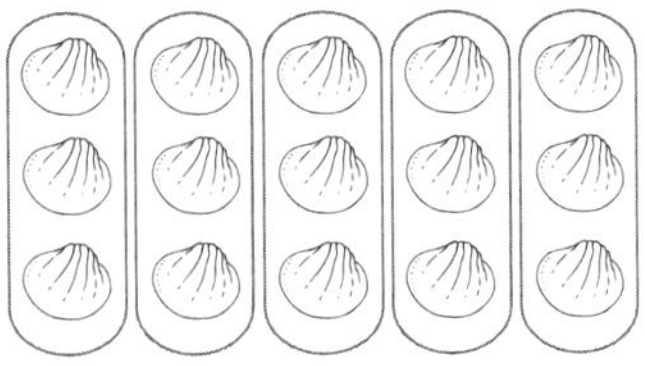

There are 5 groups of 3 .
5 x 3 = 15 There are 15 .

Divide 15 into 5 groups.
15 ÷ 5 = 3 Each group has 3 .

2. 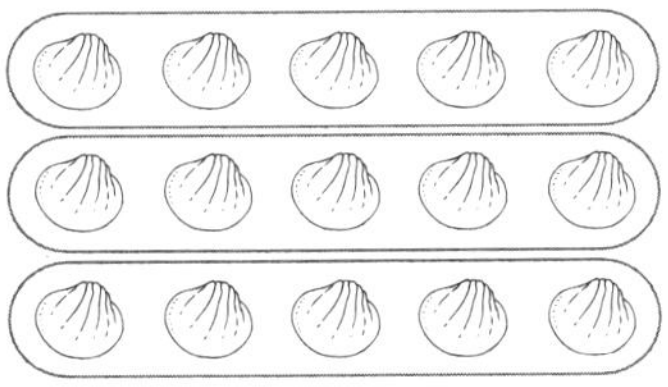

There are 3 groups of 5 .
3 x 5 = 15 There are 15 .

Divide 15 into 3 groups.
15 ÷ 3 = 5 Each group has 5 .

HINTS:

- There are 2 multiplication facts and 2 division facts for a fact family using the same 3 numbers.

e.g.
5 x 3 = 15
3 x 5 = 15
15 ÷ 3 = 5
15 ÷ 5 = 3

Write a multiplication sentence and a division sentence for each picture.

① 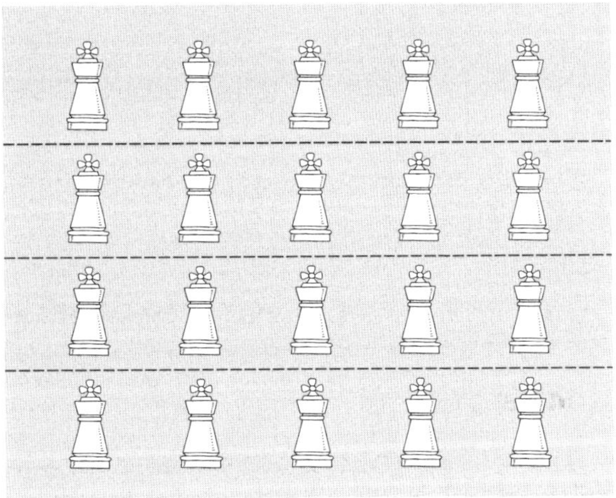

_______ X _______ = _______

_______ ÷ _______ = _______

② 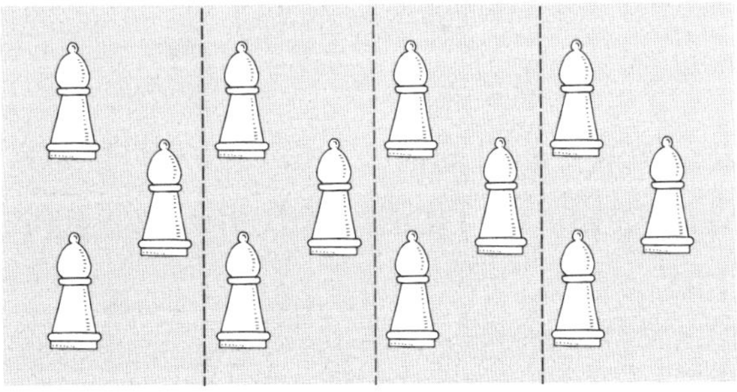

_______ X _______ = _______

_______ ÷ _______ = _______

③ 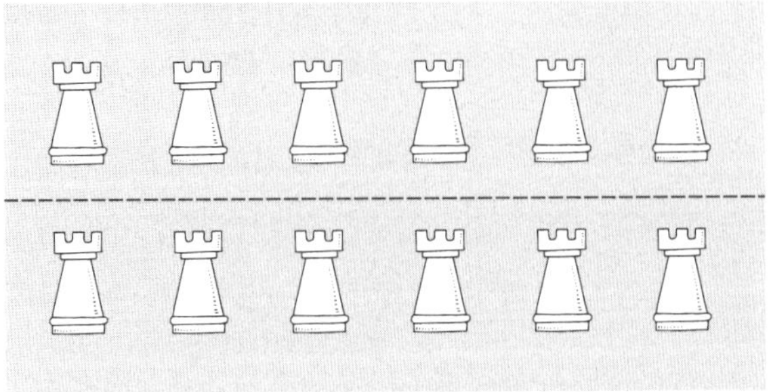

_______ X _______ = _______

_______ ÷ _______ = _______

Find the products. Then write the related multiplication and division sentences.

④ $7 \times 6 =$ ______ ______ ______ ______	⑤ $9 \times 8 =$ ______ ______ ______ ______	⑥ $4 \times 9 =$ ______ ______ ______ ______
⑦ $5 \times 8 =$ ______ ______ ______ ______	⑧ $6 \times 9 =$ ______ ______ ______ ______	⑨ $7 \times 8 =$ ______ ______ ______ ______
⑩ $9 \times 7 =$ ______ ______ ______ ______	⑪ $8 \times 6 =$ ______ ______ ______ ______	⑫ $9 \times 5 =$ ______ ______ ______ ______

Write the fact families for each group of numbers.

⑬ 5 6 30

____ X ____ = ____

____ X ____ = ____

____ ÷ ____ = ____

____ ÷ ____ = ____

⑭ 9 3 27

____ X ____ = ____

____ X ____ = ____

____ ÷ ____ = ____

____ ÷ ____ = ____

Find the quotients using multiplication facts.

⑮ 2 x 8 = 16 16 ÷ 2 = ______ 16 ÷ 8 = ______	⑯ 3 x 7 = 21 21 ÷ 3 = ______ 21 ÷ 7 = ______	⑰ 4 x 5 = 20 20 ÷ 4 = ______ 20 ÷ 5 = ______
⑱ 8 x 3 = 24 24 ÷ 3 = ______ 24 ÷ 8 = ______	⑲ 5 x 6 = 30 30 ÷ 5 = ______ 30 ÷ 6 = ______	⑳ 4 x 3 = 12 12 ÷ 4 = ______ 12 ÷ 3 = ______

Complete the multiplication and division sentences.

㉑ 7 x 8 = ______ 56 ÷ 8 = ______	㉒ 9 x 2 = ______ 18 ÷ 9 = ______	㉓ 5 x 8 = ______ 40 ÷ 8 = ______
㉔ 6 x 3 = ______ 18 ÷ 3 = ______	㉕ 5 x 7 = ______ 35 ÷ 7 = ______	㉖ 7 x 4 = ______ 28 ÷ 7 = ______

Fill in the missing numbers.

㉗ ______ x 5 = 45 45 ÷ 5 = ______	㉘ 6 x ______ = 24 24 ÷ ______ = 6	㉙ ______ x 4 = 32 32 ÷ ______ = 4
㉚ 7 x ______ = 35 35 ÷ ______ = 7	㉛ ______ x 4 = 36 36 ÷ 4 = ______	㉜ ______ x 3 = 27 27 ÷ 3 = ______
㉝ ______ x 9 = 63 63 ÷ 9 = ______	㉞ 2 x ______ = 14 14 ÷ ______ = 2	㉟ 6 x ______ = 18 18 ÷ ______ = 6
㊱ 5 x ______ = 15 15 ÷ ______ = 5	㊲ ______ x 6 = 42 42 ÷ 6 = ______	㊳ 7 x ______ = 56 56 ÷ ______ = 7

Write a multiplication sentence and a division sentence for each story.

㊴	Sally has 56 flowers. She puts 7 flowers in a vase. There are 8 vases. ______ x ______ = ______ ______ ÷ ______ = ______
㊵	Ted has 72 stamps. He puts 9 stamps on each page of his album. There are 8 pages of stamps. ______ x ______ = ______ ______ ÷ ______ = ______
㊶	8 children share 48 lollipops equally. Each child has 6 lollipops. ______ x ______ = ______ ______ ÷ ______ = ______

Solve the problems.

㊷ A bag of marbles is shared equally among 9 children. Each child has 6 marbles. If it is shared among 6 children, each child will have ______ marbles.

㊸ Jonathan puts his baseball cards equally in 5 boxes. Each box contains 9 cards. If he puts the cards in 9 boxes, each box will contain ______ cards.

Complete the puzzles.

Put 1, 2, 3, 4, 5, 6, 7, 8 or 9 in each of the nine boxes in each diagram, so that adding the numbers horizontally, vertically or diagonally will give the sum indicated for each diagram.

① sum= 12

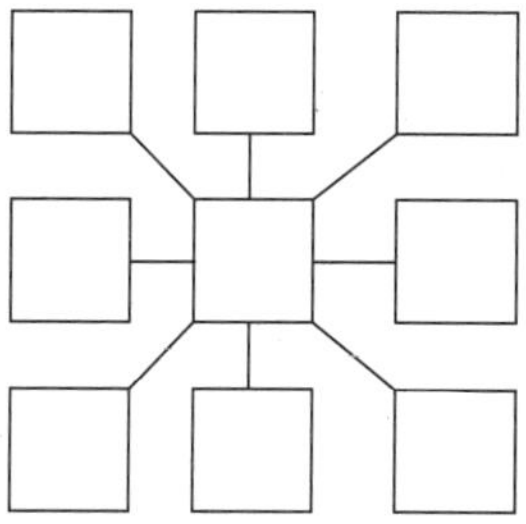

② sum= 15

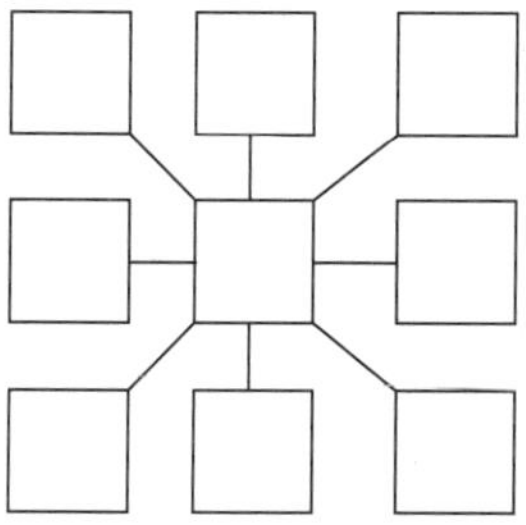

③ sum= 18

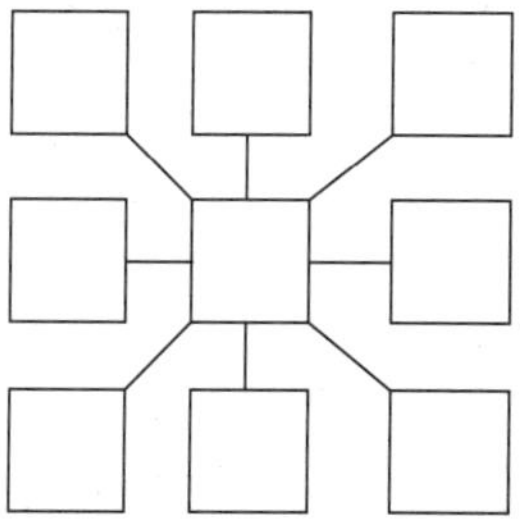

3 Division Facts to 81

EXAMPLES

Sally has 15 stickers.

1. Divide the stickers in groups of 5. How many groups are there?

   $15 \div 5 = 3$

   There are 3 groups.

2. Divide the stickers into 3 groups. How many stickers are there in each group?

   $15 \div 3 = 5$

   There are 5 stickers in each group.

HINTS:

- To divide is to share things equally into groups of the same size.
- "÷" means DIVIDE.
- Division facts can be written in 2 different ways.

  e.g. $15 \div 5 = 3$ (15 = dividend, 5 = divisor, 3 = quotient) or $5\overline{)15}$ with quotient 3 above and 15 below (align the numbers on the right-hand side)

- Do the division by recalling the multiplication facts.

  e.g. $15 \div 5 = ?$

  recall $5 \times 3 = 15$

  so $15 \div 5 = 3$

Do the division.

① $9\overline{)63}$

② $6\overline{)48}$

③ $7\overline{)42}$

④ $5\overline{)35}$

⑤ $3\overline{)24}$

⑥ $6\overline{)36}$

⑦ $2\overline{)18}$

⑧ $4\overline{)32}$

⑨ $1\overline{)5}$

⑩ $8\overline{)56}$

⑪ $6\overline{)42}$

⑫ $9\overline{)0}$

⑬ $7\overline{)63}$

⑭ $5\overline{)30}$

⑮ $3\overline{)21}$

⑯ $5\overline{)25}$

⑰ $9\overline{)45}$

⑱ $4\overline{)28}$

Write 2 division sentences for each picture.

⑲

______ ÷ ______ = ______

______ ÷ ______ = ______

⑳

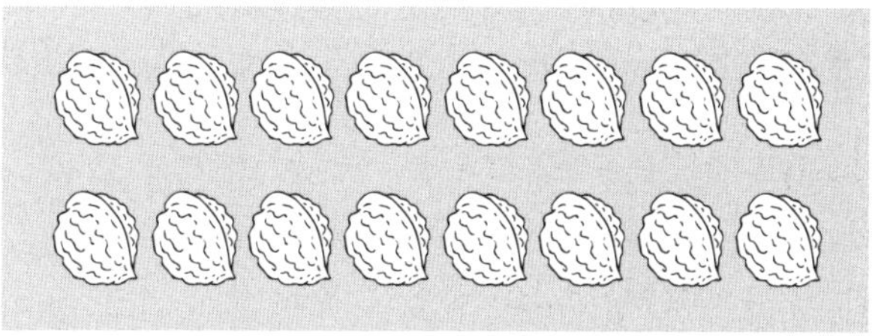

______ ÷ ______ = ______

______ ÷ ______ = ______

㉑

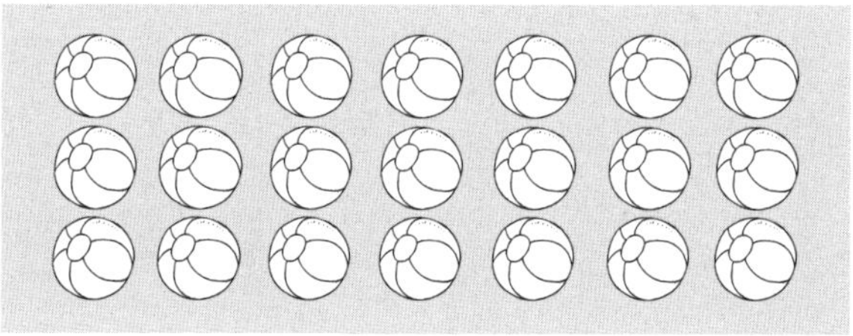

______ ÷ ______ = ______

______ ÷ ______ = ______

㉒

______ ÷ ______ = ______

______ ÷ ______ = ______

Complete the division sentences.

㉓ 63 ÷ 7 = ______

63 ÷ ______ = 7

㉖ 40 ÷ 5 = ______

40 ÷ ______ = 5

㉙ 72 ÷ 9 = ______

72 ÷ ______ = 9

㉜ 5 ÷ 1 = ______

5 ÷ ______ = 1

㉟ 3 ÷ 3 = ______

3 ÷ ______ = 3

㉔ 32 ÷ 8 = ______

32 ÷ ______ = 8

㉗ 20 ÷ 4 = ______

20 ÷ ______ = 4

㉚ 12 ÷ 2 = ______

12 ÷ ______ = 2

㉝ 35 ÷ 7 = ______

35 ÷ ______ = 7

㊱ 25 ÷ 5 = ______

25 ÷ ______ = 5

㉕ 6 ÷ 6 = ______

6 ÷ ______ = 6

㉘ 18 ÷ 3 = ______

18 ÷ ______ = 3

㉛ 64 ÷ 8 = ______

64 ÷ ______ = 8

㉞ 16 ÷ 4 = ______

16 ÷ ______ = 4

㊲ 30 ÷ 6 = ______

30 ÷ ______ = 6

Match the quotient with the division sentences in each group. Circle the correct letters.

38 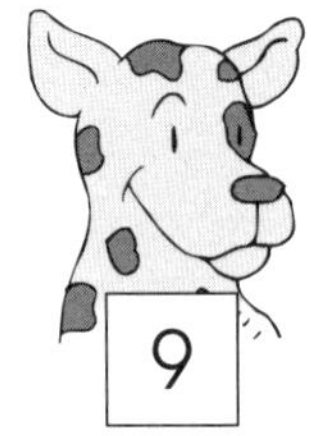

A. $54 \div 6$ | B. $56 \div 7$ | C. $18 \div 2$

39 

A. $48 \div 8$ | B. $40 \div 5$ | C. $72 \div 9$

40 

A. $63 \div 9$ | B. $21 \div 3$ | C. $35 \div 7$

41 

A. $14 \div 2$ | B. $48 \div 8$ | C. $24 \div 4$

42 

A. $45 \div 9$ | B. $10 \div 2$ | C. $24 \div 6$

43 

A. $32 \div 8$ | B. $15 \div 3$ | C. $20 \div 5$

44 

A. $20 \div 5$ | B. $27 \div 9$ | C. $24 \div 8$

45 

A. $18 \div 9$ | B. $18 \div 6$ | C. $14 \div 7$

Solve the problems. Show your work.

㊻ The gardener planted 72 pine trees in 9 rows. How many pine trees were planted in each row?

________ pine trees were planted in each row.

㊼ May puts 32 books equally on 4 shelves. How many books are there on each shelf?

㊽ Ted has 18 socks. How many pairs of socks does he have?

㊾ Mom divides 54 chocolates among Sally and her 5 friends. How many chocolates does each child get?

㊿ Tom buys 5 boxes of coloured pencils for $40. What is the price of 1 box of coloured pencils?

Solve the puzzle.

A, B, C, D, E and F participated in a badminton competition. A ⟶ B means A won the match. Find out from the diagram who did not win a single match .

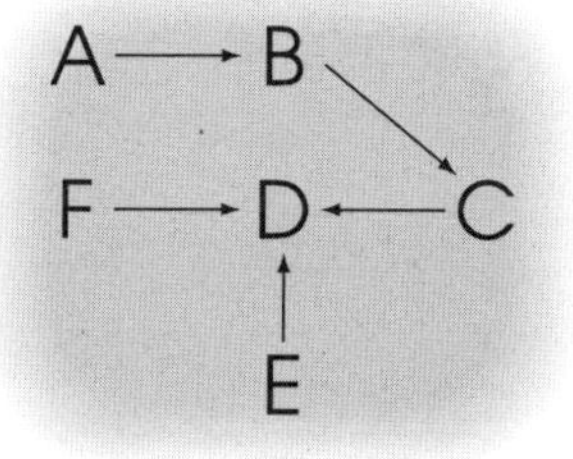

________ did not win a single match.

4 Multiplying by 10, 100 or 1000

EXAMPLES

1. 3 x 10 = 10 x 3 = 30 ← the number of zeros in the product equals the number of zeros in the factors
   3 x 100 = 100 x 3 = 300
   3 x 1000 = 1000 x 3 = 3000

2. 3 x 3 x 10 = 9 x 10 = 90

3. 3 x 30 = 3 x 3 x 10 = 9 x 10 = 90

HINTS:

- The product of multiplying a number by 10, 100 or 1000 can be found by writing 1, 2 or 3 zeros to the right of that number.

  e.g.
  3 x 10 = 10 x 3 = 30
  = 3 tens
  3 x 100 = 100 x 3 = 300
  = 3 hundreds
  3 x 1000 = 1000 x 3 = 3000
  = 3 thousands
  13 x 10 = 10 x 13 = 130
  = 13 tens
  23 x 100 = 100 x 23 = 2300
  = 23 hundreds
  33 x 1000 = 1000 x 33 = 33000
  = 33 thousands

- To calculate the product of a number and multiples of 10, 100 or 1000:
  First multiply the digits in front of the zeros. Then write the same number of zeros as in the factors at the end of the product.

  e.g. 3 x 30   3 times 3 tens
  = 3 x 3 x 10   = 9 tens
  = 9 x 10   = 90
  = 90

- Estimate the products by rounding the numbers to the nearest ten, hundred or thousand.

  e.g 56 x 7 = ? **estimate** 60 x 7 = 420
  325 x 4 = ? **estimate** 300 x 4 = 1200

Find the products mentally.

① 10 x 5 = ______

② 6 x 100 = ______

③ 7 x 100 = ______

④ 100 x 9 = ______

⑤ 8 x 10 = ______

⑥ 0 x 1000 = ______

⑦ 10 x 14 = ______

⑧ 13 x 100 = ______

⑨ 7 x 1000 = ______

⑩ 100 x 32 = ______

⑪ 25 x 100 = ______

⑫ 6 x 100 = ______

⑬ 100 x 8 = ______

⑭ 10 x 0 = ______

⑮ 1000 x 6 = ______

Find the products.

⑯ 2 x 20 = 40	⑰ 4 x 30 = 120	⑱ 3 x 20 = ____
⑲ 4 x 20 = ____	⑳ 2 x 30 = ____	㉑ 3 x 30 = ____
㉒ 2 x 40 = ____	㉓ 3 x 60 = ____	㉔ 5 x 20 = ____
㉕ 4 x 40 = ____	㉖ 5 x 30 = ____	㉗ 6 x 30 = ____
㉘ 2 x 70 = ____	㉙ 3 x 80 = ____	㉚ 4 x 60 = ____

㉛ 60 x 2	㉜ 70 x 3	㉝ 50 x 4	㉞ 30 x 6
㉟ 80 x 4	㊱ 50 x 5	㊲ 40 x 7	㊳ 90 x 2
㊴ 50 x 8	㊵ 90 x 4	㊶ 60 x 6	㊷ 30 x 9
㊸ 20 x 8	㊹ 30 x 8	㊺ 80 x 6	㊻ 60 x 9

Find the answers.

㊼ 3 x 200 = 600	㊽ 2 x 3000 = 6000	㊾ 4 x 300 = ______
㊿ 5 x 300 = ______	51 3 x 2000 = ______	52 2 x 400 = ______
53 4 x 200 = ______	54 4 x 1000 = ______	55 5 x 200 = ______
56 6 x 300 = ______	57 5 x 700 = ______	58 3 x 3000 = ______
59 5 x 2000 = ______	60 6 x 400 = ______	61 8 x 300 = ______

62 200×8	63 1000×5	64 500×8
65 400×6	66 900×2	67 700×4
68 800×3	69 5000×2	70 900×4
71 700×2	72 600×9	73 2000×3

Estimate each product by rounding the 2-digit number to the nearest ten.

(74) 53 x 6 **estimate** 50 x 6 = ______

(75) 69 x 4 **estimate** 70 x 4 = ______

(76) 72 x 3 **estimate** ______ x 3 = ______

(77) 47 x 7 **estimate** ______ x 7 = ______

(78) 34 x 5 **estimate** ______ x 5 = ______

Estimate each product by rounding the 3-digit number to the nearest hundred or rounding the 4-digit number to the nearest thousand.

(79) 420 x 5 **estimate** 400 x 5 = ______

(80) 297 x 3 **estimate** 300 x 3 = ______

(81) 2875 x 2 **estimate** 3000 x 2 = ______

(82) 1365 x 5 **estimate** 1000 x 5 = ______

(83) 673 x 4 **estimate** ______ x 4 = ______

(84) 816 x 7 **estimate** ______ x 7 = ______

(85) 367 x 5 **estimate** ______ x 5 = ______

(86) 1792 x 3 **estimate** ______ x 3 = ______

(87) 3278 x 2 **estimate** ______ x 2 = ______

(88) 571 x 8 **estimate** ______ x 8 = ______

Think and write.

How many times does "5" appear in the numbers from 1 to 100?

"5" appears ______ times.

5 Multiplying 2-Digit Numbers by 1-Digit Numbers

EXAMPLE

4 x 23 = ?

Long way:

```
   2 3   ← align the numbers on the right-hand side
x    4
   1 2   ← 4 x 3  = 12
   8 0   ← 4 x 20 = 80
   9 2   ← 12 + 80 = 92
```

Short way:

```
   2 3            1              1
x    4    →     2 3     →      2 3
                x  4          x  4
                   2           9 2
```

align the numbers on the right-hand side

4 x 3 = 12
carry 10 ones to the tens column; keep 2 ones in the ones column

9 = 4 x 2 + 1
carried over from the ones column

4 x 23 = 92

HINTS:

- To do vertical multiplication the short way:

  Align all the numbers on the right-hand side.

  Multiply the ones first.

  Then multiply the tens.

  Remember to carry 10 ones to 1 ten in the tens column.

  Remember to add the tens carried over from the ones column after multiplying the tens digit.

Multiply the long way.

①
```
   1 2
x    4
  [   ]  ← 4 x 2
  [   ]  ← 4 x 10
  [   ]
```

②
```
   2 4
x    3
  [   ]
  [   ]
  [   ]
```

③
```
   3 2
x    4
```

④
```
   1 9
x    5
```

⑤
```
   3 1
x    6
```

⑥
```
   4 7
x    6
```

Do the multiplication the short way.

⑦ 34×4	⑧ 23×3	⑨ 37×4	⑩ 25×6
⑪ 32×9	⑫ 28×2	⑬ 57×7	⑭ 48×9
⑮ 65×6	⑯ 39×5	⑰ 53×8	⑱ 67×3
⑲ 46×8	⑳ 27×4	㉑ 77×5	㉒ 39×7
㉓ 18×9	㉔ 22×6	㉕ 81×9	㉖ 52×4
㉗ 35×6	㉘ 42×8	㉙ 63×9	㉚ 95×4
㉛ 72×7	㉜ 92×3	㉝ 25×8	㉞ 58×6

㉟ 88 x 6 = ______	㊱ 74 x 9 = ______	㊲ 43 x 8 = ______
㊳ 15 x 7 = ______	㊴ 21 x 5 = ______	㊵ 98 x 2 = ______

Find the products. Then write the letters in the boxes in ⑤⑦ to see what birthday gift May wants to receive.

41) 29 x 5 = ___ s	42) 73 x 4 = ___ t	43) 86 x 3 = ___ m	44) 45 x 6 = ___ n
45) 38 x 2 = ___ o	46) 16 x 9 = ___ l	47) 52 x 7 = ___ r	48) 66 x 6 = ___ p
49) 13 x 6 = ___ b	50) 92 x 3 = ___ c	51) 78 x 6 = ___ d	52) 22 x 8 = ___ q
53) 61 x 7 = ___ u	54) 59 x 4 = ___ v	55) 33 x 9 = ___ e	56) 46 x 7 = ___ w

57)

	276	76	258	396	427	292	297	364
A								.

Estimate first. Then find the products.

58) 68 x 9	estimate: 70 x 9	59) 37 x 4	estimate
60) 51 x 6	estimate	61) 83 x 5	estimate

Solve the problems. Show your work.

⑥② Mom bought 4 boxes of chocolate for May's birthday party. There were 36 chocolates in each box. How many chocolates did Mom buy? 4 x 36 = Mom bought ______ chocolates.	36 x 4 ______
⑥③ There were 24 party hats in a bag. How many party hats were there in 3 bags?	x ______
⑥④ Mom bought 2 bags of straws with 98 straws in each bag. How many straws did Mom buy?	x ______
⑥⑤ Ted and 5 friends each contributed $18 to buy a birthday gift for May. What was the cost of the birthday gift?	x ______
⑥⑥ May put 42 cookies on a plate. How many cookies were there on 4 plates?	x ______

Solve the problem.

Show how you can move the least number of beads to change the shape of the triangle on the left-hand side to that on the right-hand side.

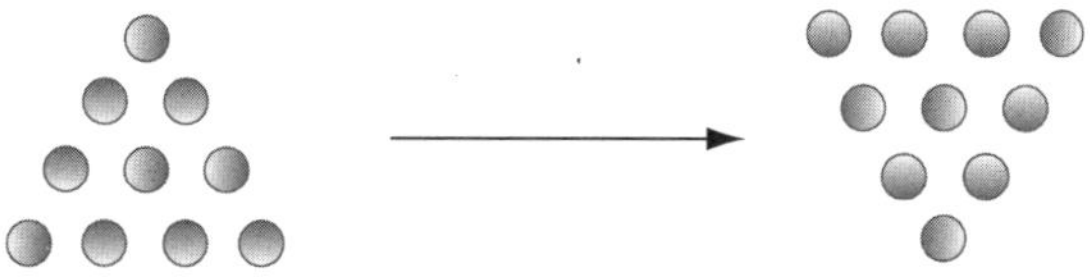

6 Multiplying 3-Digit Numbers by 1-Digit Numbers

EXAMPLE

3 x 174 = ?

Long way:

```
    1 7 4   ←— align the numbers on the right-hand side
x       3
    -----
      1 2   ←—3 x 4   = 12
    2 1 0   ←—3 x 70  = 210
    3 0 0   ←—3 x 100 = 300
    -----
    5 2 2   ←—12 + 210 + 300 = 522
```

Short way:

```
  1 7 4        1      2 1        2
x     3  →    1 7 4  →  1 7 4  →  1 7 4
-------     x     3   x     3   x     3
            -------   -------   -------
                  2       2 2     5 2 2
```

- align the numbers on the right-hand side
- 3 x 4 = 12: carry 10 ones to the tens column; keep 2 ones in the ones column
- 3 x 7 + 1 = 21 + 1 = 22 (1 carried over from the ones column): carry 2 hundreds to the hundreds column; keep 2 tens in the tens column
- 3 x 1 + 2 = 3 + 2 = 5 (2 carried over from the tens column)

3 x 174 = 522

HINTS:

- To do vertical multiplication the short way:

  Align all the numbers on the right-hand side.

  Multiply the ones first, then the tens, and finally the hundreds.

  Remember to carry 10 ones to 1 ten in the tens column and 10 tens to 1 hundred in the hundreds column.

  Don't forget to add the tens and hundreds carried over from the ones and the tens columns after multiplying the tens and hundreds digits.

Multiply the long way.

① 263 x 5

- ☐ ←— 5 x 3
- ☐ ←— 5 x 60
- ☐ ←— 5 x 200
- ☐

② 207 x 9

- ☐
- ☐
- ☐
- ☐

③ 128 x 4

- ☐
- ☐
- ☐
- ☐

④ 349 x 3

- ☐
- ☐
- ☐
- ☐

Do the multiplication the short way.

⑤ 463 x 5	⑥ 612 x 4	⑦ 575 x 2
⑧ 348 x 6	⑨ 405 x 4	⑩ 701 x 5
⑪ 315 x 3	⑫ 374 x 8	⑬ 169 x 6
⑭ 476 x 4	⑮ 502 x 9	⑯ 781 x 7
⑰ 236 x 4	⑱ 677 x 8	⑲ 564 x 7
⑳ 804 x 5	㉑ 369 x 3	㉒ 911 x 6
㉓ 749 x 2	㉔ 183 x 4	㉕ 480 x 5

㉖ 7 x 142 = ________	㉗ 9 x 313 = ________
㉘ 3 x 569 = ________	㉙ 428 x 8 = ________

Find the products. Write the letters in ㊷ to solve the riddle.

㉚ 607 x 5 c	㉛ 526 x 4 i	㉜ 238 x 6 l
㉝ 193 x 7 d	㉞ 346 x 8 e	㉟ 472 x 9 o
㊱ 845 x 2 u	㊲ 756 x 3 n	㊳ 906 x 4 m
㊴ 287 x 8 t	㊵ 632 x 7 s	㊶ 394 x 9 r

Riddle: A large reptile that lives in the rainforest.

㊷

A

3035	3546	4248	3035	4248	1351	2104	1428	2768

.

Estimate first. Then calculate the products.

㊸ 365 x 4	estimate 400 x 4	㊹ 723 x 6	estimate
㊺ 589 x 3	estimate	㊻ 912 x 2	estimate

Solve the problems. Show your work.

㊼ A bag of potato chips weighs 225 g. What is the total weight of 4 bags of potato chips? The total weight of 4 bags of potato chips is __________ .	225 x 4
㊽ A box of sugar contains 125 packets. How many packets are there in 6 boxes?	x
㊾ The capcity of one can of pop is 355 mL. How many mL of pop are there in 6 cans?	x
㊿ Ted drinks 1 box of juice each day. If the capacity of a box of juice is 250 mL, how many mL of juice does Ted drink in one week?	x

Solve the problem.

Write 2 to 11 in the circles so that the sum of the numbers at the centre and the 4 corners of each rectangle is 27.

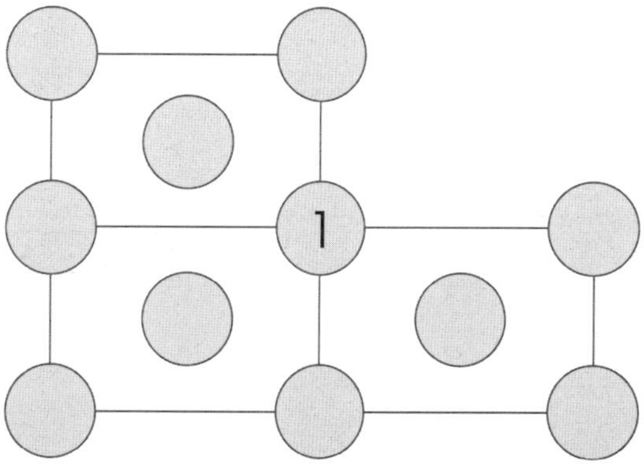

7 Multiplying 2-Digit Numbers by 2-Digit Numbers

EXAMPLES

1. 20 x 40 = 20 x 4 x 10 = 80 x 10 = 800
2. 23 x 40 = 23 x 4 x 10 = 92 x 10 = 920
3. 23 x 46 = 1058

```
      4 6  ←— align the numbers on
  x   2 3       the right-hand side
  -------
    1 3 8  ←— 3 x 46 = 138
    9 2 0  ←— 20 x 46 = 920
  -------
  1 0 5 8  ←— 138 + 920 = 1058
```

HINTS:

- To multiply a 2-digit number by another 2-digit number:

  Align the numbers on the right-hand side.

  Multiply the first 2-digit number by the ones digit and then by the tens digit of the second 2-digit number.

  Add the products to get the final answer.

- Don't forget to put a zero under the ones column when multiplying by the tens digit.
- To multiply 2 multiples of 10, multiply the digits at the tens column and write 2 zeros to the right of that product.

  e.g. 20 x 40 = 800

  2 x 4 = 8 — 2 zeros to the right of 8

Complete the multiplication.

① 35 x 17

☐ ←— 7 x 35

☐ ←— 10 x 35

☐

② 26 x 43

☐ ←— 3 x 26

☐ ←— 40 x 26

☐

③ 37 x 54

④ 81 x 42

⑤ 36 x 73

⑥ 13 x 41

Find the products.

⑦ 30 x 50 = ______	⑧ 60 x 20 = ______	⑨ 10 x 80 = ______
⑩ 40 x 70 = ______	⑪ 20 x 30 = ______	⑫ 50 x 20 = ______
⑬ 50 x 80 = ______	⑭ 40 x 90 = ______	⑮ 30 x 40 = ______
⑯ 20 x 90 = ______	⑰ 70 x 30 = ______	⑱ 60 x 70 = ______
⑲ 60 x 30 = ______	⑳ 80 x 20 = ______	㉑ 50 x 60 = ______

Do the multiplication. Show your work.

㉒ 25 x 24	㉓ 93 x 36	㉔ 45 x 64	㉕ 52 x 27
㉖ 56 x 22	㉗ 16 x 47	㉘ 82 x 37	㉙ 61 x 98
㉚ 73 x 28	㉛ 42 x 81	㉜ 38 x 55	㉝ 69 x 12
㉞ 58 x 48	㉟ 62 x 76	㊱ 32 x 28	㊲ 95 x 18

Write your answers in the puzzle below.

ACROSS

A. 25 x 25

C. 92 x 65

D. 21 x 33

G. 28 x 55

DOWN

B. 81 x 34

D. 71 x 85

E. 65 x 48

F. 21 x 41

38

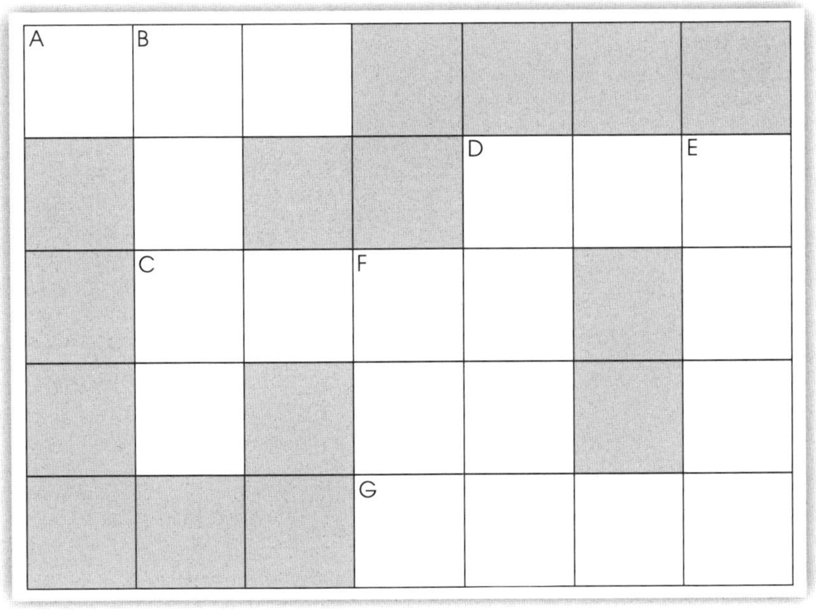

Estimate first. Then find the products.

39 $\begin{array}{r} 38 \\ \times\ 42 \\ \hline \end{array}$	estimate $\begin{array}{r} 40 \\ \times\ 40 \\ \hline \end{array}$	40 $\begin{array}{r} 92 \\ \times\ 66 \\ \hline \end{array}$	estimate
41 $\begin{array}{r} 47 \\ \times\ 59 \\ \hline \end{array}$	estimate	42 $\begin{array}{r} 73 \\ \times\ 21 \\ \hline \end{array}$	estimate
43 $\begin{array}{r} 89 \\ \times\ 14 \\ \hline \end{array}$	estimate	44 $\begin{array}{r} 63 \\ \times\ 35 \\ \hline \end{array}$	estimate

Solve the problems. Show your work.

45. There are 32 classes in May's school. Each class has 26 students. How many students are there in May's school?

There are ________ students in May's school.

46. May receives $35 pocket money each month. How much pocket money does she receive in one year?

47. There are 28 rows of 42 seats in the school theatre. How many seats are there in the school theatre?

48. Ted's school is organizing a fundraising campaign. Each of the 48 classes raises $90. What will be the total amount raised in the campaign?

How many possible routes are there for Little Squirrel to get the walnut? (Little Squirrel cannot move backward.)

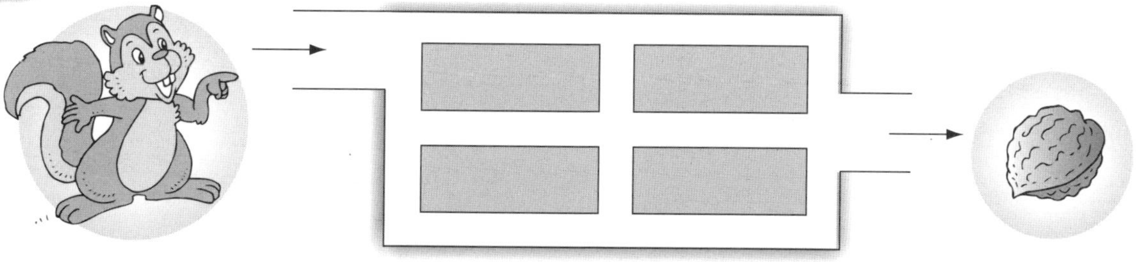

There are ________ possible routes.

8 More Multiplying and Multiples

EXAMPLES

1. How many stickers are there in all?

   5 x 4 x 3 = 20 x 3 = 60

   There are 60 stickers in all.

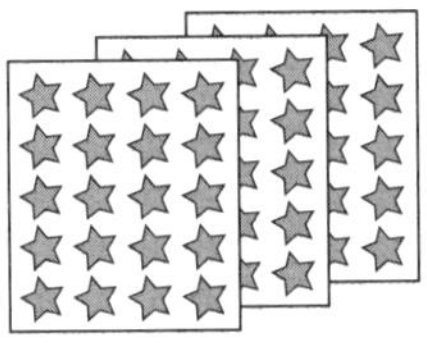

2. 5 x 4 x 3 = 5 x 12 = 60
3. Show all the multiples of 3 up to 20.

3	6	9	12	15	18
↑	↑	↑	↑	↑	↑
3 x 1	3 x 2	3 x 3	3 x 4	3 x 5	3 x 6

HINTS:

- The product of 3 factors remains the same if the order of multiplication is changed.

  e.g. 5 x 4 x 3 = 3 x 4 x 5 = 3 x 5 x 4
  = 4 x 5 x 3 = 4 x 3 x 5
  = 5 x 3 x 4
  = 60

- If possible, multiply the numbers with a product of 10, 20, 30 ... etc. first, and then multiply the 3rd number.
- Multiples of a number can be obtained by multiplying the number by 1, 2, 3 ... and so on.

Find the products.

① 2 x 3 x 6 = ________

② 5 x 6 x 7 = ________

③ 6 x 7 x 8 = ________

④ 7 x 8 x 9 = ________

⑤ 7 x 2 x 9 = ________

⑥ 6 x 3 x 4 = ________

⑦ 5 x 2 x 3 = ________

⑧ 9 x 3 x 5 = ________

⑨ 6 x 4 x 8 = ________

⑩ 7 x 2 x 8 = ________

⑪ 9 x 5 x 6 = ________

⑫ 4 x 6 x 7 = ________

⑬ 3 x 8 x 5 = ________

⑭ 6 x 2 x 9 = ________

⑮ 14 x 2 x 8 = ________

⑯ 13 x 7 x 9 = ________

⑰ 8 x 6 x 15 = ________

⑱ 11 x 3 x 7 = ________

⑲ 7 x 9 x 27 = ________

⑳ 5 x 16 x 4 = ________

㉑ 23 x 2 x 5 = ________

㉒ 6 x 8 x 31 = ________

㉓ 6 x 37 x 5 = ________

Help the students pick the balls they are going to colour. Write the numbers in the ◯ .

㉔ Ted is going to colour the balls which are multiples of 3 between 25 and 50.

㉕ May is going to colour the balls which are multiples of 4 up to 24.

㉖ Sally is going to colour the balls which are multiples of 5 and not yet coloured.

㉗ Tim is going to draw a red star on each of the balls which are multiples of 2 up to 25.

㉘ Ben is going to mark a black dot on each of the balls which are multiples of 2 between 25 and 50.

㉙ Bob is going to draw a brown dot on each of the balls which are multiples of 6.

㉚ Tom is asked to pick the balls which are multiples of 7.

Look at the 100-chart and complete the following questions.

1	2	3	4	5	6	7	8	9	10
11	12	13	14	15	16	17	18	19	20
21	22	23	24	25	26	27	28	29	30
31	32	33	34	35	36	37	38	39	40
41	42	43	44	45	46	47	48	49	50
51	52	53	54	55	56	57	58	59	60
61	62	63	64	65	66	67	68	69	70
71	72	73	74	75	76	77	78	79	80
81	82	83	84	85	86	87	88	89	90
91	92	93	94	95	96	97	98	99	100

31. The shaded numbers are multiples of ____________ .

32. Circle the multiples of 9.

33. Put a ✗ on each multiple of 10.

34. The multiples of 8 up to 60 are:

____

____________________ .

35. What is the largest multiple of 8 up to 100? ____________

36. What is the largest multiple of 9 up to 100? ____________

37. What is the largest multiple of 5 up to 80? ____________

38. What is the largest multiple of 7 up to 80? ____________

39. How many multiples of 8 are there in 100? ____________

40. How many multiples of 9 are there in 100? ____________

41. How many 3s are there in 30? ____________

42. How many 6s are there in 84? ____________

43. How many 2s are there in 30? ____________

44. How many 4s are there in 60? ____________

45. How many 5s are there in 75? ____________

List the first 5 multiples of the following numbers.

(46) 6 ______ ______ ______ ______ ______

(47) 11 ______ ______ ______ ______ ______

(48) 9 ______ ______ ______ ______ ______

(49) 12 ______ ______ ______ ______ ______

(50) 13 ______ ______ ______ ______ ______

(51) 15 ______ ______ ______ ______ ______

Solve the problems. Show your work.

(52) The children shared 2 boxes of chocolate among them. There were 5 rows of 6 chocolates in each box. How many chocolates were shared among the children?

______ chocolates were shared among the childrens.

(53) There are 3 rows of 4 tables in the school cafeteria. Each table can seat 8 students. How many students can the cafeteria hold?

(54) Mom plants 3 kinds of roses in the backyard. There are 2 rows of 6 rose bushes of each kind. How many rose bushes does Mom plant in the backyard?

(55) May drinks 2 full glasses of milk each day. The capacity of a glass is 70 mL. How many mL of milk does May drink in one week?

Just for Fun

Count the number of triangles in the diagram.

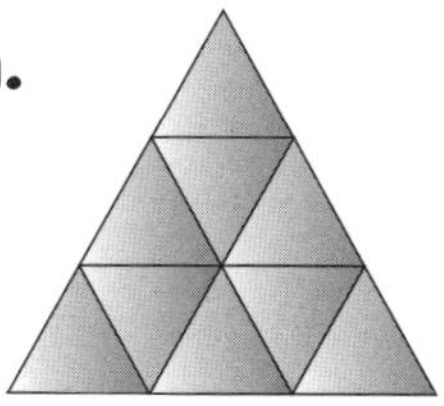

There are ______ triangles.

Midway Review

Find the answers mentally.

① 5 x 100 = ______

② 2 x 1000 = ______

③ 4 x 10 = ______

④ 10 x 6 = ______

⑤ 100 x 11 = ______

⑥ 1000 x 9 = ______

⑦ 20 x 2 = ______

⑧ 30 x 4 = ______

⑨ 200 x 3 = ______

⑩ 20 x 3 = ______

⑪ 10 x 50 = ______

⑫ 60 x 40 = ______

⑬ 400 x 9 = ______

⑭ 50 x 6 = ______

⑮ 4000 x 2 = ______

⑯ 81 ÷ 9 = ______

⑰ 54 ÷ 6 = ______

⑱ 56 ÷ 7 = ______

Write the fact families for each group of numbers.

⑲ 9 7 63

______ x ______ = ______

______ x ______ = ______

______ ÷ ______ = ______

______ ÷ ______ = ______

⑳ 5 8 40

______ x ______ = ______

______ x ______ = ______

______ ÷ ______ = ______

______ ÷ ______ = ______

Write the following.

㉑ The largest multiple of 6 up to 50 ______

㉒ The number of multiples of 5 in 40 ______

㉓ The number of multiples of 8 in 60 ______

㉔ The largest multiple of 7 up to 55 ______

Do the multiplication. Show your work.

㉕ 209 x 5	㉖ 314 x 8	㉗ 659 x 2
㉘ 562 x 3	㉙ 483 x 5	㉚ 748 x 4

㉛ 25 x 6	㉜ 37 x 8	㉝ 58 x 7	㉞ 49 x 9
㉟ 73 x 4	㊱ 45 x 3	㊲ 62 x 5	㊳ 96 x 2
㊴ 37 x 14	㊵ 53 x 28	㊶ 66 x 33	㊷ 82 x 49
㊸ 43 x 22	㊹ 75 x 52	㊺ 32 x 88	㊻ 97 x 18

Put the numbers in the right boxes.

49 27 45 28 90 30 81 35 16 64 12 21 32 6 40

㊼ Multiples of 6	㊽ Multiples of 7	㊾ Multiples of 8	㊿ Multiples of 9
______ ______	______ ______	______ ______	______ ______
______ ______	______ ______	______ ______	______ ______

Find the products. Then estimate the products to see if they are reasonable.

51. 36 x 23	estimate	52. 58 x 19	estimate
53. 673 x 4	estimate	54. 286 x 6	estimate
55. 718 x 6	estimate	56. 329 x 8	estimate

Find the answers.

57. 3 x 5 x 9 = ____________

58. 2 x 4 x 5 = ____________

59. 4 x 8 x 6 = ____________

60. 6 x 7 x 5 = ____________

61. 7 x 3 x 2 = ____________

62. 3 x 4 x 9 = ____________

Solve the problems. Show your work.

63. On Games Day 18 students from each of the 32 classes paticipated in the competitions. How many students participated in the competitions?

_______ students participated in the competitions.

64. There were 26 events on Games Day. 3 prizes were awarded for each event. How many prizes were awarded to the students?

65. The Parents' Association made 15 trays of hot dogs. There were 24 hot dogs in each tray. How many hot dogs were prepared ?

66. Each bag contains 12 buns. The parents bought 36 bags for making hamburgers. How many buns were bought in all?

67. The student helpers put 48 cups of soft drinks into each box. There were 16 boxes. How many cups of soft drinks were in the boxes?

68. May baked 2 trays of 118 cookies each for the bake sale to raise funds for Games Day. How many cookies did May bake?

69. The cookies were sold for 10¢ each in the bake sale. If all the cookies were sold out, how much did May raise in dollars?

9 Dividing Multiples of 10, 100 or 1000

EXAMPLE

3 children share 600 stickers. How many stickers does each child get?

600 ÷ 3 = 6 hundreds ÷ 3

= 2 hundreds

= 200

Each child gets 200 stickers.

$$\begin{array}{r} 200 \leftarrow \text{quotient} \\ \text{divisor} \rightarrow 3\overline{)600} \leftarrow \text{dividend} \\ \underline{600} \end{array}$$

HINTS:

- Dividing the multiples of 10, 100 or 1000 is similar to dividing other dividends, but don't forget to write the zero(s) in the quotient.

  e.g. 420 ÷ 7 =

  $$7\overline{)420} \rightarrow \begin{array}{r} 6 \\ 7\overline{)420} \\ 42 \end{array} \rightarrow \begin{array}{r} 60 \\ 7\overline{)420} \\ \underline{420} \end{array}$$

- Estimate the quotient by rounding the numbers to the nearest ten, hundred or thousand.

  e.g. 621 ÷ 2 = ?

  estimate 600 ÷ 2 = 300 — the answer should be close to 300

  There are about 300 twos in 621.

Fill in the missing numbers.

① 800 ÷ 2 = ______ hundreds ÷ 2

= ______ hundreds

= ______

② 550 ÷ 5 = ______ tens ÷ 5

= ______ tens

= ______

③ 360 ÷ 9 = ______ tens ÷ 9

= ______ tens

= ______

④ 480 ÷ 8 = ______ tens ÷ 8

= ______ tens

= ______

⑤ 600 ÷ 6 = ______ hundreds ÷ 6

= ______ hundred

= ______

⑥ 240 ÷ 4 = ______ tens ÷ 4

= ______ tens

= ______

Do the division. Then write the letters representing the answers to find what Ted says.

⑦ $9 \overline{)450}$ b	⑧ $4 \overline{)1200}$ m	⑨ $5 \overline{)50}$ s
⑩ $8 \overline{)5600}$ i	⑪ $9 \overline{)270}$ c	⑫ $2 \overline{)120}$ d
⑬ $8 \overline{)1600}$ p	⑭ $9 \overline{)630}$ f	⑮ $2 \overline{)40}$ e
⑯ $6 \overline{)3600}$ h	⑰ $7 \overline{)140}$ a	⑱ $2 \overline{)6000}$ n

⑲ 2100 ÷ 7 = ______	q	⑳ 400 ÷ 5 = ______	w
㉑ 90 ÷ 3 = ______	t	㉒ 80 ÷ 4 = ______	j
㉓ 5600 ÷ 7 = ______	g	㉔ 180 ÷ 6 = ______	l
㉕ 240 ÷ 6 = ______	y	㉖ 5400 ÷ 6 = ______	i
㉗ 400 ÷ 8 = ______	z	㉘ 60 ÷ 3 = ______	k
㉙ 300 ÷ 3 = ______	u	㉚ 200 ÷ 4 = ______	r

㉛

I like ___ ___ ___ ___ ___ ___ ___.
70 900 10 600 700 3000 800

Solve the problems. Show your work.

㉜ May puts 60 cookies equally into 2 jars. How many cookies are there in each jar? There are ______ cookies in each jar.	
㉝ Each box can hold 4 muffins. How many boxes does Mrs White need to hold 320 muffins?	
㉞ 180 boy scouts are divided into groups. Each group has 6 boy scouts. How many groups are there?	
㉟ Ted puts 900 grams of candies equally into 3 bags. How many grams of candies are there in each bag?	
㊱ How many weeks are there in 2100 days?	
㊲ Mr Stanley divides 4500 stamps equally for 5 albums. How many stamps are there in each album?	
㊳ A bag of apples costs $6. How many bags of apples can Mrs Smith buy with $60?	

Round the dividend to the nearest ten, hundred or thousand. Then estimate.

㊴ 8)‾82‾ **estimate** 8)‾80‾	㊵ 3)‾596‾ **estimate**)‾‾
㊶ 7)‾7004‾ **estimate**)‾‾	㊷ 6)‾312‾ **estimate**)‾‾

㊸ 497 ÷ 5 **estimate** ________ ÷ 5 = ________

㊹ 1888 ÷ 4 **estimate** ________ ÷ 4 = ________

㊺ 91 ÷ 3 **estimate** ________ ÷ 3 = ________

Solve the problems. Show your work.

㊻ May divides 81 flowers among 4 vases. About how many flowers are there in each vase?

________ ÷ ________ **estimate** ________ ÷ ________ = ________

There are about ________ flowers in each vase.

㊼ 8 children share 796 blocks. About how many blocks does each child get?

________ ÷ ________ **estimate** ________ ÷ ________ = ________

Each child gets about ________ blocks.

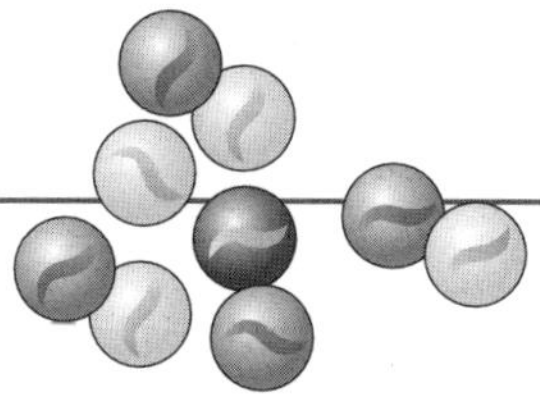

Help May share the marbles with Ted.

May has 46 yellow marbles and 154 red marbles. If May shares her marbles with Ted, how many marbles does each child get?

Each child gets ______ marbles.

10 Dividing 2-Digit Numbers with No Remainders

EXAMPLE

A bottle of juice costs \$4. How many bottles of juice can Ted buy with \$56?
Divide 56 by 4.

$4\overline{)56}$ —Divide the tens→

Tens	Ones
1	
4) 5	6
4	
1	

—Divide the ones→

Tens	Ones
1	4
4) 5	6
4	
1	6
1	6

$56 \div 4 = 14$
Ted can buy 14 bottles of juice with \$56.

HINTS:

- Dividing a 2-digit number by a 1-digit number:

  Divide the tens and then subtract.

  Bring down the ones.

  Combine the difference from the tens and the ones and then divide.

  e.g.

1	1	13
5) 65	5) 65	5) 65
5	5	5
1	15	15
		15

  $65 \div 5 = 13$

Do the division.

① $3\overline{)48}$

② $2\overline{)64}$

③ $6\overline{)84}$

④ $5\overline{)75}$

⑤ $4\overline{)72}$

⑥ $8\overline{)88}$

⑦ $3\overline{)69}$

⑧ $5\overline{)85}$

⑨ $3\overline{)42}$

⑩ $6\overline{)78}$

⑪ $2\overline{)50}$

⑫ $4\overline{)96}$

⑬ $2\overline{)32}$

⑭ $6\overline{)72}$

⑮ $5\overline{)95}$

⑯ $7\overline{)84}$

⑰ $9\overline{)99}$

⑱ $8\overline{)96}$

⑲ $4\overline{)52}$

⑳ $3\overline{)63}$

㉑ $3\overline{)81}$

㉒ $5\overline{)80}$

㉓ $2\overline{)76}$

㉔ $4\overline{)76}$

㉕ $7\overline{)91}$

㉖ $6\overline{)90}$

㉗ $5\overline{)70}$

㉘ $2\overline{)38}$

㉙ 87 ÷ 3 = ______

㉚ 74 ÷ 2 = ______

㉛ 60 ÷ 5 = ______

㉜ 68 ÷ 4 = ______

㉝ 78 ÷ 6 = ______

㉞ 39 ÷ 3 = ______

㉟ 82 ÷ 2 = ______

㊱ 95 ÷ 5 = ______

㊲ 78 ÷ 3 = ______

㊳ 98 ÷ 7 = ______

㊴ 84 ÷ 4 = ______

㊵ 84 ÷ 6 = ______

Do the division. Then put the letters in order from the greatest quotient to the smallest.

41
A. 66 ÷ 6 = ______
B. 70 ÷ 5 = ______
C. 51 ÷ 3 = ______
D. 56 ÷ 2 = ______

42 The order of the pencils : ______ , ______ , ______ , ______ .

43
A. 60 ÷ 4 = ______
B. 84 ÷ 6 = ______
C. 72 ÷ 2 = ______
D. 77 ÷ 7 = ______

44 The order of the crayons : ______ , ______ , ______ , ______ .

45
A. 58 ÷ 2 = ______
B. 75 ÷ 3 = ______
C. 68 ÷ 4 = ______
D. 80 ÷ 5 = ______

46 The order of the chocolate bars : ______ , ______ , ______ , ______ .

47
A. 92 ÷ 2 = ______
B. 88 ÷ 8 = ______
C. 91 ÷ 7 = ______
D. 84 ÷ 3 = ______

48 The order of the puzzles : ______ , ______ , ______ , ______ .

Solve the problems. Show your work.

49 5 children share 70 pencils. How many pencils does each child get?

Each child gets ________ pencils.

50 Each bag of chips costs \$2. How many bags of chips can Sally buy with \$26?

51 Mrs William buys 3 kg of meat for \$39. How much does 1 kg of meat cost?

52 A ribbon is 96 cm long. Sally cuts it into 4 equal strips. How long is each strip?

53 84 candies are packed into packets of 7. How many packets of candies are there?

Fill in the missing numbers.

①

```
     □ 8
2 ) □ 6
    6
    ----
    1 □
    □ □
    ----
```

②

```
     □ 7
□ ) 8 □
    6
    ----
    □ 1
    2 1
    ----
```

③

```
     1 □
6 ) □ □
    □
    ----
    3 □
    3 0
    ----
```

11

Dividing 2-Digit Numbers with Remainders

EXAMPLE

Sally shares 74 candies with 4 friends. How many candies does each child get? How many candies are left?

74 ÷ 5 = 14R4

↑ 14 with remainder 4

Each child gets 14 candies.
4 candies are left.

	Tens	Ones
	1	4 R 4
5)	7	4
	5	
	2	4
	2	0
		4

HINTS:

- Dividing a 2-digit number by a 1-digit number:

  Divide the tens and then subtract.

  Bring down the ones.

  Combine the difference from the tens and the ones and then divide.

  Write the remainder beside the quotient.

e.g.

```
   1            1           19          19R1
2)39   →    2)39    →   2)39    →   2)39
  2            2           2           2
  1            19          19          19
                           18          18
                            1           1
```

39 ÷ 2 = 19R1

Complete the division.

①

```
    □ □ R □
3 ) 4 7
    3
    □ □
    1 □
      □
```

②

```
    □ □ R □
4 ) 5 1
    □
    1 □
      □
      3
```

③

```
    □ □ R □
6 ) 7 9
    □
    1 □
    □ 8
      □
```

④

```
    □ □ R □
2 ) 3 7
    □
    1 □
    1 □
      □
```

⑤

```
    1 □ R □
5 ) 7 6
    □
    □ □
    □ □
      □
```

⑥

```
    □ □ R □
8 ) 9 3
    8
    □ □
      □
      □
```

Do the division. Use R to show remainders.

⑦ $6\overline{)71}$

⑧ $4\overline{)57}$

⑨ $2\overline{)33}$

⑩ $3\overline{)89}$

⑪ $5\overline{)64}$

⑫ $7\overline{)94}$

⑬ $6\overline{)85}$

⑭ $8\overline{)99}$

⑮ $2\overline{)77}$

⑯ $5\overline{)73}$

⑰ $6\overline{)81}$

⑱ $4\overline{)59}$

⑲ 44 ÷ 3 = ____________

⑳ 86 ÷ 5 = ____________

㉑ 59 ÷ 4 = ____________

㉒ 74 ÷ 6 = ____________

㉓ 66 ÷ 5 = ____________

㉔ 89 ÷ 7 = ____________

㉕ 97 ÷ 4 = ____________

㉖ 80 ÷ 3 = ____________

㉗ 75 ÷ 2 = ____________

㉘ 89 ÷ 5 = ____________

㉙ 91 ÷ 8 = ____________

㉚ 61 ÷ 4 = ____________

㉛ 70 ÷ 6 = ____________

㉜ 59 ÷ 2 = ____________

Do the division. Then find the problems with remainder 1 and write the letters in order in ⑮ to find what May buys for Ted.

㉝ $5\overline{)72}$ (s)	㉞ $4\overline{)67}$ (b)	㉟ $3\overline{)47}$ (m)	㊱ $2\overline{)55}$ (r)
㊲ $5\overline{)61}$ (a)	㊳ $7\overline{)87}$ (l)	㊴ $8\overline{)95}$ (t)	㊵ $6\overline{)73}$ (d)

㊶ 92 ÷ 7 = ______ (i)	㊷ 94 ÷ 4 = ______ (q)
㊸ 73 ÷ 2 = ______ (o)	㊹ 64 ÷ 5 = ______ (p)
㊺ 58 ÷ 3 = ______ (c)	㊻ 71 ÷ 4 = ______ (h)
㊼ 96 ÷ 5 = ______ (a)	㊽ 82 ÷ 7 = ______ (k)
㊾ 98 ÷ 8 = ______ (d)	㊿ 74 ÷ 5 = ______ (g)
(51) 90 ÷ 7 = ______ (e)	(52) 80 ÷ 6 = ______ (y)
(53) 37 ÷ 2 = ______ (r)	(54) 50 ÷ 3 = ______ (f)

(55)

A _ _ _ _ _ _ _ _ .

Solve the problems. Show your work.

56. Mrs Stanley puts 89 eggs equally in 6 boxes. How many eggs are there in each box? How many eggs are left?

    There are ________ eggs in each box. ________ eggs are left.

57. Samantha puts 97 sandwiches equally in 7 bags. How many sandwiches are there in each bag? How many sandwiches are left?

58. Ted pours 47 glasses of water equally into 3 buckets. How many glasses of water are there in each bucket? How many glasses of water are left?

59. A class of 29 students is divided into 2 groups. How many students are there in each group? How many students are left ?

Just for Fun

Read the graph and answer the questions.

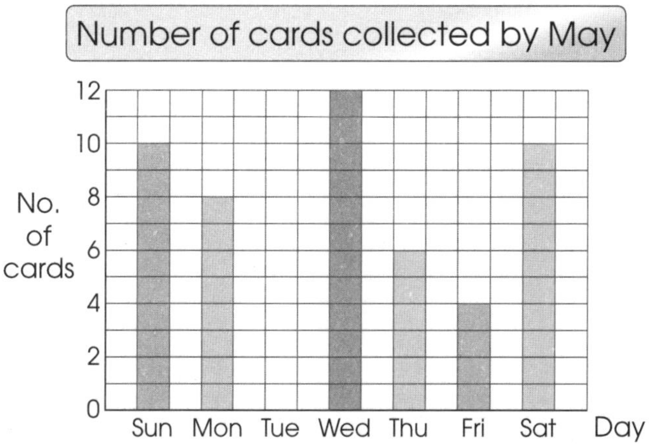

May puts all her cards into 4 packets equally. How many cards are there in each packet? How many cards are left?

There are ________ cards in each packet. ________ cards are left.

12 Dividing 3-Digit Numbers with No Remainders

EXAMPLE

Each box can hold 6 lollipops. Ted puts 738 lollipops into the boxes. How many boxes does Ted need?

```
    1             1 2            1 2 3
6 ) 7 3 8  →  6 ) 7 3 8  →  6 ) 7 3 8
    6             6 ↓            6
    1             1 3            1 3
                  1 2            1 2 ↓
                    1              1 8
                                   1 8
         bring down the tens
                                bring down the ones
```

738 ÷ 6 = 123
Ted needs 123 boxes.

HINTS:

- Dividing a 3-digit number by a 1-digit number :
  - 1st Divide
  - 2nd Multiply
  - 3rd Subtract
  - 4th Bring down

  repeat these steps until there are no more numbers to bring down
- Don't forget to do division from left to right.
- Estimate the quotient to check the answer.

  e.g. 809 ÷ 8 = ?

  estimate 800 ÷ 8 = 100 ← the answer should be close to 100

Do the division.

① 4) 476

② 3) 513

③ 684 ÷ 6 = ________

④ 972 ÷ 4 = ________

⑤ 670 ÷ 5 = ________

⑥ 608 ÷ 8 = ________

⑦ 966 ÷ 7 = ________

⑧ 870 ÷ 5 = ________

⑨ 860 ÷ 4 = ________

⑩ 931 ÷ 7 = ________

⑪ 648 ÷ 9 = ________

⑫ 558 ÷ 6 = ________

⑬ 762 ÷ 3 = ________

⑭ 567 ÷ 9 = ________

Estimate by rounding the dividends to the nearest ten or hundred. Then do the division.

⑮ $3\overline{)747}$

estimate: $3\overline{)750}$

⑯ $5\overline{)695}$

estimate:

⑰ $8\overline{)792}$

estimate:

⑱ $6\overline{)906}$

estimate:

⑲ 686 ÷ 7 = ______ estimate ______ ÷ ______ = ______

⑳ 326 ÷ 2 = ______ estimate ______ ÷ ______ = ______

㉑ 788 ÷ 4 = ______ estimate ______ ÷ ______ = ______

㉒ 915 ÷ 5 = ______ estimate ______ ÷ ______ = ______

㉓ 294 ÷ 6 = ______ estimate ______ ÷ ______ = ______

㉔ 416 ÷ 8 = ______ estimate ______ ÷ ______ = ______

㉕ 567 ÷ 3 = ______ estimate ______ ÷ ______ = ______

㉖ 891 ÷ 9 = ______ estimate ______ ÷ ______ = ______

Circle the correct answer(s).

㉗ Which problem has the smallest quotient?

A. $500 \div 4$ B. $833 \div 7$ C. $738 \div 6$

㉘ Which problem has the greatest quotient?

A. $912 \div 8$ B. $882 \div 9$ C. $672 \div 6$

㉙ Which problems have the same quotient?

A. $381 \div 3$ B. $936 \div 8$ C. $548 \div 4$ D. $762 \div 6$

㉚ Which problems have quotients smaller than 100?

A. $917 \div 7$ B. $776 \div 8$ C. $705 \div 5$ D. $528 \div 6$

㉛ Which is the best estimation for $719 \div 4$?

A. $800 \div 4$ B. $720 \div 4$ C. $700 \div 4$ D. $710 \div 4$

㉜ What is the difference between $774 \div 9$ and $882 \div 7$?

A. 50 B. 30 C. 20 D. 40

㉝ What is the sum of the quotients of $512 \div 8$ and $693 \div 9$?

A. 141 B. 153 C. 173 D. 151

㉞ What is the product of the quotients of $261 \div 3$ and $432 \div 6$?

A. 6612 B. 6274 C. 6264 D. 6192

Solve the problems. Show your work.

㉟ Mrs White sold 750 doughnuts in 5 days. How many doughnuts were sold each day?

_______ doughnuts were sold each day.

㊱ Mrs White earned $648 in 8 days. How much did Mrs White earn each day?

㊲ Ted shares 816 g of peanuts with 5 friends. How many grams of peanuts does each child get?

㊳ May uses 973 beads to make 7 bracelets. How many beads does May use to make 1 bracelet?

㊴ Ted uses 528 blocks to build 4 towers. How many blocks are there in each tower?

Which is the best buy in each group? Circle the correct answers.

		Food Depot	Brain Mart	Ray's Store
①		A 6 for 534¢	B 5 for 485¢	C 4 for 392¢
②		A 4 for 516¢	B 6 for $7.08	C 8 for $9.12

13 Dividing 3-Digit Numbers with Remainders

EXAMPLE

Mr Smith divides 538 stickers among 4 classes.
How many stickers are for each class?
How many stickers are left?

```
     1 3 4  R2 ←— remainder
 4 ) 5 3 8
     4
     ————
     1 3
     1 2
     ————
       1 8
       1 6
     ————
         2
```

538 ÷ 4 = 134R2
134 stickers are for each class.
2 stickers are left.

HINTS:

- Follow these steps to do division :

  1st Divide **2nd** Multiply
  3rd Subtract **4th** Bring down

- Use the following formula to check answers:

  Q x D + R = Dividend

  (Q = Quotient, D = Divisor, R = Remainder)

  e.g. Is 659 ÷ 3 = 219R2 correct?

  check 219 x 3 + 2 = 657 + 2
  = 659
  = Dividend

  So, 659 ÷ 3 = 219R2 is correct.

Do the division. Use R to show the remainders.

① 6) 749	② 4) 567	③ 3) 389	④ 9) 847
⑤ 8) 973	⑥ 2) 635	⑦ 7) 527	⑧ 5) 919

⑨ 3) 409	⑩ 7) 654	⑪ 6) 789	⑫ 2) 543
⑬ 9) 613	⑭ 3) 854	⑮ 4) 945	⑯ 8) 706

⑰ 479 ÷ 5 = ____________

⑱ 682 ÷ 6 = ____________

⑲ 574 ÷ 3 = ____________

⑳ 908 ÷ 8 = ____________

㉑ 729 ÷ 4 = ____________

㉒ 395 ÷ 7 = ____________

㉓ 286 ÷ 5 = ____________

㉔ 626 ÷ 4 = ____________

㉕ 486 ÷ 7 = ____________

㉖ 772 ÷ 3 = ____________

㉗ 503÷ 4 = ____________

㉘ 422 ÷ 9 = ____________

㉙ 621 ÷ 5 = ____________

㉚ 519 ÷ 2 = ____________

㉛ 734 ÷ 6 = ____________

㉜ 849 ÷ 7 = ____________

㉝ 653 ÷ 8 = ____________

㉞ 599 ÷ 6 = ____________

Estimate by rounding the dividends to the nearest ten or hundred. Then do the division.

㉟ 5) 479	estimate 5) 500	㊱ 6) 778	estimate)

㊲ 958 ÷ 8 = ______ estimate ______ ÷ ______ = ______

㊳ 579 ÷ 5 = ______ estimate ______ ÷ ______ = ______

㊴ 696 ÷ 7 = ______ estimate ______ ÷ ______ = ______

㊵ 898 ÷ 9 = ______ estimate ______ ÷ ______ = ______

Do the division. Then check the answers.

㊶ 823 ÷ 6 = 137R1 check 137 x 6 + 1 = ______

㊷ 947 ÷ 2 = ______ check ______________ = ______

㊸ 567 ÷ 4 = ______ check ______________ = ______

㊹ 775 ÷ 2 = ______ check ______________ = ______

㊺ 607 ÷ 7 = ______ check ______________ = ______

㊻ 829 ÷ 5 = ______ check ______________ = ______

㊼ 626 ÷ 8 = ______ check ______________ = ______

Solve the problems. Show your work.

48. There are 748 blocks for 5 children. How many blocks are there for each child? How many blocks are left?

    There are ______ blocks for each child. ______ blocks are left.

49. May's mother puts 429 cookies in 7 boxes. How many cookies are there in each box? How many cookies are left?

50. Ted shares 260 grams of golden raisins with 2 friends. How many grams of golden raisins does each child get? How many grams of golden raisins are left?

51. Ted puts 369 baseball cards in 5 boxes. How many baseball cards are there in each box? How many baseball cards are left?

52. Each box of candies costs \$8. How many boxes of candies can May buy with \$462? How much is left?

Look at the table and answer the question.

	Carrot	Blueberry	Banana
Number of muffins	74	276	397

Each box can hold 6 muffins. How many boxes does Mrs Smith need to hold all the muffins?

Mrs Smith needs ________ boxes to hold all the muffins.

14 Zeros in the Quotient

EXAMPLE

3 bags of flour weigh 624 grams. How heavy is 1 bag of flour?

Divide the hundreds:

```
   2
3)624
  6
```

→

Divide the tens:

```
   20  ← no groups of 3 go into 2; put a '0' in the quotient
3)624
  6
   2
   0
   2
```

→

Divide the ones:

```
   208
3)624
  6
   2
   0
   24
   24
```

$624 \div 3 = 208$

1 bag of flour weighs 208 grams.

HINTS:

- When the dividend is smaller than the divisor, write '0' in the quotient and continue to divide.

e.g. $419 \div 4 = ?$

```
   1            10            104R3
4)419   →   4)419   →   4)419
  4           4             4
              1             1
              0             0
              1             19
                            16
                             3
```

$419 \div 4 = 104R3$

Do the division. Use R to show the remainders.

① $7\overline{)729}$

② $4\overline{)826}$

③ $312 \div 3 =$ ________

④ $645 \div 6 =$ ________

⑤ $544 \div 5 =$ ________

⑥ $864 \div 8 =$ ________

⑦ $731 \div 7 =$ ________

⑧ $625 \div 6 =$ ________

⑨ $425 \div 4 =$ ________

⑩ $619 \div 3 =$ ________

⑪ $904 \div 9 =$ ________

⑫ $538 \div 5 =$ ________

⑬ $214 \div 2 =$ ________

⑭ $719 \div 7 =$ ________

⑮ $627 \div 6 =$ ________

⑯ $414 \div 4 =$ ________

Help Sally check her answers. If the answer is correct, put a ✓ in the ◯ ; otherwise put a ✗ .

⑰	709 ÷ 7 = 101R3	◯	check	____ x ____ + ____ = ____
⑱	627 ÷ 6 = 104R3	◯	check	
⑲	539 ÷ 5 = 106R4	◯	check	
⑳	423 ÷ 4 = 105R3	◯	check	
㉑	976 ÷ 9 = 108R4	◯	check	
㉒	874 ÷ 8 = 109R6	◯	check	
㉓	626 ÷ 3 = 208R2	◯	check	

Do the division. Then check the answers.

㉔ 721 ÷ 7 = ________

check

㉕ 532 ÷ 5 = ________

check

㉖ 431 ÷ 4 = ________

check

㉗ 656 ÷ 6 = ________

check

㉘ 914 ÷ 3 = ________

check

㉙ 809 ÷ 2 = ________

check

In each group, use 4 of the numbers to complete the division.

30. 103 5 518 3 538 ______ ÷ ______ = ______ R ______

31. 204 2 818 4 202 ______ ÷ ______ = ______ R ______

32. 623 2 207 3 4 ______ ÷ ______ = ______ R ______

33. 3 9 102 6 924 ______ ÷ ______ = ______ R ______

34. 7 106 4 746 2 ______ ÷ ______ = ______ R ______

Match the division sentences that have the same answers. Write the letters in the rings.

35. 549 ÷ 5

36. 753 ÷ 7

37. 623 ÷ 6

38. 617 ÷ 2

39. 628 ÷ 3

A 829 ÷ 8

B 925 ÷ 3

C 837 ÷ 4

D 767 ÷ 7

E 646 ÷ 6

Solve the problems. Show your work.

40. Ted puts 632 marbles in 6 jars. How many marbles are there in each jar? How many marbles are left?

There are ______ marbles in each jar. ______ marbles are left.

41. Each tape costs \$8. How many tapes can Mr Smith buy with \$869? How much money is left?

42. A roll of ribbon is 730 cm long. May cuts the ribbon into 7 equal strips. How long is each strip? How much ribbon is left?

43. Mrs Stanley uses 5 g of baking soda for each cake. How many cakes can she make with 544 g of baking soda? How much baking soda is left?

44. 829 batteries are packed into packets of 4. How many packets of batteries are there? How many batteries are left?

See how Sally builds her towers with blocks. Follow the pattern to add the next 2 sets of blocks.

Step 1	Step 2	Step 3	Step 4	Step 5
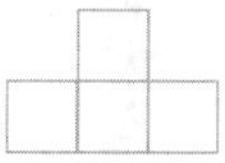	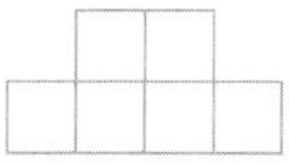			

15 Dividing 4-Digit Numbers

EXAMPLE

Uncle Sam puts 4268 oranges into 8 boxes. How many oranges are there in each box? How many oranges are left?

Divide the thousands:

```
8)4268
```

no groups of 8 in 4; move to the right and try with a bigger number

Divide the hundreds:

```
    5
8)4268
  40
   2
```

Divide the tens:

```
    53
8)4268
  40
   26
   24
    2
```

Divide the ones:

```
   533
8)4268
  40
   26
   24
    28
    24
     4
```

Write the remainder:

```
   533R4
8)4268
  40
   26
   24
    28
    24
     4
```

There are 533 oranges in each box.
4 oranges are left.

HINTS:

- Always start with the left-most number. After dividing, don't forget to check the answer.

  e.g. Is 5750 ÷ 6 = 958R2 correct?

  958 × 6 + 2 = 5748 + 2

  = 5750

  = Dividend

  So, 5750 ÷ 6 = 958R2 is correct.

Do the division.

① 9)4682

② 3)3763

③ 5)7467

④ 6)8409

⑤ 7)5709

⑥ 8)8251

⑦ $4\overline{)5803}$

⑧ $5\overline{)7478}$

⑨ $7\overline{)9074}$

⑩ $8\overline{)3982}$

⑪ 2095 ÷ 3 = ____________

⑫ 6874 ÷ 5 = ____________

⑬ 4105 ÷ 8 = ____________

⑭ 8753 ÷ 9 = ____________

⑮ 6582 ÷ 7 = ____________

⑯ 7742 ÷ 4 = ____________

⑰ 3394 ÷ 6 = ____________

⑱ 5680 ÷ 8 = ____________

⑲ 5217 ÷ 2 = ____________

⑳ 4094 ÷ 7 = ____________

㉑ 8753 ÷ 4 = ____________

㉒ 3299 ÷ 5 = ____________

㉓ 2574 ÷ 9 = ____________

㉔ 2980 ÷ 6 = ____________

㉕ 8061 ÷ 5 = ____________

㉖ 6524 ÷ 3 = ____________

㉗ 7206 ÷ 8 = ____________

㉘ 8219 ÷ 9 = ____________

㉙ 4020 ÷ 6 = ____________

㉚ 3742 ÷ 7 = ____________

㉛ 9224 ÷ 9 = ____________

㉜ 5073 ÷ 4 = ____________

㉝ 4316 ÷ 3 = ____________

㉞ 1085 ÷ 9 = ____________

See how May stores her things. Complete the table.

		No. of boxes	No. of items in each box	No. of items left
35	2068 beads	5		
36	4211 blocks	7		
37	3274 marbles	6		
38	3486 cards	3		
39	8215 matches	4		
40	5265 stickers	8		

Do the division. Then find the problems with no remainders and write the letters in order in ⑤① to complete what Sally says.

41. 6542 ÷ 6 = ________ (b)
42. 7392 ÷ 7 = ________ (s)
43. 9232 ÷ 8 = ________ (t)
44. 1509 ÷ 5 = ________ (d)
45. 6162 ÷ 3 = ________ (a)
46. 4712 ÷ 4 = ________ (m)
47. 8874 ÷ 9 = ________ (p)
48. 8755 ÷ 6 = ________ (m)
49. 7740 ÷ 8 = ________ (y)
50. 4840 ÷ 5 = ________ (s)

51. I like collecting ___ ___ ___ ___ ___ ___ .

Solve the problems. Show your work.

52. 3265 cookies were sold in 5 days. How many cookies were sold each day?

    ________ cookies were sold each day.

53. Ted can go 7560 cm in 7 minutes. How far can he go in 1 minute?

54. May uses 8 strips of ribbon for each craft item. How many craft items can she make with 8268 strips of ribbon? How many strips of ribbon are left?

55. Mr Smith puts 4286 doughnuts into boxes of 6 doughnuts. How many boxes of doughnuts are there? How many doughnuts are left?

56. May uses 9 beads to make a bracelet. How many bracelets can she make with 2086 beads? How many beads are left?

Draw the top, front and side view of the tower in the space below to show how it looks.

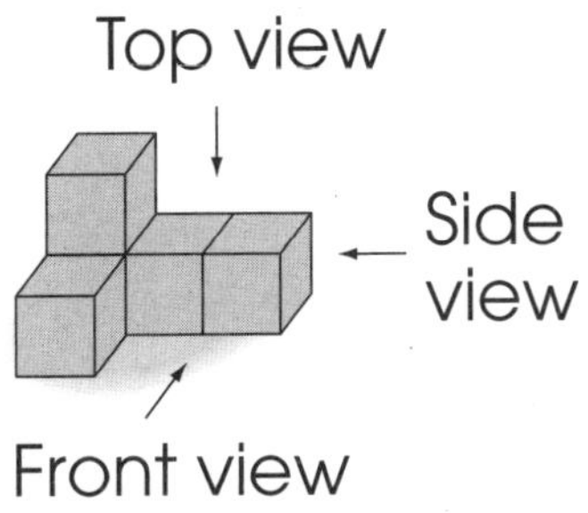

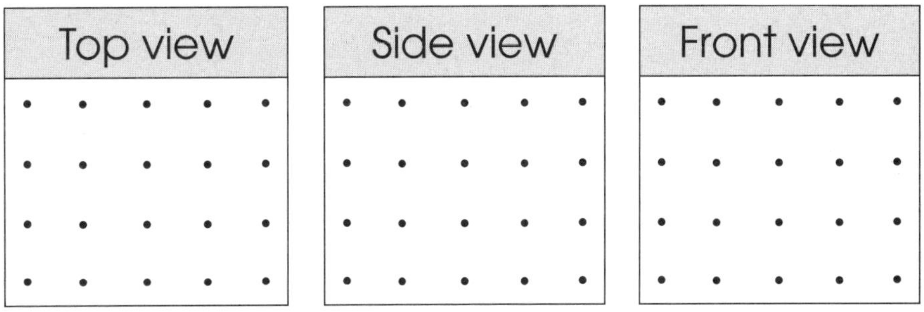

16 More Multiplying and Dividing

EXAMPLE

5 children share 8 boxes of chocolate each containing 89 chocolates. How many chocolates does each child get? How many chocolates are left?

89 x 8 = 712 ← **1st** Use multiplication to find the total number of chocolates.

712 ÷ 5 = 142 R2 ← **2nd** Use division to find the number of chocolates each child gets and the number of chocolates left.

Each child gets 142 chocolates.
2 chocolates are left.

HINTS:

- Don't think that every problem needs one operation only. Sometimes more than one operation is needed. Try to write two appropriate number sentences to solve a two-step problem.

  e.g. Sam earned $735 in a week. How much did Sam earn in 3 days?

  735 ÷ 7 = 105 ← earnings per day
  105 x 3 = 315 ← earnings in 3 days

  Sam earned $315 in 3 days.

Find the answers.

① 329 x 46 = ______

② 57 x 64 = ______

③ $2 \overline{)329}$

④ $5 \overline{)6284}$

⑤ 38 x 15 = ______

⑥ 278 x 6 = ______

⑦ 4286 ÷ 9 = ______

⑧ 301 ÷ 4 = ______

⑨ 127 x 7 = ______

⑩ 3204 ÷ 3 = ______

⑪ 3511 ÷ 8 = ______

⑫ 32 x 74 = ______

⑬ 29 x 66 = ______

⑭ 529 ÷ 5 = ______

Circle the correct answers.

⑮ Which number sentences have the same product?

A. 44×25 B. 221×5 C. 74×15 D. 22×50

⑯ Which number sentences have the same quotient?

A. $407 \div 6$ B. $527 \div 8$ C. $267 \div 4$ D. $592 \div 9$

⑰ Which number sentences have the same remainder?

A. $1068 \div 9$ B. $1159 \div 8$ C. $3758 \div 7$ D. $813 \div 6$

⑱ Which numbers, when divided by 8, have a remainder of 3?

A. 3899 B. 8753 C. 6822 D. 9395

⑲ Which numbers, when divided by 7, have a quotient of 106?

A. 739 B. 743 C. 746 D. 749

⑳ Which numbers are divisible by 6?

A. 8492 B. 784 C. 7650 D. 8184

㉑ Which number sentences have a product greater than 6000?

A. 849×8 B. 54×99 C. 74×88 D. 65×74

㉒ Which number sentences have a product that is a multiple of 10?

A. 426×5 B. 126×9 C. 75×81 D. 85×44

㉓ Which number sentences have the same answer?

A. 24×36 B. 16×37 C. $2368 \div 4$ D. $2593 \div 3$

Solve the problems. Show your work.

㉔ Each basket holds 26 apples. How many apples are there in 16 baskets?

There are ________ apples in 16 baskets.

㉕ Each basket of apples costs $7. How many baskets of apples can John buy with $200? How much money is left?

㉖ May buys 8 bags of candies each containing 128 candies. How many candies does May buy?

㉗ May shares her candies with 4 friends. How many candies does each child get? How many candies are left?

㉘ Aunt Pam sold 882 pizzas in 6 days. How many pizzas were sold each day?

㉙ Each pizza costs $4. How much money did Aunt Pam get for selling pizzas each day?

㉚ Aunt Pam uses 9 g of pepper for each pizza. How many g of pepper does she need to make 75 pizzas?

Write two number sentences to solve each problem. Show your work.

㉛ 4 girls share 6 boxes of gumballs each containing 325 gumballs. How many gumballs does each girl get? How many gumballs are left?

________ x ________ = ________

________ ÷ ________ = ________

Each girl gets ________ gumballs. ________ gumballs are left.

㉜ There are 484 sheets of paper in 2 packs. How many sheets of paper are there in 7 packs?

㉝ Mrs Stanley gives a box of stickers to her class of 36 students. Each student gets 48 stickers. If only 7 students share the stickers, how many stickers does each student get? How many stickers are left?

㉞ The total weight of 6 sacks of soil is 5910 grams. What is the total weight of 9 sacks of soil?

Find the answers.

① ▲ + ● − ▲ = 9 ● = ________

② ■ ÷ ■ + ■ ÷ ■ = ? ? = ________

Final Review

Do the division. Then find the problems with remainder 1 and write the letters in order in ㉓ to complete what May says.

① $5\overline{)76}$ r	② $7\overline{)89}$ m	③ $3\overline{)52}$ a	④ $4\overline{)67}$ y
⑤ $9\overline{)286}$ b	⑥ $3\overline{)174}$ a	⑦ $8\overline{)476}$ l	⑧ $6\overline{)325}$ c

⑨	1269 ÷ 4 = ________	t	⑩	8275 ÷ 8 = ________	q
⑪	326 ÷ 3 = ________	u	⑫	9106 ÷ 6 = ________	d
⑬	4076 ÷ 9 = ________	k	⑭	527 ÷ 5 = ________	f
⑮	3275 ÷ 7 = ________	n	⑯	4204 ÷ 2 = ________	s
⑰	8166 ÷ 5 = ________	i	⑱	6214 ÷ 3 = ________	c
⑲	736 ÷ 4 = ________	g	⑳	1088 ÷ 9 = ________	z
㉑	2816 ÷ 6 = ________	p	㉒	925 ÷ 4 = ________	e

㉓ P ___ ___ ___ ___ ___ ___ ___ makes perfect!

Do the division. Then check the answers.

㉔ 276 ÷ 9 = ________ **check** ______ x ______ + ______ = ______

㉕ 1294 ÷ 5 = ________ **check** ______ x ______ + ______ = ______

㉖ 3266 ÷ 4 = ________ **check** ______ x ______ + ______ = ______

㉗ 825 ÷ 7 = ________ **check** ______ x ______ + ______ = ______

㉘ 7086 ÷ 8 = ________ **check** ______ x ______ + ______ = ______

㉙ 6283 ÷ 6 = ________ **check** ______ x ______ + ______ = ______

㉚ 5774 ÷ 3 = ________ **check** ______ x ______ + ______ = ______

Do the multiplication.

㉛ 564 x 9	㉜ 876 x 3	㉝ 298 x 4	㉞ 763 x 5
㉟ 28 x 45	㊱ 37 x 82	㊲ 66 x 53	㊳ 21 x 78

㊴ 64 x 18 = ________	㊵ 389 x 8 = ________
㊶ 612 x 7 = ________	㊷ 34 x 34 = ________
㊸ 371 x 6 = ________	㊹ 287 x 2 = ________
㊺ 58 x 26 = ________	㊻ 49 x 51 = ________

Complete the multiplication and division sentences using each group of numb ers.

47. 6 8 162 117

___ x ___ = 936

___ ÷ ___ = 27

48. 26 1204 7 1014

___ x 39 = ___

___ ÷ ___ = 172

49. 89 609 87 801

___ x 7 = ___

___ ÷ 9 = ___

50. 4005 5 4065 9

445 x ___ = ___

___ ÷ ___ = 813

Fill in the missing numbers.

51.

6 □
x □ 9
□ 8 5
1 □ 5 0
□ 5 □ □

52.

□ 7
x 2 □
2 □ 1
□ 3 4 0
□ 5 □ 1

53.

□ □
x 4 6
3 □ 8
□ 1 2 0
2 □ □ 8

54.

□ □ 3 R □
7) □ 6 □
□
1 □
1 4
□ □
2 1
4

55.

□ □ 5 9 R □
4) □ 2 □ 7
4
2 □
2 0
3 7
3 □
1

56.

1 7 □ R □
3) 5 □ 3
□
□ □
2 1
□ □
1 □
1

Solve the problems. Show your work.

57. A roll of string is 4206 cm long. Bill cuts the string into 8 equal strips. How long is each strip? How much string is left?

    Each strip is ______ cm long. ______ cm of string is left.

58. Each magazine costs \$5. How much money does Mr Smith get from selling 427 magazines?

59. Aunt Pam puts 826 flowers equally in 6 baskets. How many flowers are there in each basket? How many flowers are left?

60. The total weight of 7 bags of sugar is 1995 grams. How heavy is 1 bag of sugar?

61. Ted buys 5 boxes of marbles. Each box has 123 marbles. How many marbles does Ted buy altogether?

62. Ted puts his marbles equally in 6 bags. How many marbles are there in each bag? How many marbles are left?

Write two number sentences to solve each problem.

63. There are 275 mL of juice in one box. May pours 6 boxes of juice equally into 4 bottles. How much juice does each bottle hold? How much juice is left?

    ______ X ______ = ______   ______ ÷ ______ = ______

    Each bottles holds ______ mL of juice. ______ mL of juice is left.

64. David and Ted have the same number of stamps making a total of 826 stamps. George has 4 times as many stamps as David. How many stamps does George have?

65. Mrs Stanley bought 86 dozens of pencils. She gave 5 pencils to each student. How many students can get the pencils? How many pencils are left?

66. The total weight of 8 boxes of crackers is 3640 grams. What is the total weight of 7 boxes of crackers?

67. Ted's mother wants to bake 56 cakes. Her oven can only bake 4 cakes every 2 hours. How long will it take her to bake all the cakes?

Section II

Overview

In Section I, students practised multiplication and division of whole numbers. In Section II, these skills are built upon. Students work with fractions and decimals, and the concept of direct proportion is introduced. In addition, students learn how to find the factors and multiples of whole numbers.

In the Geometry units, they learn to draw and analyse 3D shapes. The study of 2D shapes includes different types of quadrilaterals.

In simple measurements, students learn to measure and calculate the area of regular and irregular shapes, and to determine the capacity of containers.

Graphing includes bar graphs as well as plotting coordinates as points on a grid. The concepts of algebraic symbols and equations are introduced.

Money applications include finding sale prices in dollars and cents.

There is an emphasis throughout on developing the ability to estimate an answer before calculating it exactly.

1 Multiples

WORDS TO LEARN

Multiple - the result of multiplying a number

Common multiple - a number that is the multiple of more than one number

Least common multiple (LCM) - the smallest common multiple

e.g. Multiples of 3 are 3, 6, 9, 12, 15, 18, 21, 24, 27, 30, 33, 36.....

Multiples of 4 are 4, 8, 12, 16, 20, 24, 28, 32, 36.....

Common Multiples of 3 and 4 are 12, 24, 36, ...

The least common multiple of 3 and 4 is 12.

Which cans should Tim aim for? Write the numbers.

① Tim wants to throw the balls into every 3rd can.

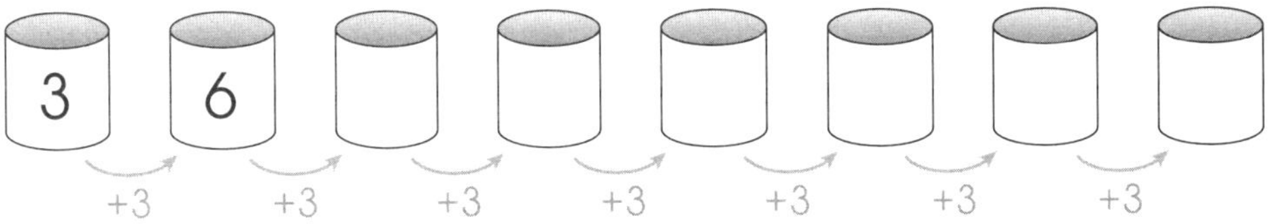

② Tim wants to throw the balls into every 6th can.

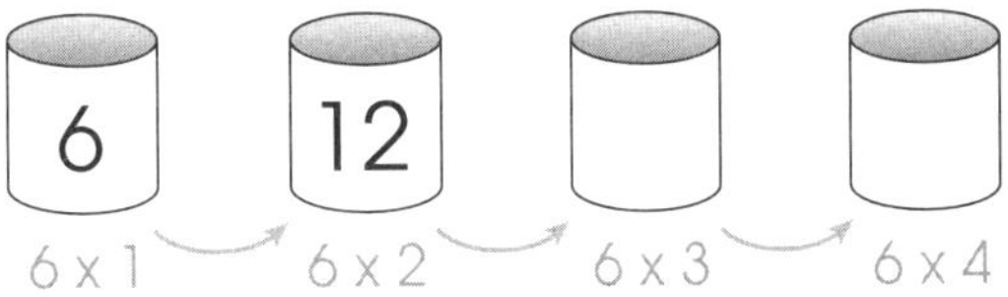

Ways to find multiples:
1. Keep adding the numbers, or
2. Multiply the numbers by 1,2,3...

Write the first five multiples of the following numbers.

③ **5** 5 , 10 , ___ , ___ , ___

④ **7** ___ , ___ , ___ , ___ , ___

⑤ **8** ___ , ___ , ___ , ___ , ___

⑥ **10** ___ , ___ , ___ , ___ , ___

⑦ **11** ___ , ___ , ___ , ___ , ___

⑧ **12** ___ , ___ , ___ , ___ , ___

Write the numbers.

⑨ Tim throws the balls into every 3rd can and every 4th can.

a. Multiples of 3: [3] [ ] [ ] [ ] [ ] [ ] [ ] [ ]

b. Multiples of 4: [4] [ ] [ ] [ ] [ ] [ ]

c. Common multiples of 3 and 4: [ ] [ ]

d. Least common multiple of 3 and 4: [ ]

Write the first 4 common multiples of the following numbers. Then find the least common multiple (LCM).

⑩ Common multiples of 4 and 8: ____ , ____ , ____ , ____

LCM of 4 and 8: ____

⑪ Common multiples of 2 and 6: ____ , ____ , ____ , ____

LCM of 2 and 6: ____

⑫ Common multiples of 8 and 12: ____ , ____ , ____ , ____

LCM of 8 and 12: ____

ACTIVITY

Answer the questions.

1. Which 2 numbers have these common multiples?
   14, 28, 42, 56, 70 ____ and ____

2. Tim eats salad on every 2nd day and eats jelly on every 7th day. When will he eat salad and jelly on the same day?
   Every ____ days.

2 Factors

WORDS TO LEARN

Factors - numbers that can be multiplied to get a product

e.g. The factors of 12: 1, 2, 3, 4, 6, 12

The factors of 18: 1, 2, 3, 6, 9, 18

Common Factors of 12 and 18: 1, 2, 3, 6

The Greatest Common Factor (GCF) of 12 and 18 is 6.

12 = 1 x 12	18 = 1 x 18
12 = 2 x 6	18 = 2 x 9
12 = 3 x 4	18 = 3 x 6

How many different piles can Tim make with 14 coins? Help him write the numbers.

① 1 pile of coins; each pile has _____ coin(s).

② 2 piles of coins; each pile has _____ coin(s).

③ 7 piles of coins; each pile has _____ coin(s).

④ 14 piles of coins; each pile has _____ coin(s).

⑤ The factors of 14 are _____, _____, _____, _____.

⑥
14 = 1 x ______
14 = 2 x ______
14 = 7 x ______
14 = 14 x ______

Find the factors of the following numbers.

⑦ The factors of 18 are: ________________________________

⑧ The factors of 24 are: ________________________________

⑨ The factors of 40 are: ________________________________

⑩ The factors of 56 are: ________________________________

Stop when you get a number you have already multiplied by.

Read what Tim and Nicky say. Then find the factors to answer their question.

⑪ Factors of 24:

_____ , _____ , _____ , _____ ,

_____ , _____ , _____ , _____

⑫ Factors of 30:

_____ , _____ , _____ , _____ ,

_____ , _____ , _____ , _____

⑬ The common factors of 24 and 30 are _____ , _____ , _____ , _____ .

⑭ Tim and Nicky could both have _____ , _____ , _____ and _____ piles.

Try these.

⑮ The factors of 12 are: __________

⑯ The factors of 18 are: __________

⑰ The common factors of 12 and 18 are: __________

⑱ The factors of 16 are: __________

⑲ The factors of 24 are: __________

⑳ The common factors of 16 and 24 are: __________

㉑ The common factors of 20 and 30 are: __________

㉒ The common factors of 32 and 40 are: __________

Help Tim and Nicky find the biggest number of piles of coins they can make. Fill in the blanks.

㉓ Factors of 20:

____ , ____ , ____ ,

____ , ____ , ____

㉔ Factors of 28:

____ , ____ , ____ ,

____ , ____ , ____

㉕ The common factors of 20 and 28 are ____ , ____ , ____ .

㉖ The greatest common factor of 20 and 28 is ____ .

㉗ The greatest number of piles of coins Tim and Nicky can both make is ____ piles.

Circle all the common factors of the numbers. The largest one is the GCF.

Try these.

㉘ The factors of 24 are ________________________ .

㉙ The factors of 36 are ________________________ .

㉚ The common factors of 24 and 36 are ________________________ .

㉛ The greatest common factor (GCF) of 24 and 36 is ________ .

Find the common factors and GCF.

㉜ 30, 45 Common factors: ________________________

GCF: ________

㉝ 60, 78 Common factors: ________________________

GCF: ________

㉞ 50, 75 Common factors: ________________________

GCF: ________

㉟ 48, 56 Common factors: ________________________

GCF: ________

Follow Tim's method to find the GCF of the following numbers.

To find the GCF of 30 and 36, keep dividing the two numbers by their common factors (except 1) until there are no more common factors between them. The product of the divisors is the GCF.

2	30	36	← common factor : 2
3	15	18	← common factor : 3
	5	6	← no common factor

GCF of 30 and 36
= 2 x 3
= 6

36.
2 | 24 40
2 | ____
2 | ____

GCF of 24 and 40
= 2 x ____ x ____
= ____

37.
2 | 18 36
 | ____
 | ____

GCF of 18 and 36
= ____ x ____ x ____
= ____

38.
2 | 48 60
 | ____
 | ____

GCF of 48 and 60
= ____ x ____ x ____
= ____

ACTIVITY

Help Tim solve the problem.

My mom has baked 54 muffins and 57 cookies. How many boxes will she need if all the boxes hold the same number of muffins and cookies?

______ boxes, each containing ______ muffins and ______ cookies.

3 Multiplication

WORDS TO LEARN

Multiplication - a short way to find a sum when the addends are the same
e.g. 5 + 5 + 5 = 3 x 5 = 15

Help Tim answer Uncle Jack's questions.

If there are 136 cars, each carrying 4 people, how many people will there be?

① 136 x 4 = ______

There will be ______ people.

```
    2          1 2          1 2
  1 3 6        1 3 6        1 3 6
x     4  →   x     4  →   x     4
  -----        -----        -----
      □          □ 4          □ 4 4
```

Try these.

② 239 x 3 = ____________

③ 193 x 5 = ____________

④ 207 x 4 = ____________

⑤ 148 x 8 = ____________

Help Tim find the number of people in the parking lot.

⑥ In the parking lot, there are 5 rows of cars. Each row has 6 cars. Each car has 2 people. How many people are there?

a. 5 x 6 x 2
= (5 x 6) x 2
= ______ x ______
= ______

b. 6 x 2 x 5
= (6 x 2) x 5
= ______ x ______
= ______

Find the number of cars in 5 rows first, and then times the number of people in each car. It is the same to find the number of people in each row, and then times the number of rows.

There are ______ people in the parking lot.

Try these.

⑦ (4 x 3) x 5 = _____

4 x (3 x 5) = _____

⑧ (9 x 6) x 3 = _____

9 x (6 x 3) = _____

⑨ (8 x 7) x 5 = _____

8 x (7 x 5) = _____

⑩ A x (B x C) = 216

(A x B) x C = _____

The answer is the same even if we change the order of multiplication.

Read what Uncle Jack says. Then help Tim find the number of seats in the waiting areas.

If a whole number is multiplied by 10, you can just add a "0" to the end of it.
e.g. 64 x 10 = 640

If a whole number is multiplied by 10, 20, 30 ....
you can multiply the number by 1, 2, 3.....
Then add a "0" to the end of the product.
e.g. 24 x 30 = 720

```
   2 4
x    3
------
   7 2
```

add '0'

⑪ In waiting area A, there are 23 rows of seats with 10 seats in each row. How many seats are there in all?

23 x 10 = _____

There are _____ seats in all.

```
   2 3
x  1 0
------
 _____
```

⑫ In waiting area B, there are 16 rows of seats with 20 seats in each row. How many seats are there in all?

16 x _____ = _____

There are _____ seats in all.

```
   1 6
x _____
------
 _____
```

Try these.

⑬ 36 x 30 = _______

⑭ 33 x 40 = _______

⑮ 18 x 50 = _______

⑯ 43 x 70 = _______

Help Uncle Jack find how many pieces of luggage are in his truck.

⑰ Uncle Jack has made 12 trips with 34 pieces of luggage on each trip. How many pieces of luggage are there?

```
  3 4        3 4        3 4        3 4        3 4
x 1 2      x 1 2      x 1 2      x 1 2      x 1 2
-----      -----      -----      -----      -----
    ☐   ➜     ☐8  ➜     6 8  ➜     6 8  ➜     6 8
                       ☐0        ☐4 0       3 4 0
                                            -----
                                            ☐
```

$34 \times 12 =$ ________

There are ______ pieces of luggage.

When you multiply the tens digit, remember to put a "0" under the ones column.

Try these.

⑱	⑲	⑳	㉑
15 x 37 =	74 x 26 =	48 x 19 =	36 x 14 =

㉒ 47 x 29 = ________

㉓ 86 x 53 = ________

㉔ 31 x 46 = ________

㉕ 25 x 66 = ________

㉖ 80 x 96 = ________

㉗ 87 x 34 = ________

㉘ 45 x 12 = ________

㉙ 39 x 28 = ________

Tim wants to know how many people are on the planes. Help him estimate first. Then do the problems.

㉚ There are 12 planes.

Each plane has 87 people.

How many people are there?

87 x 12 = ______

There are ______ people on the planes.

```
   8 7                    Estimate
 x 1 2   (rounded to)       9 0
 -----                    x 1 0
                          -----
 _____   (should be close to) _____
 _____
```

Round the numbers to the nearest tens.

Try these.

```
㉛   2 7    Estimate      ㉜   3 8    Estimate      ㉝   1 6    Estimate
   x 4 2      3 0            x 2 5                    x 5 4
   -----    x ____           -----    x ____          -----    x ____
   _____     ____            _____     ____           _____     ____
   _____                     _____                    _____
```

ACTIVITY

Tick ✔ the right answers. Mark the time you need to finish the questions.

1. 8 x 13 x 5 ☐ 522 ☐ 520
2. 6 x 19 x 5 ☐ 570 ☐ 577
3. 15 x 7 x 2 ☐ 201 ☐ 210
4. 35 x 29 x 2 ☐ 2030 ☐ 2003

I can finish in ________ minutes.

If possible, multiply the numbers with a product of 10, 20, 30... first. Then multiply the other numbers.

e.g. 15 x 6 x 2
= 15 x 2 x 6
= 30 x 6
= 180

4 Division

WORDS TO LEARN

Division - the inverse operation of multiplication

e.g. 23 ÷ 5 = 4 r 3

dividend (23), divisor (5), quotient (4), remainder (3)

```
      4      ← quotient
  5 ) 2 3    ← dividend
divisor 2 0
      ---
        3    ← remainder
```

Help Tim find the number of baseball cards in each pile.

① Tim has put 284  in 4 piles. How many  in each pile?

```
4 ) 2 8 4   ⇨        ☐        ⇨       7 ☐
              4 ) 2 8 4           4 ) 2 8 4
                  ↑                   2 8      bring
     choose the closest multiple      ---      down
     of 4                               4
                                        ☐
                                       ---
```

There are ______  in each pile.

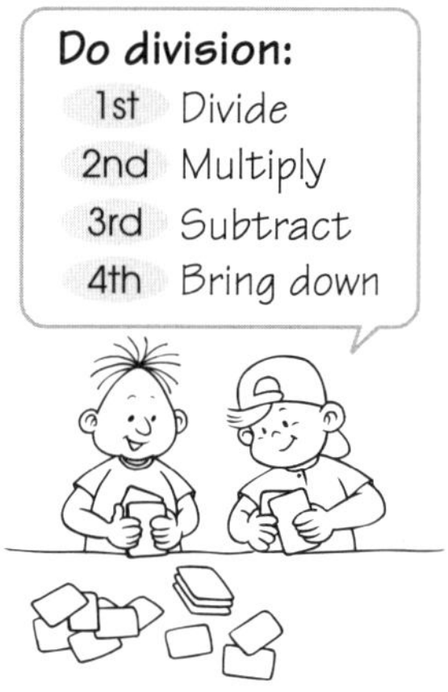

② Tim has put 234  in 8 piles. How many  in each pile?

```
8 ) 2 3 4   ⇨       ☐         ⇨       2 ☐ r ☐
              8 ) 2 3 4           8 ) 2 3 4
                  ☐                   1 6
                 ---                  ---
                                        7 4
                                        ☐
                                       ---
                                        ☐
```

There are ______  in each pile and ______  left over.

Try these.

③ 407 ÷ 6 = ________

④ 753 ÷ 9 = ________

⑤ 639 ÷ 5 = ________

⑥ 841 ÷ 3 = ________

Read what Tim says. Then help him find the number of baseball cards in each pile.

⑦ I put 31  in 12 piles.

31 ÷ 12 = ____ r ____

There are ______  in each pile

and ______  left over.

```
     □ r □
12 ) 3 1      ← 1st  Estimate how many 12 are in 31.
     □ □      ← 2nd  Multiply.
                     12 x 1 = 12
                     12 x 2 = 24
                     12 x 3 = 36
       □      ← 3rd  Subtract.
```

⑧ I put 98  in 19 piles.

98 ÷ 19 = ____ r ____

There are ______  in each pile

and ______  left over.

```
       4              5 r □
19 ) 9 8  →  19 ) 9 8
     7 6          □ □
     2 2            □
```

Greater than 19, so try a bigger quotient, 5.

Try these.

⑨ 93 ÷ 21 = __________

⑩ 56 ÷ 13 = __________

⑪ 77 ÷ 15 = __________

⑫ 81 ÷ 16 = __________

⑬ 79 ÷ 14 = __________

⑭ 69 ÷ 22 = __________

⑮ 37 ÷ 11 = __________

⑯ 47 ÷ 18 = __________

⑰ 65 ÷ 23 = __________

⑱ 76 ÷ 17 = __________

Nicky also wants to put his baseball cards in piles. Help him do the division

⑲ Divide 140  into 10 piles. How many  in each pile?

140 ÷ 10 = ______

There are ______  in each pile.

$$10\overline{)140}$$

______

$$\begin{array}{r} 1 \\ 10\overline{)140} \\ 10 \\ \hline 40 \end{array}$$

Bring down and divide again.

______

⑳ $20\overline{)375}$ r

______ 5

㉑ $15\overline{)423}$ r

______ 3

㉒ $16\overline{)312}$ r

______ 2

㉓ $17\overline{)673}$ r

______

㉔ $23\overline{)488}$ r

______

㉕ $24\overline{)509}$ r

______

㉖ 409 ÷ 16 = ________

㉗ 329 ÷ 18 = ________

㉘ 975 ÷ 31 = ________

㉙ 672 ÷ 38 = ________

See how Nicky checks his answer. Then do the questions and check the answers in the same way.

```
     1 7 r10
15 ) 2 6 5
     1 5
     -----
     1 1 5
     1 0 5
     -----
       1 0
```

Check

17 x 15 + 10

= 255 + 10

= 265

1st Multiply the quotient by the divisor.

2nd Add the remainder.

The answer is the same as the dividend. I am correct!

Check the answers

Divisor

Q x **D** + **R** = **Dividend**

Quotient Remainder

⑳ 15) 390 r ___ ... 0

Check

____ x 15 + ____

= ____

㉛ 18) 456 r ___ ... 6

Check

____ x 18 + ____

= ____

㉜ 25) 697 r ___

Check

____ x ____ + ____

= ____

㉝ 36) 866 r ___

Check

____ x ____ + ____

= ____

㉞ 525 ÷ 32 = ________

㉟ 487 ÷ 23 = ________

㊱ 730 ÷ 48 = ________

㊲ 669 ÷ 34 = ________

Read what Tim says. Then do the divisions.

38. In my class, there are 26 students and we have 3432 baseball cards in all. How many does each of us have?

$3432 \div 26 =$ ______

Each of us has ______ baseball cards.

```
      1 3 □
26 ) 3 4 3 2
     2 6
     ---
       8 3
       7 8
       ---
         5 2
         □ □
         ---
```

39.

```
             r
27 ) 4 6 7 3
     -----
         7
     -----
           3
     -----
```

40.

```
             r
21 ) 3 6 2 8
     -----
         2
     -----
           8
```

41.

```
             r
39 ) 3 2 7 4
     -------
           4
```

42.

```
             r
32 ) 2 2 7 3
     -------
           3
```

43.

```
             r
31 ) 8 0 0 4
```

44.

```
             r
35 ) 8 6 7 3
```

45. Share 4682  equally among 42 children. How many  does each child get?

________ ÷ ________ = ________

Each child gets ________  and there are ________  left over.

46. One box can hold 48 cards. How many boxes does Nicky need to hold 3068 cards?

________ ÷ ________ = ________

Nicky needs ________ boxes.

The remainder needs a box too.

47. 1782 students are going to watch baseball.

Each bus can carry 68 students. How many buses will be needed?

________ ÷ ________ = ________

________ buses will be needed.

ACTIVITY

Work out the answers by mental calculation.

1. $46 \div 46 + 1 =$ ________
2. $(36 + 36) \div 2 =$ ________
3. $56 \times 1 \div 1 =$ ________
4. $1 \times 263 \div 1 =$ ________
5. $47 \div 47 \times 47 =$ ________
6. $(623 - 623) \div 5 =$ ________

5 Direct Proportion

WORDS TO LEARN

Direct proportion - two related sets of data which increase or decrease in the same patterns

e.g. 1 🍎 for 25¢ → (x 2) → 2 🍎 for 50¢ (x 2)

The more you buy, the more you have to pay. The number of 🍎 and the cost are in direct proportion.

Help Uncle Jack find how much he has to pay for the golf balls. Complete the table and answer the questions.

①

Number of golf balls		Cost
	1	$2 x 1 = $_____
1 x 2	2	$2 x 2 = $_____
1 x 3	3	$2 x _____ = $_____
1 x 4	4	$2 x _____ = $_____
1 x 5	5	$2 x _____ = $_____

The cost of the golf balls are the multiples of 2.

② How much do 6 golf balls cost? $__________

③ How much do 14 golf balls cost? $__________

④ How many golf balls can be bought for $20? __________

⑤ Are the number of golf balls and the cost in direct proportion? __________

Read what Uncle Jack says. Then complete the table and answer the questions.

> Each player in my golf class uses 5 golf balls to practise.

⑥

Number of players	1	4	7	10	12
Number of golf balls	5				

⑦ How many golf balls does Uncle Jack need if there are 9 players? ________

⑧ How many players would it take to use up 100 golf balls? ________

Uncle Jack wants to order some magazines and books. Help him fill in the tables.

> Find the cost of 1 magazine first. $18 ÷ 3 = $6.

⑨

Number of magazines	1	2	3	5	8
Cost ($)			18		

⑩

Number of books	4	7	8	10	12
Cost ($)			64		

Find the cost for one unit first.

ACTIVITY

Read what Uncle Jack says. Then tick ✔ the right graph.

> My golf club has 2 new members every month.

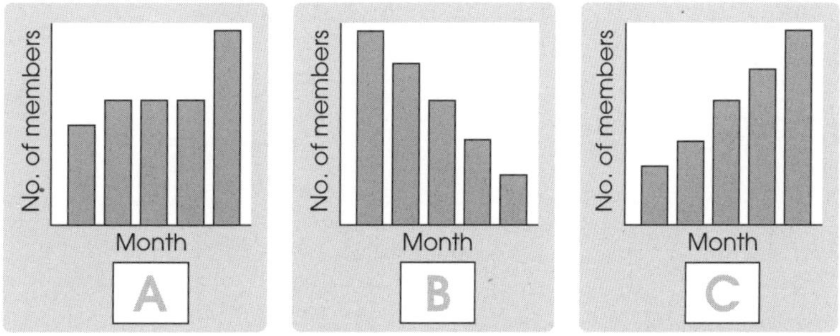

6 Fractions

WORDS TO LEARN

Fraction - a number showing a part of a whole

e.g. 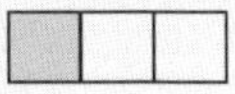 $\frac{1}{3}$ $\frac{\text{part shaded}}{\text{parts in all}}$ $\frac{1}{3}$ ← numerator, ← denominator

Proper fraction - a fraction with a numerator smaller than its denominator e.g. $\frac{3}{8}$

Improper fraction - a fraction with a numerator greater than its denominator e.g. $\frac{9}{7}$

Mixed number - a number formed by a whole number and a proper fraction e.g. $4\frac{3}{5}$

Equivalent fractions - fractions with the same value e.g. $\frac{1}{2} = \frac{2}{4}$

Simplest form - a fraction in which the numerator and denominator have only 1 as their common factor

Help Tim put his cards on the right boards. Write the fractions or mixed numbers.

① Proper Fraction

② Improper Fraction

③ Mixed Number

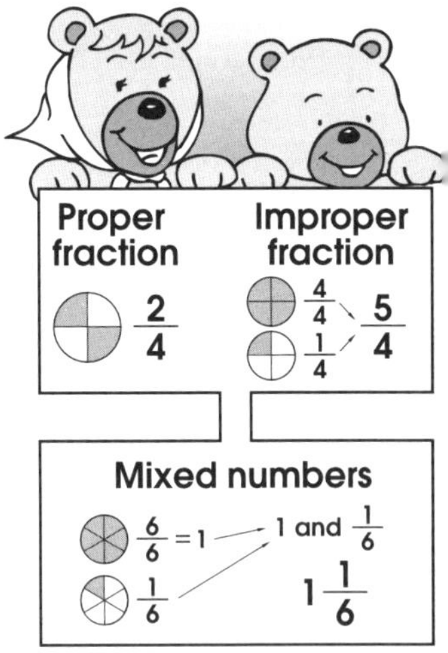

Follow Tim's method to change the improper fractions to mixed numbers.

④ $\frac{9}{7}$ = ______

⑤ $\frac{4}{3}$ = ______

⑥ $\frac{12}{5}$ = ______

⑦ $\frac{13}{4}$ = ______

$\frac{8}{6} = \frac{6}{6} + \frac{2}{6} = 1\frac{2}{6}$

or $\frac{8}{6} = 8 \div 6 = 1\frac{2}{6}$

$\frac{8}{6} \rightarrow 6\overline{)8}$ = 1 r2 (8 − 6 = 2) $\rightarrow 1\frac{2}{6}$

Read what Nicky says. Then change the mixed numbers to improper fractions.

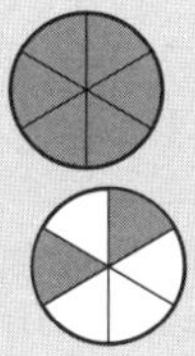

$1\frac{2}{6} = 1 + \frac{2}{6} = \frac{6}{6} + \frac{2}{6} = \frac{8}{6}$

or $1\frac{2}{6} = \frac{1 \times 6 + 2}{6} = \frac{8}{6}$

Multiply the whole number by the denominator and add the numerator.

⑧ $2\frac{1}{3} =$ ______

⑨ $3\frac{4}{7} =$ ______

⑩ $1\frac{5}{8} =$ ______

⑪ $5\frac{1}{4} =$ ______

⑫ $4\frac{5}{6} =$ ______

⑬ $7\frac{1}{3} =$ ______

Follow Tim's method to write equivalent fractions.

$\frac{1}{2}$, $\frac{2}{4}$ and $\frac{4}{8}$ are equivalent fractions.

$\frac{1}{2} = \frac{2}{4} = \frac{4}{8}$ $\quad \frac{1 \times 2}{2 \times 2} = \frac{2}{4}$ $\quad \frac{1 \times 4}{2 \times 4} = \frac{4}{8}$

⑭ $\frac{2}{3} = \frac{}{6} = \frac{}{12}$

⑮ $\frac{1}{5} = \frac{}{10} = \frac{}{15}$

⑯ $\frac{3}{4} = \frac{}{8} = \frac{}{20}$

⑰ $\frac{7}{8} = \frac{}{24} = \frac{}{40}$

Multiply the numerator and denominator by the same number to get an equivalent fraction.

Follow Tim's method to write the fractions in simplest form.

⑱ $\frac{20}{30} = \frac{}{3}$

⑲ $\frac{16}{20} = \frac{}{5}$

⑳ $\frac{12}{15} = \frac{4}{}$

㉑ $\frac{42}{54} = \frac{7}{}$

To simplify a fraction, divide the numerator and denominator by the same number.

$\frac{20}{25} = \frac{20 \div 5}{25 \div 5} = \frac{4}{5}$

Read the two cards that Uncle Jack has picked for Tim. Help Tim write the answers in simplest form.

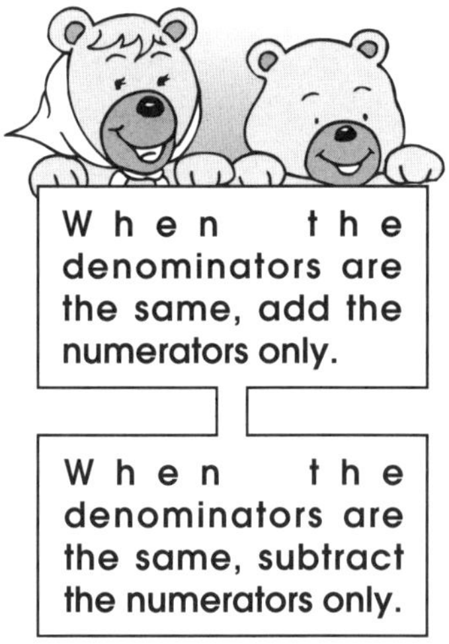

㉒ $\frac{6}{10} + \frac{2}{10} = \underline{\quad}$

㉓ $\frac{10}{12} - \frac{7}{12} = \underline{\quad}$

㉔ $\frac{6}{15} + \frac{3}{15} = \underline{\quad}$

㉕ $\frac{14}{16} - \frac{12}{16} = \underline{\quad}$

㉖ $\frac{7}{20} + \frac{5}{20} = \underline{\quad}$

㉗ $\frac{19}{24} - \frac{13}{24} = \underline{\quad}$

㉘ $\frac{2}{18} + \frac{7}{18} = \underline{\quad}$

㉙ $\frac{19}{21} - \frac{5}{21} = \underline{\quad}$

Write the mixed number in simplest form for each problem.

㉚ $\frac{6}{8} + \frac{3}{8} = \frac{9}{8} = \underline{\qquad}$

㉛ $\frac{6}{10} + \frac{9}{10} = \frac{\quad}{10} = \underline{\qquad}$

㉜ $\frac{7}{12} + \frac{9}{12} = \frac{\quad}{\quad} = \underline{\qquad}$

㉝ $\frac{5}{16} + \frac{15}{16} = \frac{\quad}{\quad} = \underline{\qquad}$

Follow Tim's method to solve the problems. Write the answers in simplest form.

㉞ $2\frac{1}{6} + 3\frac{4}{6} =$ ______

㉟ $4\frac{8}{9} - 3\frac{4}{9} =$ ______

㊱ $4\frac{2}{9} + 4\frac{1}{9} =$ ______

㊲ $3\frac{7}{12} - 1\frac{5}{12} =$ ______

Try these. Write each fraction in simplest form.

㊳ $5\frac{4}{7} + 3\frac{6}{7} =$ ______

㊴ $1\frac{8}{9} + 4\frac{4}{9} =$ ______

㊵ $2\frac{5}{8} + 1\frac{3}{8} =$ ______

Change the improper fractions to mixed numbers.

Don't forget :

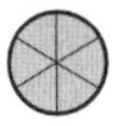 $\frac{6}{6} = 1$

Help Tim find what fraction of a pizza was left.

㊶ $2 - \frac{1}{6} = 1\frac{\square}{6} - \frac{1}{6} = 1\frac{\square}{6}$

Try these. Write each fraction in simplest form.

㊷ $4 - \frac{2}{5} =$ ______

㊸ $5 - \frac{1}{3} =$ ______

㊹ $3 - \frac{6}{10} =$ ______

㊺ $9 - \frac{9}{10} =$ ______

ACTIVITY

Find who ate which pizza. Write the letters only.

A . Nicky ate $\frac{10}{25}$ of a pizza.

B . Tim ate $\frac{36}{54}$ of a pizza.

C . Jill ate $\frac{42}{48}$ of a pizza.

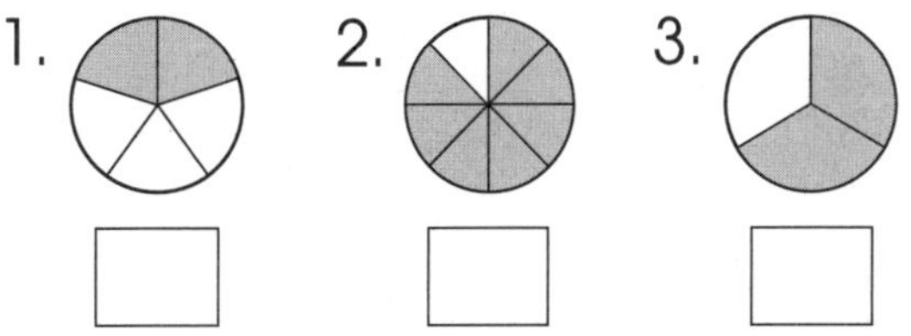

7 Decimals (Addition and Subtraction)

WORDS TO LEARN

Decimal - a numeral containing a decimal point, with the value of the digit(s) to the right of the decimal point being less than 1

e.g. ones tenths hundredths
4.65
decimal point

Read: Four and sixty-five hundredths

In fraction: $4\frac{65}{100}$

Read what the children say. Then write the decimals.

① five tenths ______

② eighty-one hundredths ______

③ eight tenths ______

④ forty-five hundredths ______

⑤ $\frac{4}{10}$ ______

⑥ $\frac{6}{100}$ ______

Write the children's heights in metres and put the measurements in order.

⑦ Tim 1 m 8 cm = ______ m

⑧ Nicky 1 m 14 cm = ______ m

⑨ Jill 97 cm = ______ m

⑩ Nancy 1 m 2 cm = ______ m

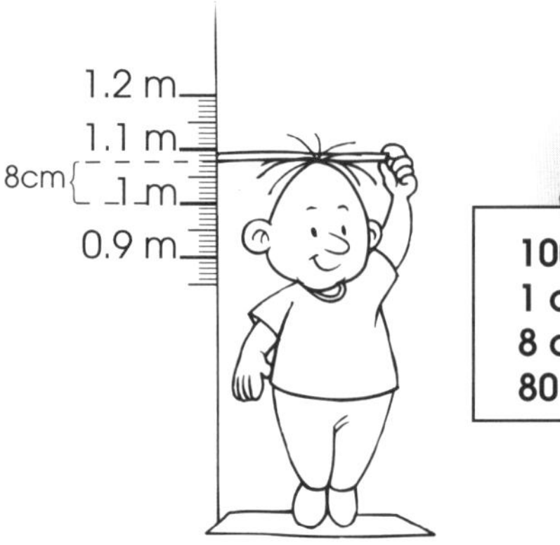

⑪ From the tallest to the shortest:

______ > ______ > ______ > ______

Read what Tim and Nicky say. Then write the children's weights in kilograms and put the readings in order.

If this block is divided into 1000 equal parts, each part is one thousandth.

□ → $\frac{1}{1000}$ or 0.001

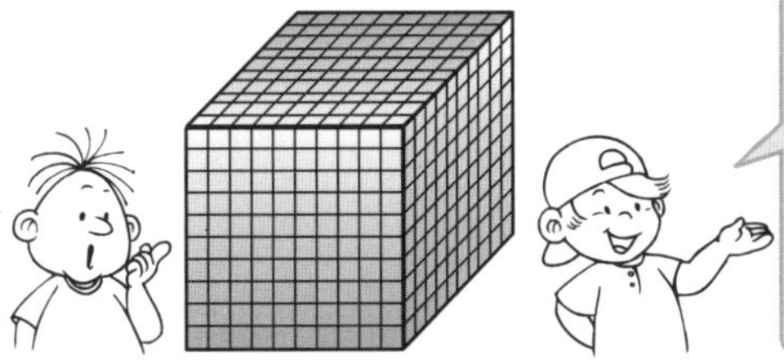

1 kg = 1000 g
1 g = 0.001 kg

$2\frac{632}{1000}$ kg can be written as 2.632 kg.

⑫	Tim	35 kg 213 g = ______ kg
⑬	Nicky	34 kg 78 g = ______ kg
⑭	Jill	34 kg 5 g = ______ kg
⑮	Nancy	35 kg 10 g = ______ kg

⑯ From the heaviest to the lightest:

______ > ______ > ______ > ______

Read what Tim says. Then compare the decimals and put >, < or = in the □ .

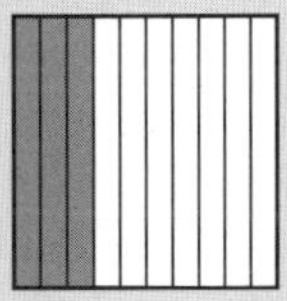

$\frac{3}{10}$ = 0.3

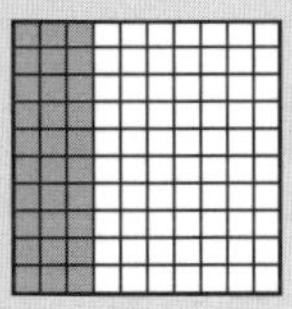

$\frac{30}{100}$ = 0.30

0.3 and 0.30 are equal.

⑰ 1.9 □ 1.90	⑱ 2.07 □ 2.70	⑲ 36.0 □ 36.00
⑳ 8.509 □ 8.5900	㉑ 4.40 □ 4.04	㉒ 26.30 □ 26.300
㉓ 6.74 □ 6.470	㉔ 4.333 □ 4.33	㉕ 12.68 □ 12.86

Help the children find how much money they have.

㉖ I had \$1.32 and Uncle Jack gave me \$0.59. How much do I have now?

1st Align the decimal points.	2nd Add hundredths.	3rd Add tenths.	4th Add ones.
$\begin{array}{r} 1.32 \\ +\ 0.59 \\ \hline \end{array}$	$\begin{array}{r} 1.32 \\ +\ 0.59 \\ \hline \square \end{array}$	$\begin{array}{r} ^{1}\ \ \ \ \\ 1.32 \\ +\ 0.59 \\ \hline \square 1 \end{array}$	$\begin{array}{r} 1.32 \\ +\ 0.59 \\ \hline \square.91 \end{array}$

Align the decimal points when you add or subtract the decimal numbers.

 has \$________ now.

㉗  had \$1.56 and spent \$0.48. How much does he have now?

$\begin{array}{r} 1.56 \\ -\ 0.48 \\ \hline \end{array}$	$\begin{array}{r} ^{4\ 16} \\ 1.\not{5}\not{6} \\ -\ 0.48 \\ \hline \square \end{array}$	$\begin{array}{r} ^{4\ 16} \\ 1.\not{5}\not{6} \\ -\ 0.48 \\ \hline \square 8 \end{array}$	$\begin{array}{r} 1.56 \\ -\ 0.48 \\ \hline \square.08 \end{array}$

 has \$________ now.

Try these.

㉘ 3.64 + 0.97 = ________

㉙ 2.48 + 9.56 = ________

㉚ 10.54 – 3.27 = ________

㉛ 12.64 + 31.49 = ________

㉜ 9.87 – 8.50 = ________

㉝ 7.63 + 12.4 = ________

㉞ 8.89 + 12.37 = ________

㉟ 10.21 – 9.88 = ________

See how Tim estimates and finds the answer. Follow his method to solve the problems.

㊱ 1.46 + 2.84 − 1.94 = ______

Round the decimals to the nearest whole number to estimate.

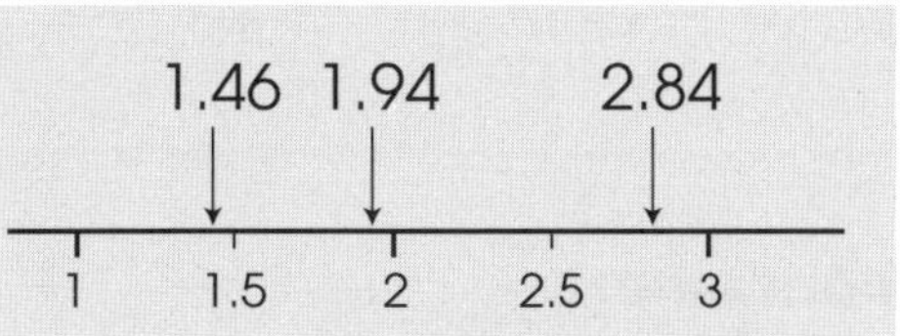

1.46 + 2.84 − 1.94 =

Estimate: 1 + 3 − 2 = 2

```
   1.46
+  2.84
  -----
   □.□□
-  1.94
  -----
   □.□□
```

Do the calculation in order.
e.g. 4 + 1 − 3 = 5 − 3
= 2

㊲ 2.43 + 1.57 − 1.15 = ______ Estimate:	㊳ 1.64 + 5.77 − 0.94 = ______ Estimate:
㊴ 12.05 − 4.47 + 6.03 = ______ Estimate:	㊵ 15.13 − 5.89 − 4.33 = ______ Estimate:
㊶ 9.97 + 0.13 + 4.56 = ______ Estimate:	㊷ 12.67 − 7.69 + 4.19 = ______ Estimate:

ACTIVITY

Each child, together with his or her pet, weighs 44.81 kg. Match the children with their pets. Write the letters only.

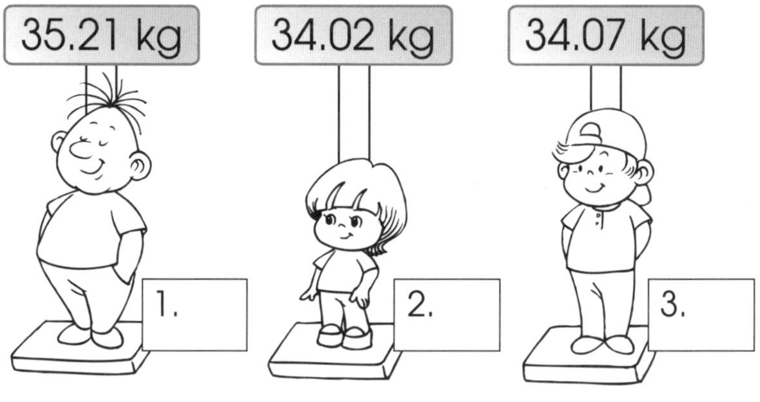

A.  9.6 kg

B.  10.74 kg

C.  10.79 kg

8 Capacity

WORDS TO LEARN

Capacity - the amount of water that a container can hold
There are 1000 millilitres (mL) in a litre (L); 1000mL = 1L.

Write the amount of liquid in each container.

①
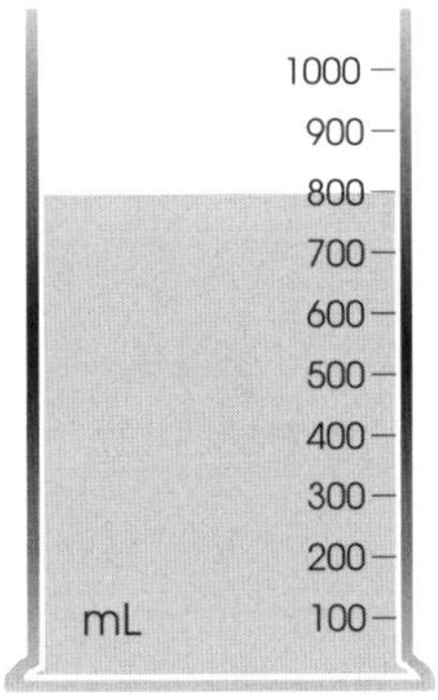

______ mL

②
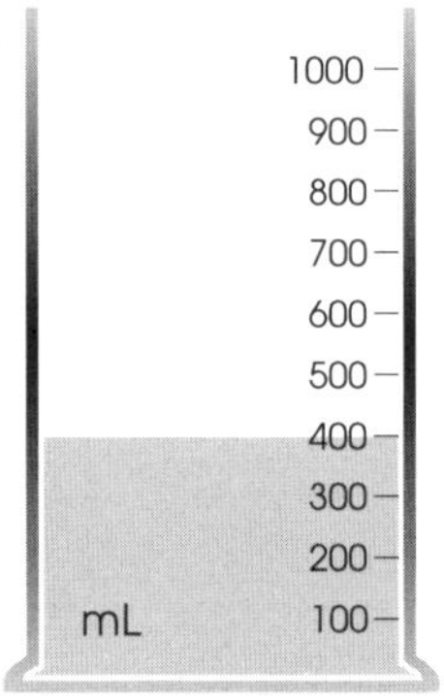

______ mL

③
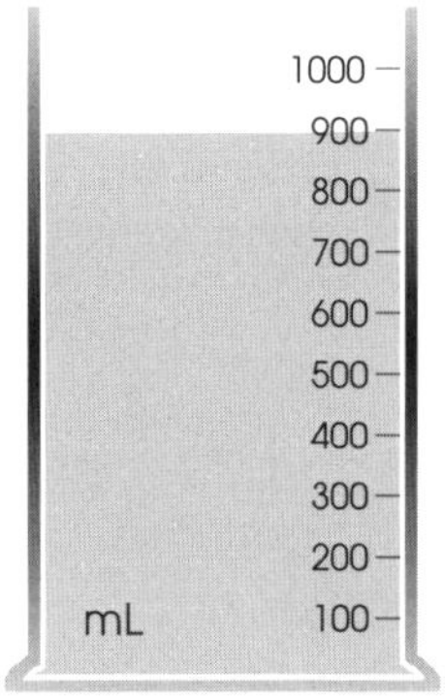

______ mL

How much water did Tim use to water his plants? Fill in the blanks.

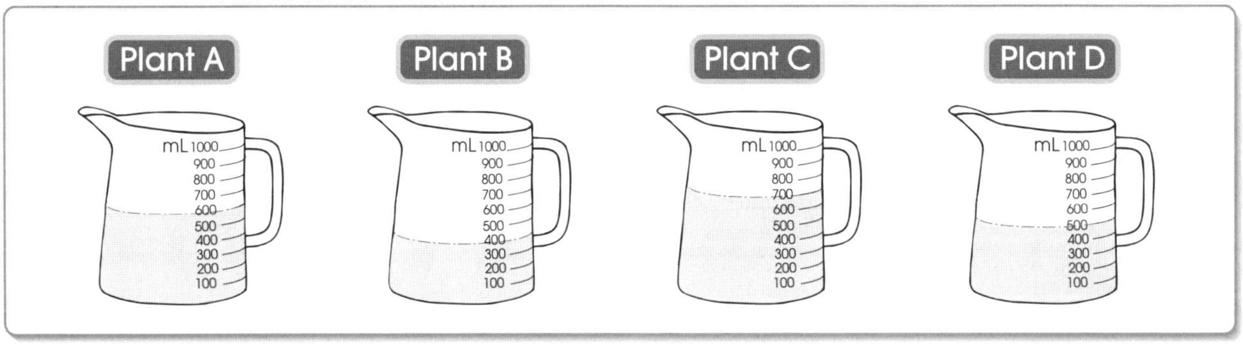

④ Plant A: 1000 mL – 600 mL = ______ mL

⑤ Plant B: ______ mL – ______ mL = ______ mL

⑥ Plant C: ______ mL – ______ mL = ______ mL

⑦ Plant D: ______ mL – ______ mL = ______ mL

⑧ Which plant needs the most water? Plant ______

⑨ Which plant needs the least water? Plant ______

Draw the water level in each container.

⑩
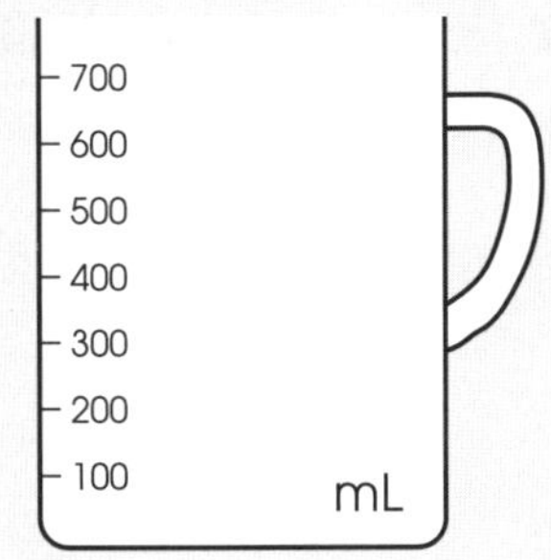

300 mL

⑪
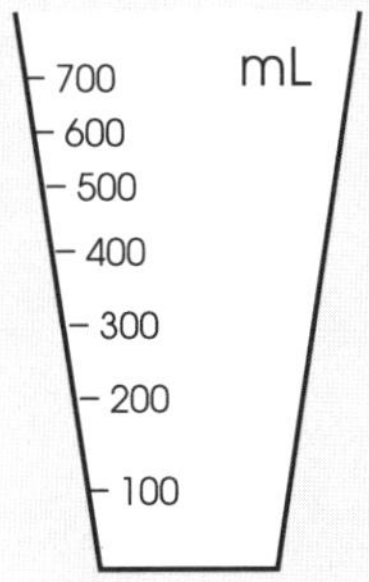

200 mL

⑫
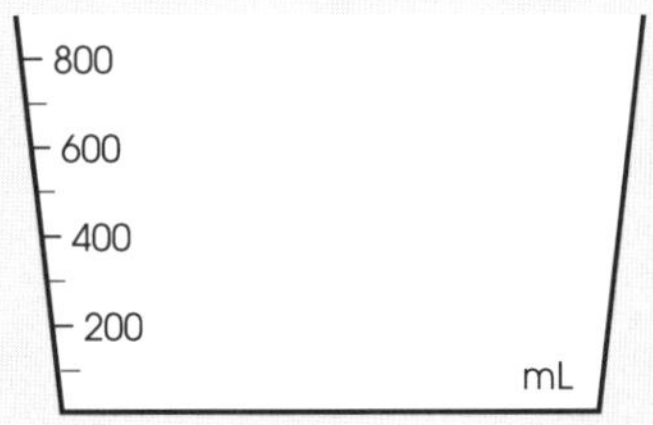

700 mL

Look at the containers and answer the questions.

1 L	=	**1000 mL**
1 mL	=	**0.001 L**

⑬ How many  of water can be poured into a  ? ________

⑭ How many  of water can be poured into a  ? ________

⑮ How many  of water can be poured into a  ? ________

⑯ How many millilitres of water can a  hold ? ________ mL

ACTIVITY

Tick ✔ the container that has a capacity of $\frac{1}{4}$ litre.

A

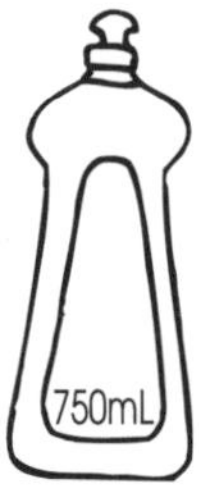

B

C

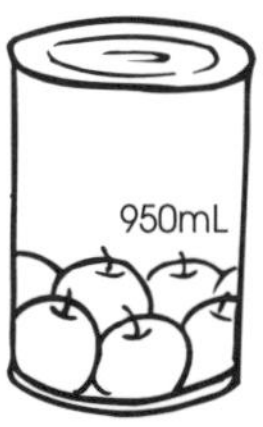

D

9 Solids

WORDS TO LEARN

Face - a flat surface of a solid

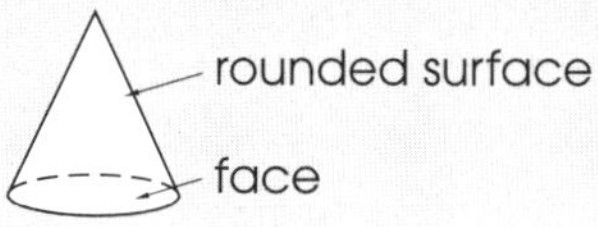

Edge - a curve or a straight line segment where two surfaces or faces meet

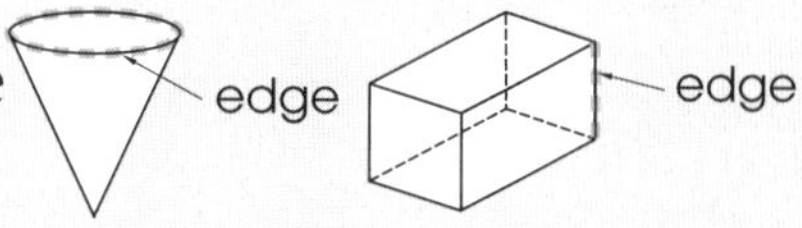

Vertex - a point where lines or edges meet

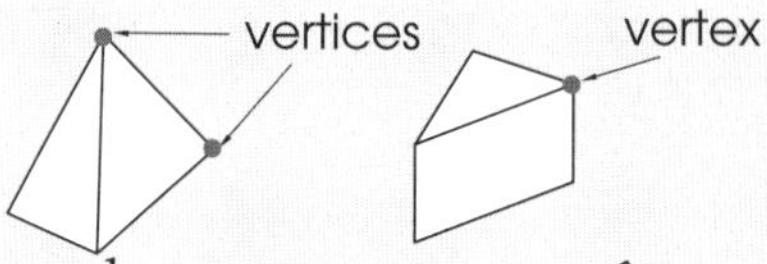

Prism - a solid shape with rectangular faces and congruent ends, named by the shape of its ends e.g

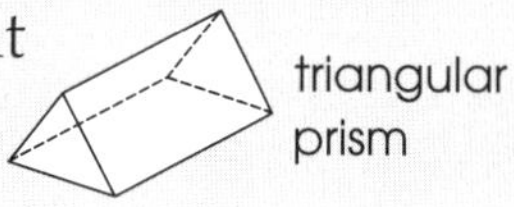

Pyramid - a solid shape with triangular faces, a common vertex and a flat base, named by the shape of its base e.g

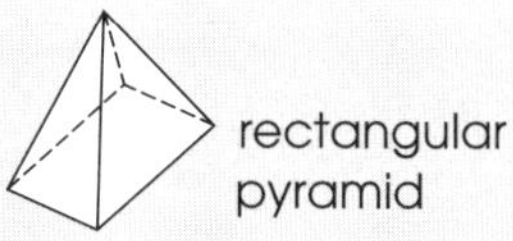

Cylinder - a solid shape with two circular ends of the same size e.g

Name the frames that Tim has built with tooth picks and plasticine.

①

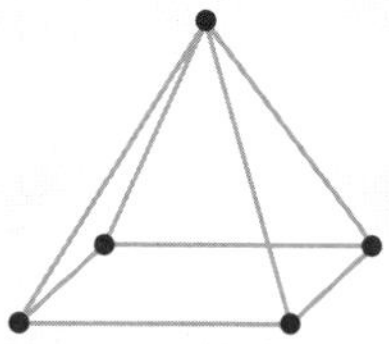

Rectangular pyramid
____

②

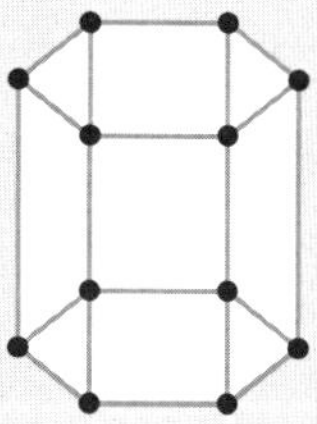

____

③

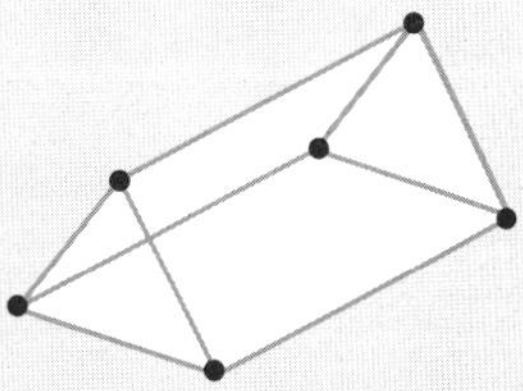

____

④

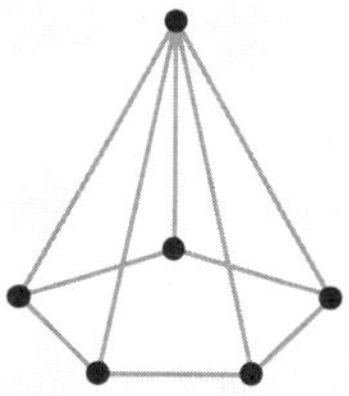

____

Prisms and pyramids are named by the shape of the ends or base.

Read what Tim says. Then complete the table.

Solid		Number of faces	Number of vertices	Number of edges
⑤ Rectangular pyramid	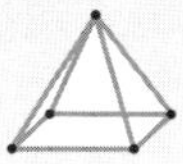			
⑥ Hexagonal pyramid				
⑦ Triangular pyramid	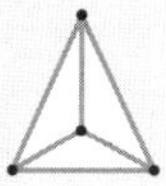			
⑧ Pentagonal prism	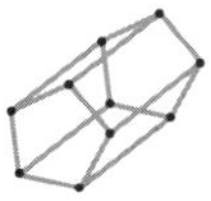			
⑨ Triangular prism	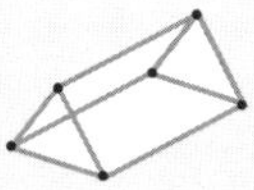			
⑩ Rectangular prism	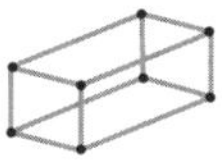			

Match the nets with the shapes. Write the letters only.

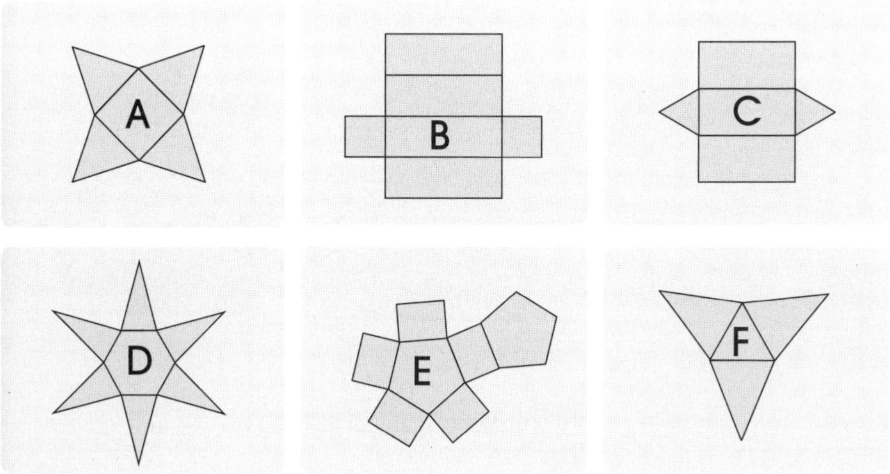

⑪ 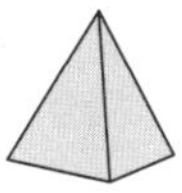 ________

⑫ 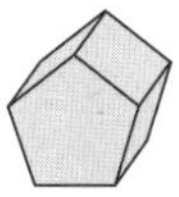 ________

⑬ 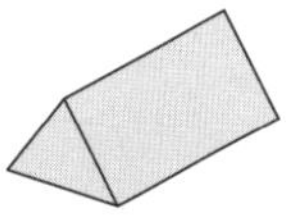 ________

⑭ 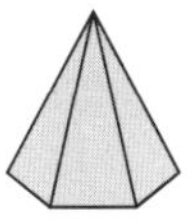 ________

⑮ 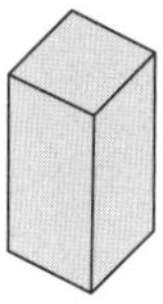 ________

⑯ 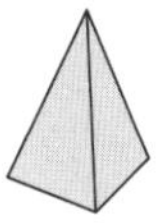 ________

Follow Tim's method to draw the pyramids.

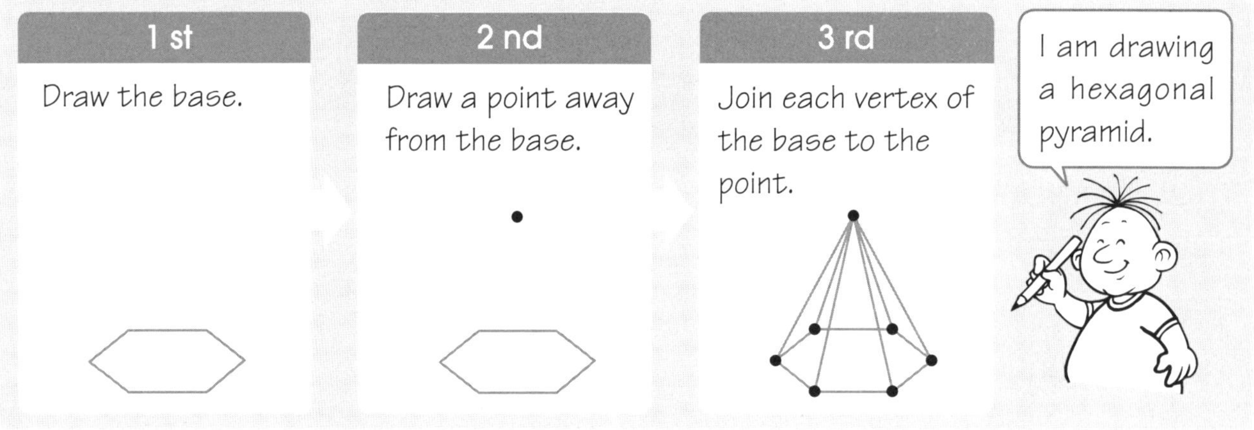

⑰ Pentagonal pyramid

⑱ Rectangular pyramid

Follow Nicky's method to draw the prisms.

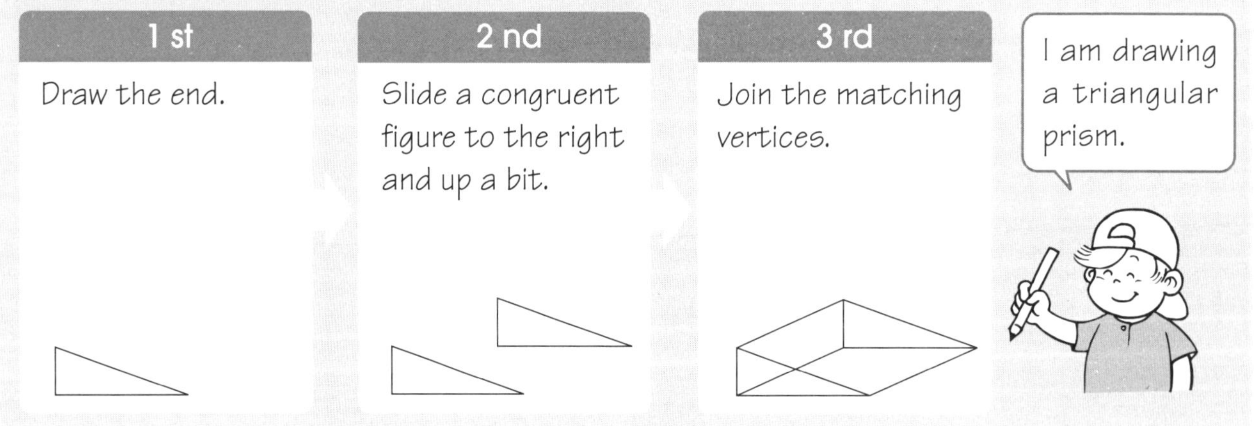

⑲ Rectangular prism

⑳ Hexagonal prism

Read what Uncle Jack says and tick ✔ the right answers.

21. 

What is the rule for finding the number of edges of a pyramid?

- [A] Number of edges = Number of sides in the base x 2
- [B] Number of edges = Number of sides in the base + 2

22. 

What is the rule for finding the number of vertices of a pyramid?

- [A] Number of vertices = Number of sides in the base – 1
- [B] Number of vertices = Number of sides in the base + 1

23. 

What is the rule for finding the number of edges of a prism?

- [A] Number of edges = Number of sides in the base + 3
- [B] Number of edges = Number of sides in the base x 3

24. 

What is the rule for finding the number of vertices of a prism?

- [A] Number of vertices = Number of sides in the base x 2
- [B] Number of vertices = Number of sides in the base + 2

ACTIVITY

Use the above formulas to answer the questions.

1. The base of a pyramid has 20 sides.

   a. How many edges ? ______ b. How many vertices ? ______

2. The base of a prism has 16 sides.

   a. How many edges ? ______ b. How many vertices ? ______

10 Pictographs

WORDS TO LEARN

Pictograph - a graph using pictures to show information

Look at the pictograph and answer the questions.

Number of Cartons of Milk Sold Last Week

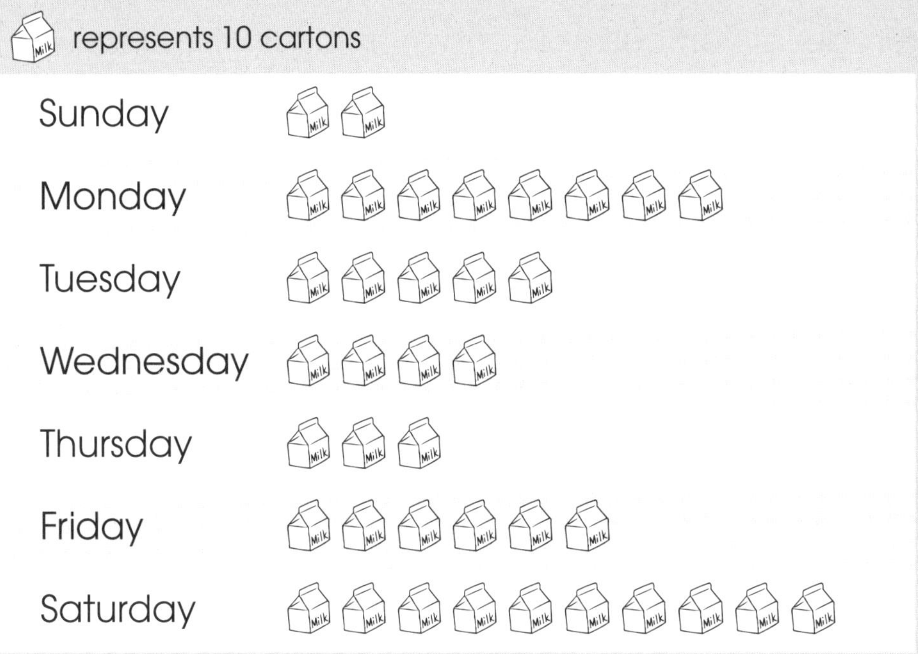

① How many cartons of milk do 7 (milk carton) represent? ____________

② How many people bought milk on Monday? ____________

③ How many people bought milk on Saturday? ____________

④ How many more people bought milk on Friday than on Thursday? ____________

⑤ On which day did the fewest people buy milk? ____________

⑥ How many people bought milk on Tuesday and Wednesday? ____________

⑦ How many cartons of milk were sold in all? ____________

Look at the table. Then complete the graph and answer the questions.

Food					
No. of people	400	600	300	400	700

Draw  **to complete the graph.**

⑧ **Favourite Food**  represents 100 people

⑨ How many  would represent 500 people? ____________

⑩ How many more people like  than  ? ____________

⑪ How many people has Uncle Jack asked? ____________

ACTIVITY

Use the clues to write the names.

Name	Number of Candies

 represents 25 candies

Nicky: I have 100 candies.

Tim: I have more than 125 candies.

Jill: I have 25 more candies than Nicky.

Midway Test

Complete the tables and answer the questions. (15 marks)

① The children's magazines are $3 each.

Number of magazines	1	2	3	5	6	10
Cost ($)	3					

② The women's magazines are $5 each.

Number of magazines	1	3	5	6	10	12
Cost ($)	5					

③ How many children's magazines can you buy for $22? ____________

④ How much do 15 women's magazines cost? $ ____________

⑤ The cost of children's magazines are in multiples of ____________ .

⑥ The cost of women's magazines are in multiples of ____________ .

⑦ The least common multiple of 3 and 5 is ____________ .

Answer the questions. (4 marks)

⑧ Tim eats sandwiches on every 4th day and eats hot dogs on every 5th day. When will he eat sandwiches and hot dogs on the same day?

Every ________ days

⑨ Nicky plays hockey on every 6th day and plays baseball on every 8th day. When will he play hockey and baseball on the same day?

Every ________ days

Find the factors of each number. Then find the greatest common factor. **(10 marks)**

⑩ 10: ______________

12: ______________

GCF of 10 and 12: ______

⑪ 16: ______________

48: ______________

GCF of 16 and 48: ______

Use short division to find the greatest common factor of the following numbers. **(6 marks)**

⑫ 20 40

GCF of 20 and 40: ______

⑬ 36 48

GCF of 36 and 48: ______

Write the decimal numbers in order from the largest to the smallest. **(6 marks)**

⑭ 6.4 3.9 5.8 4.6 4.9 5.0

____ > ____ > ____ > ____ > ____ > ____

⑮ 7.24 6.69 9.83 8.65 8.00 7.00

____ > ____ > ____ > ____ > ____ > ____

Change the fractions to decimal numbers. **(4 marks)**

⑯ $1\frac{2}{10}$ = ___ . ___

⑰ $2\frac{56}{100}$ = ___ . ___

⑱ $\frac{5}{100}$ = ___ . ___

⑲ $6\frac{205}{1000}$ = ___ . ___

Midway Test

Look at the prices of the toys. Then complete the table. (6 marks)

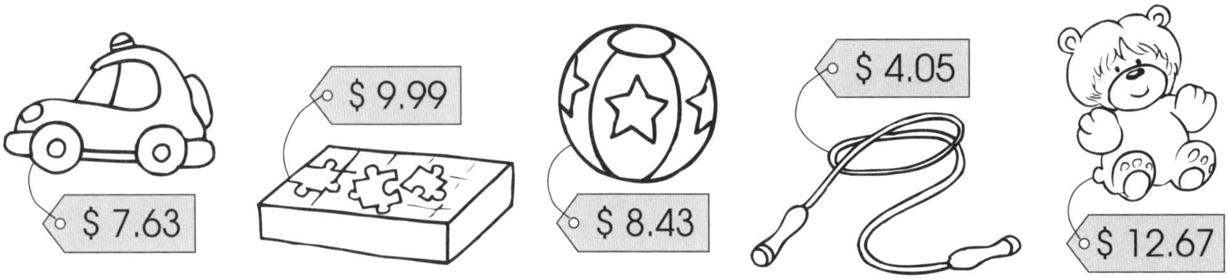

Toy	Cost	Money given	Change
	⑳ 7.63 + 12.67 $ ____	$ 25.00	㉑ 25.00 – ____ $ ____
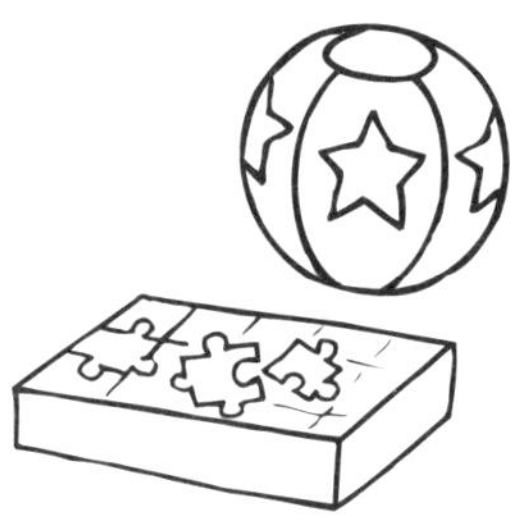	㉒ + ____ $ ____	$ 20.00	㉓ – ____ $ ____
	㉔ + ____ $ ____	$ 20.75	㉕ – ____ $ ____

Answer the questions. (10 marks)

㉖ 17×29

㉗ 56×18

㉘ 23×36

㉙ The toy store sells 13  every day. How many  are sold in 45 days?

_______ x _______ = _______

_______  are sold in 45 days.

㉚ There are 23 people. Each person has spent $15. How much money have they spent altogether?

_______ x _______ = _______

They have spent $_______ altogether.

Change the improper fractions to mixed numbers. (3 marks)

㉛ $\frac{11}{6} = \square$

㉜ $\frac{13}{8} = \square$

㉝ $\frac{12}{5} = \square$

Write the equivalent fractions. (3 marks)

㉞ $\frac{4}{5} = \frac{\square}{20}$

㉟ $\frac{12}{16} = \frac{\square}{4}$

㊱ $\frac{15}{40} = \frac{3}{\square}$

Write the answers in simplest form. (6 marks)

㊲ $\frac{5}{16} + \frac{1}{16} = \frac{\quad}{\quad} = \frac{\quad}{\quad}$

㊳ $\frac{9}{12} - \frac{3}{12} = \frac{\quad}{\quad} = \frac{\quad}{\quad}$

㊴ $4\frac{6}{15} + 5\frac{3}{15} = \frac{\quad}{\quad} = \frac{\quad}{\quad}$

㊵ $4\frac{5}{6} - 1\frac{2}{6} = \frac{\quad}{\quad} = \frac{\quad}{\quad}$

㊶ $2\frac{5}{18} + 9\frac{5}{18} = \frac{\quad}{\quad} = \frac{\quad}{\quad}$

㊷ $9\frac{17}{25} - 5\frac{7}{25} = \frac{\quad}{\quad} = \frac{\quad}{\quad}$

Complete the division to find out how many vehicles arrived at the airport. (9 marks)

㊸ 2398 people came by car. Each car could carry 4 people. At least how many cars arrived at the airport?

4) 2398

2398 ÷ ______ = ______

At least ______ cars arrived at the airport.

㊹ 3846 people came by van. Each van could carry 7 people. At least how many vans arrived at the airport?

7)

3846 ÷ ______ = ______

At least ______ vans arrived at the airport.

㊺ 7588 people came by bus. Each bus could carry 38 people. At least how many buses arrived at the airport?

)

______ ÷ ______ = ______

At least ______ buses arrived at the airport.

Put the above results in a graph and answer the questions. (6 marks)

㊻ Draw  to complete the graph.

 = 100 vehicles

Cars	
Vans	
Buses	

47. Which kind of vehicle was the most popular? ______

48. How many more cars are there than buses? ______

49. How many  would represent 800 vehicles? ______

Name the shapes and answer the questions. (6 marks)

50. 

______

51. 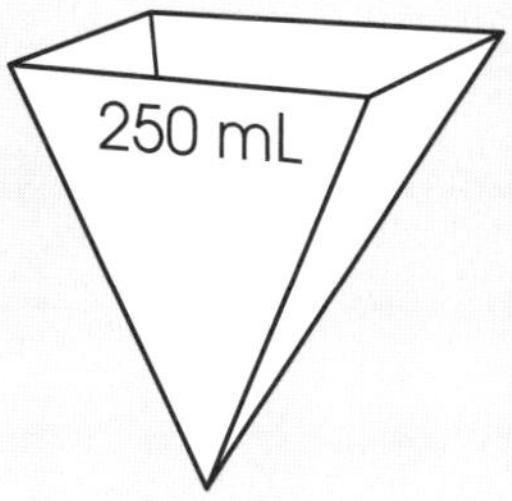

______

52. 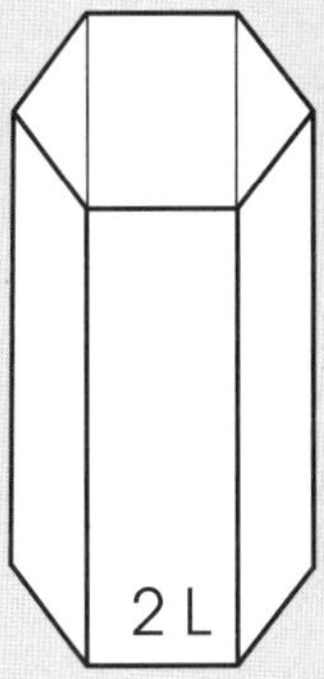

______

53. How many  of water can be poured into a  ? ______

54. How many  of water can be poured into a  ? ______

55. How many  of water can be poured into a  ? ______

Complete the table. (6 marks)

Solid	Number of faces	Number of vertices	Number of edges
Rectangular prism 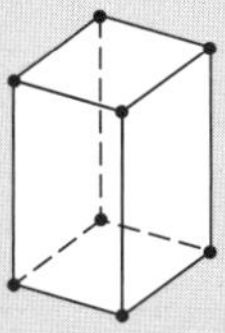	56.	57.	58.
Pentagonal pyramid 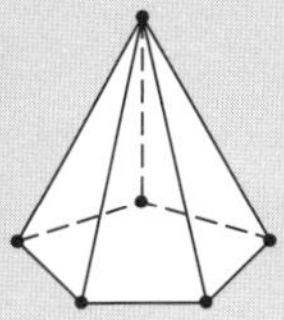	59.	60.	61.

SCORE

100

11 Brackets

WORDS TO LEARN

Brackets ( ) - signs to show which part of a problem is to be done first

e.g. $5 \times (2 + 4) = 5 \times (6)$

$= 30$

Solve the problem inside the ( ) first.

Help Lily find how many pine cones she and Nicky have.

① I collected 25 pine cones. Nicky picked 17 but gave 8 to Nancy. How many pine cones do Nicky and I have altogether now?

$25 + (17 - 8) =$ ________ + ________

$=$ ________

Lily and Nicky have ________ pine cones altogether now.

Remember to calculate the parts inside the brackets first.

Match each child with the pine cone that has the same answer. Write the letters only.

②  $(42 + 6) \div 3$

③  $(83 - 7) \div 2$

④  $4 \times (16 - 9)$

⑤  $(41 - 27) \times 6$

⑥  $(72 \div 9) \times 3$

A $59 - (25 \times 2 - 19)$

B $48 \times 2 - (36 \div 3)$

C $(56 - 29) - (47 - 36)$

D $37 + (56 \div 4 - 13)$

E $(43 - 28 \div 2) - 5$

Read what Tim says. Then help him find how many pine cones he and Nicky have.

⑦ 

> I picked 19 (pine cones) and Nicky picked 25. He gave 16 to Nancy who gave him 4 back. How many (pine cones) do Nicky and I have altogether now?

$19 + ((25 - 16) + 4) = \_\_\_\_ + (\_\_\_\_ + 4)$

$= \_\_\_\_ + \_\_\_\_$

$= \_\_\_\_$

Tim and Nicky have ______ (pine cones) altogether now.

Calculate the bracketed parts from inside out.

Do multiplication and division before addition and subtraction.

Find how many pine cones each child has collected.

⑧ $2 \times ((4 + 2) \div 3 + 9)$

=

=

⑨ $(10 - (7 - 4)) \times 3 \div 7$

=

=

⑩ $45 - (30 - (18 - 6)) \div 6$

=

=

⑪ $((14 + 35) \div 7 + 1) \times 4$

=

=

ACTIVITY

Put brackets to these 4's to produce the right answers.

1. $4 - 4 - 4 \div 4 = 1$
2. $4 \div 4 - 4 \div 4 - 4 \div 4 = 2$
3. $4 + 4 + 4 \div 4 = 3$
4. $4 \times 4 - 4 + 4 = 4$

12 More about Fractions

WORDS TO LEARN

Fraction - a number which shows a part of a whole

e.g. 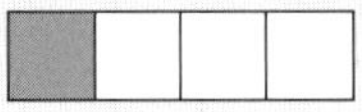 $\frac{1}{4}$ part shaded / parts in all

$\frac{1}{4}$ ← numerator / ← denominator

Follow Tim's method to compare the fractions. Put > or < in the ☐.

Which is greater, $\frac{3}{5}$ or $\frac{7}{10}$?

$\frac{3}{5} = \frac{3 \times 2}{5 \times 2} = \frac{6}{10}$ → $\frac{6}{10} < \frac{7}{10}$ → $\frac{3}{5} < \frac{7}{10}$

Use equivalent fractions with the same denominator to compare fractions.

To compare fractions, find equivalent fractions with same denominator first.

① $\frac{2}{3}$ ☐ $\frac{5}{6}$ ② $\frac{4}{7}$ ☐ $\frac{5}{14}$ ③ $\frac{3}{8}$ ☐ $\frac{11}{24}$

④ $\frac{4}{5}$ ☐ $\frac{7}{15}$ ⑤ $\frac{8}{9}$ ☐ $\frac{39}{45}$ ⑥ $\frac{5}{6}$ ☐ $\frac{11}{18}$

Follow Tim's method to solve the problems. Write the answers in simplest form.

e.g. $\frac{1}{2} + \frac{1}{4} = \frac{2}{4} + \frac{1}{4}$
$= \frac{3}{4}$

e.g. $\frac{4}{5} - \frac{7}{10} = \frac{8}{10} - \frac{7}{10}$
$= \frac{1}{10}$

1st Find the common denominator.
2nd Add or subtract the numerators.
3rd Write the fraction in simplest form.

To add or subtract fractions, find equivalent fractions with same denominator first.

⑦ $\frac{2}{5} + \frac{1}{10} = \frac{\quad}{10} + \frac{1}{10}$
$= \frac{\quad}{10} = \underline{\quad}$

⑧ $\frac{4}{7} - \frac{2}{14} = \frac{\quad}{14} - \frac{2}{14}$
$= \frac{\quad}{14} = \underline{\quad}$

⑨ $\frac{1}{3} + \frac{7}{24} = \frac{\underline{\quad}}{\underline{\quad}} + \frac{\underline{\quad}}{\underline{\quad}}$

$= \frac{\underline{\quad}}{\underline{\quad}} = \frac{\underline{\quad}}{\underline{\quad}}$

⑩ $\frac{17}{20} - \frac{3}{5} = \frac{\underline{\quad}}{\underline{\quad}} - \frac{\underline{\quad}}{\underline{\quad}}$

$= \frac{\underline{\quad}}{\underline{\quad}} = \frac{\underline{\quad}}{\underline{\quad}}$

⑪ $\frac{3}{40} + \frac{5}{8} = \frac{\underline{\quad}}{\underline{\quad}} + \frac{\underline{\quad}}{\underline{\quad}}$

$= \frac{\underline{\quad}}{\underline{\quad}} = \frac{\underline{\quad}}{\underline{\quad}}$

⑫ $\frac{5}{12} - \frac{1}{24} = \frac{\underline{\quad}}{\underline{\quad}} - \frac{\underline{\quad}}{\underline{\quad}}$

$= \frac{\underline{\quad}}{\underline{\quad}} = \frac{\underline{\quad}}{\underline{\quad}}$

Follow Tim's method to find the answers. Write the answers in simplest form.

e.g. $3 - 1\frac{2}{5} = 2\frac{5}{5} - 1\frac{2}{5}$

$= (2 - 1) + (\frac{5}{5} - \frac{2}{5})$

$= 1\frac{3}{5}$

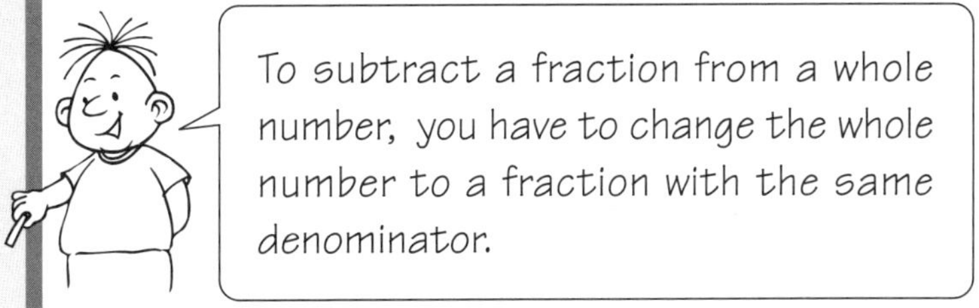

⑬ $5 - 2\frac{5}{6} = 4\frac{\underline{\quad}}{6} - 2\frac{5}{6}$

$= (4 - \quad) + (\frac{\underline{\quad}}{6} - \frac{5}{6})$

$= \underline{\quad}$

⑭ $4 - 3\frac{4}{7} = 3\frac{\underline{\quad}}{7} - 3\frac{4}{7}$

$=$

$=$

ACTIVITY

Tim is looking for a gift. He can only move horizontally or vertically, following a path with decreasing values. Colour the path.

$4\frac{3}{8}$	$4\frac{1}{4}$	$4\frac{5}{6}$	$2\frac{5}{6}$	$1\frac{23}{24}$	$1\frac{7}{8}$	$\frac{8}{9}$
$4\frac{7}{8}$	$3\frac{1}{8}$	$3\frac{1}{16}$	$2\frac{1}{2}$	$1\frac{7}{8}$	$1\frac{1}{4}$	$1\frac{1}{2}$
$5\frac{1}{16}$	$3\frac{3}{4}$	$3\frac{3}{8}$	$2\frac{7}{8}$	$1\frac{15}{16}$	$\frac{3}{4}$	$\frac{1}{2}$

13 Decimals (Multiplication and Division)

WORDS TO LEARN

Decimal - a numeral containing a decimal point, with the value of the digits to the right of the decimal point being less than 1
e.g. 0.65, 4.328, 5.4 ...

Read what Tim says and help him find the answers.

If each pack of baseball cards costs $2.50, how much should I pay for 3 packs?

	$ 2.50	2 decimal places
x	3	
	$ 7.50	2 decimal places

1st Multiply.

2nd Count the number of decimal places in the question.

3rd Place the same number of decimal places in the answer.

①  should pay $________ for 3 packs of baseball cards.

② If each pack of baseball cards costs $2.18, how much should  pay for 4 packs?

	2.18
x	4
	______

 should pay $________ for 4 packs of baseball cards.

Try these.

③ 40.8 x 2 = ______

④ 15.4 x 3 = ______

⑤ 18.7 x 5 = ______

⑥ 21.65 x 4 = ______

⑦ 12.63 x 5 = ______

⑧ 31.48 x 3 = ______

Help the children do the division.

⑨ 

I want to share $3.40 with Nicky. How much can each of us get?

	Divide.	Put a decimal point in the quotient.
2) 3.4 0	2) 3 4 0	2) 3.4 0

1st

Divide in the same way as with whole numbers.

2nd

Put a decimal point in the quotient directly above the decimal point in the dividend.

Each of them can get $________ .

⑩ 

I want to share $4.55 with Nancy. How much can each of us get?

	Divide.	Put a decimal point in the quotient.	Round the quotient to the nearest hundredth.
2) 4.5 5	2) 4 5 5	2) 4.5 5	

Each of them can get $________ . (rounded to the nearest hundredth)

Round a decimal to the nearest hundredth: If the thousandth digit is more than 5, round it up and add 1 to the hundredth digit. If it is 4 or less, leave it out.

Try these. Round the answers to the nearest hundredth.

⑪ 13.64 ÷ 2 = ________

⑫ 19.20 ÷ 3 = ________

⑬ 12.95 ÷ 5 = ________

⑭ 19.85 ÷ 6 = ________

⑮ 18.26 ÷ 4 = ________

⑯ 21.37 ÷ 7 = ________

Follow Tim's method to solve the problems.

```
                               2.5
2 ) 5  →  2 ) 5.0  →  2 ) 5.0
                              4 ↓
                              1 0
                              1 0
```

Whole numbers divided by whole numbers:

1st
Add a decimal point to the last digit of the dividend.

2nd
Add zeros to the dividend until your answer has no remainders or you have enough decimal places.

⑰ 5) 8.☐

⑱ 4) 5.☐☐

⑲ 4) 43.☐☐

⑳ 12) 27.☐☐

㉑ 8) 17.☐☐☐

See how Nicky estimates and follow his method to solve the problems.

```
       3.0 1              Estimate
4 ) 12.0 4                     3
    12           →        4 ) 12
         4                    12
         4
```

12.04 is about 12.

$12 \div 4 = 3$

The quotient should be about 3.

㉒ $27.93 \div 7 =$ ______

Estimate:

㉓ $56.08 \div 8 =$ ______

Estimate:

㉔ $36.24 \div 12 =$ ______

Estimate:

㉕ $65.56 \div 11 =$ ______

Estimate:

Find how much money the children have.

㉖  ,  and  each have $1.65 and  has $1.25.

How much money do they have in all?

$1.65 x 3 + $1.25 = $ ______ + $ ______

= $ ______

They have $ ________ in all.

Do multiplication and division before you do addition and subtraction.

Try these.

㉗ 2.64 ÷ 4 + 2.4

= ______ + ______

= ______

㉘ 4.16 x 3 – 3.78

= ______ – ______

= ______

㉙ 15.63 – 14.58 ÷ 3

= ______ – ______

= ______

㉚ 15.89 + 5.06 x 4

= ______ + ______

= ______

ACTIVITY

Which is the best buy? Tick ✔ the right boxes.

1.

- ☐ A 3 for $ 2.00
- ☐ B 5 for $ 2.85
- ☐ C 7 for $ 4.58

2.

- ☐ A 2 for $ 2.95
- ☐ B 3 for $ 3.85
- ☐ C 5 for $ 6.28

14 Averages

WORDS TO LEARN

Average - the sum of a set of numbers divided by the total number of addends

e.g. The average of 3, 7, 8 and 18 is 9.

$$\text{Average} = \frac{\text{Total value in the group}}{\text{Total number of addends}} = \frac{3 + 7 + 8 + 18}{4} = 9$$

Tim practised shots on goal last week. Read his record and help him find his average score.

SUN	MON	TUE	WED	THU	FRI	SAT
6	8	9	7	6	7	6

Find average
1st Add the numbers.
2nd Divide the sum by the total number of addends.

① Add : 6 + 8 + 9 + 7 + 6 + 7 + 6 = ______

② Divide : ______ ÷ 7 = ______

③ Tim's average score was ______ .

Tim recorded the number of goals his hockey team scored in different games last month. Help him find the average score.

Game	1	2	3	4	5	6	7	8
Number of goals	4	5	3	1	0	2	5	4

④ Add : ___ + ___ + ___ + ___ + 0 + ___ + ___ + ___ = ______

⑤ Divide : ______ ÷ ______ = ______

⑥ The average score was ______ .

Look at the table and find the average distance that the children have to travel from home to the arena.

Tim	Nicky	Nancy	Jill	Lily	George	Mark
3.4 km	1.8 km	7.3 km	6.4 km	2.4 km	2.9 km	2.4 km

⑦ Add : ____ + ____ + ____ + ____ + ____ + ____ + ____ = ____

⑧ Divide : ____ ÷ ____ = ____

⑨ The average distance is ____ km .

Find the average of each group and round it to the nearest hundredth.

⑩ 20 cm, 15 cm, 18 cm, 20 cm, 26 cm, 19 cm, 23 cm, 22 cm ________ cm

⑪ 45 L, 38 L, 63.4 L, 5.9 L, 4.7 L, 15.9 L ________ L

⑫ 17.64 kg, 25.37 kg, 15.13 kg, 26.49 kg, 18.06 kg ________ kg

⑬ \$4.69, \$16.30, \$10.58, \$9.87, \$12.63 \$ ________

ACTIVITY

Tick ✔ the right answers.

The average height of the hockey team is 135 cm. If Nicky or George joins the team, how will the average change?

1. Nicky is 140 cm tall. The average height will be

☐ raised. ☐ lowered. ☐ the same.

2. George is 134 cm tall. The average height will be

☐ raised. ☐ lowered. ☐ the same.

15 Algebraic Symbols

WORDS TO LEARN

Algebraic symbol - a letter or a symbol to represent an unknown number

Equation - a mathematical sentence with an equal sign (=)

e.g. Tim had y candies. He ate 2 and had 7 left.
How many candies did he have at first?

$y - 2 = 7$

$y = 9$

Nancy and Tim are playing games. Read what they say. Then find the unknown figures.

What is the value of y if the problems, down and across, have the same result?

	6	
5	+	y
	3	

$5 + y = 6 + 3$
$5 + y = 9$
Which number plus 5 is 9?
1, 2, 3, ④... $y = 4$

①

	12	
5	+	z
	7	

z = ___

②

	4	
k	+	6
	15	

k = ___

③

	m	
4	+	7
	11	

m = ___

Try these.

④

	36	
21	–	m
	16	

m =

⑤

	7	
4	x	14
	n	

n =

Pay attention to the operation signs:
+ – x ÷

⑥

	18	
p	÷	9
	2	

p =

⑦

	q	
17	+	18
	26	

q =

⑧

	18	
24	÷	r
	3	

r =

Use algebraic symbols to express the following questions. Tick ✔ the right boxes.

I had \$$x$. My mom gave me \$5 more. Now I have \$$(x + 5)$.

⑨ Nancy has y candies and Tim has 7. How many candies do they have in all?

☐ $y + 7$ ☐ $y - 7$ ☐ $y \times 7$

⑩ Tim is x years old. How old was he 4 years ago?

☐ $x + 4$ ☐ $x - 4$ ☐ $x \div 4$

⑪ Nicky bought k hot dogs at \$2 each. How much did he pay?

☐ $k + 2$ ☐ $k \div 2$ ☐ $k \times 2$

⑫ Nancy shared m stickers with 3 of her friends. How many stickers does each get?

☐ $m + 4$ ☐ $m \div 4$ ☐ $m \times 4$

⑬ The box has n rows of 6 muffins. How many muffins are there?

☐ $n \div 6$ ☐ $n + 6$ ☐ $n \times 6$

ACTIVITY

Read what Uncle Jack says. Tick ✔ the right equation.

I got 2 report cards every year. When I was 8, I had 6 in all. How many report cards did I have when I was y years old?

☐ A Number of report cards = $(y - 8) \times 2$

☐ B Number of report cards = $(y - 8) + 6$

☐ C Number of report cards = $(y - 8) \times 2 + 6$

16 Quadrilaterals

WORDS TO LEARN

Quadrilateral - a figure with 4 straight sides

e.g.

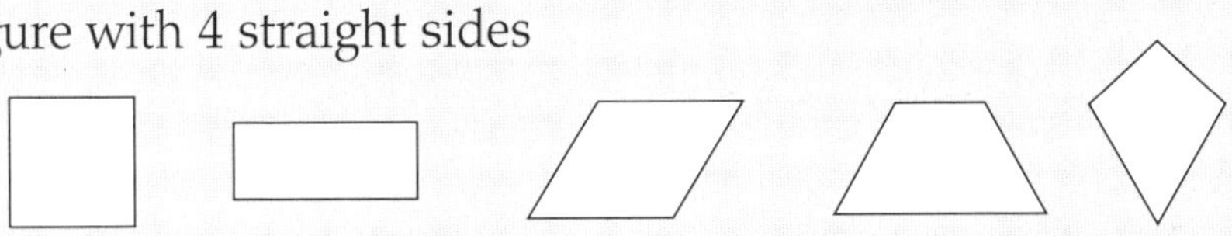

Opposite sides - sides that are facing each other

Opposite angles - angles that are facing each other diagonally

e.g.

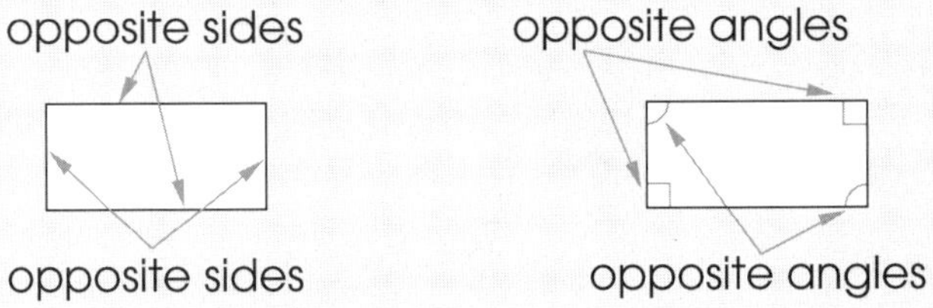

Look at the children's kites and answer the questions.

① Which kites have 4 equal sides? ____________

② Which kites have opposite sides parallel? ____________

③ Which kite has no parallel sides? ____________

④ Which kite has only 1 pair of opposite sides parallel? ____________

⑤ Which kites have 4 equal angles? ____________

Help Tim tick ✔ the properties of each quadrilateral.

	all sides equal	opposite sides equal	opposite sides parallel	only 1 pair of opposite sides parallel	all angles equal	only 1 pair of opposite angles equal
⑥ Rectangle						
⑦ Parallelogram						
⑧ Square						
⑨ Rhombus						
⑩ Kite						
⑪ Trapezoid						

See what shapes Tim can make with these geo-strips. Tick ✔ the right answers.

⑫ 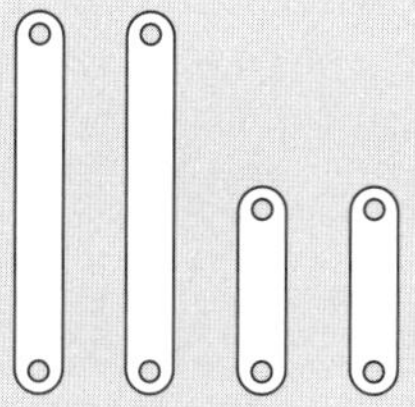

- ☐ Square
- ☐ Parallelogram
- ☐ Rectangle
- ☐ Trapezoid
- ☐ Rhombus
- ☐ Kite

⑬ 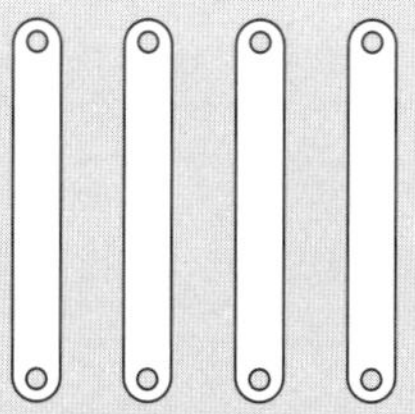

- ☐ Square
- ☐ Parallelogram
- ☐ Rectangle
- ☐ Trapezoid
- ☐ Rhombus
- ☐ Kite

ACTIVITY

Answer the question.

How many trapezoids can you find in this figure?

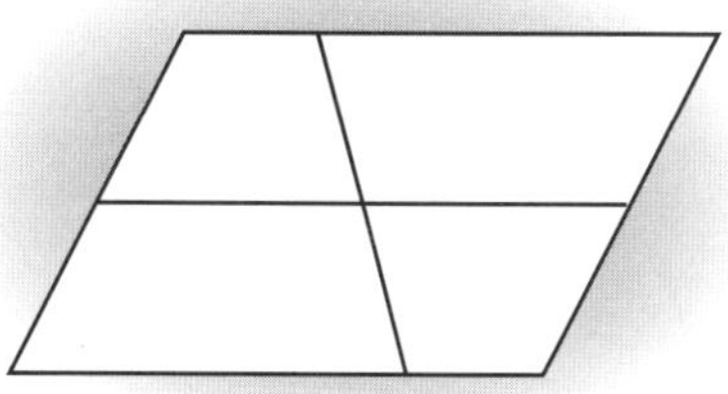

There are ________ trapezoids.

17 Area

WORDS TO LEARN

Area - the number of square units of a surface

e.g. 1cm × 1cm square ← Area = 1 cm^2 1m × 1m square ← Area = 1 m^2

Tim used some stickers to measure the size of the cards. Help him write the numbers and tick ✔ the right answer.

Card A

Card B

Card C

① ________  are needed to cover Card A.

② ________  are needed to cover Card B.

③ ________  are needed to cover Card C.

④ Which card has the largest area?

☐ Card A ☐ Card B ☐ Card C

Tim used different stickers to measure the area of his book. Help him write the number of stickers and tick ✔ the right answer.

⑤ 

⑥ 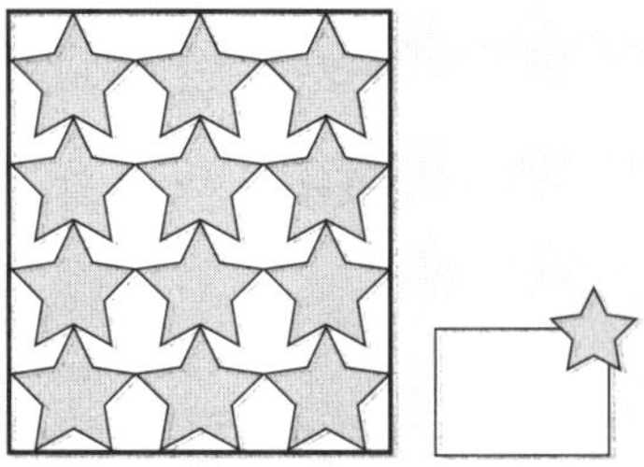

⑦ 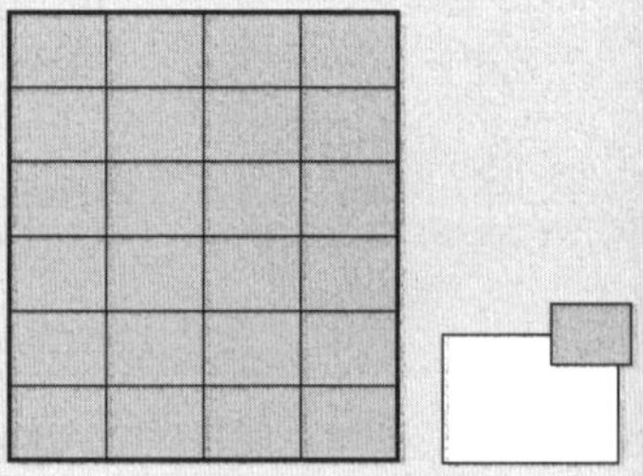

⑧ Which one of these shapes measures the area best?

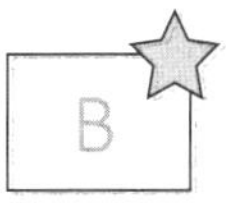

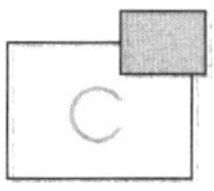

Read what Tim says and find the area of each shape by counting the number of squares. Then answer the questions.

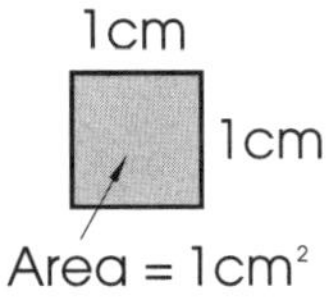

A square with sides of 1 cm has an area of 1 square centimetre (1 cm^2).

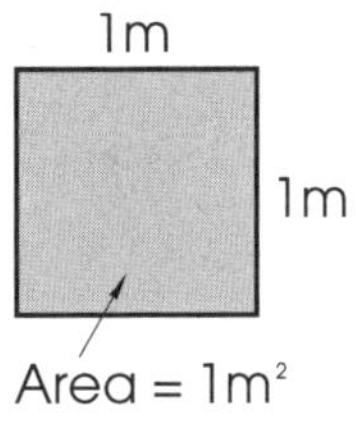

A square with sides of 1 m has an area of 1 square metre (1 m^2).

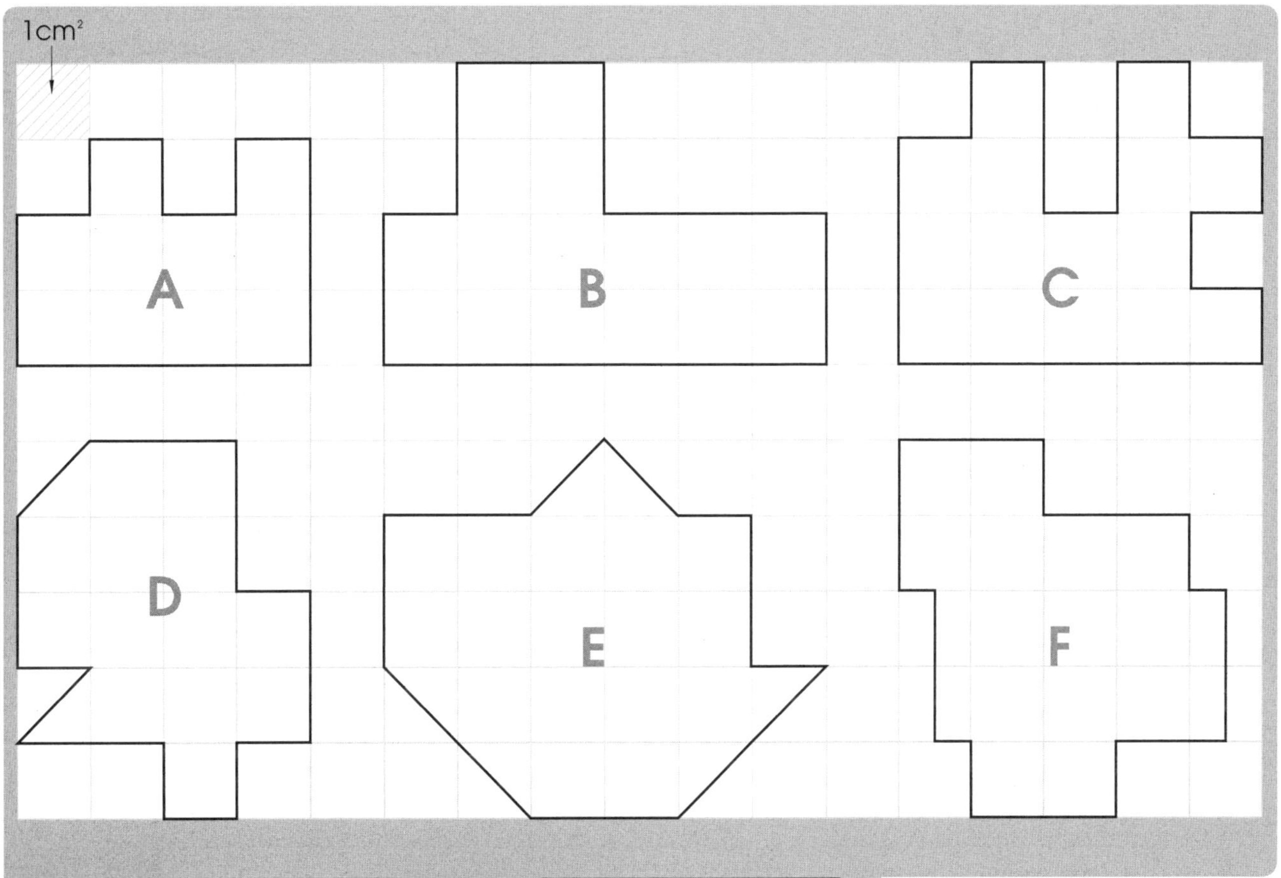

⑨ A ____ cm^2

⑩ B ____ cm^2

⑪ C ____ cm^2

⑫ D ____ cm^2

⑬ E ____ cm^2

⑭ F ____ cm^2

⑮ Which figure has the largest area? ______

⑯ Which figure has the smallest area? ______

⑰ Which two figures have the same area? ______ and ______

Tim used some wires to make different shapes. Help him find the area of each shape.

1cm²

⑱

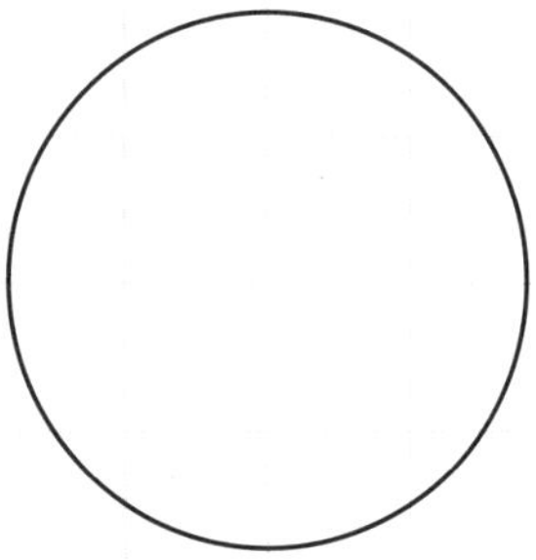

Approximately ______ cm²

⑲

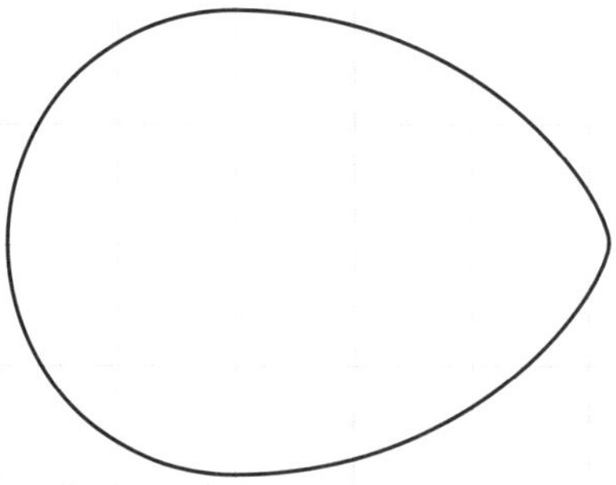

Approximately ______ cm²

⑳

Approximately ______ cm²

㉑

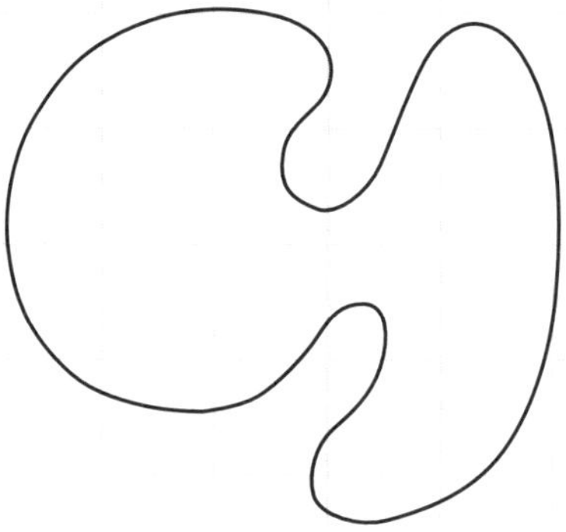

Approximately ______ cm²

Count only the squares that are more than half covered.

Count the squares to complete the table.

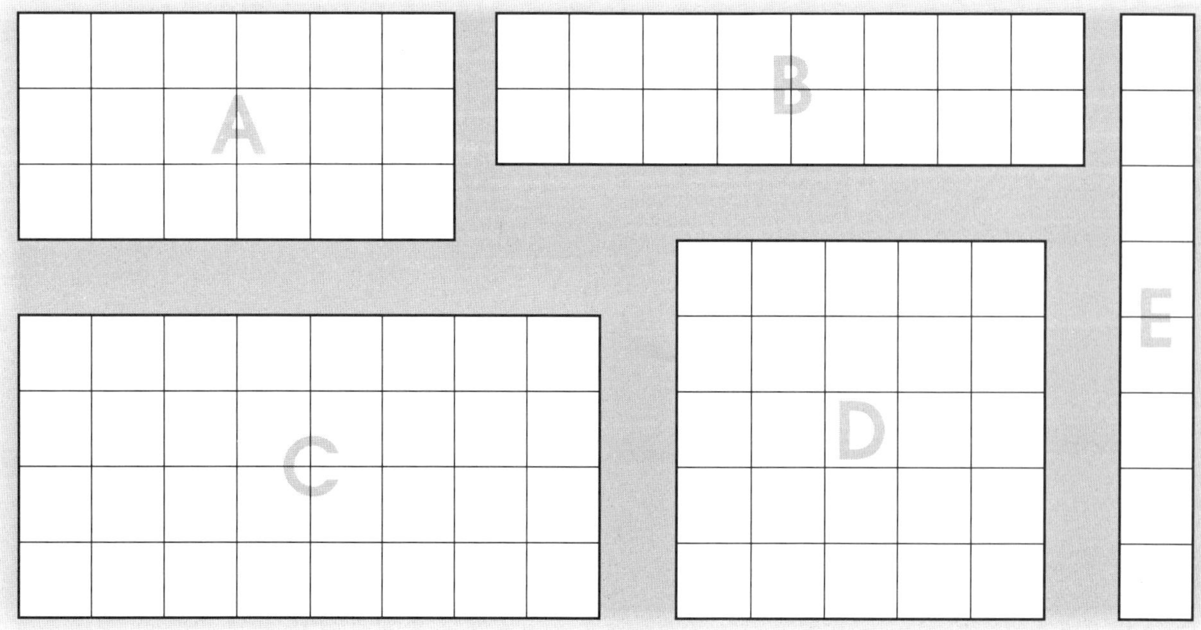

22	A	B	C	D	E
Length (cm)					
Width (cm)					
Area (cm²)					

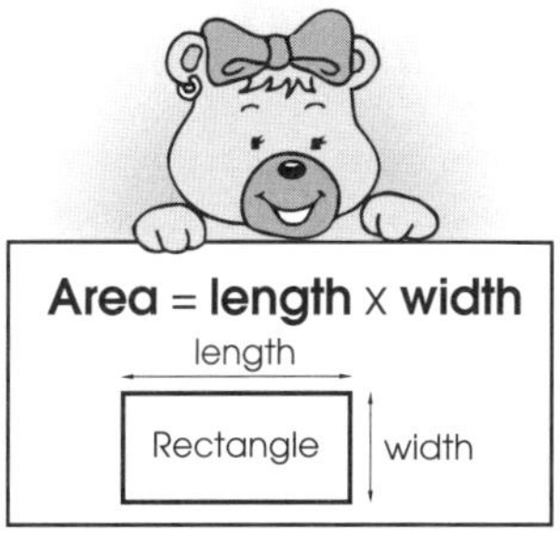

You can use this formula to find the area of a rectangle.

Use the formula to find the area of each rectangle.

23. 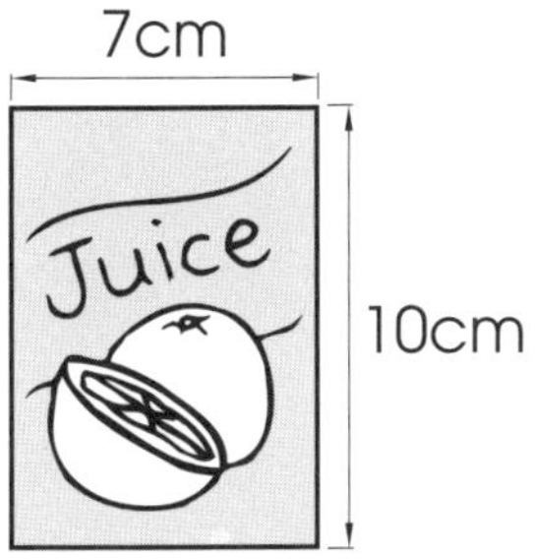

Area = ________ cm²

24. 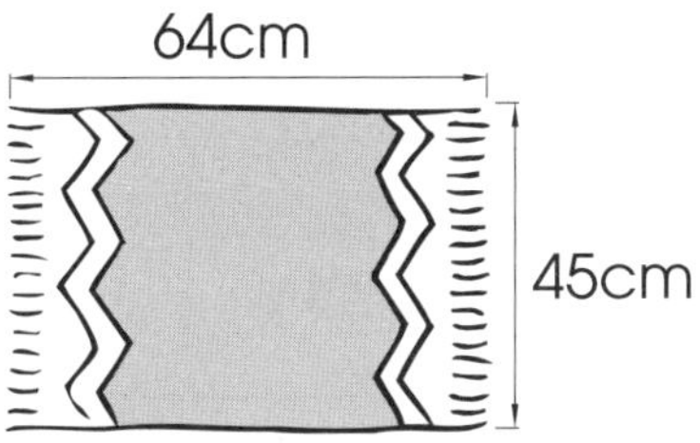

Area = ________ cm²

25. 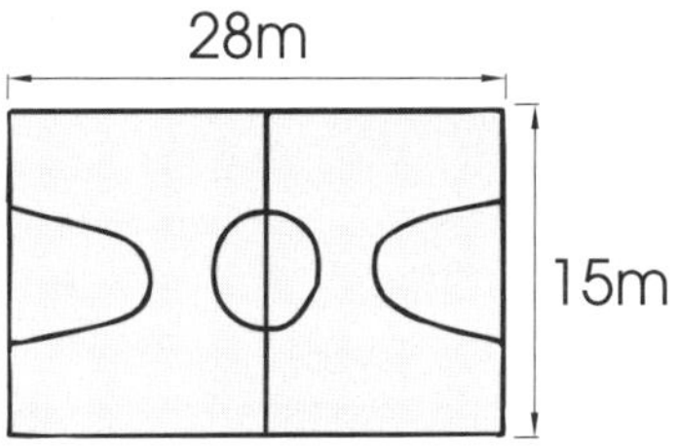

Area = ________ m²

26. 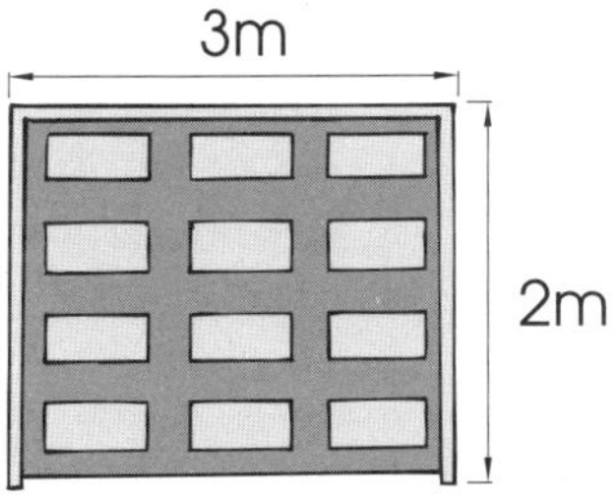

Area = ________ m²

27. 

Area = ________ cm²

28. 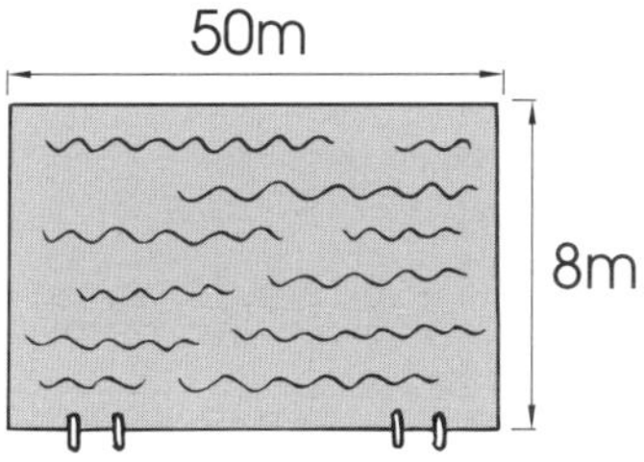

Area = ________ m²

ACTIVITY

Find the area of Tim's house.

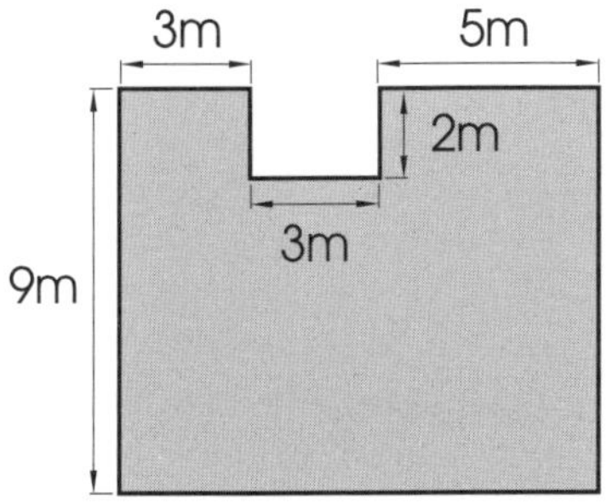

You can draw 2 lines in my house to split it into 3 rectangles.

Area = ________ m²

18 Compound Bar Graphs

WORDS TO LEARN

Compound bar graph - a graph using bars to show two or more figures in the same group

Axis - the frame of a graph showing the scale

Tim has recorded the attendance at the local hockey matches. Help him complete the bar graph and answer the questions.

Week	1	2	3	4	5	6
Number of People	500	700	400	200	400	1000

① Attendance at Local Hockey Matches

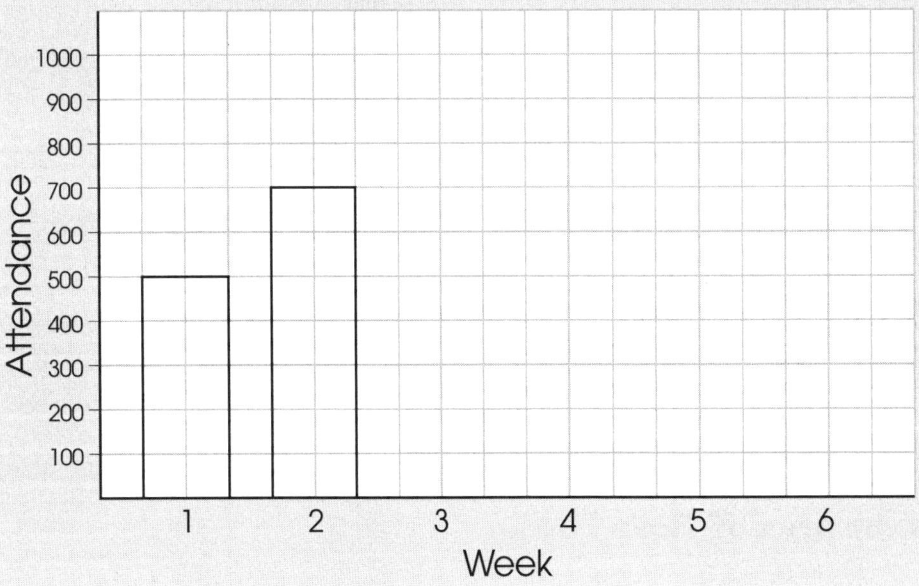

The bars are of the same width and are evenly spaced out.

② Which week had an attendance closest to 900? ________

③ How many more people were there in week 2 than week 4? ________

④ How many bars are in the graph? ________

Study the graph and answer the questions.

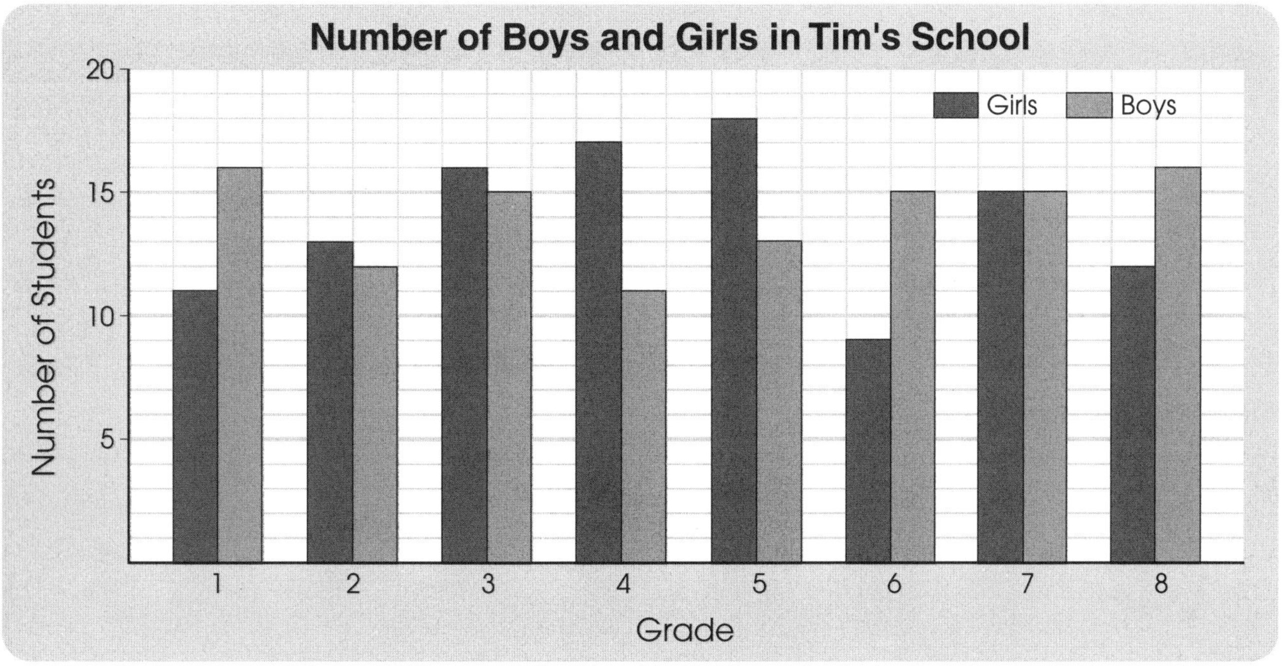

⑤ How many girls are in Grade 7? ________

⑥ How many boys are in Grade 8? ________

⑦ How many students are in Grade 4? ________

⑧ Which Grade has the fewest girls? ________

⑨ Which 2 Grades have 16 boys? ________ and ________

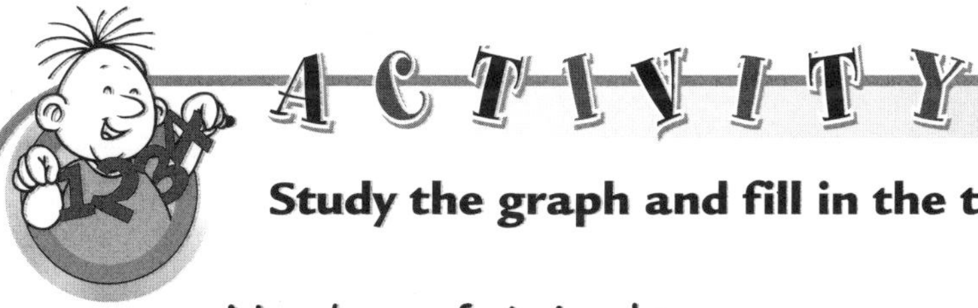

Study the graph and fill in the table.

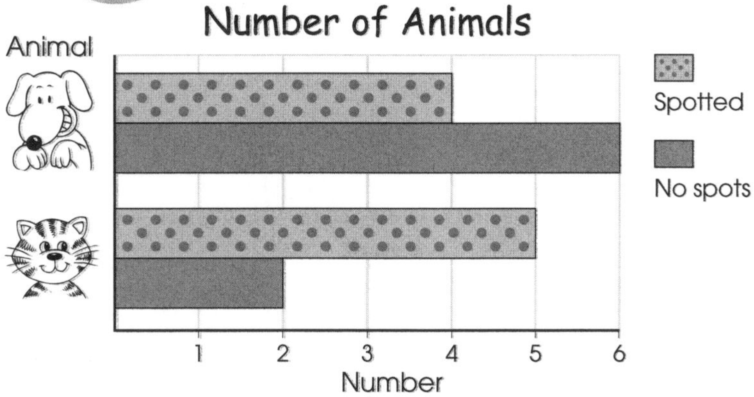

	Spotted	No spots

19

Money

WORDS TO LEARN

\$ - dollar sign ¢ - cent sign

e.g. 78¢ = \$ 0.78

\$ 0.78 (dollars . cents)

Help Tim and Nicky find how much money they have. Estimate first. Then find the amount in dollars.

①

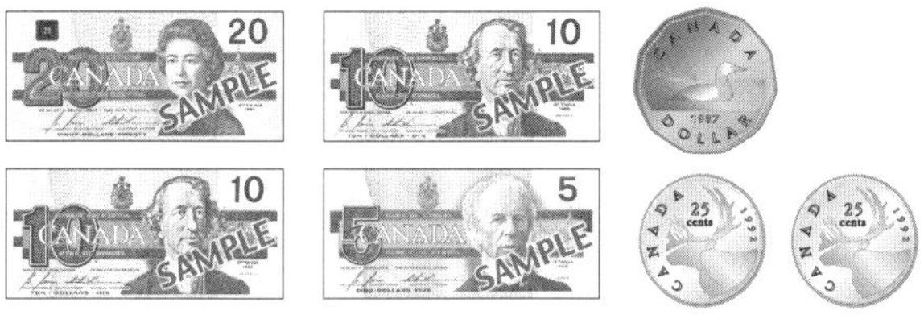

Estimate \$ ______ Actual Amount \$ ______

②

Estimate \$ ______ Actual Amount \$ ______

Many items at ABC Toy Shop are on sale now. Write how much can be saved and the reduced prices.

See how the children pay for their toys. Help the cashier give them the changes with the fewest coins. Write the numbers of coins in each change.

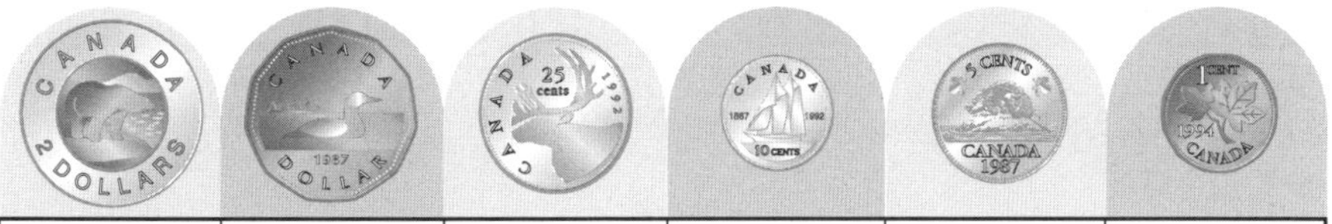

⑧ 						
⑨ 						

Try these.

⑩
```
   5.00
 - 2.35
 ------
```

⑪
```
   16.83
 +  9.79
 -------
```

Don't forget to put the decimal point in the answer.

⑫
```
   10.00
 -  9.51
 -------
```

⑬
```
   20.00
 - 16.47
 -------
```

⑭
```
   4.98
 + 5.64
 ------
```

ACTIVITY

Tick ✔ 3 items that you can buy for exactly $20.

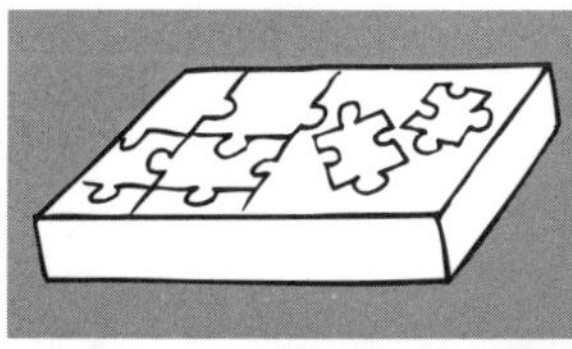
$6.61 ☐

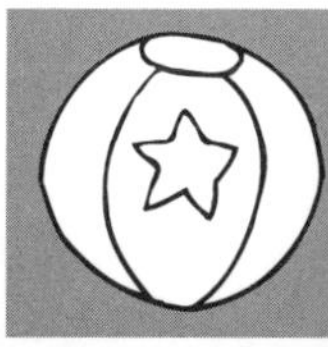
$4.39 ☐

$6.34 ☐

$3.58 ☐

$8.67 ☐

$9.27 ☐

20 Coordinates

WORDS TO LEARN

Coordinates	-	a pair of numbers or letters to locate a place on a map (The order of the pair must be (unit across, unit up).)
Legend	-	a table showing the meaning of all the symbols on a map
Grid	-	a set of uniformly spaced horizontal and vertical lines

Tim has put his toys on a grid. Draw the pictures or write the coordinates to answer the questions.

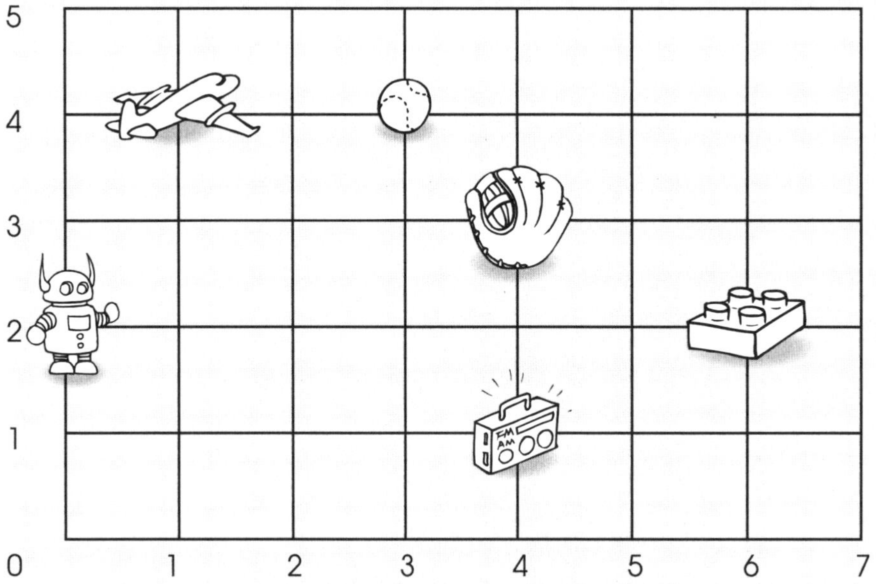

① What do you find at (1, 4)? ☐

② What do you find at (4, 3)? ☐

③ Where is the  ? ______

④ Where is the  ? ______

⑤ What do you find 2 blocks down and 3 blocks to the right of the  ? ☐

Tim wants to make a treasure map. Follow his instruction to draw the things on the map.

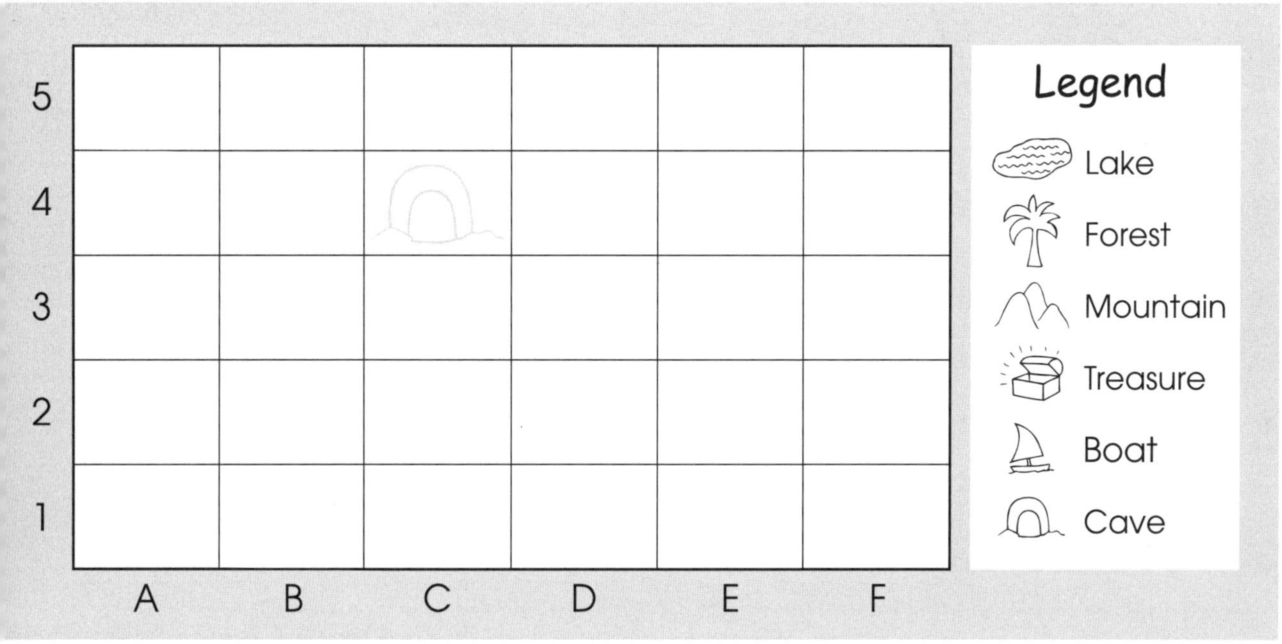

⑥ Draw a cave in block (C, 4) and block (A, 5).

⑦ Draw a boat in block (F, 1) and block (D, 2).

⑧ Draw a lake covering block (B, 3) and block (C, 3).

⑨ Draw a forest in block (F, 3) and block (B, 2).

⑩ Draw a mountain in block (D, 3) and block (E, 4).

⑪ Draw the treasure in block (B, 4).

Read the coordinates and write the letters to see what Tim wants to act.

						!
(3, 2)	(2, 1)	(5, 2)	(0, 0)	(1, 3)	(4, 0)	

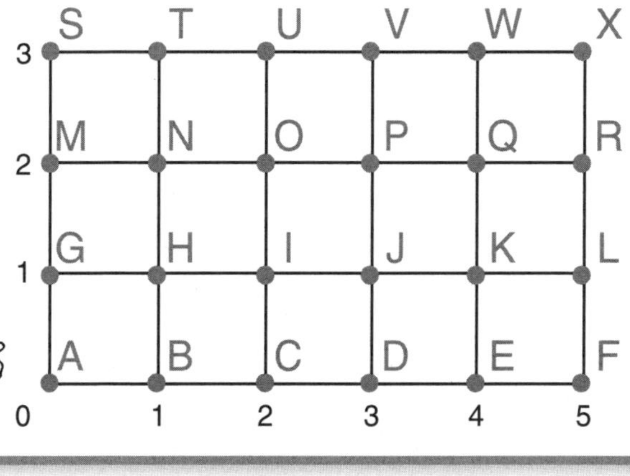

Final Test

Find the costs and the changes. (8 marks)

\$4.99 

\$1.69 

\$2.18 

\$3.29 

① 5 boxes of 

Cost	Change
\$ 4.99	\$ 50.00
x ______	−\$ ______
\$ ______	\$ ______

② 6 bags of 

Cost	Change
\$ 2.18	\$ 20.00
x ______	−\$ ______
\$ ______	\$ ______

③ 7 baskets of 

Cost	Change
\$ ______	\$ 25.00
x ______	−\$ ______
\$ ______	\$ ______

④ 9 packets of 

Cost	Change
\$ ______	\$ 50.00
x ______	−\$ ______
\$ ______	\$ ______

How much will each person pay? Round the answers to the nearest hundredth. (4 marks)

⑤ 1 bag of  is shared equally between 2 people.

\$ 2.18 ÷ ______ = \$ ______

Each person will pay \$ ______ .

⑥ 1 basket of  is shared equally among 5 people.

\$ ______ ÷ ______ = \$ ______

Each person will pay \$ ______ .

Find the answers. (8 marks)

⑦ 2.94 ÷ 2 = ________

⑧ 62 ÷ 8 = ________

⑨ 13.08 ÷ 3 = ________

⑩ 55 ÷ 4 = ________

⑪ 49.14 ÷ 9 = ________

⑫ 76 ÷ 5 = ________

⑬ 26.82 ÷ 6 = ________

⑭ 105 ÷ 2 = ________

Find the averages. (2 marks)

⑮ 4 g, 0 g, 32 g, 14 g, 17 g, 19 g, 26 g

The average weight is ________ g.

⑯ 46 km, 59 km, 37 km, 18 km, 30 km, 38 km

The average distance is ________ km.

Find the average height and weight of the children. (2 marks)

Height (m)	1.43	1.41	1.38	1.42	1.46
Weight (kg)	35.21	34.07	34.02	35.07	36.43

⑰ The average height of the children is ________ m.

⑱ The average weight of the children is ________ kg.

Final Test

Compare the fractions. Put in >, < or =. (6 marks)

⑲ $\frac{4}{6}$ ☐ $\frac{11}{18}$

⑳ $\frac{9}{32}$ ☐ $\frac{3}{8}$

㉑ $\frac{5}{16}$ ☐ $\frac{15}{48}$

㉒ $\frac{12}{21}$ ☐ $\frac{4}{7}$

㉓ $\frac{10}{45}$ ☐ $\frac{4}{9}$

㉔ $\frac{11}{12}$ ☐ $\frac{31}{36}$

Solve the problems. (8 marks)

㉕ $60 \div ((23 - 17) \times 5)$

=

=

㉖ $(37 - (26 - 19)) \times 2$

=

=

㉗ $56 + (68 - 19) \div (14 \div 2)$

=

=

㉘ $(27 + 29) \div (8 - 4)$

=

=

Find the answers in simplest form. (20 marks)

㉙ $\frac{5}{12} + \frac{1}{2} =$

=

㉚ $\frac{5}{8} - \frac{7}{16} =$

=

㉛ $\frac{9}{25} + \frac{1}{5} =$

=

㉜ $\frac{11}{40} + \frac{3}{8} =$

=

㉝ $1\frac{2}{9} + 2\frac{1}{3} =$

=

㉞ $5\frac{5}{6} - 3\frac{1}{12} =$

=

35. $7\frac{3}{4} - 2\frac{5}{12} =$

$=$

36. $6 - 3\frac{5}{8} =$

$=$

37. $5 - 4\frac{8}{9} =$

$=$

38. $2\frac{7}{10} + 5\frac{3}{20} =$

$=$

Find the area of each shape. (6 marks)

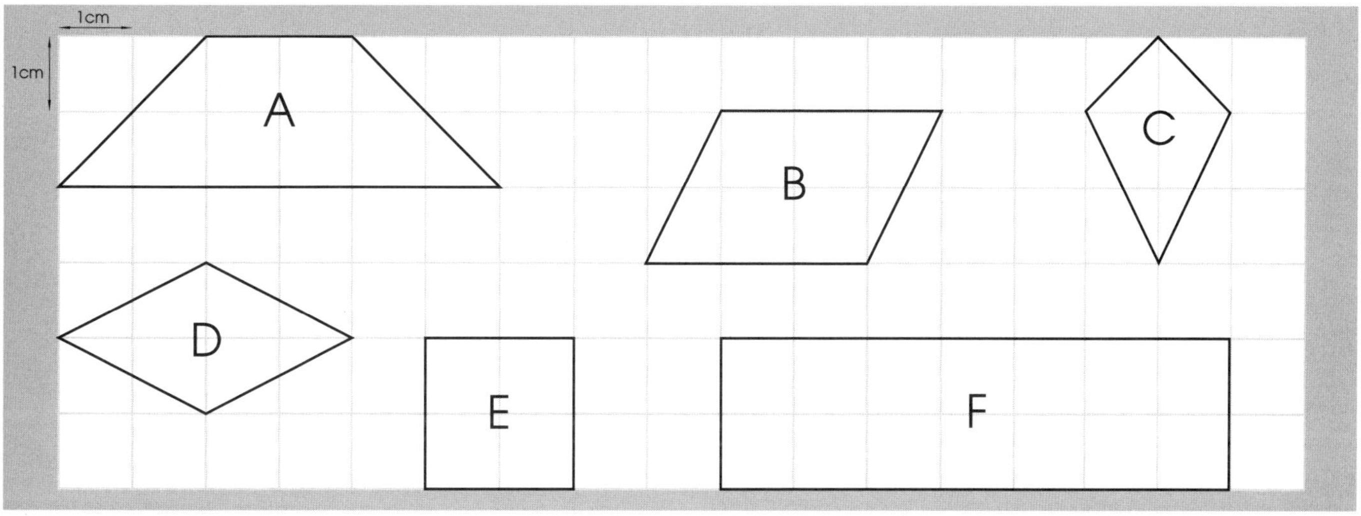

39. Square = ________ cm^2

40. Kite = ________ cm^2

41. Parallelogram = ________ cm^2

42. Rhombus = ________ cm^2

43. Trapezoid = ________ cm^2

44. Rectangle = ________ cm^2

Look at the above shapes and answer the questions. Write the letters only. (7 marks)

45. Which shapes have 4 equal sides? ____________

46. Which shapes have opposite sides parallel? ____________

47. Which shape has only 1 pair of opposite sides parallel? ____________

Final Test

Find the area of each rectangle. (4 marks)

⑱

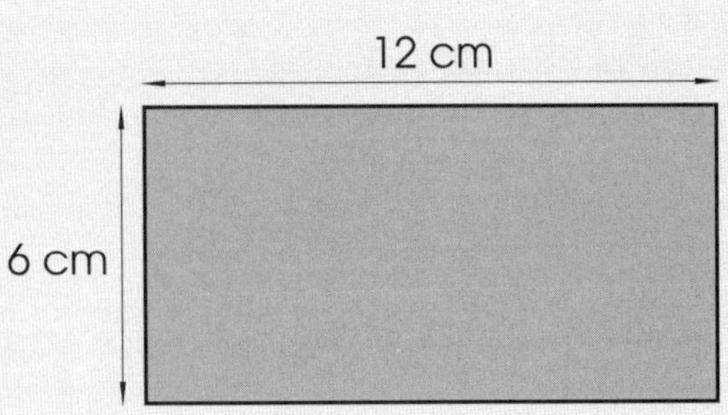

Area = ______ cm^2

⑲

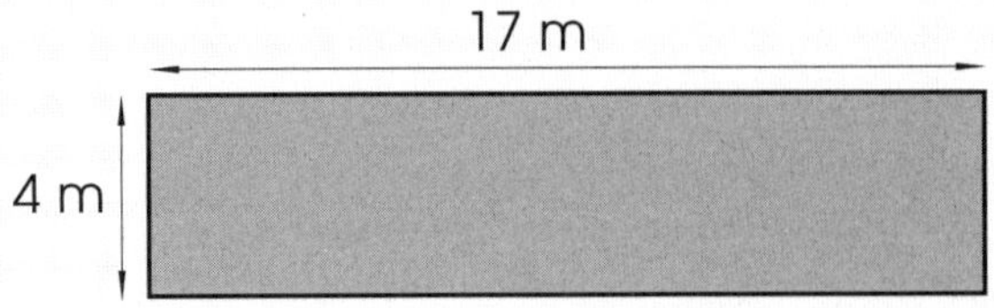

Area = ______ m^2

⑳

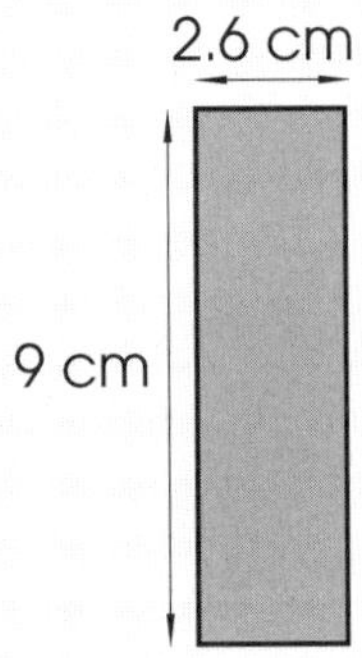

Area = ______ cm^2

㉑

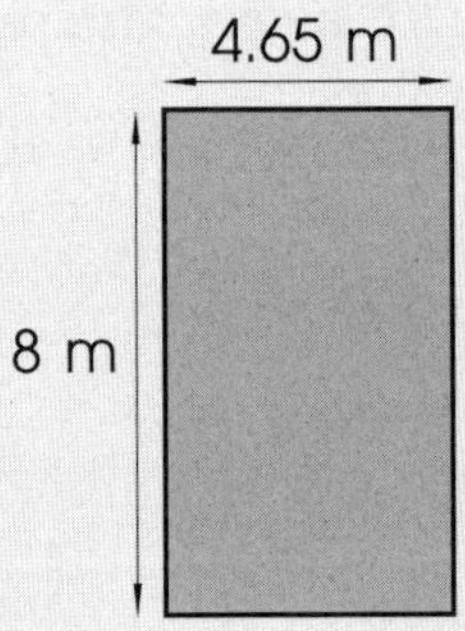

Area = ______ m^2

Use algebraic symbols to express the following questions. Tick ✔ the right answers. (4 marks)

52. Tim is m years old. How old was he 2 years ago?

   A $(m + 2)$ years old   B $(m - 2)$ years old   C $(m \div 2)$ years old

53. Tim shares $\$x$ with 2 friends. How much money does each child get?

   A $\$ (x + 3)$ B $\$ (x \div 3)$ C $\$ (x - 3)$

54. Nicky bought y boxes of cereal at \$3.99 each. How much did he pay?

   A $\$ (y \times 3.99)$ B $\$ (y + 3.99)$ C $\$ (y \div 3.99)$

55 Tim has $\$x$ and Nicky has \$10. How much money do they have in all?

A $\$ (x - 10)$ B $\$ (x \div 10)$ C $\$ (x + 10)$

Read the map and answer the questions. (7 marks)

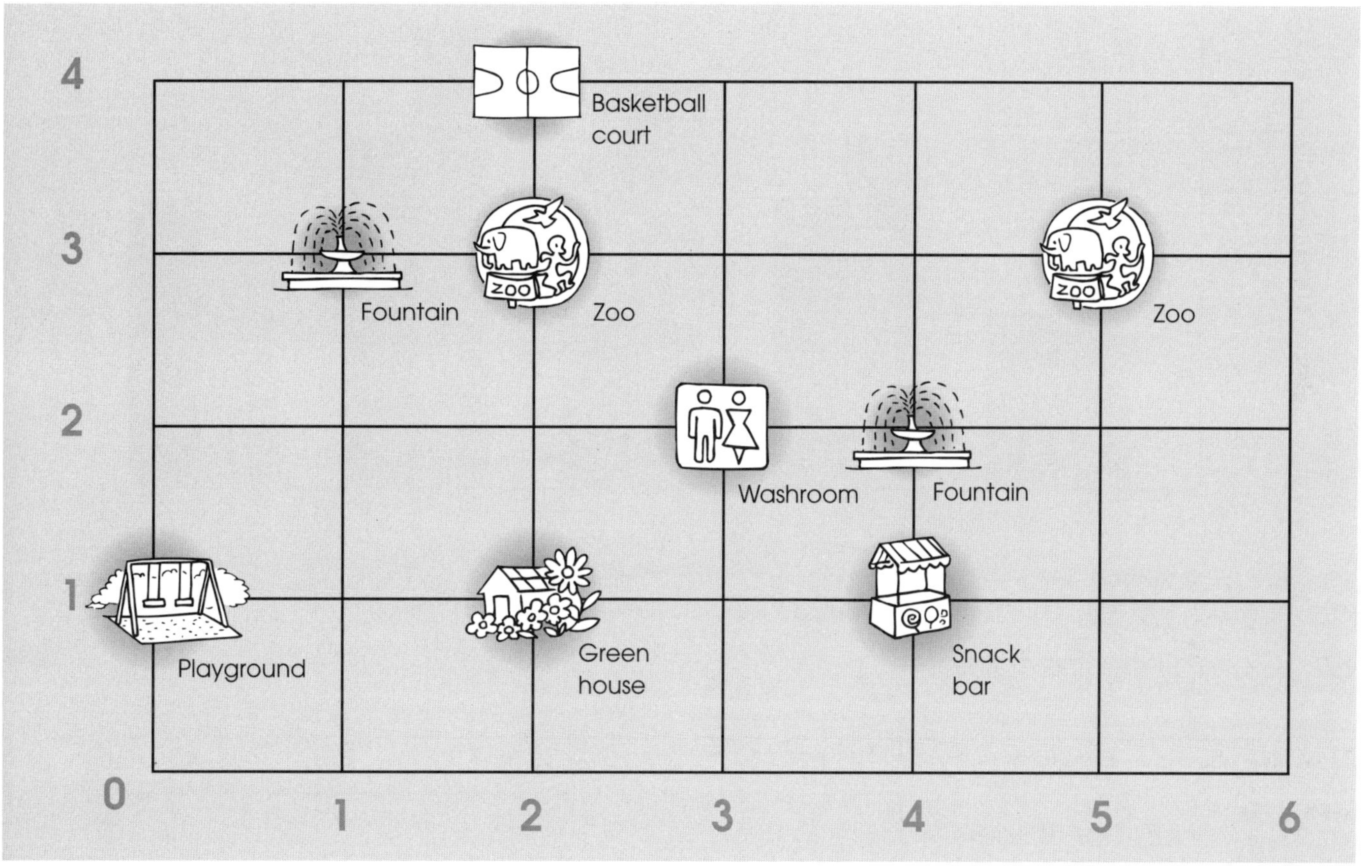

56 Where are the zoos? ________ and ________

57 Where is the playground? ________

58 What do you find at (2, 4)? ________

59 What do you find at (3, 2)? ________

60 What do you find 2 blocks to the right of the green house? ________

61 What do you find 1 block up and 2 blocks to the left of the washroom? ________

Final Test

Read the bar graph to complete the table and answer the questions.
(14 marks)

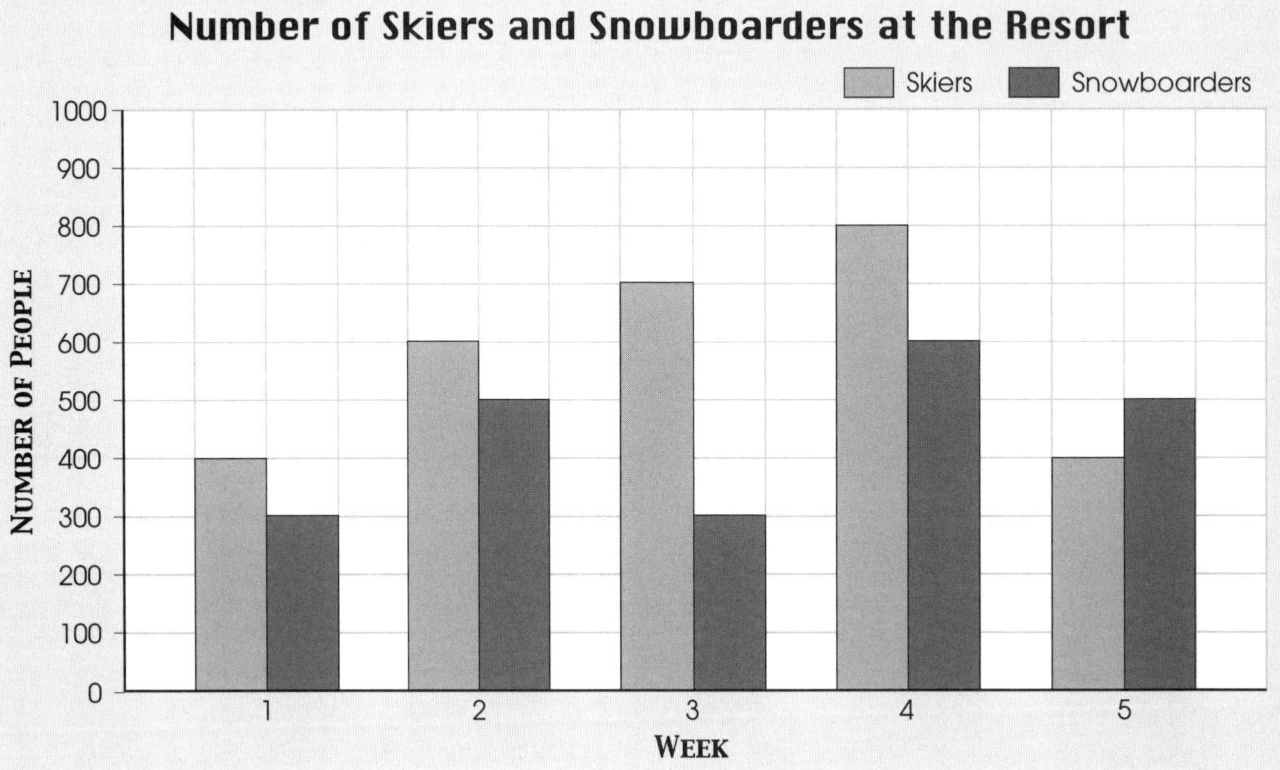

62. Complete the table.

Week	1	2	3	4	5
Number of skiers					
Number of Snowboarders					

63. In which week were there most people skiing? ________

64. In which week were there fewest people snowboarding? ________

65. In which week were there 900 people at the resort? ________

66. How many more skiers than snowboarders were there in week 3? ________

SCORE

100

Section III

Overview

In Section II, arithmetic skills were developed and practised.

In Section III, all four arithmetic operations and mixed operations are applied in the context of word problems using whole numbers and decimals.

Emphasis is placed on careful reading and translating into mathematical "language". Answers are written in full sentences using appropriate units and students are encouraged to check whether or not their answers are reasonable.

The relationship between fractions and decimals is explored in context.

Equations are introduced as a way to represent real-life situations mathematically. Solving a word problem often involves solving an equation.

UNIT 1

Numeration

EXAMPLE

Emily and Gabe estimate the number of stickers they have altogether to the nearest 10. Emily says 180 and Gabe says 170. The number of stickers they have altogether is 178. Who gives a better estimation?

Round 178 to the nearest 10 → 180

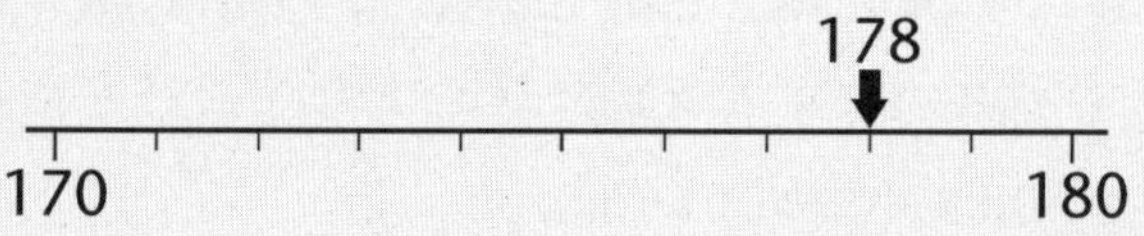

Answer : Emily gives a better estimation.

Use the table below to solve the problems. Show your work.

Name	Emily	Gabe	Doug	Megan	Clare	Elaine
No. of Stickers	2000	1245	2650	1225	2700	945

① Who has the most stickers? How many? Write in words.

Answer : ______ has the most stickers. ______ stickers.

② Who has the fewest stickers? How many? Write in words.

Answer : ______

③ Who has 50 stickers more than Doug?

Answer : ______

④ Who has 700 stickers fewer than Clare?

Answer : ______

⑤ Doug buys one pack of stickers each week. In each pack there are 10 stickers. He starts with 2650 stickers. How many stickers will he have after 4 weeks?

Answer : ______

⑥ If Elaine gives 100 stickers to her friends each week, how many stickers will she have after 3 weeks?

Answer :

⑦ If each week Emily gives 100 stickers to Megan, how many stickers will each of them have after 3 weeks?

Answer :

⑧ If Gabe gives 5 stickers to Megan each week, how long will it take for them to have the same number of stickers?

Answer :

⑨ If Doug buys 60 stickers each week and gives 10 to Emily, how many stickers will each of them have after 4 weeks?

Answer :

⑩ How long will it take Emily to give away all her stickers if she gives 400 away each week?

Answer :

CHALLENGE

Penny has 30 stickers and Tanya has 35 stickers. Penny buys 6 stickers every week and Tanya buys 5 stickers every week. How many weeks will it take for them to have the same number of stickers?

Answer :

UNIT 2 Addition and Subtraction of Whole Numbers

EXAMPLE

Emily ran 1462 m. Gabe ran 1287 m. How much farther did Emily run than Gabe?

Think : how much farther ... than ... ➠ Subtraction problem

Write : 1462 – 1287 = 175

Answer : Emily ran 175 m farther than Gabe.

Estimate the answer in each situation by rounding the number of marbles to the nearest 100. Show your work.

① Gabe has 428 marbles. He gives Emily 99 marbles. How many marbles has he left?

Answer : He has about ______ marbles left.

② Emily has 183 green marbles and 214 blue marbles. How many green and blue marbles does Emily have altogether?

Answer : ______

③ Jill has 507 marbles but gives 197 to her brother. How many marbles has she left?

Answer : ______

④ Mark buys a bag of 89 marbles. He adds it to his collection of 280 marbles. How many marbles does he have altogether?

Answer : ______

⑤ Joe has 317 marbles and buys a bag of 88 marbles. Wayne gives 95 marbles to Joe. How many marbles does Joe have?

Answer : ______

⑥ Which children have about 300 marbles in the end?

Answer : ______

The table shows how many metres Emily travelled on her bike last week. Use the table to solve the problems. Show your work.

	SUN	MON	TUE	WED	THU	FRI	SAT
Distance (m)	876	328	829	515	372	686	1425

⑦ How far did Emily travel altogether on the weekend?

Answer : ____________________

⑧ How far did Emily travel altogether on Monday and Tuesday?

Answer : ____________________

⑨ How far did Emily travel altogether on Wednesday, Thursday and Friday?

Answer : ____________________

⑩ How far did Emily travel altogether last week?

Answer : ____________________

⑪ How much farther did Emily travel on Saturday than on Thursday?

Answer : ____________________

⑫ How much farther did Emily travel on Friday than on Monday?

Answer : ____________________

⑬ If Emily wanted to travel 700 m on Monday, how much farther would she have to travel?

Answer : ____________________

⑭ If George travelled 288 m more than the distance Emily travelled on Tuesday, how far did he travel?

Answer : ____________________

- ***For question 10, you may make use of the answers from questions 7, 8 and 9.***

The table shows the number of cans collected by each group in the past two weeks. Use the table to answer the questions. Show your work.

Group	A	B	C	D	E
No. of cans collected in week 1	651	394	1823	973	574
No. of cans collected in week 2	479	503	795	885	931

⑮ How many more cans did Group A collect in week 1 than in week 2?

Answer : ______________________

⑯ How many more cans did Group E collect in week 2 than in week 1?

Answer : ______________________

⑰ How many cans did Group A collect in all?

Answer : ______________________

⑱ How many cans did Group B collect in all?

Answer : ______________________

⑲ How many cans did Group C collect in all?

Answer : ______________________

⑳ How many cans did Group D collect in all?

Answer : ______________________

㉑ How many cans did Group E collect in all?

Answer : ______________________

㉒ Put the groups in order from the one with the most cans to the one with the fewest.

Answer : ______________________

㉓ How many more cans did Group C collect than Group B?

Answer : ______________________

㉔ How many more cans did Group E collect than Group A?

Answer : ______________________

Solve the problems. Show your work.

A total of one thousand five hundred sixty-seven people attended the first day of a tennis tournament. The next day, one thousand eight hundred twelve people attended. The ticket sales were six thousand seven hunderd eight dollars for the first day and seven thousand eight hundred twelve dollars for the second day.

㉕ What was the difference in attendance between the two days?

Answer : ______________________

㉖ How many people attended the two-day tournament?

Answer : ______________________

㉗ If six hundred eighty men and one hundred seventy-five children attended the first day of the tournament, how many women were there?

Answer : ______________________

㉘ What was the difference in the ticket sales between the two days?

Answer : ______________________

CHALLENGE

①

No. of blocks	1	10	100	1000
Weight (g)	100	1000		

② If the weight of the blocks is 2000 g, how many blocks are there?

Answer : ______________________

UNIT 3

Multiplication and Division of Whole Numbers

EXAMPLE

Emily buys 125 grams of candies each week. How many grams of candies will Emily have altogether after 5 weeks?

Think : 5 groups of 125

Write : $5 \times 125 = 625$

Answer : Emily will have 625 grams of candies after 5 weeks.

Emily and Gabe are helping out on Uncle Smith's farm. Solve the problems. Show your work.

① Emily picks 300 cobs of corn and splits them into 5 piles. How many cobs of corn are there in each pile?

Answer : There are ______ cobs of corn.

② Gabe picks 48 apples off each of 9 trees. How many apples does Gabe pick altogether?

Answer : ______

③ Emily has 3 baskets. Each basket holds 163 carrots. How many carrots does Emily have?

Answer : ______

④ Gabe picks 8 baskets of strawberries. Each basket holds 132 strawberries. How many strawberries are picked?

Answer : ______

⑤ There are 135 apple trees. Emily picks 6 apples from each tree. How many apples does Emily pick?

Answer : ______

⑥ There are 260 blueberries. If they were shared among 4 children, how many blueberries would each child get?

Answer : ______

⑦ Gabe picks 328 apples. The apples are packed in bags with 9 in each bag. How many apples will be left over?

Answer : ______________________

⑧ Emily pulls up carrots. Every time she has pulled 8, she ties them together. If she pulls up 230 carrots, how many carrots will not be tied up?

Answer : ______________________

⑨ Gabe picks 6 tomatoes from each plant. If he picked 163 tomatoes, how many tomatoes did he pick from the last plant?

Answer : ______________________

⑩ Emily and 4 of her friends are sharing 121 cherries equally among them. How many cherries will be left over?

Answer : ______________________

⑪ Gabe and 3 of his friends are sharing 207 peanuts equally among them. How many peanuts will be left over?

Answer : ______________________

⑫ Gabe has a bucket with 320 cherries in it. If he puts them into 6 boxes evenly, how many cherries will be left over?

Answer : ______________________

⑬ Emily puts 315 onions in 8 bags. How many onions are left over?

Answer : ______________________

⑭ Gabe puts 124 pears in boxes. Each box holds 9 pears. How many boxes does he need?

Answer : ______________________

⑮ Emily picks 156 strawberries and packs 8 in each basket. How many baskets does she need?

Answer : ______________________

⑯ Each box holds 6 potatoes. Gabe puts 215 potatoes into boxes. How many boxes does he need?

Answer : ______________________

- ***For questions 14, 15 and 16, don't forget that the remainder needs a container too.***

Elaine and Winston have gone with their class to a fruit farm. See how their teacher, Mrs Winter, put them into groups. Solve the problems.

Group **A** :11 students	Group **B** :13 students	Group **C** :12 students

⑰ If each student in Group A was allowed to pick 14 apples, how many apples were picked?

Answer : ______________________

⑱ If each bag holds 7 apples, how many bags are needed to hold all the apples picked by Group A?

Answer : ______________________

⑲ If each student in Group B was allowed to pick 45 strawberries, how many strawberries were picked?

Answer : ______________________

⑳ If each basket holds 9 strawberries, how many baskets are needed to hold all the strawberries picked by Group B?

Answer : ______________________

㉑ If each student in Group C was allowed to pick 36 peaches, how many peaches were picked?

Answer : ______________________

2-digit number × *2-digit number*

Example: 22 × 14

$$\begin{array}{r} 22 \\ \times\ 14 \\ \hline 88 \\ 220 \\ \hline 308 \\ \hline\hline \end{array}$$

1st *Multiply by the ones.*

2nd *Multiply by the tens and put a 0.*

3rd *Add the product.*

㉒ Groups A and C met together at the cherry trees. Each of the students was allowed to pick 36 cherries. How many cherries were picked in all?

Answer : ______________________

㉓ Groups B and C met together at the blueberry bushes. Each of the students was allowed to pick 48 blueberries. How many blueberries were picked in all?

Answer : ______________________

㉔ Groups A and B met together at the raspberry plants. Each of the students was allowed to pick 85 raspberries. How many raspberries were picked in all?

Answer : ______________________

Help the farm owner, Mr Smith, solve the problems. Show your work.

㉕ An apple costs 34¢. What is the total cost of 25 apples?

Answer : ____________________

㉖ A bag of potatoes costs $4.00. How many bags of potatoes can be bought with $102.00?

Answer : ____________________

㉗ What is the cost of 98 baskets of strawberries if each basket costs $6.00?

Answer : ____________________

㉘ Each box of cherries costs $5.00. Is $173.00 enough to buy 34 boxes of cherries?

Answer : ____________________

㉙ A bag of corn weighs 826 grams. What is the mass of 6 bags of corn?

Answer : ____________________

㉚ Mr Stanley pays with a $100 bill for 9 big bags of onions and gets $37.00 back. How much does each bag of onions cost?

Answer : ____________________

㉛ Each bag of potatoes weighs 95 grams. What is the mass of 17 bags of potatoes?

Answer : ____________________

CHALLENGE

Emily and 3 of her friends earned $38.00 each for helping on the farm. If they were paid altogether in $5 bills, how much change would they have to give back?

Answer : ____________________

UNIT 4

Mixed Operations of Whole Numbers

EXAMPLE

Emily has 80 marbles. Gabe has 134 marbles. They put their marbles together and then divide them equally. How many marbles does each child get?

1st Find the total number of marbles : 80 + 134 = 214

2nd Each child gets : 214 ÷ 2 = 107

Answer : Each child gets 107 marbles.

Look at the jars of marbles and solve the problems. Show your work.

① How many marbles are red or blue?

Answer : ______________________

② If the green marbles were shared among 5 people, how many would each person get?

Answer : ______________________

③ If Emily takes 113 marbles from each jar, how many marbles will she have?

Answer : ______________________

④ If Gabe takes 176 yellow marbles, how many yellow marbles will be left?

Answer : ______________________

⑤ If Gabe puts the purple marbles into 3 bags equally, how many purple marbles will there be in each bag? How many purple marbles will be left?

Answer : ______________________

⑥ Emily took a jar and split the marbles into 7 groups. Each group had 36 marbles and 4 marbles were left over. Which jar did Emily take?

Answer : ____________________

⑦ Gabe took 2 marbles from a jar and split the rest of the marbles into 4 equal shares of 62 marbles each. Which jar did Gabe take?

Answer : ____________________

⑧ Gabe made 6 piles of 65 yellow marbles. When he was done, how many yellow marbles were left in the jar?

Answer : ____________________

⑨ Emily took the purple marbles and divided them equally among 7 children. Then each child put 10 back into the jar. How many marbles did each child actually get?

Answer : ____________________

⑩ Emily had 236 marbles, and Gabe had 432 marbles. They put the marbles together and divided them into 4 equal shares. How many marbles were there in each share?

Answer : ____________________

⑪ Ray had 300 white marbles. He took 30 and divided the rest among 5 children. How many marbles did each child get?

Answer : ____________________

⑫ Emily had 8 bags of 56 marbles each. Gabe gave her 39 marbles. How many marbles did Emily have?

Answer : ____________________

⑬ Ray put his marbles equally into 6 bags and 4 marbles were left. If each bag had 72 marbles, how many marbles would Ray have?

Answer : ____________________

⑭ Gabe had 5 jars of 56 marbles each. If he split all his marbles equally into 4 jars, how many marbles would be in each jar?

Answer : ____________________

- ***Questions 6 to 14 are two-step problems. First split each problem into 2 parts. Then solve the first part before working on the other.***

Emily and Gabe have been playing video games. Look at their scores and solve the problems. Show your work.

• Space Bonkers •

High Score

1st	Gabe	3260
2nd	Emily	2870
3rd	Emily	1980
4th	Gabe	980
5th	Gabe	910

Castle Adventure

High Score

1st	Emily	5620
2nd	Emily	5490
3rd	Gabe	5060
4th	Emily	4830
5th	Gabe	4700

⑮ What is the difference between the first and last highest scores in Space Bonkers?

Answer : The difference is __________.

⑯ What is the difference between the first and last highest scores in Castle Adventure?

Answer : __________

⑰ If Ray scored 470 in each of 6 rounds of Space Bonkers, what would his total score be?

Answer : __________

⑱ Can Ray beat the 1st highest score in Space Bonkers?

Answer : __________

⑲ If Jane scored 830 in each of 7 rounds of Castle Adventure, what would her total score be?

Answer : __________

⑳ Can Jane beat the 1st highest score in Castle Adventure?

Answer : __________

㉑ If Emily got 63 points every minute, what would her total score be in 15 minutes?

Answer : __________

㉒ If Emily got 972 points in 9 minutes, how many points would she get in 1 minute?

Answer : __________

Solve the problems. Show your work.

㉓ 234 cherries were eaten by 6 birds. If each bird ate the same number of cherries, how many cherries did each bird eat?

Answer : ______

㉔ There were 6 trees. Each tree had 32 birds in it. How many birds were there?

Answer : ______

㉕ 233 birds were in the tree and 69 more joined them. How many birds were there altogether?

Answer : ______

㉖ 8 crows ate 134 cherries each. How many cherries did they eat altogether?

Answer : ______

㉗ A crow ate 108 cherries from one tree and 156 cherries from another. How many cherries did the crow eat altogether?

Answer : ______

㉘ If a crow ate 333 cherries evenly from 9 trees, how many cherries did it eat from 1 tree?

Answer : ______

㉙ There were 763 cherries. If 319 cherries were eaten, how many cherries would be left over?

Answer : ______

㉚ There were 872 cherries, but 427 turned bad. How many good cherries were there?

Answer : ______

CHALLENGE

Emily buys 6 bags of milk for her 4 cats. Each bag holds 2 L of milk. Each cat drinks 1 L in a week. After feeding the cats for 1 week, Emily has 2 L of milk left. Is this story correct or not? Explain.

Answer : ______

UNIT 5 Averages

EXAMPLE

Emily's Math test scores are 80, 70, 60 and 74. What is her average score?

Total score : 80 + 70 + 60 + 74 = 284 **Number of addends :** 4

Average : 284 ÷ 4 = 71

Answer : Her average score is 71.

Emily and her friends are playing video games. Use the table to solve the problems. Show your work.

Game	1st	2nd	3rd	4th
Emily	1230	758	1080	980
Joe	866	1008	982	520
Peter	790	562	1682	858

① What is Emily's average score?

Answer : Her average score is ______.

② What is Joe's average score?

Answer : ______

③ What is Peter's average score?

Answer : ______

④ What is the difference in the average scores between Emily and Joe?

Answer : ______

⑤ What is the difference in the average scores between Emily and Peter?

Answer : ______

⑥ What is the difference in the average scores between Joe and Peter?

Answer : ______

Solve the problems. Show your work.

⑦ Gabe has an average of 200 marbles in 4 jars, which 4 of these jars are his?

Answer : ______________________

⑧ If all the above jars belonged to Gabe, what would be the average number of marbles in each jar?

Answer : ______________________

⑨ Wayne has an average of 90¢ in 4 piggy banks, which 4 of these piggy banks are his?

Answer : ______________________

⑩ If all the above piggy banks belonged to Wayne, what would be the average amount in each piggy bank?

Answer : ______________________

CHALLENGE

Emily got these scores on the English tests : 76, 92, 80 and 72.

① What is her average score?

Answer : ______________________

② If Emily got 0 on the next test, what would be her average score?

Answer : ______________________

UNIT 6 Fractions

EXAMPLE

Emily coloured $\frac{1}{8}$ of a circle. Gabe coloured $\frac{3}{8}$ of the circle. Who coloured more?

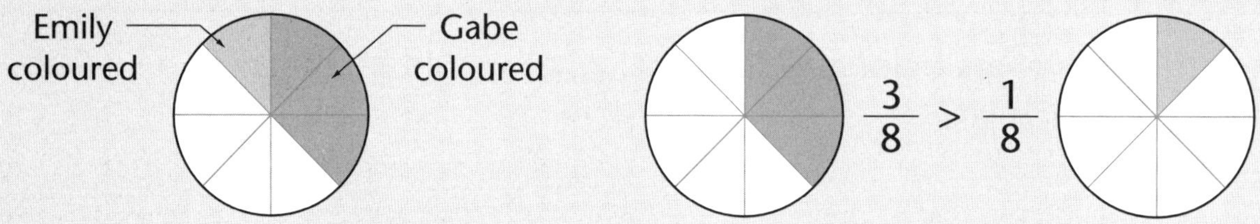

Answer : Gabe coloured more.

Emily asked some classmates about their favourite fruits. Use her table to solve the problems. Show your work.

Fruit	Apple	Orange	Banana	Grape	Peach
No. of classmates	4	2	1	3	2

① How many classmates did Emily ask?

Answer : Emily asked ______ classmates.

② What fraction of her classmates prefer apples?

Answer : ______

③ What fraction of her classmates prefer bananas?

Answer : ______

④ What fraction of her classmates prefer oranges or grapes?

Answer : ______

⑤ What fraction of her classmates do not like oranges?

Answer : ______

⑥ What fraction of her classmates do not like bananas or grapes?

Answer : ______

Colour the pictures and solve the problems.

⑦ Emily has 8 apples. $\frac{3}{8}$ are red and the rest green. What fraction of the apples are green?

Answer : ____________________

⑧ Gabe has 9 apples. $\frac{2}{9}$ are yellow, $\frac{3}{9}$ green and the rest red. What fraction of the apples are red?

Answer : ____________________

⑨ Judy has 12 leaves. $\frac{1}{6}$ are red, $\frac{3}{6}$ yellow and the rest green. What fraction of the leaves are green?

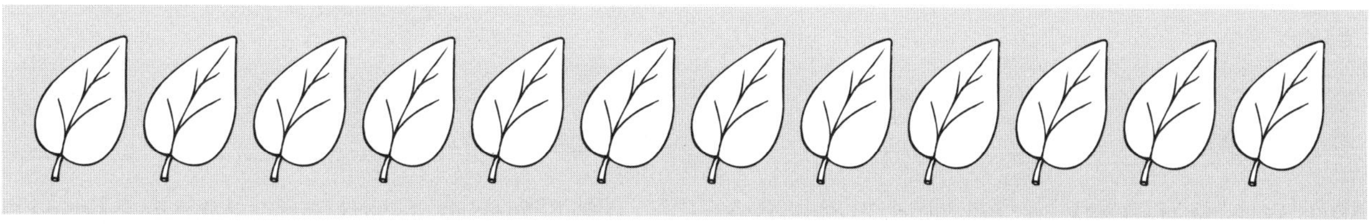

Answer : ____________________

⑩ Mrs Tina has 15 peppers. $\frac{1}{3}$ are green, $\frac{1}{5}$ red and the rest yellow. What fraction of the peppers are yellow?

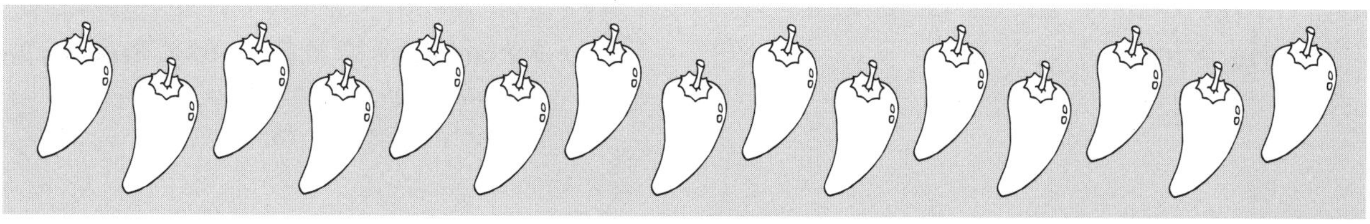

Answer : ____________________

Solve the problems. Show your work.

Mrs Winter ordered 2 party pizzas for her class. Each pizza had 24 slices.

Hawaiian Pizza

Emily, Gabe, Judy, Wayne, Michael	Each ate **1** slice
Eva, Ivan, Ron	Each ate **2** slices

Pepperoni Pizza

Emily, Judy, Eva, Raymond, George, John	Each ate **1** slice
Sally, Michael, Tim, Alexander	Each ate **2** slices

⑪ How many slices of Hawaiian pizza were eaten?

Answer : ______________________

⑫ What fraction of the Hawaiian pizza was eaten?

Answer : ______________________

⑬ What fraction of the pepperoni pizza was eaten?

Answer : ______________________

⑭ What fraction of the pepperoni pizza was left over?

Answer : ______________________

⑮ How many slices of pizzas were there in all?

Answer : ______________________

⑯ How many slices of pizzas did Emily eat in all?

Answer : ______________________

⑰ What fraction of the pizzas were eaten by Emily?

Answer : ______________________

⑱ What fraction of the pizzas were eaten by Michael?

Answer : ______________________

⑲ What fraction of the pizzas were eaten by the children?

Answer : ______________________

- *For questions 17 to 19, you may make use of the answer in question 15.*

Write a mixed number to show how many pizzas each person has. Then solve the problems.

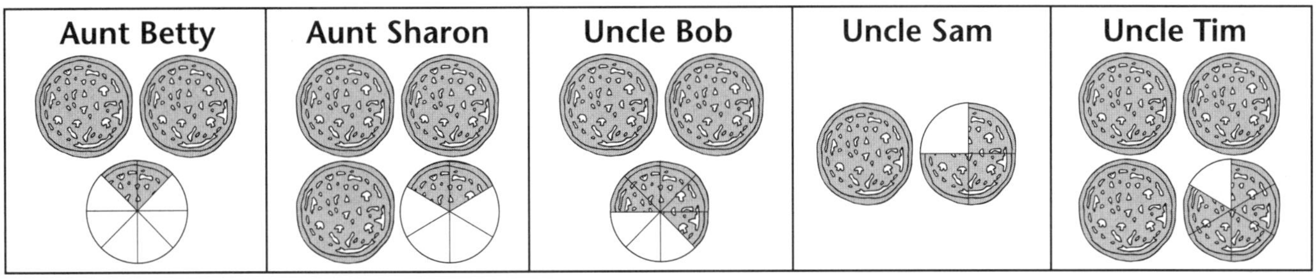

⑳ Aunt Betty has ________ pizzas.

㉑ Aunt Sharon has ________ pizzas.

㉒ Uncle Bob has ________ pizzas.

㉓ Uncle Sam has ________ pizzas.

㉔ Uncle Tim has ________ pizzas.

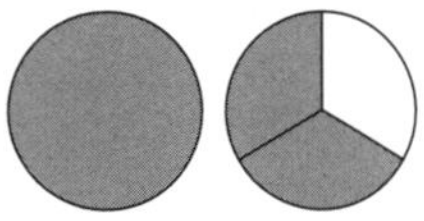

There are 1 whole pizza and $\frac{2}{3}$ of a pizza.

There are $1\frac{2}{3}$ pizzas.

There are one and two-third pizzas.

㉕ Who has more pizzas, Aunt Betty or Uncle Bob? Explain.

Answer : ______________________________

㉖ Who has more pizzas, Aunt Sharon or Uncle Tim? Explain.

Answer : ______________________________

CHALLENGE

Mr Stanley ate $\frac{1}{2}$ of a pie. Yvon ate $\frac{2}{4}$ of a pie. George ate $\frac{4}{8}$ of a pie. They said that they had eaten the same amount of a pie. Are they correct? Colour the pies below to prove your answer.

Mr Stanley : 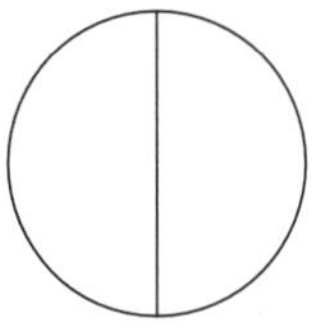 Yvon : 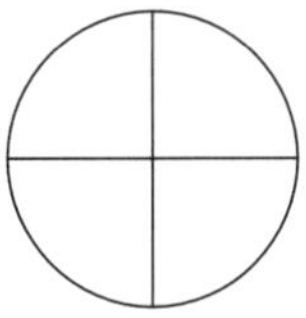 George : 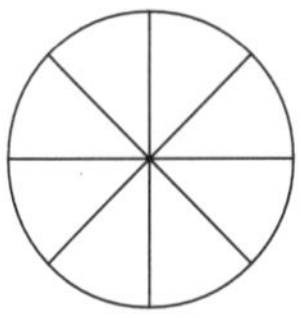

Answer : ______________________________

MIDWAY REVIEW

Solve the problems. Show your work.

The children in Mrs Frek's class sold apples for charity. Mrs Frek divided the children into 3 groups and gave each group a box for collecting money.

① There were 24 boxes of apples. Each box had 36 apples. How many apples were there in all?

Answer : ____________________

② Mrs Frek divided the apples equally into 3 groups. How many apples were in each group?

Answer : ____________________

③ Emily's group had 5 children. Each child sold 39 apples. How many apples did they sell in all?

Answer : ____________________

④ Doug's group had 6 children. Each child sold 38 apples. How many apples did they sell in all?

Answer : ____________________

⑤ Emily said if her group sold 30 more apples, they would beat Doug's group. Was she correct? Explain.

Answer : ____________________

⑥ Gabe's group had 6 children. They sold 252 apples in all. How many apples did each child sell?

Answer : ____________________

⑦ How many more apples did Gabe's group sell than Emily's group?

Answer : ____________________

⑧ How many apples did Emily's group and Gabe's group sell in all?

Answer : ____________________

⑨ Which group sold the most apples?

Answer : ____________________

⑩ How many apples did the children sell in all?

Answer : ____________________

⑪ What is the average number of apples each group sold?

Answer : ____________________

Use the information on P.22 to complete the table.

⑫

	Emily's group	Doug's group	Gabe's group
No. of children in each group			
No. of apples Mrs Frek gave each group			
No. of apples sold			
No. of apples left over			
No. of apples each child sold (on average)			

⑬ How many apples were left over in all?

Answer : ______________________

⑭ Emily sold 40 apples. 17 of them were green. What fraction of the apples that Emily sold were green?

Answer : ______________________

⑮ Doug sold 38 apples. 20 of them were green. What fraction of the apples that Doug sold were not green?

Answer : ______________________

⑯ Emily's group collected $54.00, Doug's group $63.00 and Gabe's group $81.00. How much more money did Gabe's group collect than Emily's group?

Answer : ______________________

⑰ How much money did the three groups collect in all?

Answer : ______________________

⑱ How much did each group collect on average?

Answer : ______________________

Solve the problems. Show your work.

Gabe and his friends went to the store to buy lemonade mix.

⑲ Which container holds the greatest amount of lemonade mix? How much? Write in words.

Answer : ______________________

⑳ What is the total amount of lemonade mix in A and F?

Answer : ______________________

㉑ How much more does D hold than B?

Answer : ______________________

㉒ Which container holds 952 g less than D?

Answer : ______________________

㉓ Which 2 containers hold about the same amount as B?

Answer : ______________________

㉔ Which container holds about half the amount in D?

Answer : ______________________

㉕ Gabe bought 936 g of lemonade in 3 identical containers. Which container was it?

Answer : ______________________

㉖ Emily bought 1648 g of lemonade mix in 2 different containers. Which 2 containers were they?

Answer : ______________________

㉗ Doug bought 8 cans of A. How many grams of lemonade mix were there altogether?

Anwer : ______________________

Circle the correct answer in each problem.

(28) Gabe made 9 jugs of lemonade. There were 7650 mL of lemonade. How many millilitres of lemonade were there in each jug?

A. 850 mL B. 950 mL C. 1050 mL D. 1150 mL

(29) Gabe sold 3142 mL of lemonade in the morning and 4 L in the afternoon. How many millilitres of lemonade did he sell altogether?

A. 3146 mL B. 3542 mL C. 7142 mL D. 3172 mL

(30) How much more millilitres of lemonade did he sell in the afternoon than in the morning?

A. 1858 mL B. 142 mL C. 1142 mL D. 858 mL

(31) Emily sold 152 cups of lemonade in 4 hours. How many cups of lemonade did she sell in 1 hour on average?

A. 148 cups B. 38 cups C. 28 cups D. 48 cups

(32) A cup of lemonade costs 25¢. If the children sold 89 cups, how much money would they make?

A. $22.15 B. $22.25 C. $21.25 D. $21.15

(33) Gabe had 65 cups of lemonade. Emily had 15 cups fewer than Gabe. How many cups of lemonade did Emily have?

A. 50 cups B. 55 cups C. 60 cups D. 70 cups

(34) Doug had 100 cups of lemonade more than Emily. How many cups of lemonade did Emily have?

A. 155 cups B. 160 cups C. 150 cups D. 170 cups

UNIT 7 Introduction to Decimals

EXAMPLE

Robert finished the race in 15.6 seconds. Ricky finished the race in 16.5 seconds. James finished the race in 15.9 seconds. Who finished the race in the shortest time?

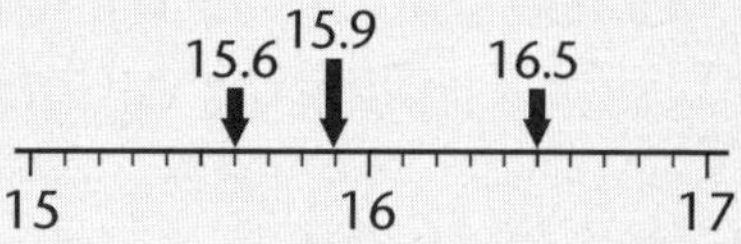

Think : Put the numbers on the number line.

Write : 15.6 < 15.9 < 16.5

Answer : Robert finished the race in the shortest time.

Emily recorded the results of the race. Look at the table and solve the problems. Show your work.

	Robert	Raymond	Ricky	Winston	George
Time (s)	15.6	19.5	18.7	15.9	17.8

① Who was the first to finish the race?

was the first to

Answer : finish the race.

② Who was the last to finish the race?

Answer :

③ Write out the race results.

	Name
1st	
2nd	
3rd	
4th	
5th	

④ If Doug joined the race and finished in 16.7 seconds, where would he be placed?

Answer :

⑤ If Gabe joined the race and finished in nineteen and two-tenths seconds, where would he be placed?

Answer :

1 5.6

1 Ten ***5 Ones*** ***6 Tenths***

15.6 means fifteen and six-tenths.

The table shows the height of the children. Use the table to solve the problems. Show your work.

	Jason	Judy	Emily	Nicky	Gabe	Sally
Height	1.25 m	1.18 m	1.05 m	1.20 m	1.28 m	1.08 m

- *To compare the decimals with the same whole number parts:*
  First compare the tenths digit. If they are the same, then compare the hundredths digit.

⑥ Who is taller than Jason?

Answer :

⑦ Who is shorter than Sally?

Answer :

⑧ Who is shorter than Nicky, but taller than Sally?

Answer :

⑨ Who is taller than Nicky, but shorter than Gabe?

Answer :

⑩ Write the names in order of height from the tallest to the shortest.

Answer :

⑪ How many children are there with a height above 1.23 m?

Answer :

⑫ How many children are there with a height below 1.10 m?

Answer :

⑬ If Nicky says his height is 1.2 m instead of 1.20 m, is he correct? Explain.

Answer :

⑭ If Sally says her height is 1.80 m instead of 1.08 m, is she correct? Explain.

Answer :

Uncle Sam has a lot of containers. Help him decide which container he should use to hold each type of juice. Write the letters in the boxes.

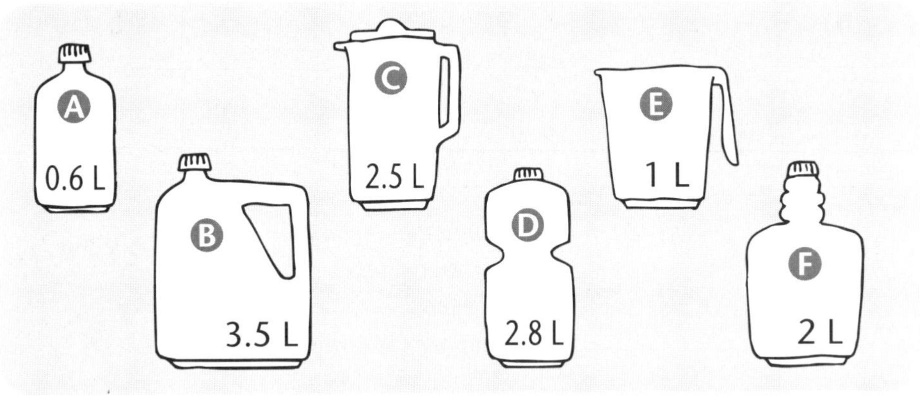

Container

⑮ Two and thirty-eight hundredths of a litre of apple juice. ☐

⑯ One and sixty-seven hundredths of a litre of grape juice. ☐

⑰ Seventy-nine hundredths of a litre of orange juice. ☐

⑱ Two and seven tenths of a litre of pineapple juice. ☐

⑲ Sixty hundredths of a litre of papaya juice. ☐

⑳ Three and two hundredths of a litre of lemon juice. ☐

Look at the containers again and solve the problems.

㉑ Which containers have a capacity greater than 1.5 L?

Answer : ______________________

㉒ How many containers have a capacity smaller than 2.15 L?

Answer : ______________________

㉓ Which containers have a capacity greater than 1.5 L but smaller than 3.15 L?

Answer : ______________________

Read the clues. Write the names and times of the children in the race.

- Albert came third.
- John had a time of 10.8 minutes.
- Sue came after Peter and took exactly 20.4 minutes.
- Peter had a time of 15.8 minutes.
- Jack took 1.2 minutes more than Larry who was sixth.
- Lisa came in 0.6 minute faster than Albert who took 11.2 minutes.
- Jack's time was 12 minutes longer than Lisa's.
- Lisa won the race.

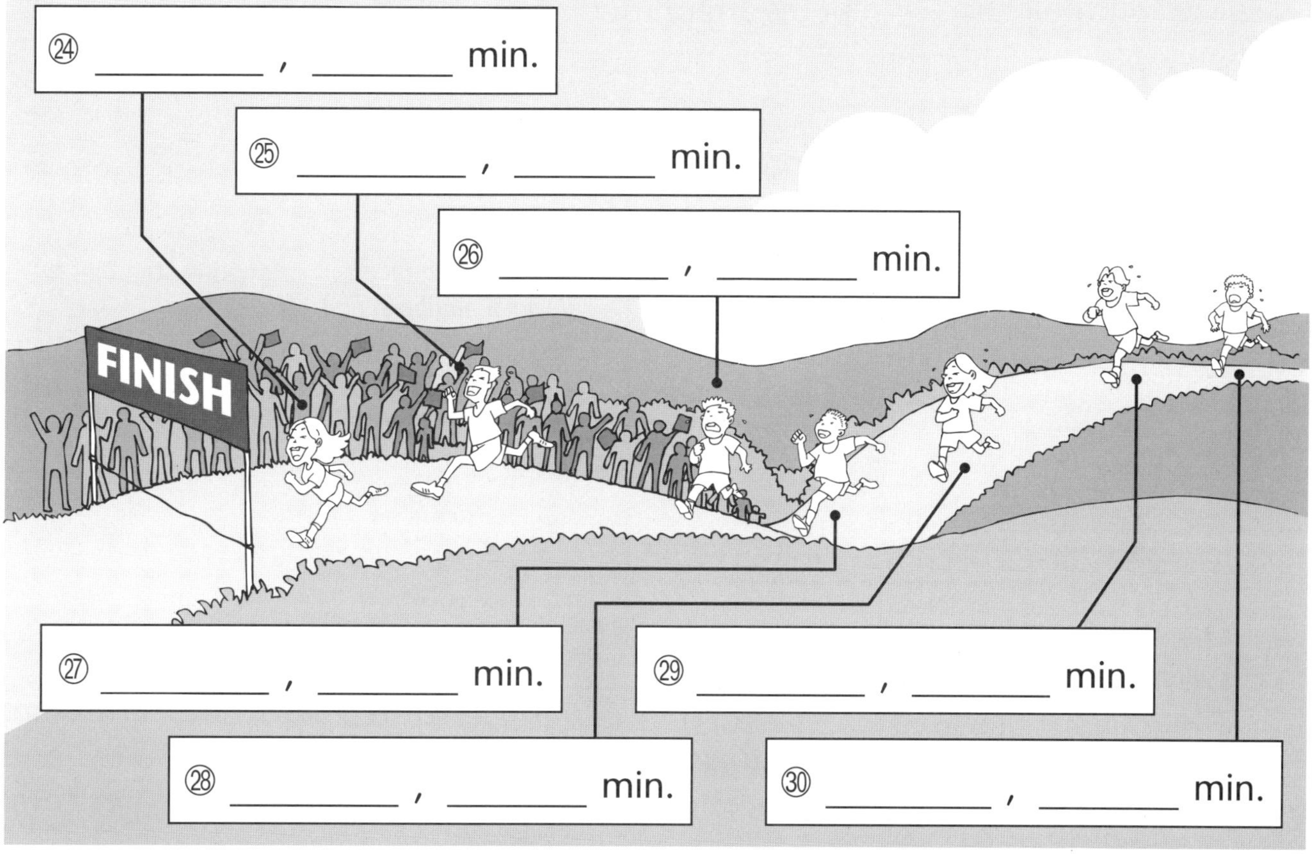

CHALLENGE

If Gabe entered the race and came in half way between John and Lisa, what would be his time? Draw a number line to show your answer.

Answer : ____________________

UNIT 8 Addition and Subtraction of Decimals

EXAMPLE

Judy swam one lap in 1.6 minutes and another lap in 1.8 minutes. How long did it take her altogether?

Think : altogether → addition

Write : $1.6 + 1.8 = 3.4$

Answer : It took her 3.4 minutes altogether.

Solve the problems. Show you work.

- *To add or subtract decimal numbers, first line up the decimal points and then place a decimal point in the answer.*
  e.g. $2.5 + 4.7 = 7.2$

$$\begin{array}{r} 2.5 \\ +\ 4.7 \\ \hline 7.2 \end{array}$$

① Judy swims the first lap in 1.5 minutes and the next two in 3.7 minutes. How long does it take her to swim 3 laps?

Answer : It takes her ______ minutes.

② On Wednesday, Judy practised swimming for 1.3 hours. On Thursday she practised for 2.5 hours. How long did she practise altogether?

Answer : ______

③ How much longer did Judy practise swimming on Thursday than on Wednesday?

Answer : ______

④ Judy swims 3 laps. Her times are 1.45 minutes, 1.37 minutes and 1.61 minutes. What is her total time?

Answer : ______

⑤ What is the time difference between Judy's best 2 laps?

Answer : ______

⑥ Judy beat her best time by 0.4 minute. If her best time used to be 1.62 minutes, what is her new best time?

Answer : ______________________

⑦ Kate took 80.1 seconds to finish the race. Judy swam 6.3 seconds faster than Kate. What was Judy's time?

Answer : ______________________

⑧ Judy swam 1.68 km in the morning, and 1.07 km in the afternoon. How many kilometres did she swim in all?

Answer : ______________________

⑨ Judy can swim 3.8 km without stopping. Her friend can swim 2.95 km without stopping. How much farther can Judy swim than her friend?

Answer : ______________________

⑩ Judy raced against Emily. Judy's time was 74.2 seconds. Emily's time was 80.3 seconds. By how many seconds did Emily lose the race?

Answer : ______________________

⑪ Justin entered a race. He finished the 2-lap race in 89.7 seconds. If he swam the 1st lap in 42.9 seconds, how long did it take him to swim the 2nd lap?

Answer : ______________________

⑫ Sally entered a 3-lap race. She swam the 1st lap in 1.23 minutes, the 2nd in 1.45 minutes and finished the race in 4.05 minutes. How long did it take her to swim the 3rd lap?

Answer : ______________________

Solve the problems. Show your work.

Distance from St. Mount	
Littleton	1.25 km
Jonesville	1.88 km
Ashmorly	2.59 km
Peterston	4.45 km
Shelby	6.48 km
Jacob	8.67 km

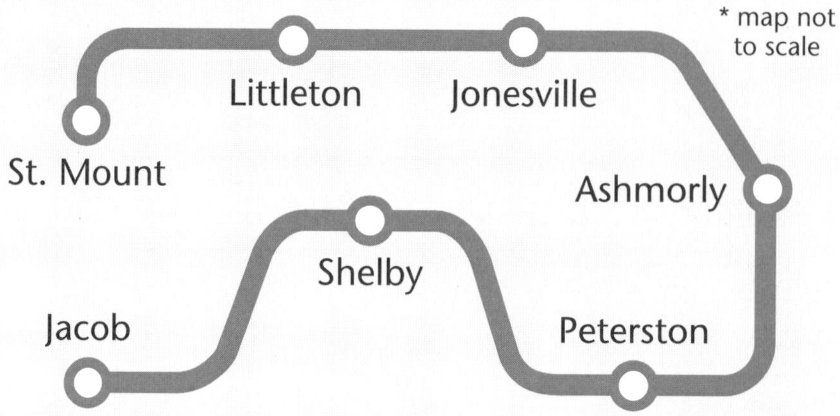

⑬ What is the distance between Littleton and Jonesville?

Answer : ______

⑭ What is the distance between Peterston and Jacob?

Answer : ______

⑮ Which station, Ashmorly or Shelby, is closer to Peterston?

Answer : ______

⑯ Which station, Peterston or Jacob, is closer to Shelby?

Answer : ______

⑰ What is the distance from Ashmorly to the nearest station?

Answer : ______

⑱ Judy lives in Littleton and works in St. Mount. If she takes the subway to work and back, how far does she travel a day?

Answer : ______

⑲ Emily travelled 3.2 km. If she started at Littleton, which station did she arrive at?

Answer : ______

⑳ May travelled 2.57 km. If she started at Peterston, which station did she arrive at?

Answer : ______

㉑ Which two stations are closest to each other?

Answer : ______

Solve the problems. Show your work.

Railway Fares	
Adult	**$1.86**
Student (with student I.D.)	**$1.28**
Child (12 years or under)	**$0.95**
Senior (age 65 or over)	**$0.95**
Infant (in arms)	**free**
Party ticket (2 adults and 3 children)	**$5.80**

22. Amy is 12 years old. If Mr Von, Mrs Von and Amy took the railway, how much would be their fares?

Answer : ______________________

23. If Mr Von had $3.19, how much more would he need to pay for their fares?

Answer : ______________________

24. George forgot to bring his student I.D. How much more money does he need to pay for the adult ticket instead of the student ticket?

Answer : ______________________

25. If 2 adults and 3 children bought a party ticket instead of paying the exact fares, how much money would they save?

Answer : ______________________

26. Mr and Mrs Smith are seniors and they have two grandchildren who are 3 years old and 4 months old. If they took the train with their grandchildren, how much would their fares be?

Answer : ______________________

CHALLENGE

Look at the above railway fares again.

Uncle Sam is 35 years old. His father is 32 years older than he. His mother is 4 years younger than his father. Uncle Sam has a son and twin daughters who are 3 years old and 6 months old. Uncle Sam's wife, Susan, is 3 years younger than he. If Uncle Sam takes the train with his parents, wife and children, what tickets should he buy? How much should he pay?

Answer : ______________________

UNIT 9 Relationship between Fractions and Decimals

EXAMPLE

Judy and her friends had pizza for lunch.

a. What fraction of the pizza was eaten?

Answer : $\frac{3}{10}$ of the pizza was eaten.

b. How much of the pizza was eaten?

Answer : 0.3 of the pizza was eaten.

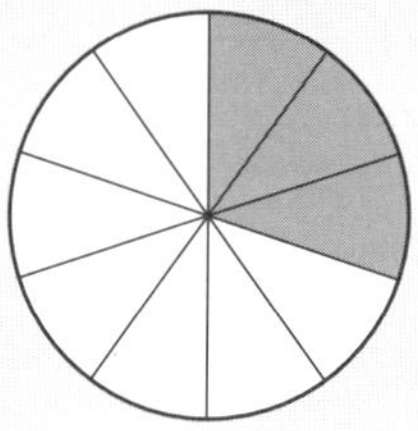

Fraction → $\frac{3}{10} = 0.3$ ← Decimal number

Look at the candies. Solve the problems.

A $\frac{4}{10}$ kg	B $\frac{10}{4}$ kg	C $\frac{7}{10}$ kg	D $\frac{3}{10}$ kg	E $\frac{10}{7}$ kg
F $\frac{10}{5}$ kg	G $\frac{10}{3}$ kg	H $\frac{10}{10}$ kg	I $\frac{1}{10}$ kg	J $\frac{9}{10}$ kg

① Which bag of candies weighs 0.3 kg?

Answer : Bag ______ weighs 0.3 kg.

② Which bag of candies weighs 0.7 kg?

Answer : ______

③ Which bag of candies weighs 0.1 kg?

Answer : ______

④ Which bag of candies weighs ten tenths of a kilogram?

Answer : ______

⑤ Which bag of candies weighs nine tenths of a kilogram?

Answer : ______

⑥ Which bag of candies weighs four tenths of a kilogram?

Answer : ______

The children sold cookies for charity. Read the announcement. Then colour the diagrams to show the cookies sold and solve the problems.

The cookie sale is over. The third winner is Emily Von who sold one and two-tenths boxes of cookies. The second winner, Wayne Smith, sold three and six-tenths boxes and the first winner is David Winter who sold four and nine-tenths boxes of cookies.

⑦ **Boxes of Cookies Sold by Each Child**

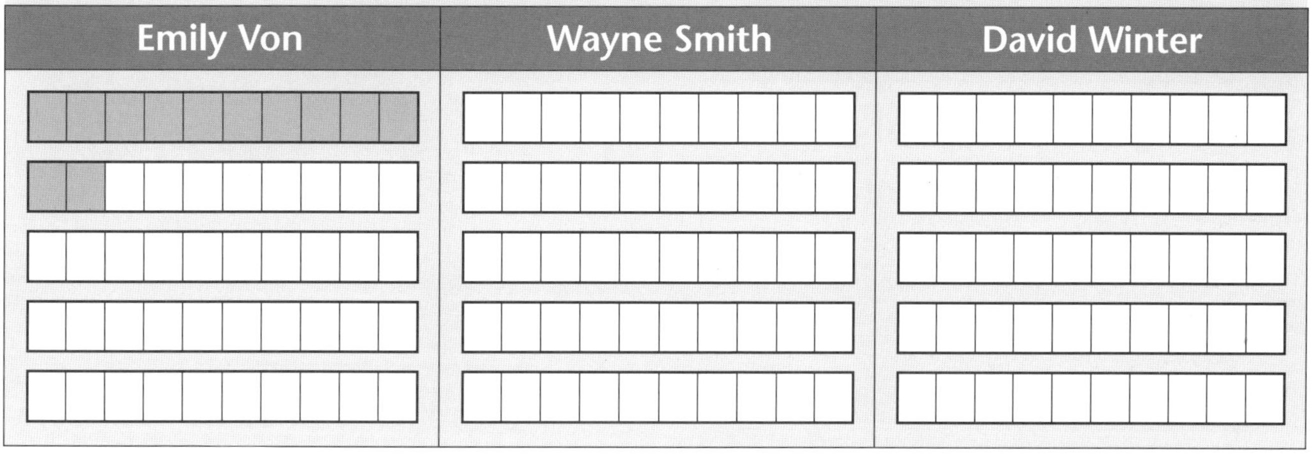

⑧ Write the number of boxes of cookies Emily sold as a fraction.

Answer : ________________

⑨ Write the number of boxes of cookies Wayne sold as a fraction.

Answer : ________________

⑩ Write the number of boxes of cookies David sold as a fraction.

Answer : ________________

Two and seven-tenths means

2.7 or $2\frac{7}{10}$.

ones — 2.7 — *tenths*; *decimal point*

⑪ Three-tenths of a box of cookies is chocolate flavour. What fraction is not chocolate flavour?

Answer : ________________

Use your calculator to put the answers in decimal numbers.

⑫ Emily saved $\frac{4}{5}$ of her allowance for charity. How much of her allowance was saved?

Answer : ______

⑬ Gabe ate $\frac{3}{4}$ of his pie. How much of his pie was eaten?

Answer : ______

⑭ George drank $\frac{12}{25}$ of a glass of water. How much of a glass of water did he drink?

Answer : ______

⑮ Elaine spent $\frac{13}{20}$ of a lesson doing classwork. How much of a lesson did she spend on classwork?

Answer : ______

⑯ How much of a box of eggs was eaten?

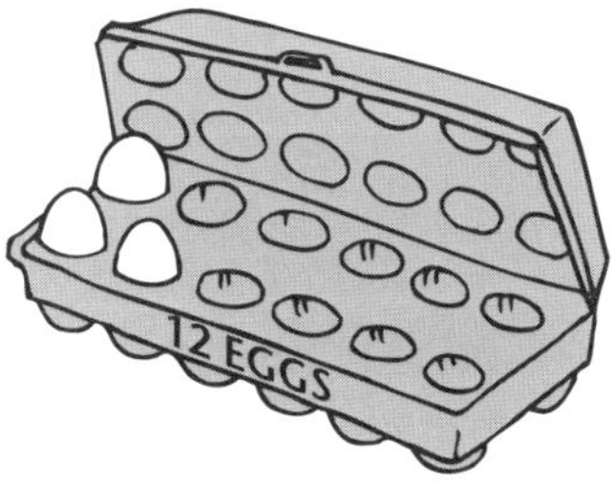

Answer : ______

- *$\frac{4}{5}$ on a calculator is entered as 4 ÷ 5.*
- *You will get the answer by pressing these keys:*

4 **÷** **5** **=**

⑰ How much of a box of chocolates is left over?

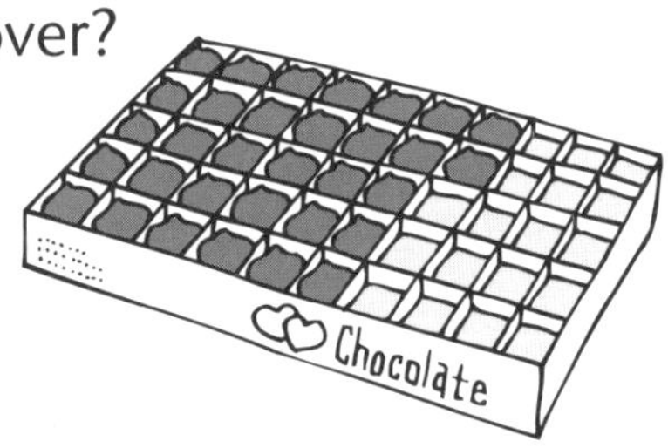

Answer : ______

⑱ How much of a bag of buns was eaten?

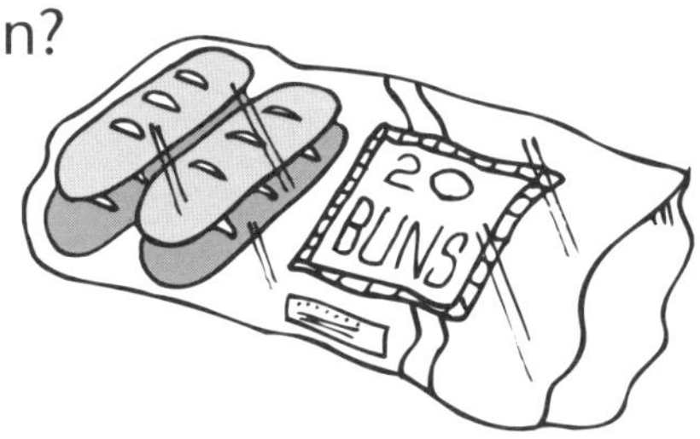

Answer : ______

⑲ 3 cupcakes are left over. How much of a box of cupcakes is left over?

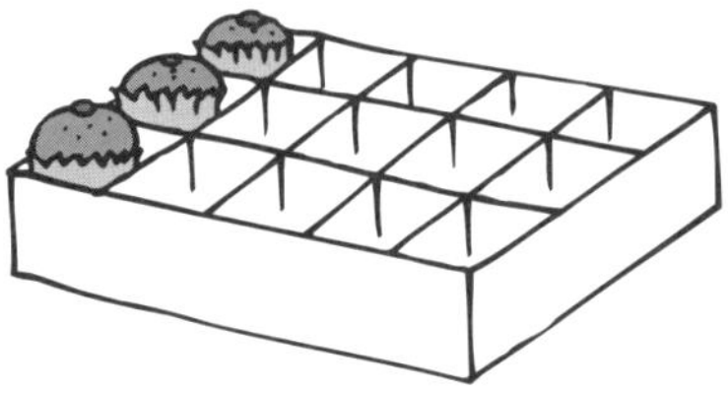

Answer : ______

Look at the recipe. Write each fraction or decimal in words to complete what Mrs Max says.

Hot Fudge

- $1\frac{3}{10}$ cups of all-purpose flour
- $\frac{1}{10}$ cup of brown sugar
- 1.5 teaspoons of baking powder
- 0.7 cup of skim milk
- $\frac{2}{10}$ cup of cocoa powder
- 1.4 cups of boiling water
- 1.8 teaspoons of vegetable oil

To make hot fudge, you need these :

⑳ ______________________ cups of all-purpose flour.

㉑ ______________________ of a cup of brown sugar.

㉒ ______________________ teaspoons of baking powder.

㉓ ______________________ of a cup of skim milk.

㉔ ______________________ of a cup of cocoa powder.

㉕ ______________________ cups of boiling water.

㉖ ______________________ teaspoons of vegetable oil.

CHALLENGE

① Emily has $\frac{17}{20}$ of a box of chocolates. George has 0.68 of a box of chocolates. Who has more chocolates?

Answer : ______________________

② Emily has $1\frac{1}{5}$ boxes of pencils. Elaine has 1.25 boxes of pencils. Who has more pencils?

Answer : ______________________

UNIT 10 **Patterns**

EXAMPLE

What are the next 3 numbers in the pattern?

2, 5, 8, 11, 14, ?, ?, ?

Think : 2, 5, 8, 11, 14 The numbers increase by 3 each time.

+3 +3 +3 +3

Answer : The next 3 numbers are 17, 20 and 23.

Complete the tables and solve the problems.

① Judy put some money in her piggy bank each week. She saved 5¢ in the 1st week, 10¢ in the 2nd week, 15¢ in the 3rd week and so on. How much would she save in the 7th week?

Week	1	2	3	4	5	6
Amount (¢)	5					

Answer : She saved ¢ in the 7th week.

② Nicky collected 2 stickers in the first week, 4 stickers in the 2nd week and 6 stickers in the 3rd week. How many stickers did he collect in the 7th week?

Week	1	2	3	4	5	6
No. of stickers	2					

Answer :

③ Gabe bought 5 marbles. Each week after that he bought 2 more marbles than the week before. How many marbles did he buy in the 8th week?

Week	1	2	3	4	5	6
No. of marbles	7					

Answer :

④ Emily saw 2 birds in her backyard on Sunday, 3 birds on Monday, 5 birds on Tuesday and 8 birds on Wednesday. How many birds would Emily see on Saturday?

Day	Sun	Mon	Tue	Wed	Thu	Fri	Sat
No. of birds	2						

Answer : ______

⑤ Mrs Winter had 100 pencils. Every week she gave 10 pencils to her students. How many pencils did she have after 7 weeks?

Week	1	2	3	4	5	6
No. of pencils left	90					

Answer : ______

⑥ A nickel weighs about 4 grams. How many nickels weigh 32 grams?

No. of Nickels	1	2	3	4	5	6
Weight (g)	4					

Answer : ______

⑦ Joe is building a tower with his blocks. Each layer has 1 more block than the one above it. How many blocks are needed for 7 layers?

Layer	1	2	3	4	5	6
No. of blocks in all	1	3	6			

Answer : ______

⑧ Joe ran a 6-lap race. He finished the first lap in 15 seconds. After that, for every lap, he took 5 seconds more than the time for the previous lap. How long did Joe take to complete the race?

Lap	1st	2nd	3rd	4th	5th	6th
Time for each lap (s)	15					

Answer : ______

Draw the missing figures. Then use 'pattern', 'size', 'shape' or 'orientation' to answer the questions.

⑨ a.

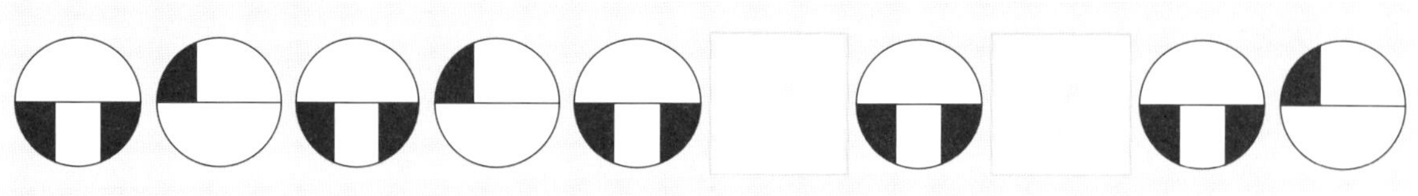

b. Which two attributes do these figures have in common?

Answer : All the figures have the same ______ and ______.

⑩ a.

b. Which two attributes do these figures have in common?

Answer : ______

⑪ a.

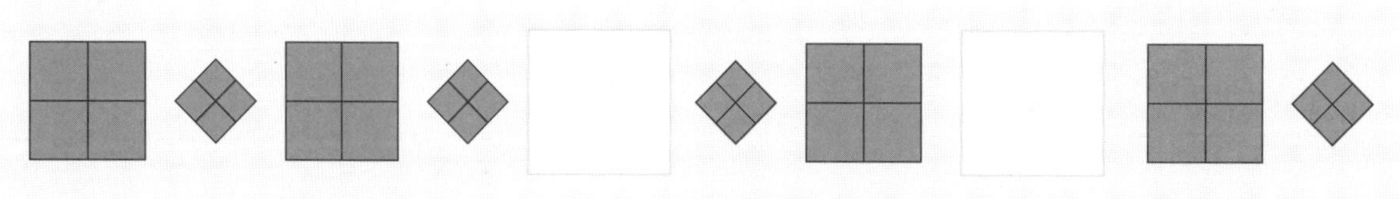

b. Which two attributes do these figures have in common?

Answer : ______

⑫ a.

b. Which two attributes do these figures have in common?

Answer : ______

⑬ a.

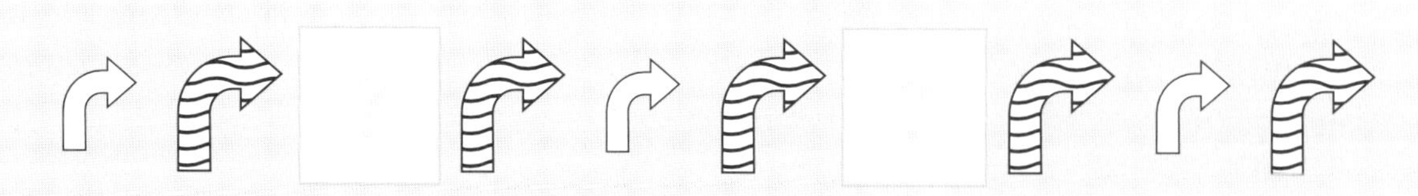

b. Which two attributes do these figures have in common?

Answer : ______

Look at the calendar. Then complete the tables and solve the problems.

September						
SUN	MON	TUE	WED	THU	FRI	SAT
		1	2	3	4	5
6	7	8	9	10	11	12
13	14	15	16	17	18	19
20	21	22	23	24	25	26
27	28	29	30			

- *You can solve the problems more easily by putting some marks on the calendar.*

⑭ Emily walks her dog on September 1. After that, she will walk it every 3 days.

Day	1st	2nd	3rd	4th	5th
Date	Sept. 1	Sept. 4			

⑮ Which date is the 8th time that Emily walks her dog in September?

Answer : ________________

⑯ Emily plays basketball every Wednesday.

Day	1st	2nd	3rd	4th	5th
Date	Sept. 2				

⑰ Which date is the 1st time that Emily plays basketball in October?

Answer : ________________

CHALLENGE

On Monday, Judy bought 10 candies and ate 3. The next day, she bought 12 candies and ate 6. The following day she bought 14 candies and ate 9. If this pattern continued, how many candies would Judy buy and eat on Thursday?

Answer : ________________

UNIT 11 Equations

EXAMPLE

At first Emily had 12 marbles, but Gabe hid some of her marbles. Emily had 8 marbles left. How many marbles did Gabe hide?

Think : What number is taken from 12 to make 8?

Write : $12 - ? = 8$

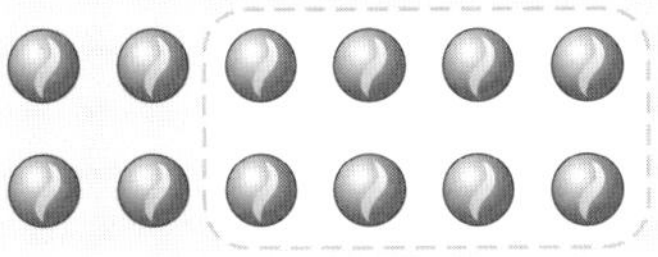

Answer : Gabe hid 4 marbles.

Use the pictures to solve the problems. Show your work.

① Gabe started with 15 marbles. After Emily hid some of his marbles, there were 9 left. How many marbles did Emily hide?

____ – ? = ____

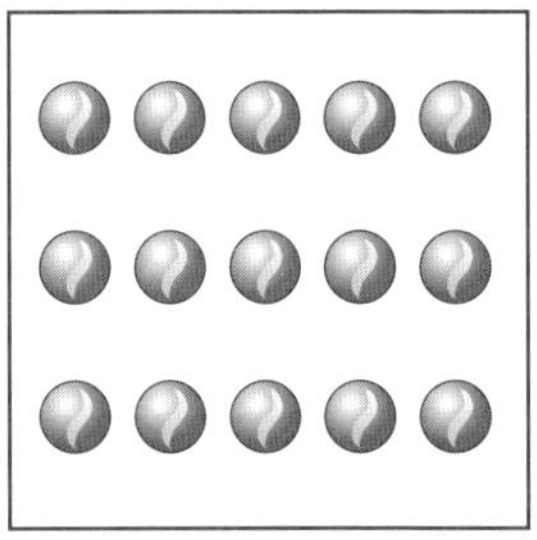

Answer : Emily hid ______ marbles.

② Emily started with 20 marbles. After Gabe hid some of her marbles, there were 12 left. How many marbles did Gabe hide?

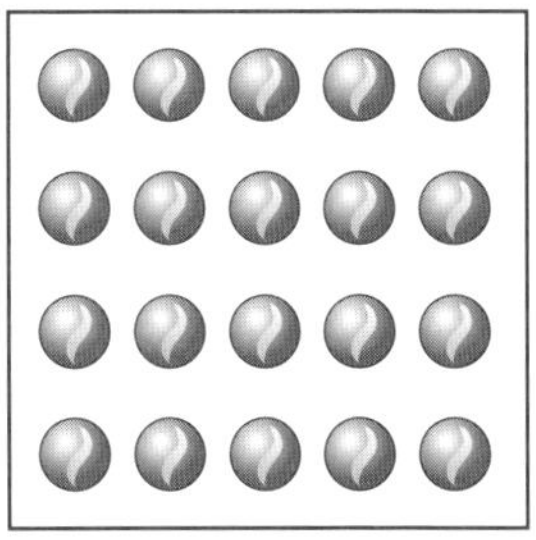

Answer : ______

③ Gabe had 9 marbles. Emily and Gabe had 12 marbles altogether. How many marbles did Emily have?

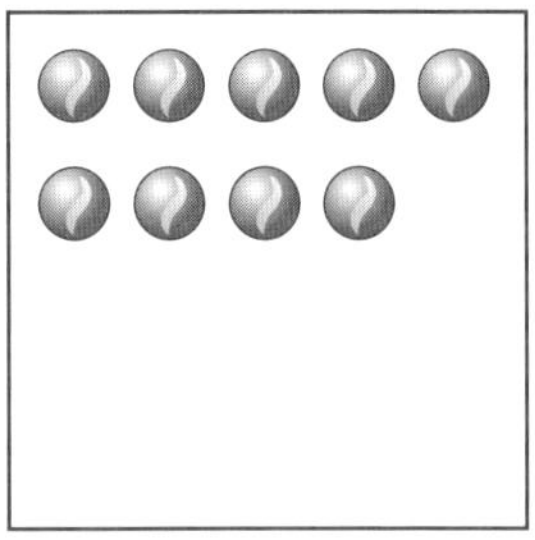

Answer : ______

④ Emily had 12 marbles. Gabe and Emily had 18 marbles altogether. How many marbles did Gabe have?

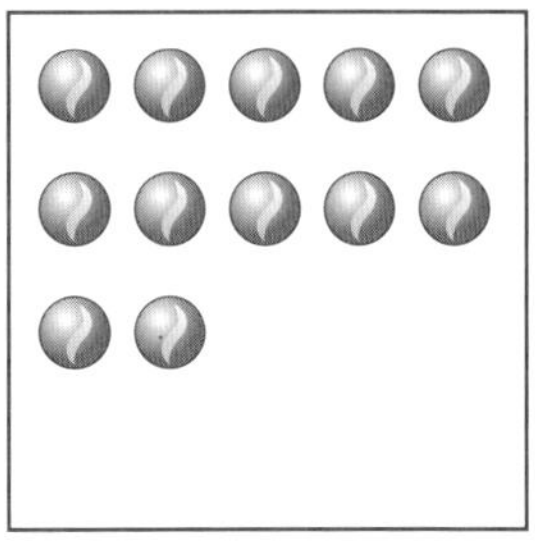

Answer : ______

Write an equation with a ? to solve each problem.

⑤ Gabe has 9 pencils. How many pencils does he need to bring his total up to 15 pencils?

___ + ? = ___

Answer : ______

⑥ Emily had 20 pencils. She gave some to Gabe and has 15 left. How many pencils did she give to Gabe?

Answer : ______

⑦ Gabe ate 6 candies and has 8 left. How many candies did Gabe have to start with?

Answer : ______

⑧ Gabe gave 8 candies to David. Then David has 21 candies. How many candies did David have to start with?

Answer : ______

⑨ Emily started with 27 candies and ended up with 19 candies. How many candies did she eat?

Answer : ______

⑩ The total cost of a candy and a pencil is 45¢. A candy costs 16¢. What is the cost of a pencil?

Answer : ______

⑪ The cost of a sticker is 5¢ more than a candy. If the cost of a sticker is 16¢, what is the cost of a candy?

Answer : ______

⑫ Emily bought a candy with 50¢ and got 21¢ back. How much does a candy cost?

Answer : ______

⑬ Gabe bought some pencils and got 8¢ back. The pencils cost 67¢. How much did Gabe pay?

Answer : ______

⑭ Gabe ate 12 candies and had 29 left. How many candies did he have to start with?

Answer : ______

⑮ If Emily gives David 5 stickers, David will have 63 stickers. How many stickers does David have?

Answer : ______

⑯ If Gabe gives Emily 39¢, he will have 36¢ left. How much does Gabe have?

Answer : ______

Swap the shapes for numbers to solve the problems.

■ 3	▲ 4	● 8	★ 9	⬢ 12	♥ 15

⑰ What is the sum of ■ , ▲ and ● ?

Answer : ____________________

♥ + ▲ – ● means
15 + 4 – 8.
15 + 4 – 8 = 19 – 8 = 11
♥ + ▲ – ● = 11

- *For questions 23 to 25, first write an equation with '?'. Then solve it to find the answer.*

⑱ What is the difference between ⬢ and ★ ?

Answer : ____________________

⑲ What is the sum of ♥ , ■ , ★ and ▲ ?

Answer : ____________________

⑳ How much more is ♥ than ● ?

Answer : ____________________

㉑ How much more is the sum of ⬢ and ● than ♥ ?

Answer : ____________________

㉒ How much more is the sum of ■ and ♥ than ⬢ ?

Answer : ____________________

㉓ What number plus ▲ equals the sum of ■ and ★ ?

Answer : ____________________

㉔ What number plus ● equals the sum of ▲ and ★ ?

Answer : ____________________

㉕ What number subtracted from ★ equals the sum of ■ and ▲ ?

Answer : ____________________

Read the clues. Write the height and weight of the children.

- Brixby is 5 cm shorter than Sandy, but 2 kg heavier than she.
- Guster is 3 cm taller than Sandy, but 1 kg lighter than she.
- Woodly is as heavy as Guster.
- Thorborn is shorter than Woodly. Their difference in height is 2.5 cm.
- The total weight of Sandy and Brixby is the same as the total weight of Boltrun and Thorborn. Boltrun is as heavy as Thorborn.
- The difference in height between Sandy and Woodly is the same as the difference in height between Boltrun and Guster. Boltrun is taller than Guster.

		Height (cm)	Weight (kg)
	Sandy	130	30
26	Woodly	128	
27	Brixby		
28	Guster		
29	Boltrun		
30	Thorborn		

CHALLENGE

Reston had a box of chocolates. He shared it equally with 5 of his friends and each friend gave 1 chocolate back to him. Then he shared the chocolates with Jane and each of them got 4. How many chocolates did Reston have at the beginning?

Answer : ______

FINAL REVIEW

Emily and her cousins are building towers out of blocks. Each block is 1.5 cm high.

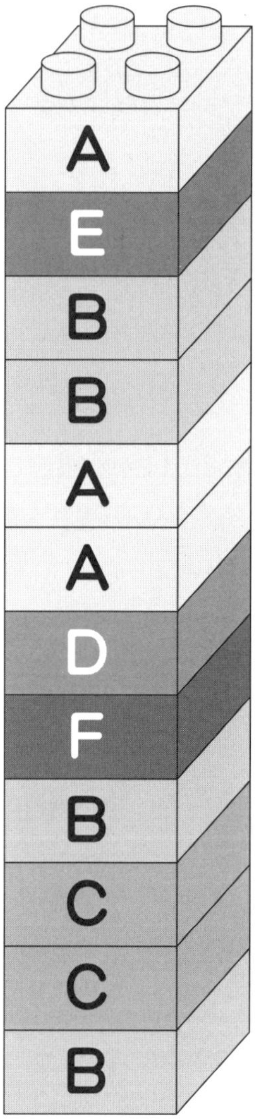

① What fraction of the blocks in the tower have a letter A on them?

Answer : ______________________

② Write the answer for question 1 as a decimal number in words.

Answer : ______________________

③ If Emily stacks up all the blocks with A on them, how tall will the tower be?

Answer : ______________________

④ Emily builds another tower by using the blocks with B and C on them. What fraction of the blocks from the first tower does she use?

Answer : ______________________

⑤ How tall is the tower that is built with blocks B and C?

Answer : ______________________

⑥ Emily's cousin, James, builds each tower with 7 blocks. Complete his table.

No. of towers	1	2	3	4	5	6	7
No. of blocks	7						

⑦ James wants to build 11 towers. How many blocks does he need?

Answer : ______________________

⑧ James tries to stack up all his 7-block towers. Each tower is 10.5 cm tall. Complete the table.

No. of stacked-up towers	1	2	3	4	5	6	7
Height of new tower (cm)	10.5						

⑨ James wants to have a new tower 94.5 cm tall, how many 7-block towers does he need?

Answer : ____________________

⑩ Would it be easy for James to make a tower 94.5 cm tall? Explain.

Answer : ____________________

⑪ If each block weighs about 65 grams, how heavy will 14 blocks be?

Answer : ____________________

⑫ If Emily shares 952 blocks with 3 cousins, how many blocks will each child get?

Answer : ____________________

⑬ If four-fifths of a bag of blocks are red, how much of a bag of blocks is red? Write in decimal number.

Answer : ____________________

⑭ Emily built her first tower in 2.45 minutes and the next one in 3.16 minutes. How long did she take to build the two towers?

Answer : ____________________

⑮ How much more time did Emily spend on building the second tower than the first one?

Answer : ____________________

FINAL REVIEW

Emily got a big box of building blocks. There were 1500 blocks in it.

⑯ Emily made a house with 623 blocks. How many blocks were left?

Answer : ______

⑰ Emily divided the remaining blocks into piles. She put 200 blocks in each pile. Complete the table.

No. of piles	1	2	3	4
No. of blocks	200	400		

⑱ What was the maximum number of piles that Emily got?

Answer : ______

⑲ How many blocks were left?

Answer : ______

⑳ James took Emily's blocks to build 3 cars. Each car was made up of 375 blocks. How many blocks did James need?

Answer : ______

㉑ Did he have enough blocks left over to make another car?

Answer : ______

㉒ Emily used $\frac{4}{15}$ of a box of blocks to build her tower. James used $\frac{7}{15}$ of the same box of blocks to build his tower. Who used more blocks? Explain.

Answer : ______

㉓ $\frac{3}{10}$ of a box of blocks is yellow, $\frac{1}{10}$ blue, $\frac{4}{10}$ green and $\frac{2}{10}$ red. Write the colours in order from the most to the fewest.

Answer : ______

㉔ James built a tower with 25 blocks. Then he took off 7 blocks. What fraction of the blocks were left?

Answer : ______

㉕ If a 16-block tower is 0.16 m tall, how tall will a 32-block tower be?

Answer : ______

㉖ How many 16-block towers are needed to make a new tower 0.64 m tall?

Answer : ______

Each block has 4 vertical faces. Emily put some stickers on each face.

Face 1

Face 2

Face 3

Face 4

	No. of blocks	1	2	3	4	5
㉗	No. of stickers on Face 1	2	4			
㉘	No. of stickers on Face 2	1	2			
㉙	No. of stickers on Face 3	5	10			
㉚	No. of stickers on Face 4	3	6			
㉛	Total no. of stickers	11				

㉜ If Emily used 88 stickers, how many blocks with stickers would there be?

Answer : ____________________

㉝ If Emily wanted to have 9 blocks with stickers, how many stickers would she need?

Answer : ____________________

㉞ If Emily wanted to have 7 stickers on face 2, how many more stickers would she need for each block?

Answer : ____________________

㉟ Look at Emily's stickers. Which two attributes do the stickers have in common?

Answer : ____________________

㊱ If each sticker costs 15¢, how much will Emily pay for the stickers on 1 block?

Answer : ____________________

㊲ How much will Emily pay for the stickers on 3 blocks?

Answer : ____________________

Circle the correct answer in each problem.

38 Which of these pizzas has had $\frac{1}{8}$ eaten?

A. 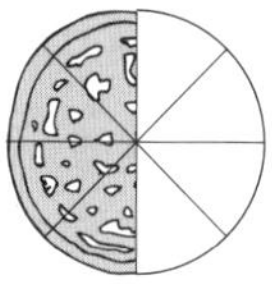 B. 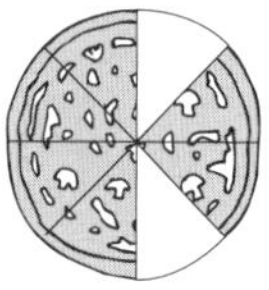 C. 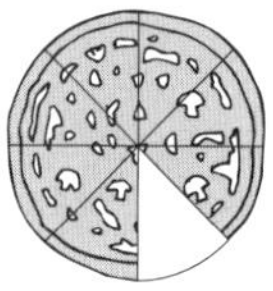 D. 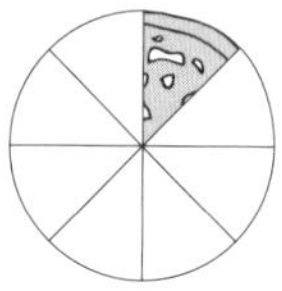

39 Which of these equations could be used to check whether 120 ÷ 5 = 24?

A. 120 – 24 = 96 B. 120 × 5 = 600 C. 24 × 5 = 120 D. 24 + 5 = 29

40 Which shape is next in this pattern?

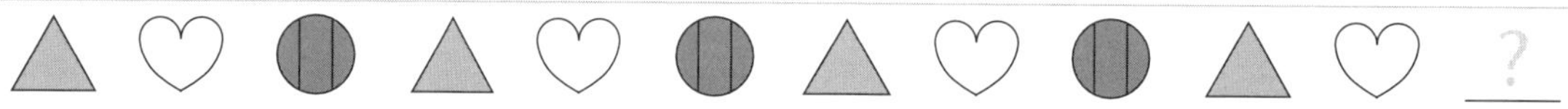

A.  B.  C. 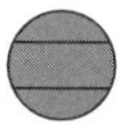 D. 

41 Gabe had 200 stickers and Emily had 150. They put them together and then shared them equally. Which two operations should be used to find the number of stickers that each child had?

A. –, ÷ B. +, ÷ C. +, × D. –, ×

42 What is the answer for question 41?

A. 175 B. 125 C. 150 D. 700

43 Which number is next in this pattern?

80	75	70	65	60	55	?

A. 65 B. 50 C. 40 D. 45

44 Which decimal number has the same value as $\frac{12}{16}$?

A. 1.33 B. 0.25 C. 0.75 D. 0.70

Section IV

Overview

Word problems in Section III were solved using the four basic arithmetic operations.

In Section IV, the problems involve measurement of area, length, perimeter, volume and time as well as money applications.

Spatial concepts are expanded to include measurement of angles using a protractor and applying transformations (rotation, reflection, translation) to shapes. Graphing applications include pictographs, bar graphs and coordinate plotting.

Tree diagrams are used to illustrate possible outcomes such as flipping a coin and tossing a die so that probabilities can be calculated.

Writing answers in full sentences with appropriate units is stressed throughout.

UNIT 1 Length

EXAMPLE

Mandy's school is 1 km from her home. Every day she walks to school and back. How far does she walk in metres?

Think : 1 km = 1000 m

Distance (in metres) : 1000 × 2 = 2000

Answer : She walks 2000 m.

Check ✓ the correct units. Then solve the problems. Show your work.

Irene goes painting in the countryside. She brings along some brushes, pencils, 3 sheets of drawing paper, a box of water colours, a stool and a drawing board.

		mm	cm	dm	m	km
①	Irene is 11 years old. She is about 110 ______ tall.					
②	She has a brush which is about 3 ______ long.					
③	The countryside is about 10 ______ from her home.					
④	She has to take a bus which is about 12 ______ long.					
⑤	She reads a book on the bus. It is about 5 ______ thick.					

⑥ One of Irene's brushes is 15 cm long. How many mm long is it?

Answer : It is ______ long.

⑦ The drawing paper is 3 dm wide. How many cm wide is it?

Answer : ______

⑧ Her stool is 80 cm high. How many dm high is it?

Answer : ______

⑨ A tube of water colour is 70 mm long. How many cm long is it?

Answer : ______

- ***Remember :***

1 cm = 10 mm
1 dm = 10 cm
1 m = 10 dm
1 m = 100 cm
1 km = 1000 m

⑩ Irene sees a lake in the countryside. It is about 1 km across. How many m across is it?

Answer : ______________________

⑪ A boy is fishing in the lake. He is about 135 cm tall. How many mm tall is he?

Answer : ______________________

⑫ There is a tree. It is about 12 m away from Irene. How many dm is it away from her?

Answer : ______________________

⑬ The tree in Irene's picture is 200 mm tall. How many dm tall is it?

Answer : ______________________

⑭ Irene can see 2 houses, one red and one yellow. The red house is 8 m tall and the yellow house is 750 cm. Which house is taller? How many dm taller?

Answer : ______________________

⑮ A kite is flying 120 m above ground. Another kite is flying 300 dm higher. How many m is it above ground?

Answer : ______________________

⑯ 2 dogs, one white and one black, are running in the field. The white dog can run 120 m and the black dog 1300 dm in 10 seconds. Which dog runs farther? How many cm farther?

Answer : ______________________

⑰ There are 2 trails in the countryside. One is shorter than the other by 3000 m. The longer trail is 15 km. How many km is the shorter trail?

Answer : ______________________

⑱ Irene uses 2 pencils to draw a picture. One of her pencils is 15 cm long. The other is 20 mm longer. How many cm long is the other pencil?

Answer : ______________________

CHALLENGE

Irene has 75 sheets of paper. She lays them end to end on the floor. If 4 sheets of paper are 112 cm long, how long will her line of paper be in cm, dm and m?

Answer : ______________________

UNIT 2 Time

EXAMPLE

Jane flew from Sydney, Australia to Tokyo, Japan. She took off at 2:00 p.m. and landed at noon the next day. How long was the flight?

No. of hours from 2:00 p.m. to midnight : 12 – 2 = 10

No. of hours from midnight to noon : 12

Total no. of hours : 10 + 12 = 22

Answer : The flight was 22 hours.

Solve the problems. Show your work.

Irene's grandparents live in Vancouver. They come to visit Irene and her parents in Toronto every year.

① This year, Irene's grandparents arrived at noon on August 28 and left on September 22 at noon. How many days did they stay in Toronto?

Answer : They stayed for ______ days.

② They took off at 2:10 p.m. Toronto time and arrived at 7:28 p.m. How long was the flight?

Answer : ______

③ Every morning they took 20 minutes to walk to a park from home. They stayed there for one and a quarter hours. How many minutes did they stay in the park?

Answer : ______

- ***Remember :***

  1 minute is 60 seconds.
  1 hour is 60 minutes.
  1 day is 24 hours.
  1 week is 7 days.
  1 year is 52 weeks.
  1 year is 365 days (366 days in a leap year).

④ They left home for the park at quarter to eight. When did they return home?

Answer : ______

⑤ Grandma needed three quarters of an hour to take a bath. How many minutes did she need in a week?

Answer : ______

Irene does similar things every morning on weekdays. This is a time line of her morning.

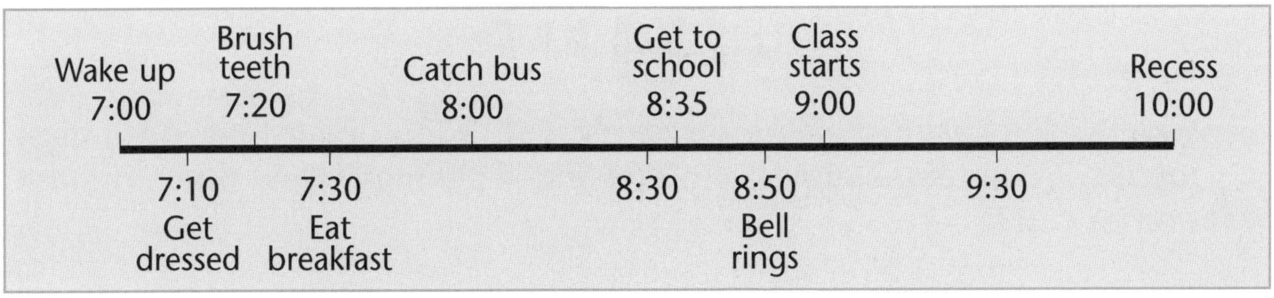

⑥ How long after she wakes up does Irene get dressed?

Answer : ____________________

⑦ If Irene gets out of bed 6 minutes after she wakes up, what time does she get out of bed?

Answer : ____________________

⑧ How long does Irene spend on the school bus every morning?

Answer : ____________________

⑨ Will she be late for school if the bus comes at 8:30?

Answer : ____________________

⑩ If Irene has French at 9:35 and it goes on until recess, how long is her French class?

Answer : ____________________

⑪ If Irene leaves home 8 minutes before her bus comes, what time does she leave home?

Answer : ____________________

CHALLENGE

Look at Irene's time line again. If lunch is 1 hour and 45 minutes after recess starts, how much time does Irene have between breakfast and lunch?

Answer : ____________________

UNIT 3 Operations with Money

EXAMPLE

Mrs Collins paid for some groceries with 3 ten-dollar bills, 4 toonies, 1 loonie, 3 quarters, 2 dimes, 1 nickel and 4 pennies. How much did the groceries cost?

No. of dollars : $10 \times 3 + 2 \times 4 + 1 \times 1 = 39$

No. of cents : $25 \times 3 + 10 \times 2 + 5 \times 1 + 1 \times 4 = 104$

Total cost : $39 + 1.04 = 40.04$

Answer : The groceries cost $40.04.

Solve the problems. Show your work.

Irene and Alan were helping their teacher count the money for the class book orders.

① Janice's order had 1 loonie, 1 quarter and 2 dimes. Which book did she order?

Answer : She ordered ______________.

② Paul's order had 2 five-dollar bills, 1 quarter and 2 dimes. Which book did he order?

Answer : ______________

③ Gary paid with 1 five-dollar bill, 1 toonie and 5 dimes. Which book did he order?

Answer : ______________________

④ Jessie paid with 2 toonies, 3 quarters, 2 dimes and 4 pennies. Which book did she order?

Answer : ______________________

⑤ Liam's order had 1 ten-dollar bill, 1 toonie, 1 loonie and 4 nickels. Which book did he order?

Answer : ______________________

⑥ Joan's order had 2 toonies, 1 loonie and 1 quarter. Which book did she order?

Answer : ______________________

⑦ Leslie paid with 1 ten-dollar bill, 3 loonies, 3 quarters, 1 dime and 2 pennies. What was his order?

Answer : ______________________

⑧ Brian paid with 2 five-dollar bills, 1 toonie, 3 dimes, 1 nickel and 1 penny. What was his order?

Answer : ______________________

Fill in the blanks.

The following students ordered several books each. Show how they paid with the smallest number of bills and coins.

	Name	Order	Bill			Coin					
			$20	$10	$5	$2	$1	25¢	10¢	5¢	1¢
⑨	Barry	$20.34	1								
⑩	Wendy	$18.17									
⑪	Ash	$12.73									
⑫	Rica	$8.48									
⑬	Tara	$11.36									
⑭	Kaitlin	$32.40									
⑮	Justin	$41.70									

Solve the problems. Show your work.

Irene and Alan helped their teacher give change to their classmates. Calculate how much change each person received and write the smallest number of bills and coins for the change.

⑯ Peter's books cost \$5.73 and he gave a ten-dollar bill.

Answer : ____________________

⑰ Jackie's books cost \$11.35 and she gave \$15.00.

Answer : ____________________

⑱ Lillian's books cost \$18.43 and she gave a \$20 bill.

Answer : ____________________

⑲ Ryan's books cost \$22.14 and he gave \$23.00.

Answer : ____________________

⑳ James gave \$30.00 for his books that cost \$21.15.

Answer : ____________________

㉑ Lisa gave a \$20 bill for her books that cost \$12.88.

Answer : ____________________

㉒ Randy gave \$10.00 for his books that cost \$4.71.

Answer : ____________________

㉓ Tony gave \$15.00 for his books that cost \$13.82.

Answer : ____________________

Another book fair was held in Birchway Public School. The students could buy books, posters and stationery there.

24. Steven bought 2 comic books. Each book cost $1.47. How much did he pay?

Answer : ______________________

25. Mimi bought a book for $3.99 and a poster for $1.25. How much did she pay?

Answer : ______________________

26. Delia bought 3 books. They cost $2.75, $3.99 and $4.16. How much did she pay?

Answer : ______________________

27. Mandy bought 3 posters that were $2.60 each. How much did she pay?

Answer : ______________________

28. Jasmine bought 2 books that cost $3.74 and $4.19. She also bought a bookmark for $0.81. How much did she pay?

Answer : ______________________

29. John bought a big dictionary for $21.32 and a poster for $2.60. How much did he pay?

Answer : ______________________

30. Mike bought 3 books. They cost $5.72, $3.69 and $2.15. He also bought a rollerball pen for $4.30. He received $0.14 change. How much did he give the cashier?

Answer : ______________________

CHALLENGE

Jennie has $25.00. She wants to buy some posters that are $2.25 each. How many can she buy? Show your thinking.

Answer : ______________________

UNIT 4 Area and Perimeter

EXAMPLE

Dave drew a rectangle and an irregular shape.

a. Find the perimeter and the area of the rectangle.

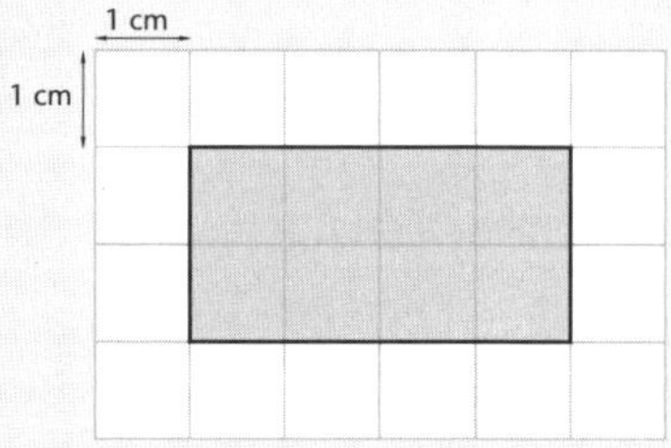

Perimeter : 4 + 2 + 4 + 2 = 12

Area : 2 rows of 4 squares

$2 \times 4 = 8$

Answer : The perimeter is 12 cm and the area is 8 cm^2.

b. Find the area of the irregular shape.

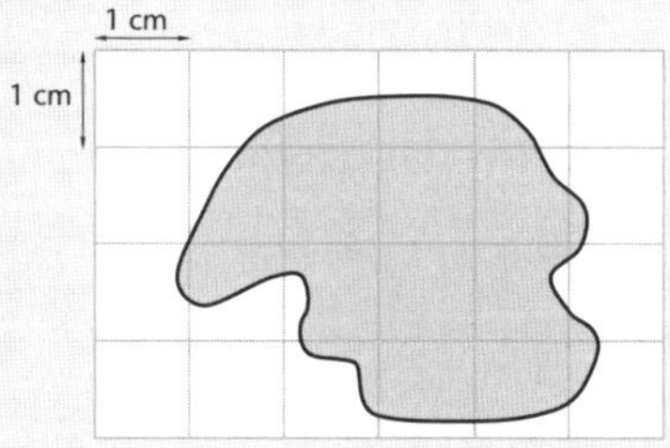

Count : 3 squares are completely inside the shape, and 6 squares are mostly inside the shape.

Area : 3 + 6 = 9

Answer: The area is about 9 cm^2.

Measure and answer.

Irene has some magnets of different shapes. Help her measure the perimeter of each magnet with a ruler with millimetres.

① 

② 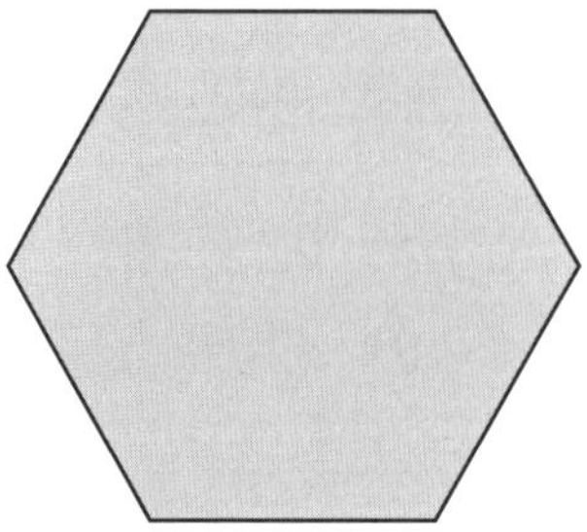

Answer : Its perimeter is ____________ .

Answer : ____________

③

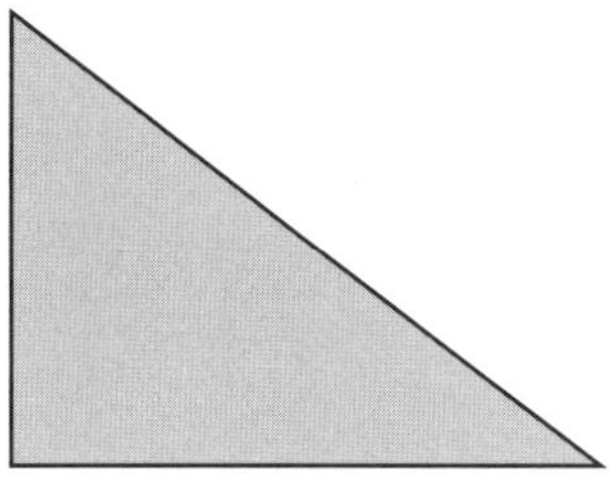

Answer : ______

④

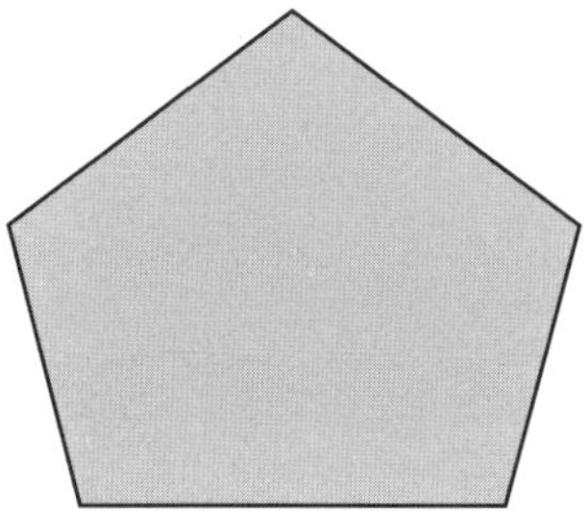

Answer : ______

⑤

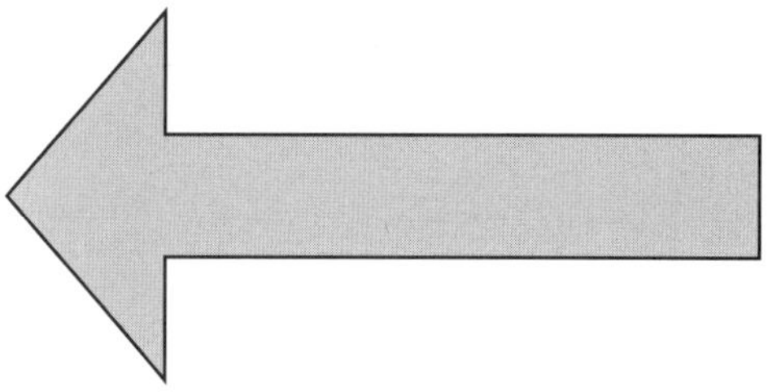

Answer : ______

⑥

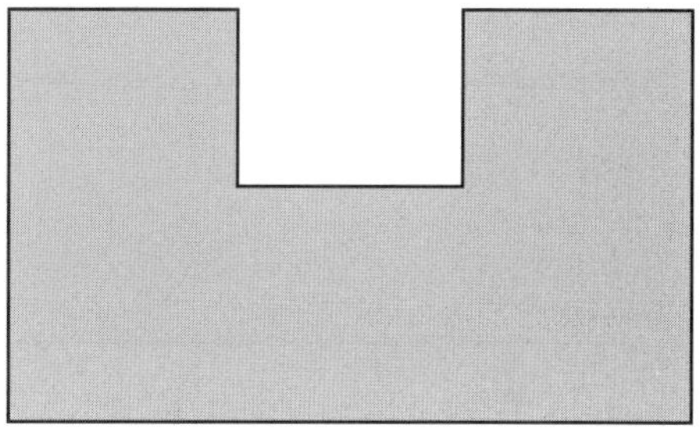

Answer : ______

Solve the problems. Show your work.

Irene is measuring the furniture and some of the things in her bedroom with a tape.

⑦ There is a rectangular photograph on the wall. The length and width of the photograph are 30 cm and 20 cm. What is its perimeter?

Answer : ______

⑧ There is a square-shaped noticeboard. One of its sides is 60 cm. What is its perimeter?

Answer : ______

⑨ There is a triangular pennant on the noticeboard. Two of its sides are 36 cm long and the other is 24 cm. What is its perimeter?

Answer : ______

⑩ Irene's bedroom is a big rectangle. Two of the walls are 8 m long and the other two are 6 m long. What is the perimeter of her bedroom?

Answer : ________________

⑪ Irene's bed is 3 m long and 1.2 m wide. What is the perimeter of her bed?

Answer : ________________

⑫ There is a window with a height of 9 dm and a width of 16 dm. What is the perimeter of the window in metres?

Answer : ________________

⑬ Irene has a rug with 5 sides of equal lengths. The perimeter of the rug is 350 cm. What is the length of each side of the rug?

Answer : ________________

Draw the shapes and solve the problems.

Irene wants to find out the areas of the magnets she has collected. Help her draw the magnets on the grids and write their areas.

⑭ Magnet A is a rectangle with a length of 4 cm and a width of 3 cm.

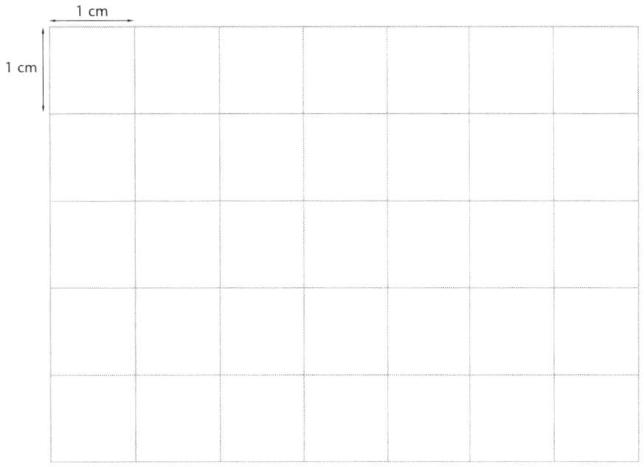

Answer : ________________

⑮ Magnet B is a square with a perimeter of 12 cm.

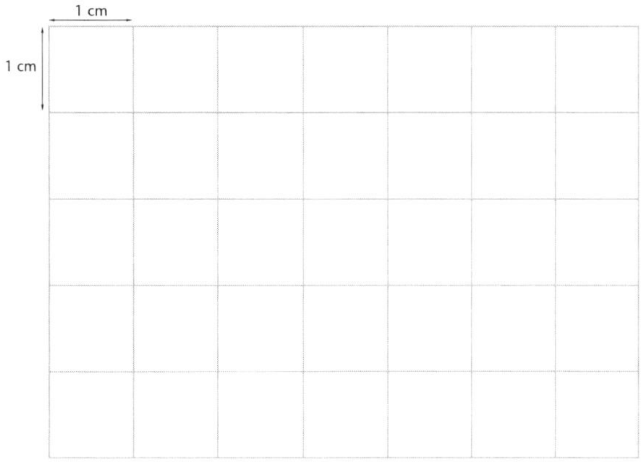

Answer : ________________

⑯ Magnet C looks like a letter T. The width of the magnet is 5 cm and the height is 6 cm. The strokes are 1 cm wide.

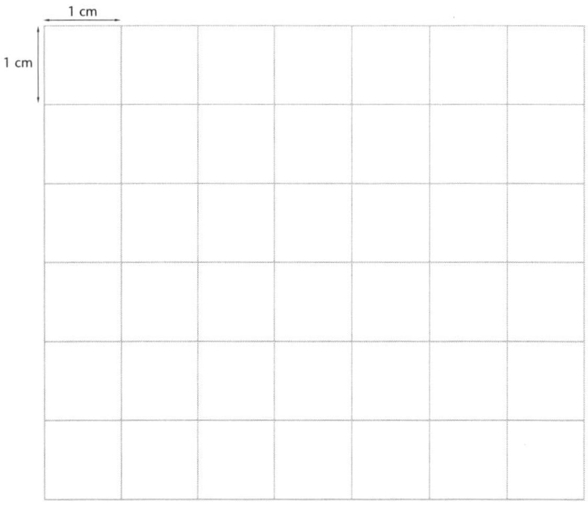

Answer : ______________________

⑰ Magnet D looks like a letter L with a width of 5 cm and a height of 6 cm. The strokes are 2 cm wide.

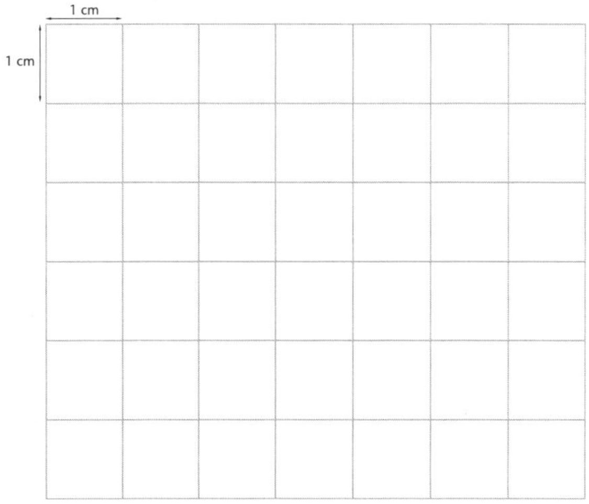

Answer : ______________________

⑱ Compare the area and perimeter of magnets C and D.

Answer : ______________________

⑲ Magnet E looks like a cross ✝. The width is 5 cm and the height is 6 cm. The strokes are 1 cm wide.

Answer : ______________________

⑳ Magnet F looks like a letter □ with a width of 3 cm and a height of 4 cm. The strokes are 1 cm wide.

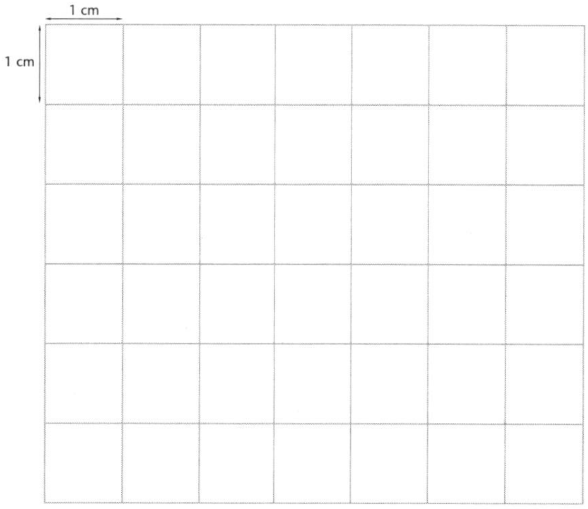

Answer : ______________________

㉑ Compare the area and perimeter of magnets E and F.

Answer : ______________________

Irene's mother has baked some cookies of irregular shapes.

㉒ What is the area?

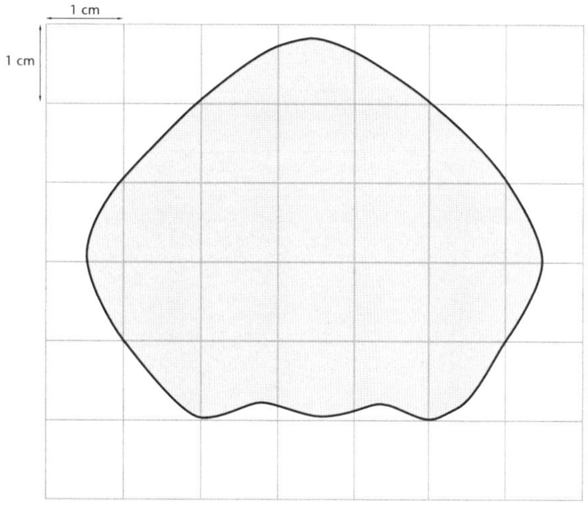

Answer :

㉓ What is the area?

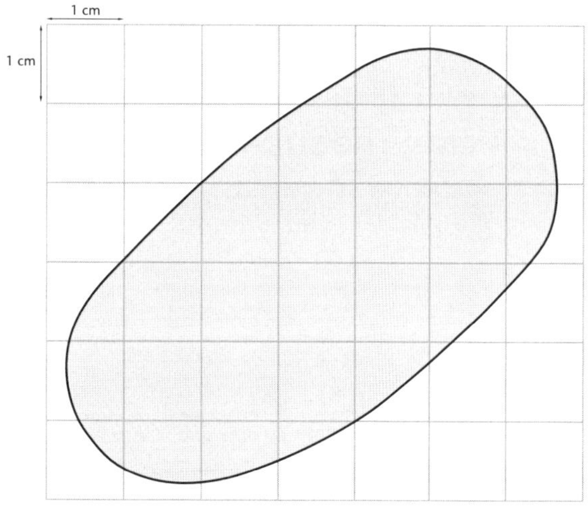

Answer :

㉔ What is the area?

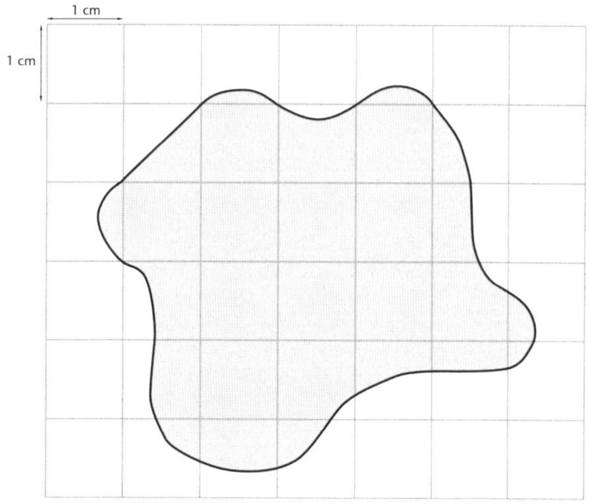

Answer :

㉕ What is the area?

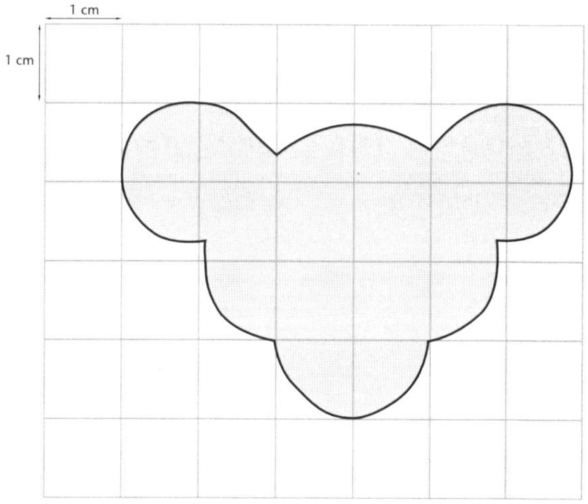

Answer :

Solve the problems. Show your work.

Irene is helping her dad build a new run for their dog. They have to decide how much fence to put around the run and how much space to give the dog.

㉖ The pen has an area of 12 m^2, and there is a rectangular kennel which is 2 m long and 1 m wide.

a. What is the area of the kennel?

Answer :

b. How much space is left in the pen for the dog to run in?

Answer : ______________________

㉗ The pen has 2 sides of 4 m and 2 sides of 3 m. If there is 12 m of fencing, how much more fencing is needed?

Answer : ______________________

㉘ The pen has 2 sides of 4 m and 2 sides of 3 m. If the longer side is lengthened by 1 m and the shorter side shortened by 1 m, what will be the difference in area between these 2 pens?

Answer : ______________________

㉙ Irene wants to enclose a rectangular pen with 12 m of fencing.

a. Draw as many different rectangles or squares as you can on the grid with the above measurement.

b. Colour the pen with the biggest area.

c. How did Irene get the biggest area with a 12-m fence?

Answer : ______________________

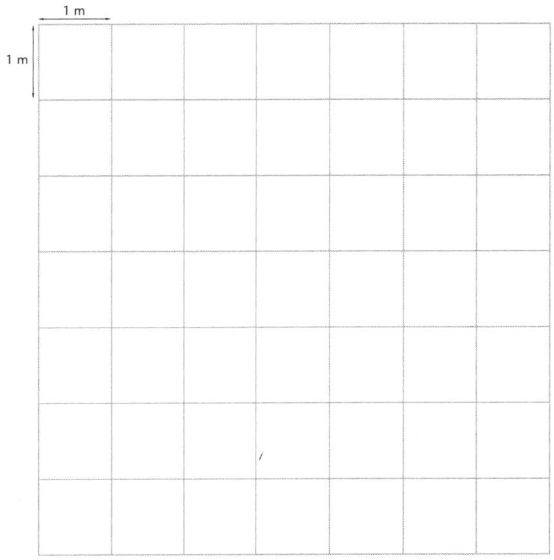

CHALLENGE

The backyard of Tom's house is rectangular in shape with a perimeter of 42 m. If the length is twice as long as the width, how long is each side?

Answer : ______________________

UNIT 5 Capacity, Volume and Mass

EXAMPLE

a. Irene has built a straight tower of blocks. The volume of each block is 1 cm^3.

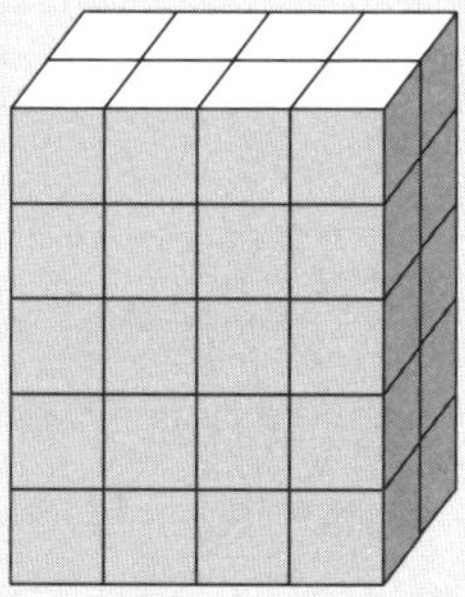

i. What is the volume of the tower?

Think : There are 5 layers of 8 blocks.

Volume of the tower : $1 \times 8 \times 5 = 40$

Answer : The volume of the tower is 40 cm^3.

ii. Each block has a mass of 10 g. What is the mass of the tower?

Mass : $10 \times 40 = 400$

Answer : The mass of the tower is 400 g.

b. Irene has a small bucket which can hold 6 bottles of water. If the capacity of each bottle is 500 mL, what is the capacity of the bucket in L?

Capacity in mL : $500 \times 6 = 3000$

Write : 1000 mL = 1 L → 3000 mL = 3 L

Answer : The capacity of the bucket is 3 L.

Irene cannot decide what units to use for the following. Help her check ✓ the correct units.

	Event	Unit					
		g	kg	cm^3	m^3	mL	L
①	Pouring some cough syrup into a spoon						
②	Measuring how much water a bath tub can hold						
③	Finding how heavy a watermelon is						
④	Calculating the space occupied by a fridge						
⑤	Finding how heavy a pencil is						
⑥	Measuring how much space a recorder occupies						
⑦	Recording the amount of water in a glass						

Solve the problems. Show your work.

Irene has some small blocks that are 1 cm^3 in volume. She and her friends are building some towers with the blocks at home.

⑧ Irene has built a straight tower. What is the volume of her tower?

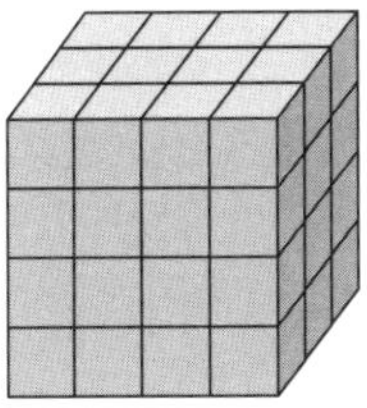

Answer : The volume ______.

⑩ Look at Peter's tower. What is its volume?

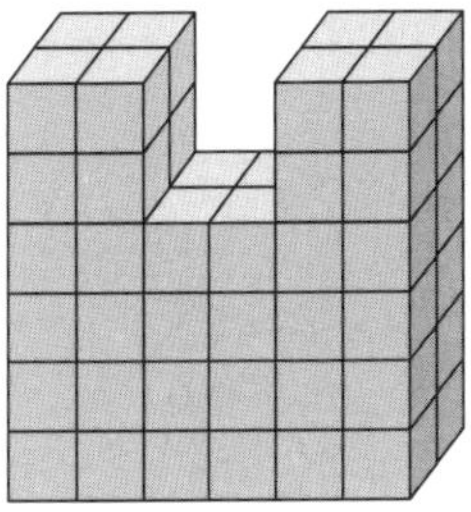

Answer : ______

⑨ Allan has built a block pyramid. What is its volume?

Answer : ______

⑪ Look at Gigi's tower. What is its volume?

Answer : ______

The children found some containers and a 1-L jug in the basement. They are trying to find the capacity of each container with the jug.

⑫ Irene can fill the 1-L jug with 4 glasses of water. What is the capacity of each glass?

Answer : ______

⑭ Irene fills a glass using 5 egg cups of water. What is the capacity of each egg cup?

Answer : ______

⑬ 20 glasses of water can fill a bucket. What is the capacity of the bucket in L?

Answer : ______

- ***Remember:***

  1 L = 1000 mL

  1 mL = 0.001 L

⑮ What is the capacity of 1 bucket and 10 glasses in L?

Answer : ______________________

⑯ There is a big mug which can hold half a jug of water. What is the capacity of the mug?

Answer : ______________________

⑰ Irene can fill 5 bottles with 1 jug of water. What is the capacity of each bottle?

Answer : ______________________

⑱ How many glasses of water can fill a tub with a capacity of 250 L?

Answer : ______________________

Irene and Alan are hungry. They go to the supermarket to buy some snacks.

⑲ Irene has enough money to buy 4 bags of cookies that weigh 21 g each or 1 big bag that weighs 80 g. Which would give her more cookies?

Answer : ______________________

⑳ Alan's favourite candies come in little bags of 43 g each and big bags of 150 g each. Which would give him more candies, 3 little bags or 1 big bag?

Answer : ______________________

㉑ Sixteen 50-g packets of potato chips cost the same as five 165-g packets of potato chips. Which have more potato chips?

Answer : ______________________

Mr Smith has made a big scale to weigh the animals on his farm. He only knows that the mass of a rabbit is 1 kg and every animal of the same kind weighs the same. Look how he weighs his animals and solve the problems.

㉒ What is the mass of the cat?

Answer : ______

㉓ What is the mass of the dog?

Answer : ______

㉔ What is the mass of the pig?

Answer : ______

㉕ What is the mass of the calf?

Answer : ______

㉖ How many rabbits would be needed to balance a calf?

Answer : ______

㉗ How many rabbits would be needed to balance 2 cats and 1 dog?

Answer : ______

㉘ How many dogs would be needed to balance a calf?

Answer : ______

㉙ How many cats would be needed to balance a calf?

Answer : ______

㉚ How many cats must be added to 6 dogs in order to balance a calf?

Answer : ______

㉛ If Mr Smith puts 6 cats on one side of the scale and a pig on the other side, which side will weigh more?

Answer : ______

㉜ Is it possible to balance a calf, 6 dogs and 4 cats? Explain.

Answer : ______

CHALLENGE

John, Ben and Tim are playing on a teeter-totter. John has a mass of 50 kg. Ben is 6 kg heavier than Tim. If John can balance Ben and Tim together, what is the mass of Tim?

Answer : ______

UNIT 6 Two- and Three-Dimensional Figures

EXAMPLE

Irene can see many signs of different shapes on her remote control.

a. How many of them are quadrilaterals?

Think : Quadrilaterals are polygons having 4 straight sides.

Count : 11 quadrilaterals

Answer : There are 11 quadrilaterals.

b. Which of the solids on the right are prisms and which are pyramids?

Think : Pyramids have triangular faces standing on a base and meeting at a vertex.

Prisms have congruent ends and straight sides.

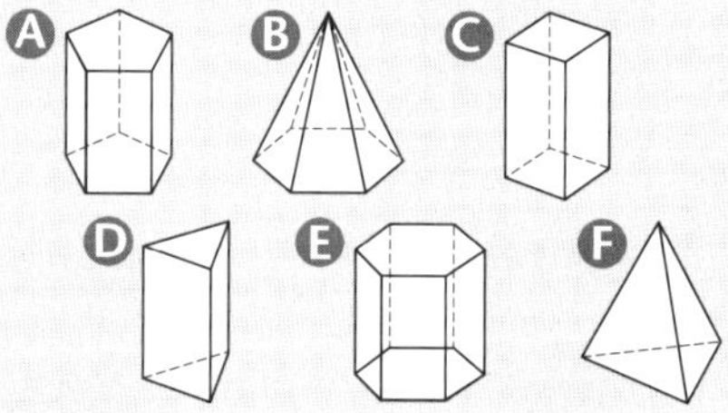

Answer : A, C, D and E are prisms. B and F are pyramids.

Count and colour. Show your thinking and answer the questions.

Irene's teacher has several boxes of shapes. She wants Irene to sort and colour them. Help Irene finish her work.

① Irene has to sort out all the rectangles and colour them red.

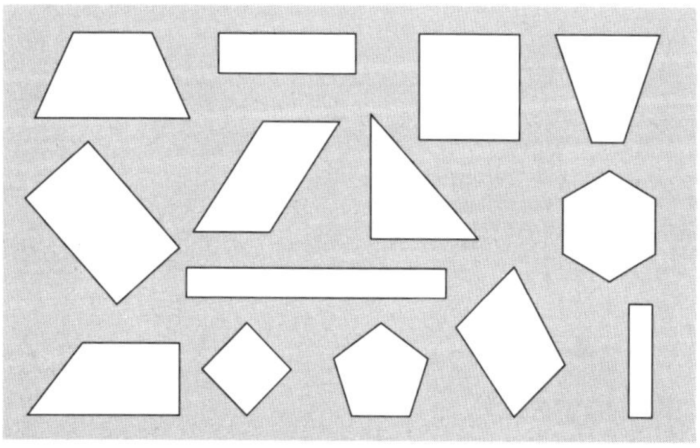

- *A quadrilateral has 4 straight sides, 4 angles and 4 vertices.*

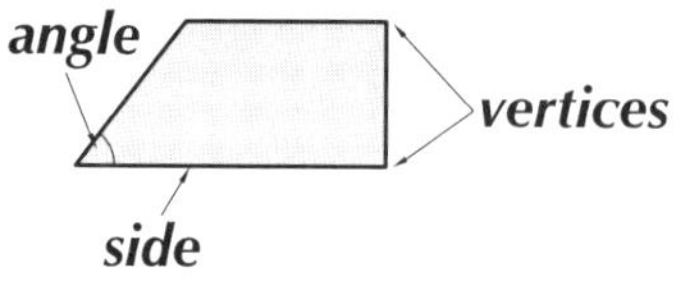

a. How do you know they are rectangles?

Answer : __________

b. How many shapes in the box are not quadrilaterals? Explain.

Answer : __________

② Irene has to sort out all the pentagons from a box of polygons. Colour them green. Is the shape marked A a pentagon? Explain.

Answer : ______________________

③ Irene has to sort out all the hexagons from a box of polygons. Colour them yellow. How do you know they are hexagons?

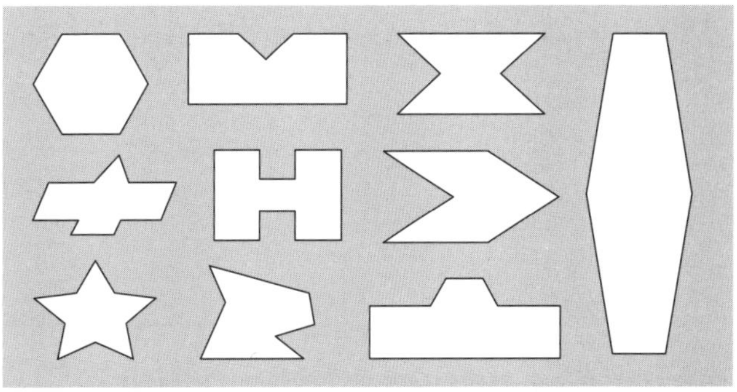

Answer : ______________________

④ Irene has to colour the rhombuses brown and the parallelograms blue. What are the similarities and differences between a rhombus and a parallelogram?

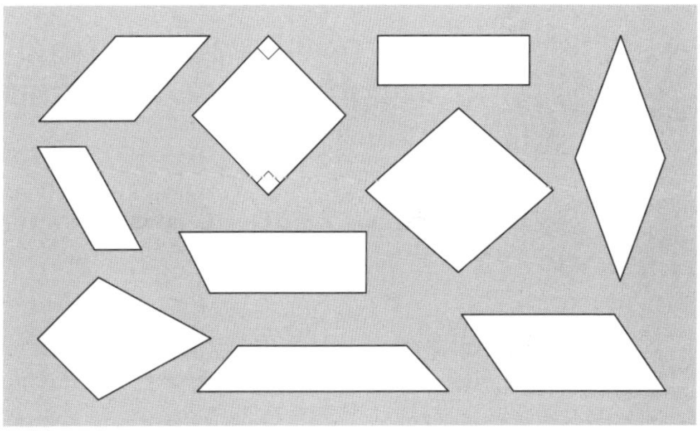

Answer : ______________________

Write the names of the polygons.

Irene is making some shapes for her teacher. Read what she says and write the shape she is making.

⑤ 'This shape has 4 right angles. Two of its sides are longer than the others.'

Answer : ______________________

⑥ 'This quadrilateral has 4 equal sides but the angles are not right angles.'

Answer : ______________________

⑦ 'This shape has 5 straight sides and 5 angles.'

Answer : ______________________

⑧ 'This shape has 6 angles and 6 vertices. The sides are equal in length.'

Answer : ______________________

⑨ 'I can get these 2 congruent shapes by cutting a rectangle into halves from corner to corner.'

Answer : ____________________

⑩ 'This quadrilateral has all the sides equal in length and all the angles equal in size.'

Answer : ____________________

⑪ 'This shape has 2 pairs of parallel lines. The opposite sides and angles are equal.'

Answer : ____________________

⑫ 'This shape has 8 angles and 8 vertices. All its sides are equal in length.'

Answer : ____________________

Write the names of the solids.

- *A prism has congruent ends and straight sides.*

e.g.

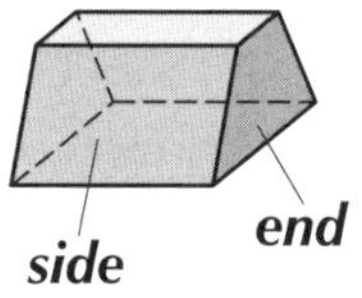

- *A pyramid has a base and the edges meet at a vertex.*

e.g.

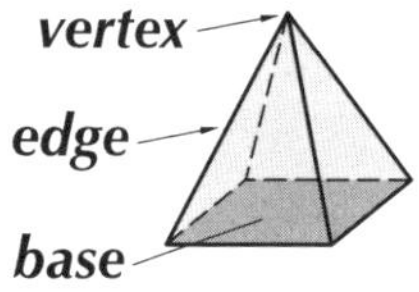

- *A cone has a round base and a curved surface.*

e.g.

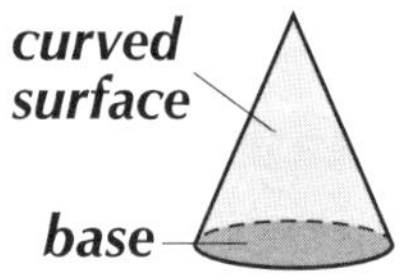

⑬ There is a box which has congruent ends and straight sides. What kind of solid is it?

Answer : ____________________

⑭ In the box there is a container which has a square base and 4 edges meeting at a vertex. What kind of solid is it?

Answer : ____________________

⑮ In the box there is a big die with 6 faces. The edges are equal in length and they meet at right angles. What kind of solid is it?

Answer : ____________________

⑯ Irene finds a hat for the snowman. The base of the hat is round and it has a curved surface which comes to a point. What does the hat look like?

Answer : ____________________

⑰ Irene finds a rod for the snowman, too. The rod has two circular ends and it is straight and long. What kind of solid is it?

Answer : ______________________

⑱ Irene makes a big snow ball for the head of the snowman. What kind of solid is it?

Answer : ______________________

⑲ Irene's mother gives her a chocolate bar. The side view of the bar is a rectangle. The ends are triangles. What kind of solid is it?

Answer : ______________________

⑳ Irene's mother also gives her a candy. The candy has 4 faces. Each face looks like a triangle. What kind of solid is it?

Answer : ______________________

Complete the table.

㉑ Irene wants to make a summary of the solids she saw today. Help her complete the table.

Solid	Number of faces	Number of curved surfaces	Number of straight edges	Number of vertices
Cylinder				
Cube				
Rectangular prism				
Sphere				
Cone				
Rectangular pyramid				
Triangular prism				
Tetrahedron				

CHALLENGE

Irene has 2 nets for making 2 solids. What solids is she going to make?

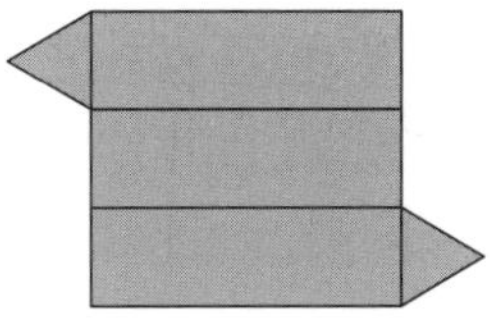

Answer : ______________________

Answer : ______________________

Solve the problems. Show your work.

Irene is helping her father build a rectangular flower bed. The width of the flower bed is 3 m and the perimeter is 16 m.

① Draw a sketch to show the shape and sides of the flower bed.

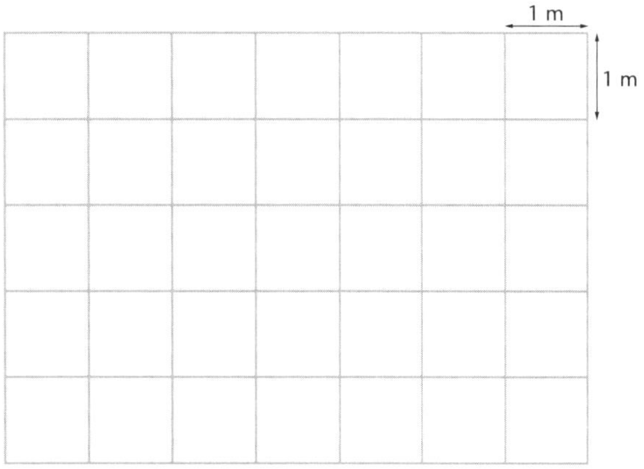

② Irene's dad wants to build a brick edging around the outside of the flower bed. If the edging costs $80.00 for 5 m, how much does it cost for 1 m?

Answer : ____________________

③ What is the total cost for the edging?

Answer : ____________________

④ Special soil in 15-kg bags costs 40¢ per kg. How much does Irene's dad pay for 1 bag of special soil?

Answer : ____________________

⑤ How much does he pay for 35 bags of special soil?

Answer : ____________________

⑥ Irene's dad started digging at 9:45 in the morning. He worked for 4 hours with two 25-minute breaks. When did he finish working?

Answer : ____________________

⑦ What is the area of the flower bed?

Answer : ____________________

⑧ Is the flower bed bigger or smaller if it is a 4-m square?

Answer : ____________________

⑨ Irene will grow 12 flowers on 1 m^2 of land. How many flowers will there be on the flower bed?

Answer : ____________________

⑩ Rose food costs $8.89 a box plus a tax of $1.33. How much will Irene's dad pay for 1 box of rose food?

Answer : ____________________

⑪ If Irene's dad paid for the rose food with a $10 bill and a quarter, what was the change?

Answer : ____________________

Mr Smith is going to build a path leading to the front door of his house with either bricks or slabs. He is now browsing in a shop selling construction materials.

⑫ There are 3 piles of bricks in the shop. The volume of each brick is 1000 cm^3. What is the volume of each pile of bricks?

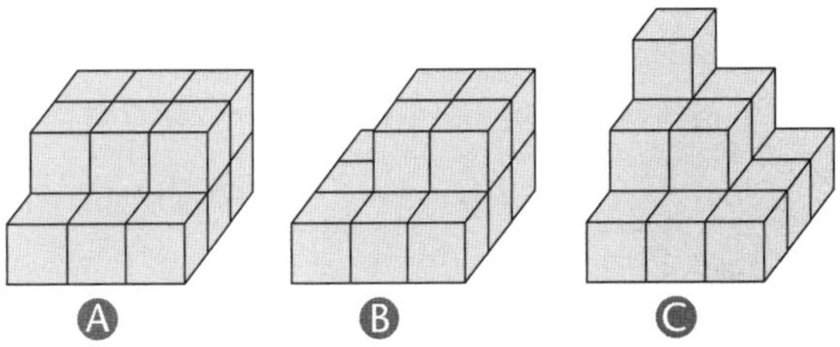

Answer : ______

⑬ If the 3 piles of bricks are to be stacked in a straight tower with 4 bricks in each layer, how many layers will there be? How many bricks will be left over?

Answer : ______

⑭ If each brick is 10 cm high, what will be the height of the brick tower in metres?

Answer : ______

⑮ What will be the volume of the brick tower in cm^3?

Answer : ______

⑯ The bricks cost 50¢ each in this shop. They cost 10 for $4.50 in AA shop. Which offers a better deal? Explain your thinking.

Answer : ______

⑰ 9 slabs can cover an area of 1 m^2. If the path is 10 m^2, how many slabs should Mr Smith buy?

Answer : ______

⑱ Each slab costs $3.00 and the shop charges $25.50 for delivery. How much will Mr Smith pay for the slabs including delivery?

Answer : ______

⑲ Mr Smith is paying for some tools which cost $37.28 including tax with a $50 bill. What is the fewest number of bills and coins he receives as change?

Answer : ______

Jenny and Mike are playing in the backyard. Their mother brings them some cold drinks and snacks.

⑳ Look at the containers of the cold drinks and snacks. Write what 3-dimensional shapes you can see.

Answer :

㉑ The diagrams below are the labels found on the containers of TT biscuits and BB chocolates. What are their areas?

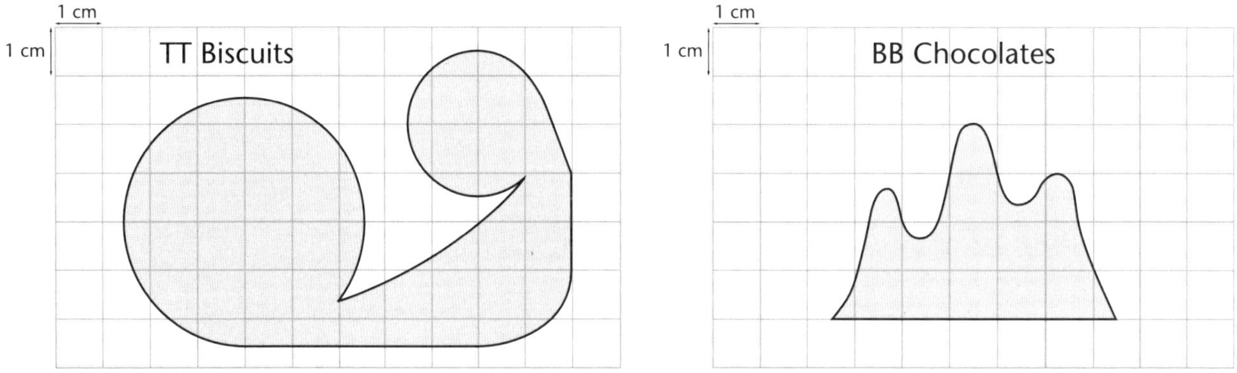

Answer :

㉒ Jenny has a jug which can hold 5 boxes of apple juice. If each box of apple juice is 400 mL, how many litres of juice can the jug hold?

Answer :

㉓ Jenny's mother has made 80 ice cubes each weighing 25 g. What is the total weight of the ice cubes in kg?

Answer :

㉔ The ice cubes took 25 minutes to melt in a jug of juice. Jenny's mother made the juice at 1:38 p.m. When would all the ice cubes melt?

Answer :

Circle the correct answer in each problem.

25. Irene walks her dog around a regular pentagonal field with each side 230 m long. What is the perimeter of the field?

A. 1380 m B. 1150 m C. 1610 m D. 920 m

26. Irene gets paid $4.00 an hour to walk her neighbour's dog. She walks for 30 minutes on each weekday and 1 hour on Saturdays and on Sundays. How much does she earn each week?

A. $21.00 B. $28.00 C. $24.00 D. $18.00

27. Irene wanted to weigh her dog. She and her dog both stepped onto a scale. The scale reading was 55 kg. If Irene weighed 41.5 kg, how much did her dog weigh?

A. 96.5 kg B. 9.65 kg C. 13.5 kg D. 1.35 kg

28. Emily uses a glass which is a cylinder to cut cookies out of dough. What shape are the cookies?

A. square B. round C. hexagonal D. pentagonal

29. If Emily spent $5.00 to make 100 cookies, how much would she spend to make 1000 cookies?

A. $50.00 B. $0.50 C. $500.00 D. $100.00

30. What shape can be made with the net?

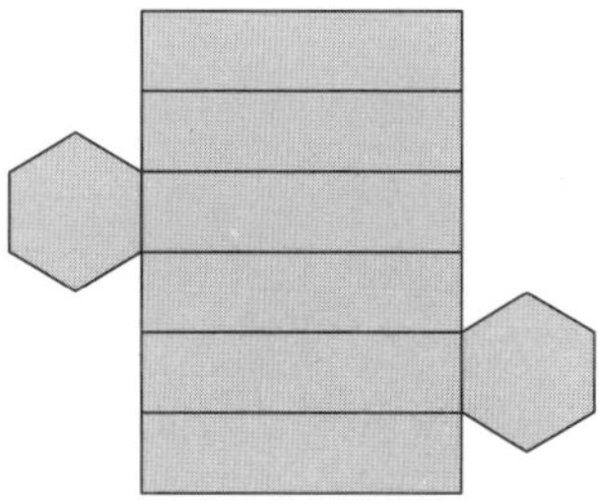

A. a hexagonal pyramid
B. a pentagonal prism
C. a cylinder
D. a hexagonal prism

31. Peter has 3 $5 bills, 2 twoonies, 1 loonie, 3 quarters, 4 nickels and 13 pennies. How much money does he have?

A. $20.13 B. $21.08 C. $20.08 D. $21.13

32. It is 10:35 a.m. and Jenny has been out of bed for 2 hours 40 minutes. When did Jenny get out of bed?

A. 7:55 a.m. B. 8:55 a.m. C. 7:00 a.m. D. 8:00 a.m.

UNIT 7 Angles

EXAMPLE

Which angle is equal to the angle on the left?

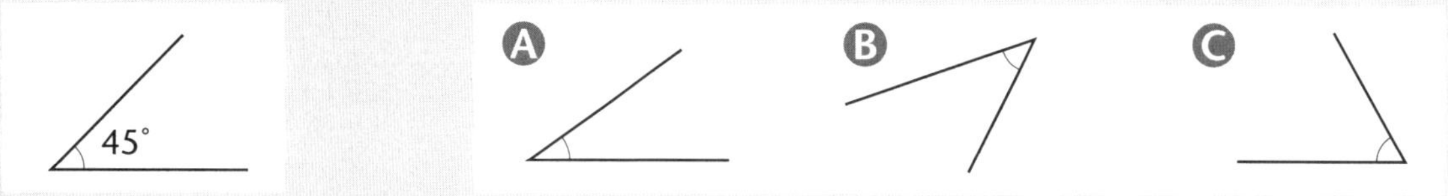

Measure the angles A, B and C with a protractor.

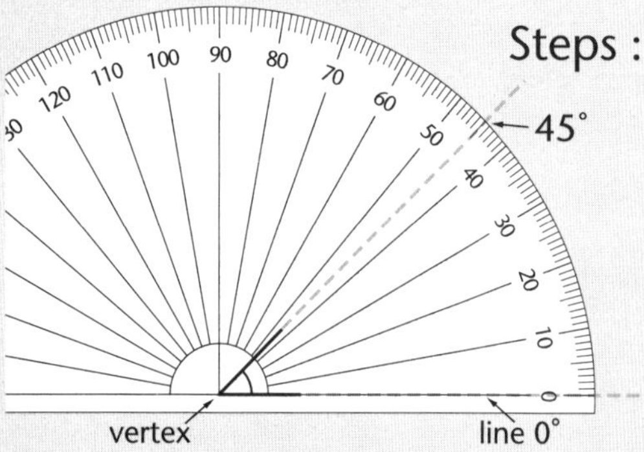

Steps :
1. Lengthen the line segments, if necessary.
2. Place line 0° on one of the line segments and the centre at the vertex.
3. Record the angle in degrees (°) between the line segments.

Answer : Angle B is 45°. It is equal to the angle on the left.

Solve the problems.

① Measure and mark the angles which show how the rocket flies.

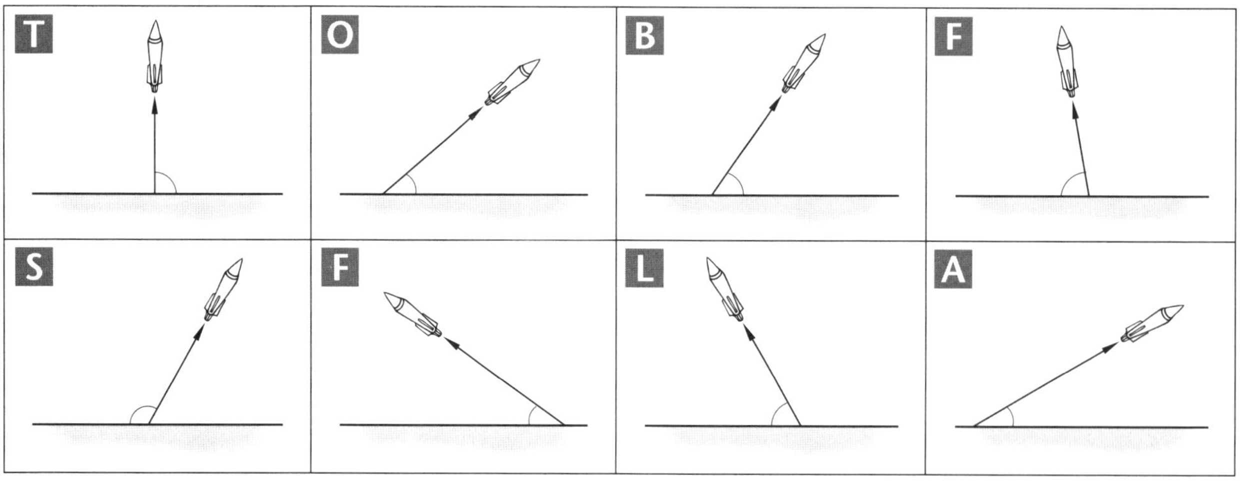

② Which angle above is greater than a right angle?

Answer : ______ is greater than a right angle.

③ The sum of which 3 angles above equals the angle of a straight line?

Answer : ______

④ Write the letters represented by the angles to see what Alan is saying.

55°	60°	30°	120°	90°	40°	80°	35°

Draw the clock hands. Measure and mark the angles on the clock.

Irene is playing with a toy clock.

⑤ If it is 3 o'clock, what angle is made by the clock hands?

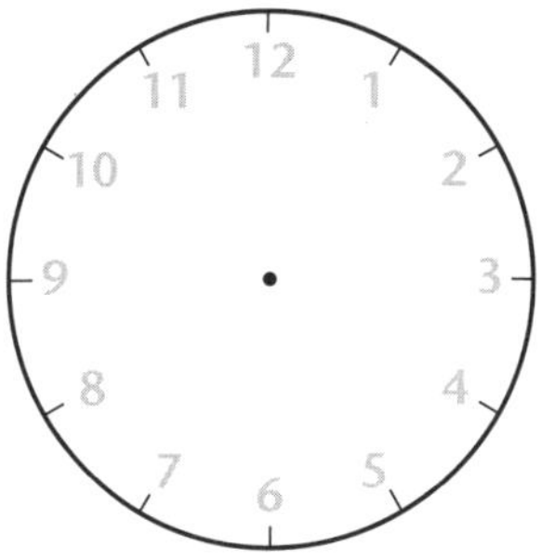

⑥ The hour hand is at 6. Where is the minute hand if the angle between the clock hands is 180°?

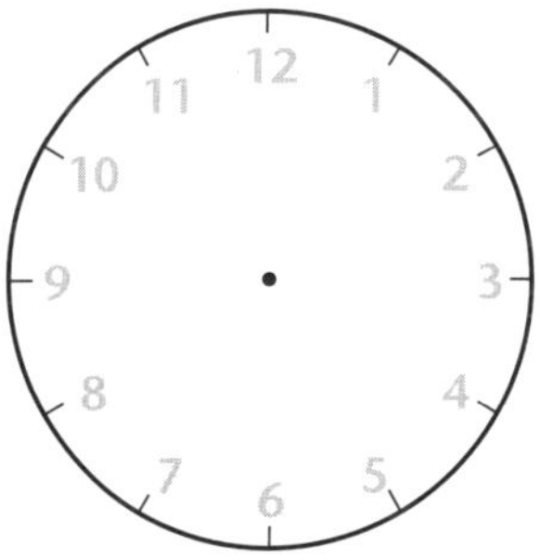

⑦ It is 9:00. What angle is made by the clock hands?

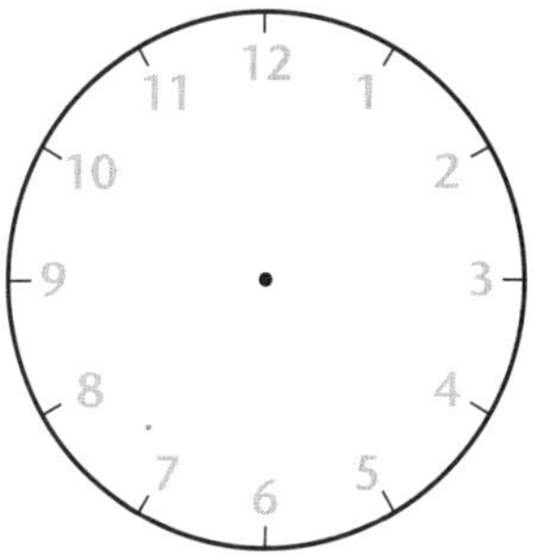

⑧ Irene turns the clock to 7:00 and then to 8:00. What is the difference in the angles between the hands?

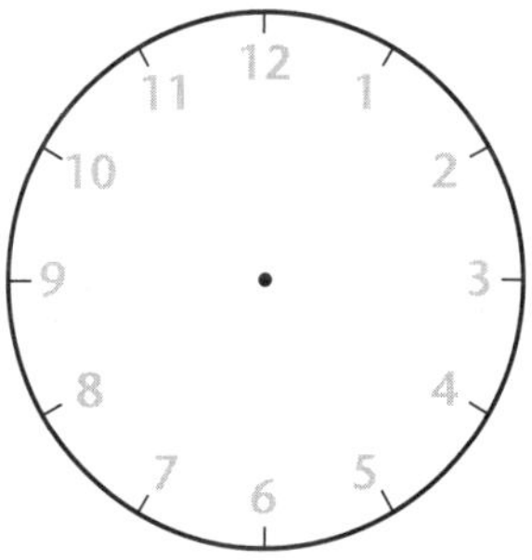

CHALLENGE

Try Irene's toy clock. If its hour hand doesn't move as the minute hand moves, after 3 o'clock, when will the hands of the clock be next at 90°?

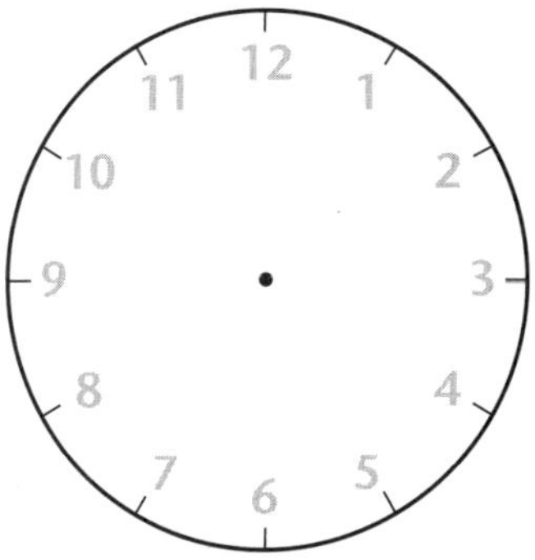

Answer : ____________________

UNIT 8 Transformations

EXAMPLE

Irene and Alan are playing with a set of plastic letters. They wonder how the letter E looks like if they slide it, turn it and flip it.

a. Sliding the letter (translation)

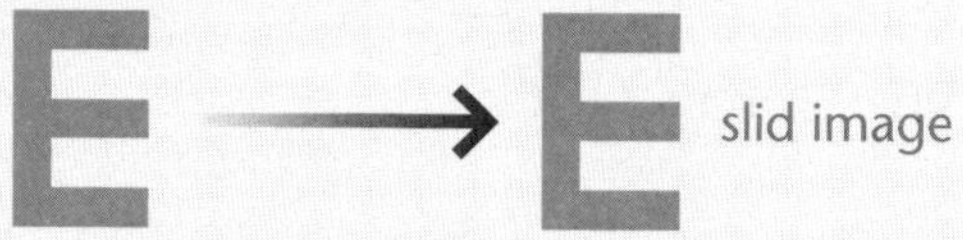

b. Making $\frac{1}{4}$ turn of the letter (rotation)

c. Flipping the letter (reflection)

Write the transformations.

Irene and Alan have slid, turned and flipped some of their letters. Write what transformations they used.

①

Answer : They used ______________________.

②

Answer : ______________________

③
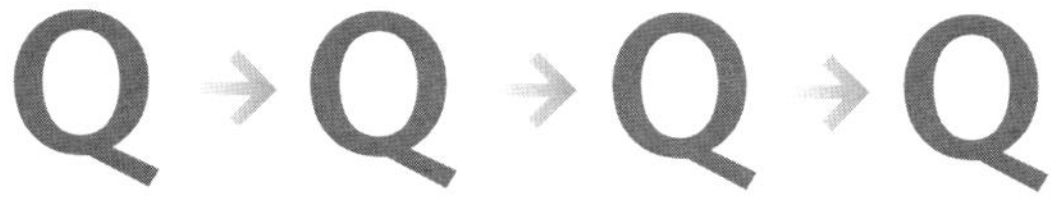

Answer : ______________________

④

Answer : ______________________

⑤
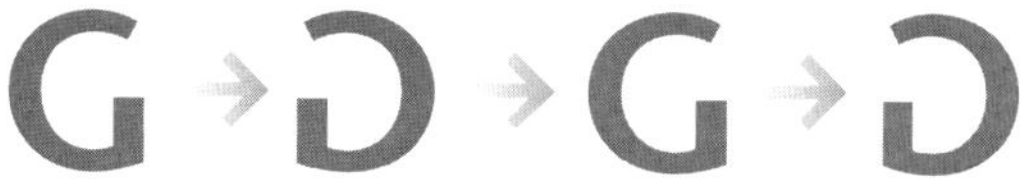

Answer : ______________________

⑥

Answer : ______________________

Draw the images and solve the problems.

Alan has made some shapes on a geoboard with elastic bands. He asks Irene to transform the shapes.

⑦ Irene has to flip the shape over the line l.

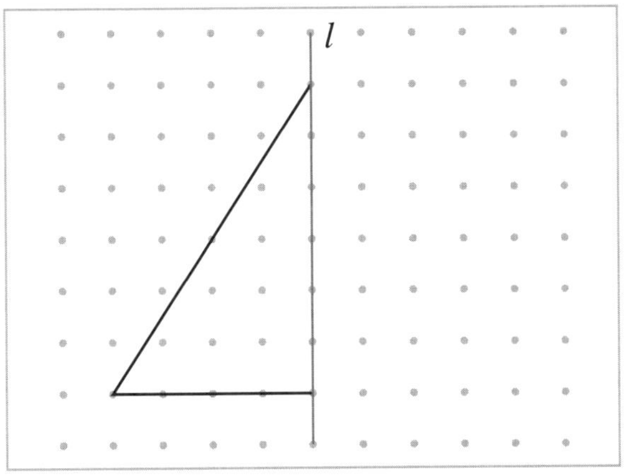

⑧ Irene has to flip the shape over the line l.

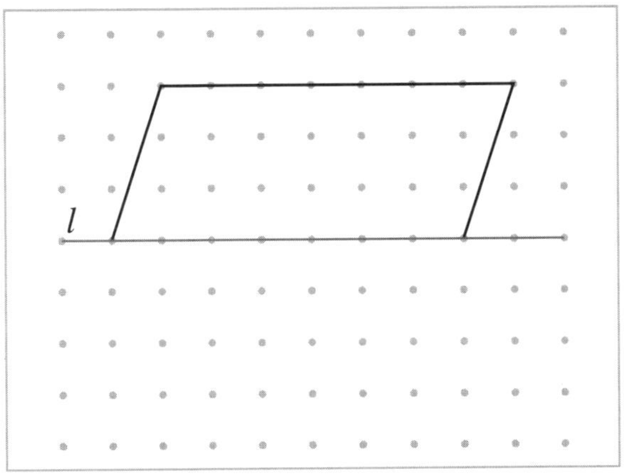

⑨ Irene has to slide the shape horizontally so that the image of point E is at E_1.

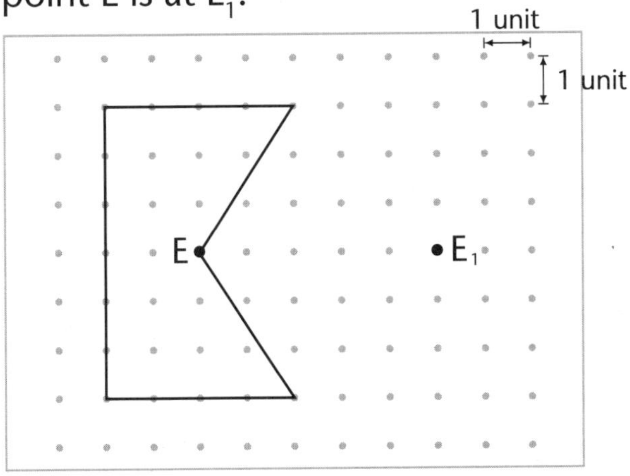

⑩ Irene has to slide the shape vertically so that the image of point X is at X_1.

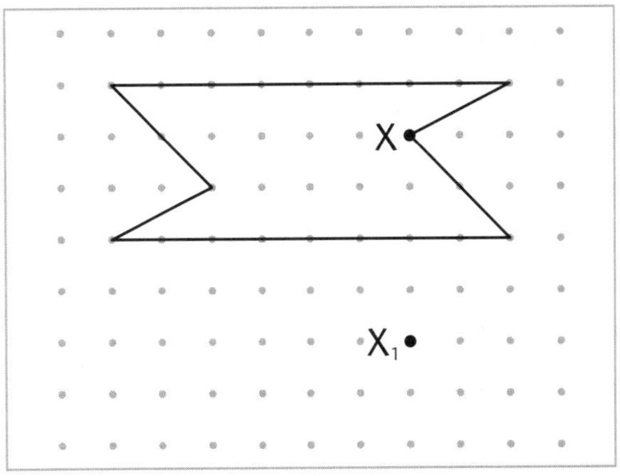

⑪ What transformation did Irene use to make the image of the shape?

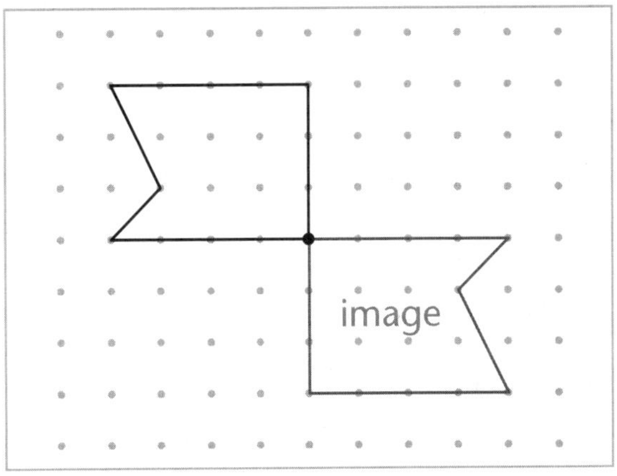

Answer : ____________________

⑫ How many units is the shape slid horizontally in question 9?

Answer : ____________________

⑬ Are the shapes and their images congruent?

Answer : ____________________

Look at the cards that Irene placed and solve the problems.

⑭ What transformation is used to form the pattern?

Answer : ____________________

⑮ How would you describe this pattern?

Answer : ____________________

⑯ What is the next card in the pattern?

Answer : ____________________

⑰ If there were 20 cards, how many would look like  ?

Answer : ____________________

⑱ What would the 13th card in the pattern look like?

Answer : ____________________

⑲ How many cards would you need to repeat the pattern 6 times?

Answer : ____________________

⑳ If you only used every 2nd card, which cards would be in the pattern?

Answer : ____________________

㉑ If you only used every 2nd card, would the transformation be the same? Explain.

Answer : ____________________

㉒ If this pattern only used $\frac{1}{2}$ turned cards, how many cards would be in the pattern?

Answer : ____________________

㉓ What would cards 1 to 4 look like in a mirror if you stand a mirror on the bottom side of them? Draw the hearts in the boxes.

㉔ If this pattern started at 2 and turned $\frac{1}{4}$ clockwise, how would it look? Draw the hearts in the boxes.

Help Alan find the lines of symmetry that each shape has.

㉕ Which of the following shapes has the most lines of symmetry?

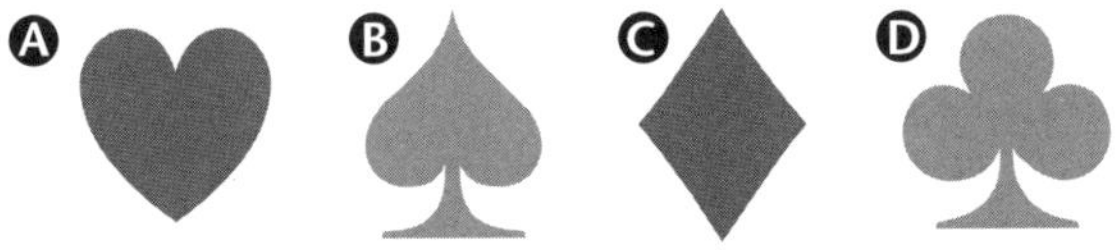

Answer : ____________________

㉖ How many lines of symmetry does a diamond  have?

Answer : ____________________

㉗ How many lines of symmetry does a heart  have?

Answer : ____________________

㉘ Which has more lines of symmetry, a diamond or a square? Explain.

Answer : ____________________

㉙ If Irene cut a square in half down the middle, how many lines of symmetry could Alan draw on each half?

Answer : ____________________

㉚ If Irene cut a square in half from corner to corner, how many lines of symmetry could Alan draw on each half?

Answer : ____________________

㉛ Irene has drawn a flower. Draw all the lines of symmetry on the flower.

CHALLENGE

Count the number of lines of symmetry on these 2 shapes. Predict the number of lines of symmetry that a decagon (10 sides) would have.

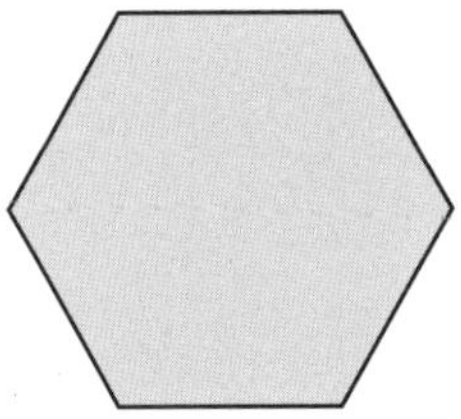

Hexagon

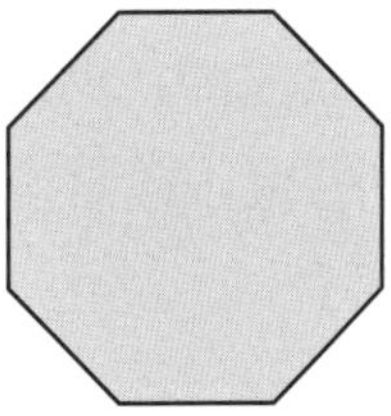

Octagon

Answer : ____________________

UNIT 9 Coordinate Systems

EXAMPLE

Look at the mail boxes in Parkway Building. Mr Brown lives in A3 and Mr Green lives in E5. Write what each of them receives today.

Think : Mr. Brown's mail box is in column A row 3. There is a tax return in box A3. Mr Green's mail box is in column E row 5. There are some coupons in box E5.

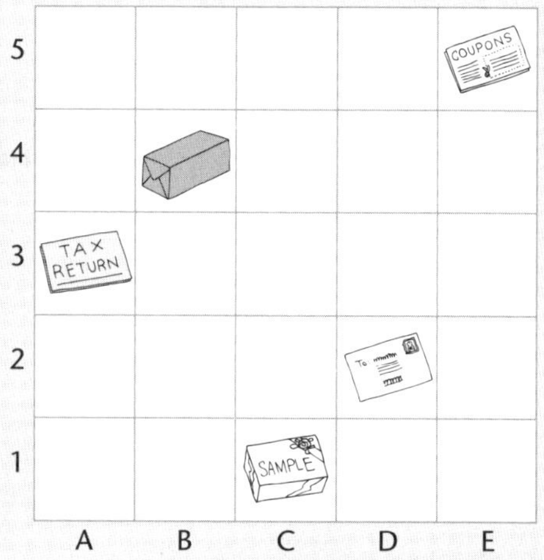

Answer : Mr Brown receives a tax return and Mr Green receives some coupons.

Draw the shapes and solve the problems.

Irene is drawing some shapes on a grid. Help her finish the drawing.

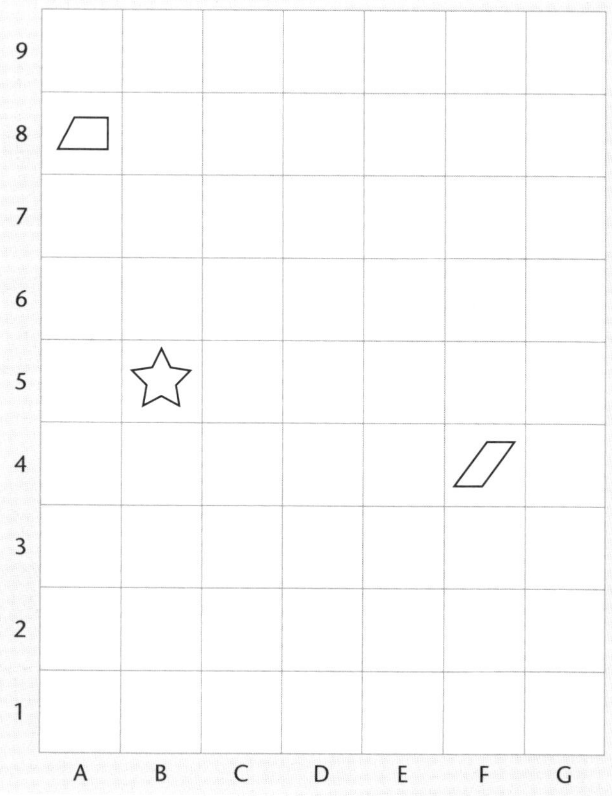

① Draw a circle in D4, a square in A1, a triangle in B2, a rhombus in C7, a rectangle in G7, and a black square in E5.

② What are the locations of  and  ?

Answer : ______________________

③ How many rows and columns are there on the grid?

Answer : ______________________

Solve the problems. Show your work.

Irene and Alan are playing a fishing game. They take turns to catch the fish. The one with the highest score wins the game.

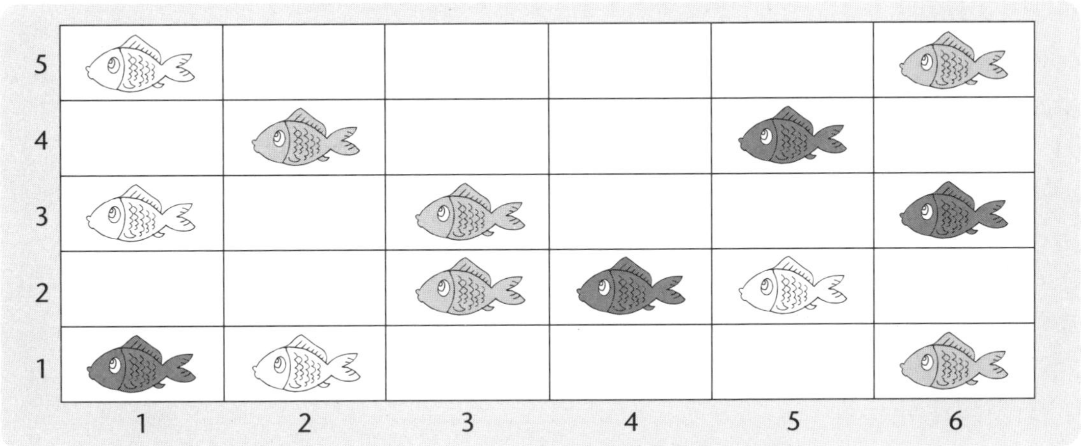

④ What are the ordered pairs of all the  ?

Answer : ______________________

⑤ What are the ordered pairs of all the  ?

Answer : ______________________

⑥ What are the ordered pairs of all the  ?

Answer : ______________________

⑦ Irene catches 3 fish. They are at (2, 1), (5, 4) and (6, 5). What is her score?

Answer : ______________________

⑧ Alan catches 2 fish. One is 2 units down from (1, 3) and the other is 2 units right from (3, 2). What is his score?

Answer : ______________________

⑨ Who is the winner?

Answer : ______________________

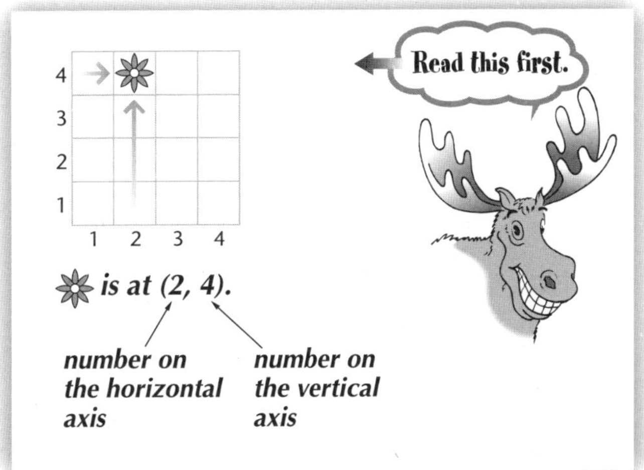

Irene is helping Alan draw a picture. She has made a grid with the horizontal and vertical lines numbered. Then she gives Alan these instructions. Read what she says and finish the picture for Alan.

⑩ Plot the ordered pairs on the grid.
(3, 1), (3, 5), (1, 5), (3, 7), (9, 7), (9, 9), (10, 9), (10, 7), (12, 7), (14, 5), (12, 5), (12, 1), (8, 1), (8, 4), (6, 4), (6, 1)

⑪ Join the ordered pairs (3, 1), (3, 5) ... (6, 1) in order with straight lines.

⑫ What have you drawn?

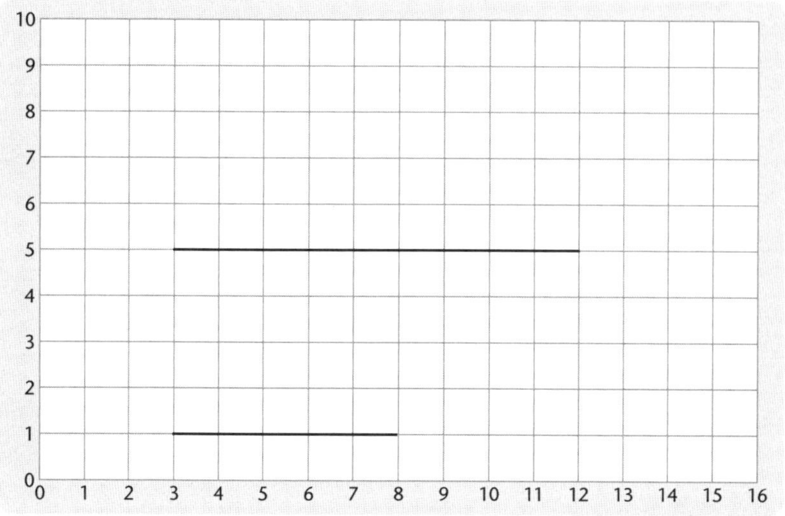

Answer : ______________________

⑬ If each of the squares on the grid is 1 cm^2, what is the area of the picture?

Answer : ______________________

⑭ If Alan wants to add a big square window on the right of the door, what are the ordered pairs of the window?

Answer : ______________________

Look at the triangle that Alan drew on the grid. Solve the problems.

⑮ What are the ordered pairs of the vertices?

Answer : ______________________

⑯ Which are the 2 ordered pairs for the line of symmetry of the triangle – (0, 4) and (5, 0), (6, 4) and (2, 0) or (3, 5) and (3, 0) ?

Answer : ______________________

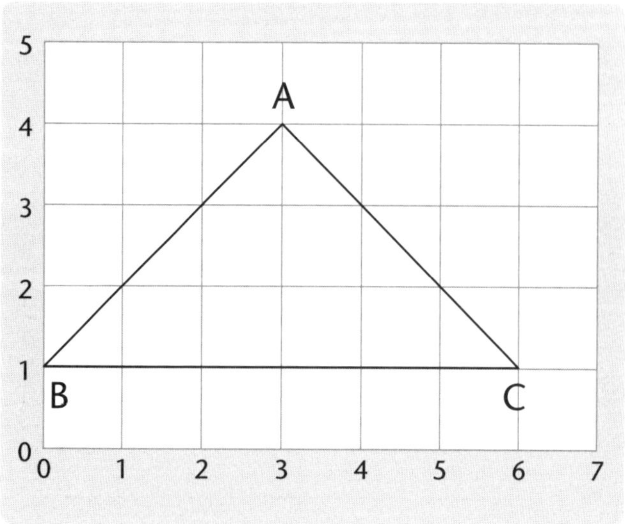

Look at Alan's picture on the grid. Solve the problems.

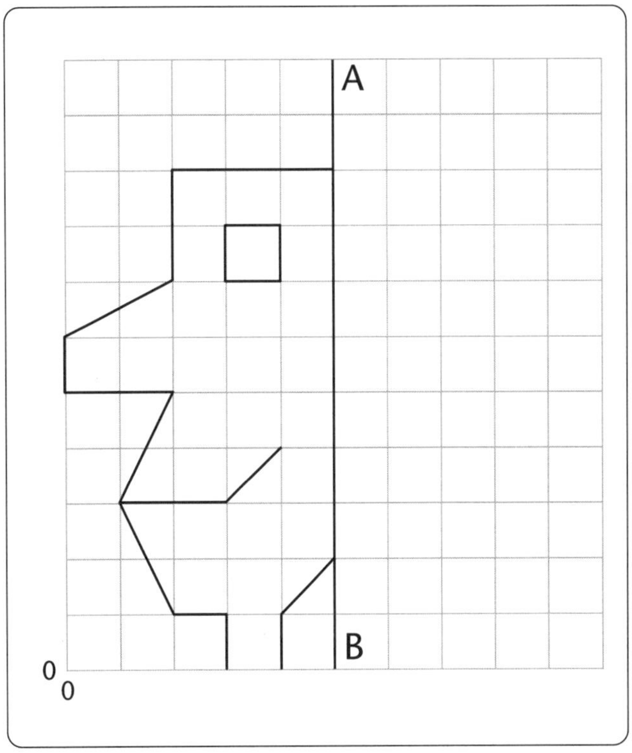

⑰ Label the horizontal and vertical axes.

⑱ Alan is going to describe his picture to Irene so she can copy it.

a. Which 4 ordered pairs will Alan give to describe the eye?

Answer : ______________________

b. Which 2 ordered pairs show the top of the head?

Answer : ______________________

c. Which 3 ordered pairs show the mouth?

Answer : ______________________

d. Which 4 ordered pairs are used to make the nose?

Answer : ______________________

CHALLENGE

① Look at Alan's picture again. If his picture was slid 4 units right and 1 unit up, which 4 ordered pairs would make the nose?

Answer : ______________________

② If the picture was flipped over the line AB, which 4 ordered pairs would make the eye?

Answer : ______________________

UNIT 10 Probability

EXAMPLE

a. Peter is tossing a loonie. What is the probability that he will get a head?

Think : There are 2 possible outcomes : head or tail.

Answer : The probability that he will get a head is 1 out of 2.

b. Jenny is tossing 2 loonies at a time. What is the probability that she will get 2 heads? Draw a tree diagram to explain your thinking.

Think : There are 4 possible outcomes : HH, HT, TH, TT.

Answer : The probability that she will get 2 heads is 1 out of 4.

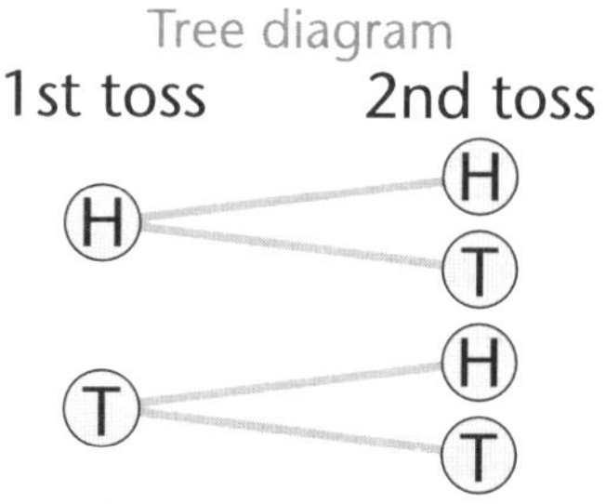

Check ✓ the right boxes.

Read each of these events and decide, following the probability rules, if the outcomes are likely or unlikely.

	Event	Outcomes	
		Likely	Unlikely
①	Irene rolls a die and gets a 6 twice in 12 rolls.		
②	Alan rolls a 6 three times in a row.		
③	Irene flips a coin 10 times and gets heads 3 times.		
④	Alan rolls a die 10 times and does not get a 1.		
⑤	Irene flips a coin 10 times and gets heads 5 times.		

Solve the problems. Show your thinking.

⑥ Alan has a die. If he rolls the die, how many possible outcomes will there be?

Answer : There will be ______.

⑦ What is the probability that he will roll a 2?

Answer : ______

⑧ What is the probability that he will roll a 6?

Answer : ______

⑨ What is the probability that he will get a number less than 4?

Answer : ______

⑩ What is the probability that he will roll a 1 or a 2?

Answer : ______

⑪ What is the probability that he will get an even number?

Answer : ______

⑫ What is the probability that he will not roll a 3?

Answer : ______

- *The number of possible outcomes stays the same but the number of desired outcomes changes.*

⑬ Write 'equally probable', 'less probable', 'more probable' or 'not probable' for the following.

a. Rolling a 2 or rolling a 6.

Answer : ______

b. Rolling a number less than 4 or a 4.

Answer : ______

c. Rolling a number less than 4 or a number larger than 4.

Answer : ______

d. Rolling a number larger than 6.

Answer : ______

e. Never rolling a 1.

Answer : ______

Irene has made 2 spinners. Spinner A is divided into 4 equal sectors while spinner B is divided into 4 sectors of different sizes.

Spinner A 

Spinner B 

⑭ For spinner A, what is the probability of spinning a  ?

Answer : ______________________________

⑮ For spinner A, what is the probability of spinning a  ?

Answer : ______________________________

⑯ For spinner B, what is the probability of spinning a  ?

Answer : ______________________________

⑰ For spinner B, what is the probability of spinning a  ?

Answer : ______________________________

⑱ What is the probability of spinning a  on spinner B?

Answer : ______________________________

⑲ If you want to spin a , which spinner should you use? Explain.

Answer : ______________________________

⑳ If you do not want to spin a , which spinner should you use? Explain.

Answer : ______________________________

㉑ If you want to spin , which spinner should you use?

Answer : ______________________________

Irene's cousin, Jenny, has 4 balls – 1 red, 1 yellow and 2 blue. She puts the red ball and a blue ball in a bag and the rest in another bag. Then she asks Alan to pick a ball from each bag.

㉒ Draw a tree diagram to show the possible outcomes.

1st bag	2nd bag	Result
Red	Blue	(R , B)
		( )
Blue		( )
		( )

㉓ How many possible outcomes are there?

Answer : ______

㉔ What is the probability of picking a red ball and a blue ball?

Answer : ______

㉕ Alan says that he has a better chance of picking 2 blue balls. Is he correct? Explain.

Answer : ______

㉖ What is the probability of picking 2 red balls?

Answer : ______

㉗ If Jenny put all the balls in a bag, would picking a red ball or a blue ball be equally likely?

Answer : ______

CHALLENGE

Help the children decide where to put each letter on this spinner.

- Irene spun it 8 times and got 4 As.
- Alan only got 2 Cs when he spun it 8 times.
- Steve got 2 Bs and 2 Ds when he spun it 16 times.

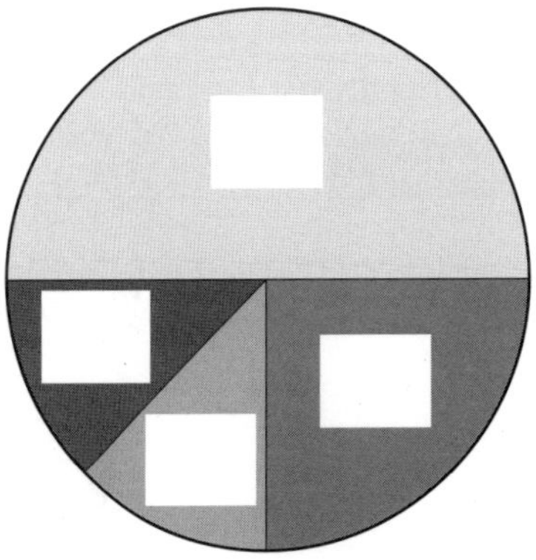

UNIT 11 Pictographs and Bar Graphs

EXAMPLE

Irene did a survey to find the favourite drinks of the Grade 4 students.

Drink	Coke	Apple juice	Orange juice	Milkshake	Lemonade
No. of students	10	8	12	15	7

a. Make a tally chart to show her record.

Drink	No. of Students
Coke	卌 卌
Apple juice	卌 ///
Orange juice	卌 卌 //
Milkshake	卌 卌 卌
Lemonade	卌 //

* To make a tally chart, the numbers are counted in 5s (卌).

b. Draw a vertical bar graph to show the information.

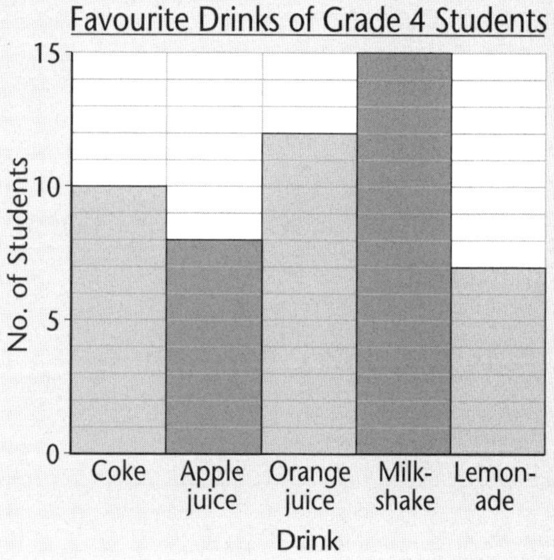

Solve the problems. Show your work.

Irene and Alan did a survey to find out in which months their friends had their birthdays.

Month	Jan	Feb	Mar	Apr	May	Jun	Jul	Aug	Sep	Oct	Nov	Dec
No. of people surveyed by Alan	3	4	4	6	3	6	6	4	4	2	2	8
No. of people surveyed by Irene	7	6	5	6	5	4	8	6	7	5	0	0

① How many people were surveyed?

Answer : ______ people were surveyed.

② Who surveyed more people? How many more?

Answer : ______

③ Make a tally chart for their findings and draw a bar graph to show the information.

Month	No. of People
Jan	
Feb	
Mar	
Apr	
May	
Jun	
Jul	
Aug	
Sep	
Oct	
Nov	
Dec	

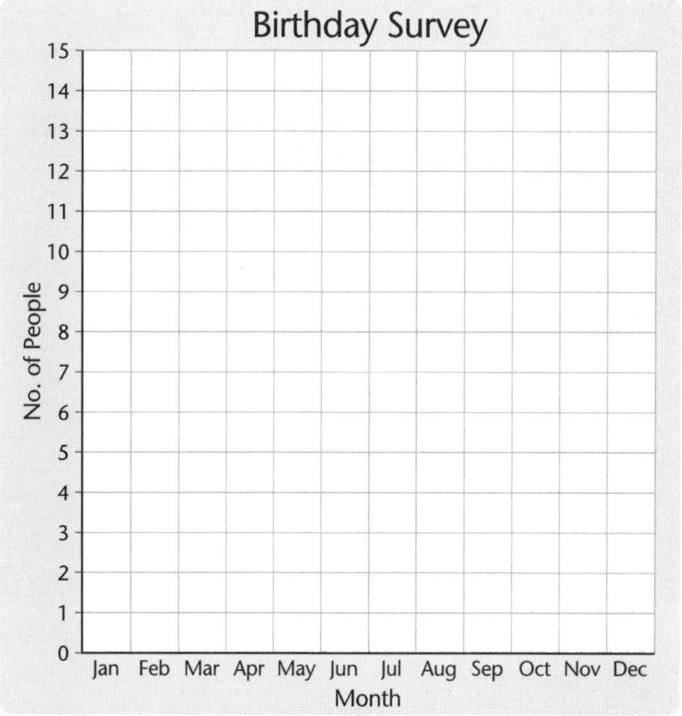

④ What is the title of this graph?

Answer : ____________________

⑤ What is the label of the horizontal axis?

Answer : ____________________

⑥ What is the label of the vertical axis?

Answer : ____________________

⑦ Which month had the fewest birthdays?

Answer : ____________________

⑧ Which month had the most birthdays?

Answer : ____________________

⑨ What is the difference between the most and the fewest birthdays?

Answer : ____________________

⑩ How many months had 10 or more birthdays?

Answer : ____________________

⑪ Can you tell the age of the people surveyed from the graph?

Answer : ____________________

⑫ Does the graph show in which year the people were born?

Answer : ____________________

For their next survey, Irene and Alan asked 6 local businesses how many birthday parties they had in 1999. Burger Palace had 60 brithday parties. Taco Place 45, Swimming Pool 80, Game Room 55, Party Pizza 70 and Movie Masters 90.

⑬ Use their information to make a tally chart.

Venue	No. of Birthday Parties
Burger Palace	
Taco Place	
Swimming Pool	
Game Room	
Party Pizza	
Movie Masters	

⑭ Draw a horizontal bar graph to show their information. Label the horizontal and vertical axes and give a title to the graph.

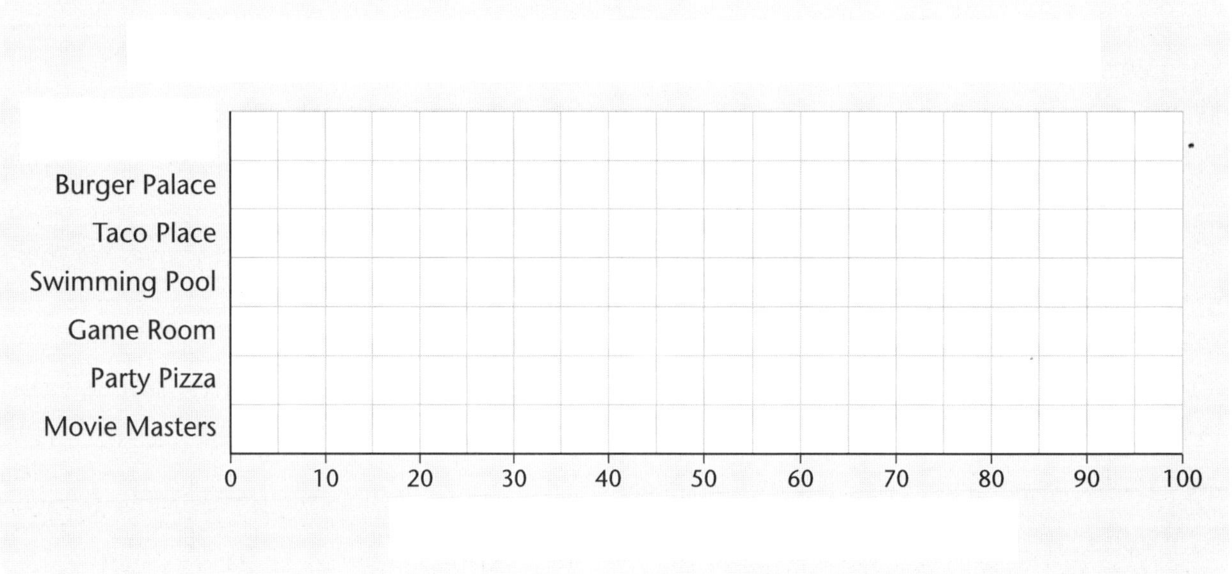

⑮ Which place held the fewest birthday parties?

Answer : ______________________

⑯ Which place held the most birthday parties?

Answer : ______________________

⑰ How many more birthday parties were held in Game Room than in Taco Place?

Answer : ______________________

⑱ How many birthday parties were there altogether?

Answer : ______________________

⑲ Make a pictograph to show the same information.

Venues for Birthday Parties	☺ = 10 parties
Burger Palace	
Taco Place	
Swimming Pool	
Game Room	
Party Pizza	
Movie Masters	

⑳ What is the best way to show 5 parties on the pictograph?

Answer : ______

㉑ How many people chose to have their party at a restaurant?

Answer : ______

㉒ How many people preferred to have their party at an activity centre?

Answer : ______

㉓ What fraction of the parties took place at the Swimming Pool?

Answer : ______

CHALLENGE

Irene drew a horizontal bar graph to show the weekly income of 4 people, A, B, C and D. Alan drew a circle graph to show the same information.

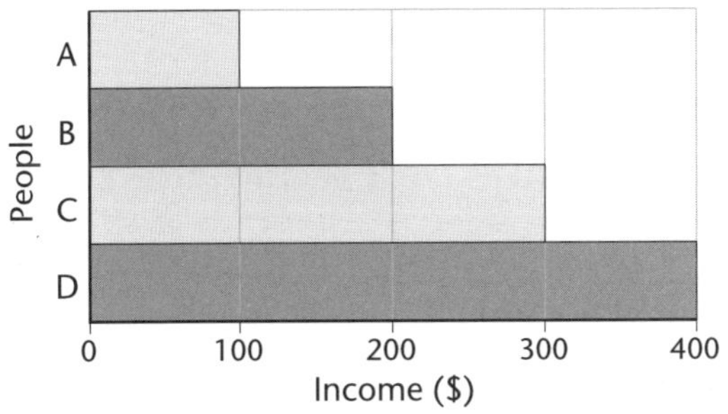

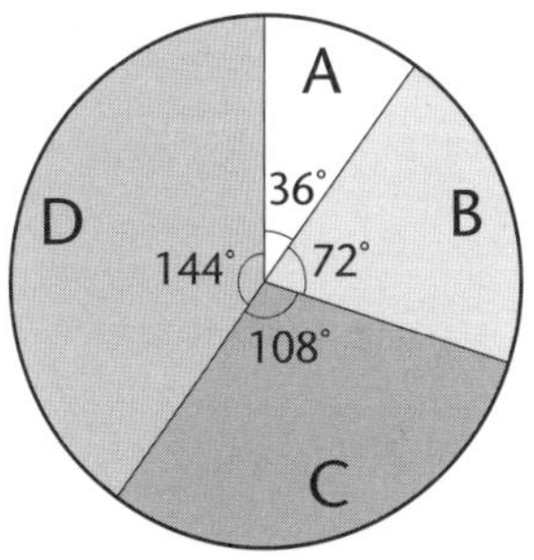

① Do these two graphs match? Explain.

Answer : ______

② What does the whole circle represent?

Answer : ______

FINAL REVIEW

Solve the problems. Show your work.

Irene is showing Peter how to draw a shape on a grid. Read her instructions and help Peter draw the shape and answer the questions.

① Mark these points on the grid:
A (1, 0), B (1, 6),
C (4, 6), D (4, 0)

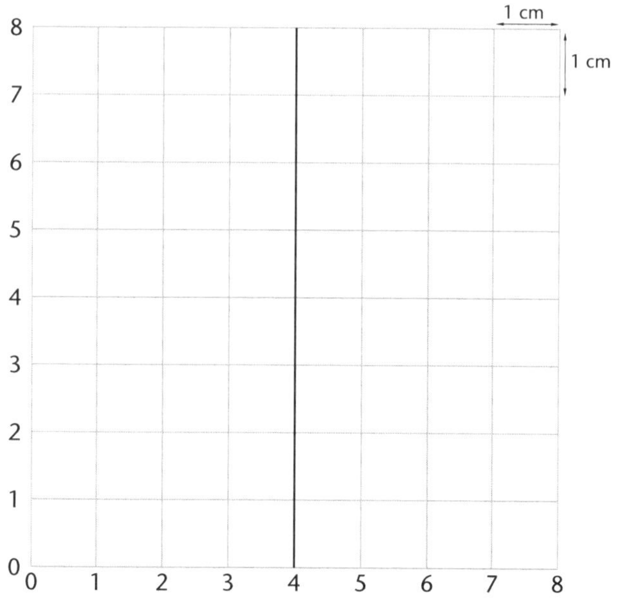

② Join the points A, B, C and D in order with straight lines.

③ What shape have you drawn?

Answer : __________

④ Reflect the shape over the black line and mark A′, B′, C′ and D′ for the images of A, B, C and D.

⑤ Which ordered pairs are now used to describe the location of the image A′, B′, C′ and D′?

Answer : __________

⑥ What is the area of the shape ?

Answer : __________

⑦ What is the perimeter of the shape?

Answer : __________

⑧ Can you tell whether the image is a flipped image or a slid image by looking at the labelled vertices? Explain your thinking.

Answer : __________

⑨ Which is larger in area, the shape itself or the triangle bounded by the straight lines AB, BB′ and B′A?

Answer : __________

Irene has made these shapes out of cardboard of different thickness.

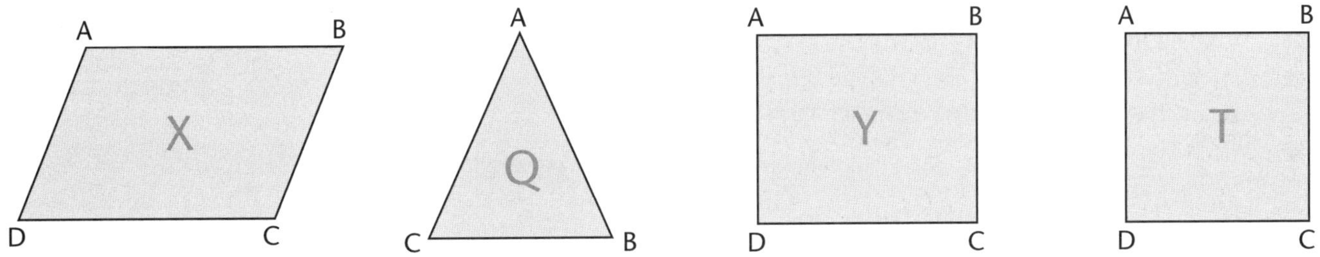

⑩ Write the names of each shape.

Answer : ______________________________

⑪ Put the shapes in order from the one with the greatest perimeter to the one with the smallest perimeter.

Answer : ______________________________

⑫ Each of the shapes weighs about 2 g. How many sets of these shapes would be needed to weigh 1 kg?

Answer : ______________________________

⑬ If Irene wanted to make a rectangular prism, which shapes would she use? How many of each shape would she use?

Answer : ______________________________

⑭ If Irene wanted to make a pyramid, which shapes would she use? How many of each shape would she use?

Answer : ______________________________

⑮ Draw the $\frac{1}{4}$ turn clockwise rotation of shapes X and Q in the spaces below.

X	Q

FINAL REVIEW

Irene and Alan played a game of dice and recorded their rolls on a tally chart.

⑯ Complete the tally chart.

a. Irene and Alan rolled twenty-four 1s.

b. They rolled eighteen 2s.

c. They rolled twenty-one 3s.

d. They rolled sixteen 4s.

e. They rolled twenty-two 5s and twenty-two 6s.

Roll	Tally
1	
2	
3	
4	
5	
6	

⑰ How many die rolls were made?

Answer : ____________________

⑱ Which number was rolled most often?

Answer : ____________________

⑲ Which number was rolled least often?

Answer : ____________________

⑳ How many more 1s were rolled than 3s in the game?

Answer : ____________________

㉑ The volume of the die is $8cm^3$. What is the volume of 500 dice?

Answer : ____________________

㉒ A container can hold 500 dice. What is its capacity in L?

Answer : ____________________

㉓ If each die roll and the recording of it took 10 seconds, how long did Irene and Alan take to create the tally chart?

Answer : ____________________

㉔ If they started at 11:04 a.m., when would they finish? (correct to the nearest minute)

Answer : ____________________

㉕ Use the tally chart to create a vertical bar graph.

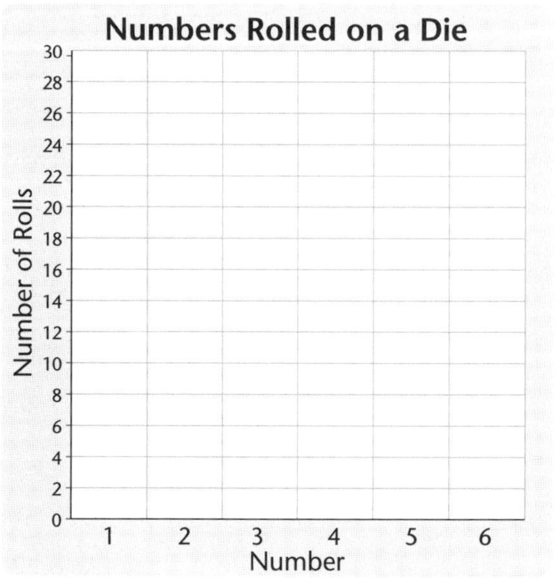

㉖ If the game followed probability rules, what results would they expect to see?

Answer :

㉗ After playing the game, Irene and Alan made a spinner. Look at their spinner. How would the spin results compare to the dice results? Explain your thinking.

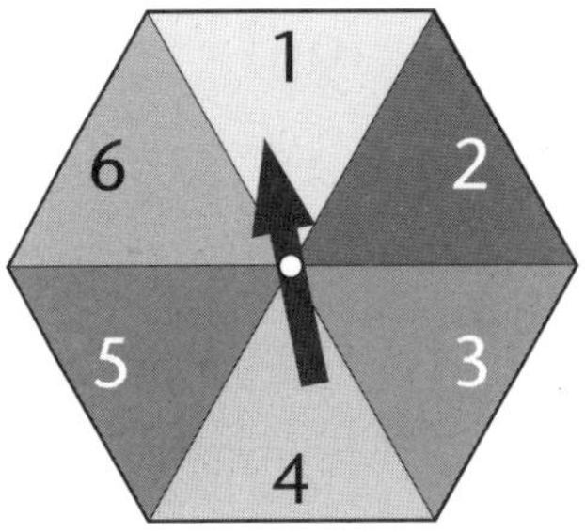

Answer :

㉘ What is the probability of landing on a 4?

Answer :

㉙ What is the probability of landing on a number greater than 4?

Answer :

㉚ What is the probability of landing on a number less than 4?

Answer :

㉛ You are going to make another spinner. The probability of landing on each number on your spinner is 1 out of 8. Draw your spinner with a protractor in the space below.

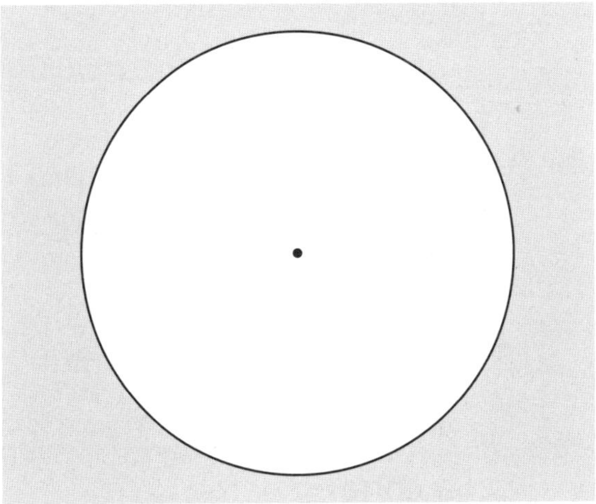

㉜ What is the size of each angle at the centre of Irene and Alan's spinner?

Answer :

㉝ What is the size of each angle at the centre of your spinner?

Answer :

㉞ If your spinner is the base of a solid, what can that solid be?

Answer :

Circle the correct answer in each problem.

35. It is 6 a.m. Which of these angles show the angle between the two hands on a clock?

A. 90° B. 120°

C. 45° D. 180°

36. Irene is sewing a seam that is 31 cm long. How many mm is that?

A. 3.1 mm B. 310 mm

C. 0.31 mm D. 3100 mm

37. There are 52 cards in a deck of playing cards. What is the probability of pulling a ♦ out of a deck?

A. 1 out of 4 B. 1 out of 13

C. 1 out of 26 D. 1 out of 56

38. In a pictograph, 65 cars are shown like this: 

Which of these is true?

A.  represents 5 cars.

B.  represents 2 cars.

C.  represents 10 cars.

D.  represents 3 cars.

39. Which of these containers has the largest capacity?

A. 

B. 

C. 

D. 

40. Alan spends about 2 hours and 20 minutes reading newspapers each week. How long does he take to read the newspapers each day?

A. 15 minutes B. 30 minutes

C. 25 minutes D. 20 minutes

41. A man can dig a hole in 45 minutes. If he finished digging at 12:08 p.m., when did he start digging the hole?

A. 12:53 p.m. B. 11:23 a.m.

C. 11:08 a.m. D. 11:37 p.m.

42. Irene made 4 shapes on a geoboard with elastic bands. Which of these is a trapezoid?

A. 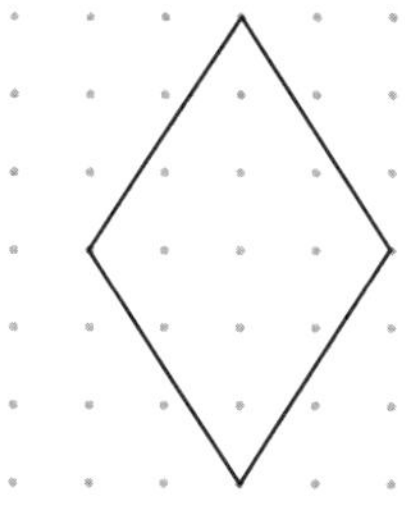

B. 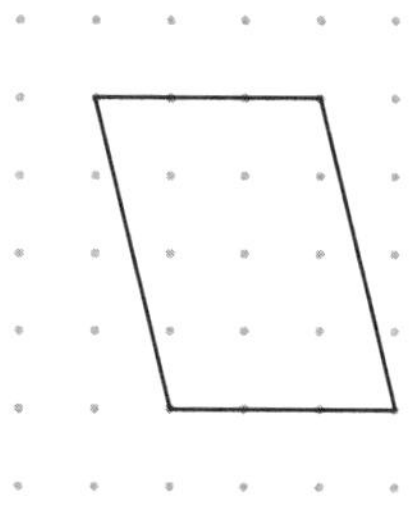

C. 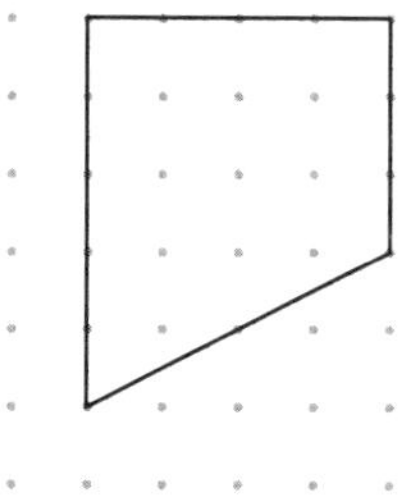

D. 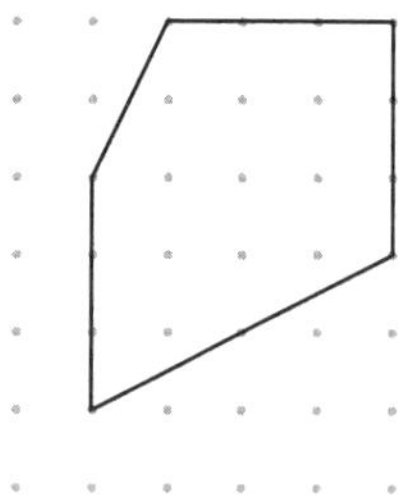

43. Which of these solid shapes has 4 vertices, 4 faces and 6 edges?

A. a tetrahedron

B. a square-based pyramid

C. a rectangular prism

D. a cone

Parents' Guide

1. *Multiplication of Whole Numbers*

- When multiplying 2-digit numbers by 2-digit numbers, remind children to put a zero under the ones column when multiplying by the tens digit.
- Encourage children to check if their answers are reasonable by rounding the numbers to the nearest ten or hundred, and estimating the products.

<u>Example</u> 57 x 12 = ?

57 → Round up to 60; 12 → Round down to 10

Estimated product
= 60 x 10
= 600
The answer of 57 x 12 should be close to 600.

- To calculate the product of a number and multiples of 10, just multiply the number by the digits in front of the zeros in the multiples, then add the same number of zeros in the factors at the end of the product.

<u>Example</u> 25 x 300 = 7500

25 x 3 = 75 add 2 zeros

- Even if the order of multiplication changes, the product remains the same.

<u>Example</u> 5 x 9 x 6 = 9 x 6 x 5 = 9 x 5 x 6 = 6 x 5 x 9 = 6 x 9 x 5 = 5 x 6 x 9 = 270

2. *Division of Whole Numbers*

- Remind children to write a "0" in the quotient before they continue to divide if the dividend is smaller than the divisor.

<u>Example</u> 323 ÷ 3 = ?

$$3\overline{)323} \text{ quotient } 1;\ 3 \quad \longrightarrow \quad 3\overline{)323} \text{ quotient } 10;\ 3,\ 23$$

Write a "0" in the quotient directly above 2, as 2 is smaller than 3; bring down 23 and continue to divide.

$$\longrightarrow \quad 3\overline{)323} \text{ quotient } 107R2;\ 3,\ 23,\ 21,\ 2$$

107 x 3 + 2 = 323, so 323 ÷ 3 = 107R2 is correct.

- Encourage children to check the answers by using multiplication and addition.
- In solving story problems using division, give the appropriate answer according to the requirement of the question.

<u>Example</u> A box can hold 6 cakes. How many boxes are needed to hold 15 cakes?

15 ÷ 6 = 2R3
3 boxes are needed. ← The answer is not 2 but 3, since the 3 cakes left over also need 1 box.

3. *Multiples and Factors*

- Multiples of a number can be formed by using repeated addition or multiplication. Using a number chart or a number line may be helpful.
- Children learn how to use multiplication and division to find the factors of a number, identify the common factors of two numbers, and determine their greatest common factor. When using multiplication to find the factors, children should write the multiplication sentences in order, starting with the smallest factor and stop when reaching a number they have already used for multiplication.

4. Mixed Operations and Brackets

- Remind children to perform the operations one at a time in the correct order :
  - Do all operations in the brackets first.
  - Then do multiplication and division in the order they occur from left to right.
  - Lastly, do addition and subtraction in the order they occur.

5. Fractions

- Children learn how to identify proper and improper fractions and mixed numbers. Make sure children understand that the numerical value of a fraction equals 1 if its numerator and denominator are equal, and that any whole number can be written as an improper fraction with the denominator equal to 1.
- Practising how to find the equivalent fractions using multiplication/division first helps children grasp the skills of simplifying fractions easily. Make sure they understand that equivalent fractions have the same value.
- When adding/subtracting mixed numbers, either add/subtract the whole numbers and fractions separately, or change the mixed numbers to improper fractions before calculating. Remind children to reduce the sums/differences to lowest terms (simplest form) and change improper fractions back to mixed numbers.
- When adding/subtracting fractions of unlike denominators, first write equivalent fractions with a common denominator. Then add/subtract the numerators and leave the denominator the same.

6. Addition and Subtraction of Decimals

- To do addition or subtraction, align the decimal points. Remember to put the decimal point in the answer.
- Remind children that only the zero at the end of the decimals can be deleted without affecting the numerical value of the decimal numbers.

  Example $2.50 = 2.5$ $2.00 = 2$ but $2.05 \neq 2.5$

7. Multiplication and Division of Decimals

- Multiply or divide the decimals as with whole numbers. Remind children that :

  a. The number of decimal places in the product is the same as that in the question. The zeros at the end of the product can be deleted after locating the decimal point.

  Example

  $$\begin{array}{r} 2.48 \\ \times \quad 5 \\ \hline 12.40 \end{array}$$

  2.48 ← 2 decimal places; 12.40 ← 2 decimal places

  So $2.48 \times 5 = 12.40 = 12.4$

  b. The decimal point in the quotient is directly above the one in the dividend. Don't forget to add a zero before the decimal point if necessary. If there is a remainder, add zeros to the right of the dividend and continue to divide until the remainder is zero or you have enough decimal places.

Example

```
                   8              8 4               0.8 4
5 ⟌4.2   →   5 ⟌4.2   →   5 ⟌4.2 0   →   5 ⟌4.2 0
               4 0            4 0               4 0
                              ────              ────
                                2 0               2 0
                                2 0               2 0
```

Add a "0" and bring down to continue the division.

Add a "0" to locate the decimal point.

8. *Length, Perimeter and Area*

- Children should remember the relationship between millimetre (mm), centimetre (cm), decimetre (dm), metre (m), and kilometre (km).
- Help children select the most appropriate standard unit to measure length and perimeter, and learn to measure with precision.
- In using grid paper with 1 cm^2 squares to find the area of an irregular shape, remind children that we can only find the approximate value of the area by counting the number of squares covered by the shape. To simplify our counting, a square that is more than half covered is counted as a whole, and a square that is less than half covered is not counted.

9. *Capacity, Volume and Mass*

- Children should remember the relationship between millilitre (mL), litre (L), cubic centimetre (cm^3), cubic metre (m^3), and also the relationship between gram (g) and kilogram (kg).
- Parents should help children visualize and select the most appropriate standard unit to measure different volumes through everyday examples.

10. *2- and 3- Dimensional Figures*

- Children should be familiar with the properties of different quadrilaterals, pyramids and prisms to help them identify, sort and classify 2-D shapes and 3-D solids. They should also practise how to sketch the solids and their nets, and make skeletons for 3-D solids.

11. *Angles*

- To measure an angle, put the 0° line of the protractor on one of the arms of the angle with the centre of the protractor at the vertex of the angle; then record the angle in degrees by taking the reading on the other arm of the angle. Remind children that lengthening the line segments forming the two arms of the angle doesn't alter the measurement of the angle.

12. *Transformations*

- Encourage children to describe transformations using reflections, rotations or translations, and identify the transformation undergone from the image produced. Practising drawing images helps children understand the characteristics of different transformations.
- Remind children that a 2-D shape may have more than one line of symmetry.

13. Coordinate Systems

- Remind children that when describing the location of an object on a grid, its ordered pair should be given by writing the number on the horizontal axis first, followed by the number on the vertical axis.

14. Patterns

- Using a calculator may help children explore and recognize mathematical relationships in some number patterns.
- Advise children to make observations carefully, as some patterns are created by changing two or more attributes (e.g. size, orientation, shape) of the figures.

15. Algebraic Symbols and Equations

- Children should know that a letter or a symbol in a mathematical sentence or an equation represents an unknown number.
- At this stage, children find the unknown number by systematic trial only.

16. Pictographs and Bar Graphs

- Children learn that data collected in a survey are recorded using a tally chart or displayed using an appropriate graph.
- Make sure children know the quantity each picture represents in drawing a pictograph, and are able to recognize what is represented by each bar in a bar graph.
- Parents should try to discuss with children the important features of the graph and help them read and interpret the data it represents.

17. Probability

- Children practise drawing tree diagrams to show all the possible outcomes of a simple probability problem.
- Children compare the probability of different events using expressions such as more probable, equally probable, and less probable; or describe the probability of an event happening using words such as likely or unlikely.
- Do not ask children to express the probability of an event mathematically using a fraction at this stage. Encourage them to describe the probability as number of favourable outcomes out of the total number of possible outcomes.

  <u>Example</u> The probability of getting a 2 by rolling a die is 1 out of 6.

1 Multiplication Facts to 81

1. 12   2. 30   3. 63   4. 24
5. 12   6. 28   7. 0   8. 5
9. 36   10. 49   11. 18   12. 14
13. 40   14. 27   15. 45   16. 0
17. 32   18. 81   19. 9 , 3 ; 27 ; 3 , 9 ; 27
20. 6 , 2 ; 12 ; 2 , 6 ; 12   21. 4 , 5 ; 20 ; 5 , 4 ; 20
22. 7 , 3 ; 21 ; 3 , 7 ; 21   23. 63   24. 10
25. 3   26. 0   27. 32   28. 35
29. 8   30. 36   31. 48   32. 21
33. 20   34. 18   35. 0   36. 48
37. 56   38. 0   39. 4 ; 28   40. 8 ; 8
41. 1 ; 9   42. 0 ; 0   43. B   44. C
45. A   46. B   47. 20 ; 25 ; 30 ; 40 ; 45
48. 18 ; 36 ; 45 ; 63 ; 72   49. 14 ; 21 ; 42 ; 49 ; 63
50. 2 ; 4 ; 6 ; 8   51. 0 ; 5
52. 0   53. 7 x 4 = 28 ; 28
54. 8 x 9 = 72 ; 72   55. 6 x 3 = 18 ; 18
56. 7 x 8 = 56 ; 56   57. 4 x 6 = 24 ; 24

Just for Fun

1.
```
  4
2 1 5
  3
```
2.
```
  1
2 3 4
  5
```
3.
```
  2
1 5 4
  3
```

2 Multiplication and Division Fact Families

1. – 3. (Suggested answers)
1. 4 , 5 ; 20 ; 20 , 4 ; 5   2. 3 , 4 ; 12 ; 12 , 4 ; 3
3. 6 , 2 ; 12 ; 12 , 2 ; 6
4. 42 ; 6 x 7 = 42 ; 42 ÷ 6 = 7 ; 42 ÷ 7 = 6
5. 72 ; 8 x 9 = 72 ; 72 ÷ 8 = 9 ; 72 ÷ 9 = 8
6. 36 ; 9 x 4 = 36 ; 36 ÷ 9 = 4 ; 36 ÷ 4 = 9
7. 40 ; 8 x 5 = 40 ; 40 ÷ 8 = 5 ; 40 ÷ 5 = 8
8. 54 ; 9 x 6 = 54 ; 54 ÷ 6 = 9 ; 54 ÷ 9 = 6
9. 56 ; 8 x 7 = 56 ; 56 ÷ 8 = 7 ; 56 ÷ 7 = 8
10. 63 ; 7 x 9 = 63 ; 63 ÷ 9 = 7 ; 63 ÷ 7 = 9
11. 48 ; 6 x 8 = 48 ; 48 ÷ 8 = 6 ; 48 ÷ 6 = 8
12. 45 ; 5 x 9 = 45 ; 45 ÷ 9 = 5 ; 45 ÷ 5 = 9
13. 5 , 6 ; 30 ; 6 , 5 ; 30 ; 30 , 6 ; 5 ; 30 , 5 ; 6
14. 9 , 3 ; 27 ; 3 , 9 ; 27 ; 27 , 3 ; 9 ; 27 , 9 ; 3
15. 8 ; 2   16. 7 ; 3   17. 5 ; 4   18. 8 ; 3
19. 6 ; 5   20. 3 ; 4   21. 56 ; 7   22. 18 ; 2
23. 40 ; 5   24. 18 ; 6   25. 35 ; 5   26. 28 ; 4
27. 9 ; 9   28. 4 ; 4   29. 8 ; 8   30. 5 ; 5
31. 9 ; 9   32. 9 ; 9   33. 7 ; 7   34. 7 ; 7
35. 3 ; 3   36. 3 ; 3   37. 7 ; 7   38. 8 ; 8
39. – 41. (Suggested answers)
39. 8 , 7 ; 56 ; 56 , 7 ; 8   40. 9, 8 ; 72 ; 72 , 9 ; 8
41. 8 , 6 ; 48 ; 48 , 8 ; 6
42. 9   43. 5

Just for Fun

1.
```
2 3 4
6 1 5
7 8 9
```
2.
```
1 2 3
6 5 4
7 8 9
```
3.
```
1 2 3
5 9 4
6 7 8
```

3 Division Facts to 81

1. 7   2. 8   3. 6   4. 7
5. 8   6. 6   7. 9   8. 8
9. 5   10. 7   11. 7   12. 0
13. 9   14. 6   15. 7   16. 5
17. 5   18. 7   19. 27 , 9 ; 3 ; 27 , 3 ; 9
20. 16 , 8 ; 2 ; 16 , 2 ; 8   21. 21 , 3 ; 7 ; 21 , 7 ; 3
22. 28 , 7 ; 4 ; 28 , 4 ; 7   23. 9 ; 9   24. 4 ; 4
25. 1 ; 1   26. 8 ; 8   27. 5 ; 5   28. 6 ; 6
29. 8 ; 8   30. 6 ; 6   31. 8 ; 8   32. 5 ; 5
33. 5 ; 5   34. 4 ; 4   35. 1 ; 1   36. 5 ; 5
37. 5 ; 5   38. A ; C   39. B ; C   40. A ; B
41. B ; C   42. A ; B   43. A ; C   44. B ; C
45. A ; C   46. 72 ÷ 9 = 8 ; 8
47. 32 ÷ 4 = 8 ; There are 8 books on each shelf.
48. 18 ÷ 2 = 9 ; He has 9 pairs of socks.
49. 54 ÷ 6 = 9 ; Each child gets 9 chocolates.
50. 40 ÷ 5 = 8 ; The price of 1 box of coloured pencils is $8.

Just for Fun

D

4 Multiplying by 10, 100 or 1000

1. 50   2. 600   3. 700   4. 900
5. 80   6. 0   7. 140   8. 1300
9. 7000   10. 3200   11. 2500   12. 600
13. 800   14. 0   15. 6000   18. 60
19. 80   20. 60   21. 90   22. 80
23. 180   24. 100   25. 160   26. 150
27. 180   28. 140   29. 240   30. 240
31. 120   32. 210   33. 200   34. 180
35. 320   36. 250   37. 280   38. 180
39. 400   40. 360   41. 360   42. 270
43. 160   44. 240   45. 480   46. 540
49. 1200   50. 1500   51. 6000   52. 800
53. 800   54. 4000   55. 1000   56. 1800
57. 3500   58. 9000   59. 10000   60. 2400
61. 2400   62. 1600   63. 5000   64. 4000
65. 2400   66. 1800   67. 2800   68. 2400
69. 10000   70. 3600   71. 1400   72. 5400
73. 6000   74. 300   75. 280   76. 70 ; 210
77. 50 ; 350   78. 30 ; 150   79. 2000   80. 900
81. 6000   82. 5000
83. 700 ; 2800   84. 800 ; 5600
85. 400 ; 2000   86. 2000 ; 6000
87. 3000 ; 6000   88. 600 ; 4800

Just for Fun

20

5 Multiplying 2-Digit Numbers by 1-Digit Numbers

1. 8 ; 40 ; 48   2. 12 ; 60 ; 72
3. 8 ; 120 ; 128   4. 45 ; 50 ; 95
5. 6 ; 180 ; 186   6. 42 ; 240 ; 282
7. 136   8. 69   9. 148   10. 150
11. 288   12. 56   13. 399   14. 432
15. 390   16. 195   17. 424   18. 201
19. 368   20. 108   21. 385   22. 273
23. 162   24. 132   25. 729   26. 208
27. 210   28. 336   29. 567   30. 380
31. 504   32. 276   33. 200   34. 348
35. 528   36. 666   37. 344   38. 105
39. 105   40. 196   41. 145   42. 292
43. 258   44. 270   45. 76   46. 144
47. 364   48. 396   49. 78   50. 276
51. 468   52. 176   53. 427   54. 236
55. 297   56. 322   57. computer
58. 612 ; 630   59. 148
```
  40
x  4
 160
```
60. 306
```
  50
x  6
 300
```
61. 415
```
  80
x  5
 400
```
62. 144 ; 144 ; 144
63. 3 x 24 = 72 ;
There were 72 party hats in 3 bags.
```
  24
x  3
  72
```
64. 2 x 98 = 196 ;
Mom bought 196 straws.
```
  98
x  2
 196
```
65. 5 x 18 = 90 ;
The cost of the birthday gift was $90.
```
  18
x  5
  90
```

66. 4 x 42 = 168 ;
There were 168 cookies.

  42
x 4
 168

Just for Fun

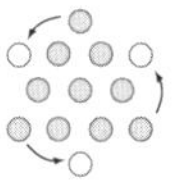

6 Multiplying 3-Digit Numbers by 1-Digit Numbers

1. 15 ; 300 ; 1000 ; 1315
2. 63 ; 0 ; 1800 ; 1863
3. 32 ; 80 ; 400 ; 512
4. 27 ; 120 ; 900 ; 1047

5. 2315	6. 2448	7. 1150	8. 2088
9. 1620	10. 3505	11. 945	12. 2992
13. 1014	14. 1904	15. 4518	16. 5467
17. 944	18. 5416	19. 3948	20. 4020
21. 1107	22. 5466	23. 1498	24. 732
25. 2400	26. 994	27. 2817	28. 1707
29. 3424	30. 3035	31. 2104	32. 1428
33. 1351	34. 2768	35. 4248	36. 1690
37. 2268	38. 3624	39. 2296	40. 4424
41. 3546	42. crocodile		

43. 1460 ; 1600

44. 4338
 700
x 6
4200

45. 1767
 600
x 3
1800

46. 1824
 900
x 2
1800

47. 4 x 225 = 900 ; 900 g ; 900

48. 6 x 125 = 750 ;
There are 750 packets in 6 boxes.
 125
x 6
 750

49. 6 x 355 = 2130 ;
There are 2130 mL of pop in 6 cans.
 355
x 6
2130

50. 7 x 250 = 1750 ;
Ted drinks 1750 mL of juice in one week.
 250
x 7
1750

Just for Fun

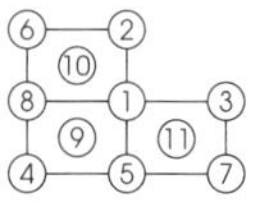

7 Multiplying 2-Digit Numbers by 2-Digit Numbers

1. 245 ; 350 ; 595
2. 78 ; 1040 ; 1118
3. 148 ; 1850 ; 1998
4. 162 ; 3240 ; 3402
5. 108 ; 2520 ; 2628
6. 13 ; 520 ; 533

7. 1500	8. 1200	9. 800	10. 2800
11. 600	12. 1000	13. 4000	14. 3600
15. 1200	16. 1800	17. 2100	18. 4200
19. 1800	20. 1600	21. 3000	

22. 25 x 24: 100 ; 500 ; 600
23. 93 x 36: 558 ; 2790 ; 3348
24. 45 x 64: 180 ; 2700 ; 2880
25. 52 x 27: 364 ; 1040 ; 1404
26. 56 x 22: 112 ; 1120 ; 1232
27. 16 x 47: 112 ; 640 ; 752
28. 82 x 37: 574 ; 2460 ; 3034
29. 61 x 98: 488 ; 5490 ; 5978
30. 73 x 28: 584 ; 1460 ; 2044
31. 42 x 81: 42 ; 3360 ; 3402
32. 38 x 55: 190 ; 1900 ; 2090
33. 69 x 12: 138 ; 690 ; 828
34. 58 x 48: 464 ; 2320 ; 2784
35. 62 x 76: 372 ; 4340 ; 4712
36. 32 x 28: 256 ; 640 ; 896
37. 95 x 18: 760 ; 950 ; 1710

38.

A 6	B 2	5				
	7			D 6	9	E 3
	C 5	9	F 8	0		1
	4		6	3		2
			G 1	5	4	0

39. 38 x 42: 76 ; 1520 ; 1596 ; 1600

40. 92 x 66: 552 ; 5520 ; 6072 ; 90 x 70: 6300

41. 47 x 59: 423 ; 2350 ; 2773 ; 50 x 60: 3000

42. 73 x 21: 73 ; 1460 ; 1533 ; 70 x 20: 1400

43. 89 x 14: 356 ; 890 ; 1246 ; 90 x 10: 900

44. 63 x 35: 315 ; 1890 ; 2205 ; 60 x 40: 2400

45. 32 x 26 = 832 ; 832
26 x 32: 52 ; 780 ; 832

46. 12 x 35 = 420 ;
She receives $420 in one year.
35 x 12: 70 ; 350 ; 420

47. 28 x 42 = 1176 ;
There are 1176 seats in the school theatre.
42 x 28: 336 ; 840 ; 1176

48. 48 x 90 = 4320 ;
The total amount raised will be $4320.
90 x 48: 720 ; 3600 ; 4320

Just for Fun

9

8 More Multiplying and Multiples

1. 36	2. 210	3. 336	4. 504
5. 126	6. 72	7. 30	8. 135
9. 192	10. 112	11. 270	12. 168
13. 120	14. 108	15. 224	16. 819
17. 720	18. 231	19. 1701	20. 320
21. 230	22. 1488	23. 1110	

24. 27 ; 30 ; 33 ; 36 ; 39 ; 42 ; 45 ; 48
25. 4 ; 8 ; 12 ; 16 ; 20 ; 24
26. 5 ; 10 ; 15 ; 25 ; 35 ; 40 ; 50
27. 2 ; 4 ; 6 ; 8 ; 10 ; 12 ; 14 ; 16 ; 18 ; 20 ; 22 ; 24
28. 26 ; 28 ; 30 ; 32 ; 34 ; 36 ; 38 ; 40 ; 42 ; 44 ; 46 ; 48 ; 50
29. 6 ; 12 ; 18 ; 24 ; 30 ; 36 ; 42 ; 48
30. 7 ; 14 ; 21 ; 28 ; 35 ; 42 ; 49
31. 8

32. – 33.

1	2	3	4	5	6	7	8	9	10
11	12	13	14	15	16	17	18	19	20
21	22	23	24	25	26	27	28	29	30
31	32	33	34	35	36	37	38	39	40
41	42	43	44	45	46	47	48	49	50
51	52	53	54	55	56	57	58	59	60
61	62	63	64	65	66	67	68	69	70
71	72	73	74	75	76	77	78	79	80
81	82	83	84	85	86	87	88	89	90
91	92	93	94	95	96	97	98	99	100

34. 8 , 16 , 24 , 32 , 40 , 48 , 56
35. 96 36. 99 37. 80 38. 77
39. 12 40. 11 41. 10 42. 14
43. 15 44. 15 45. 15
46. 6 ; 12 ; 18 ; 24 ; 30 47. 11 ; 22 ; 33 ; 44 ; 55
48. 9 ; 18 ; 27 ; 36 ; 45 49. 12 ; 24 ; 36 ; 48 ; 60
50. 13 ; 26 ; 39 ; 52 ; 65 51. 15 ; 30 ; 45 ; 60 ; 75
52. 2 x 5 x 6 = 60 ; 60
53. 3 x 4 x 8 = 96 ; The cafeteria can hold 96 students.
54. 3 x 2 x 6 = 36 ; Mom plants 36 rose bushes in the backyard.
55. 7 x 2 x 70 = 980 ; May drinks 980 mL of milk in one week.

Just for Fun

13

Midway Review

1. 500 2. 2000 3. 40 4. 60
5. 1100 6. 9000 7. 40 8. 120
9. 600 10. 60 11. 500 12. 2400
13. 3600 14. 300 15. 8000 16. 9
17. 9 18. 8
19. 9 , 7 ; 63 ; 7 , 9 ; 63 ; 63 , 7 ; 9 ; 63 , 9 ; 7
20. 5 , 8 ; 40 ; 8 , 5 ; 40 ; 40 , 5 ; 8 ; 40 , 8 ; 5
21. 48 22. 8 23. 7 24. 49
25. 1045 26. 2512 27. 1318 28. 1686
29. 2415 30. 2992 31. 150 32. 296
33. 406 34. 441 35. 292 36. 135
37. 310 38. 192

39. $\begin{array}{r} 37 \\ \times\ 14 \\ \hline 148 \\ 370 \\ \hline 518 \end{array}$ 40. $\begin{array}{r} 53 \\ \times\ 28 \\ \hline 424 \\ 1060 \\ \hline 1484 \end{array}$ 41. $\begin{array}{r} 66 \\ \times\ 33 \\ \hline 198 \\ 1980 \\ \hline 2178 \end{array}$ 42. $\begin{array}{r} 82 \\ \times\ 49 \\ \hline 738 \\ 3280 \\ \hline 4018 \end{array}$

43. $\begin{array}{r} 43 \\ \times\ 22 \\ \hline 86 \\ 860 \\ \hline 946 \end{array}$ 44. $\begin{array}{r} 75 \\ \times\ 52 \\ \hline 150 \\ 3750 \\ \hline 3900 \end{array}$ 45. $\begin{array}{r} 32 \\ \times\ 88 \\ \hline 256 \\ 2560 \\ \hline 2816 \end{array}$ 46. $\begin{array}{r} 97 \\ \times\ 18 \\ \hline 776 \\ 970 \\ \hline 1746 \end{array}$

47. 6 ; 12 ; 30 ; 90 48. 21 ; 28 ; 35 ; 49
49. 16 ; 32 ; 40 ; 64 50. 27 ; 45 ; 81 ; 90

51. $\begin{array}{r} 36 \\ \times\ 23 \\ \hline 108 \\ 720 \\ \hline 828 \end{array}$ $\begin{array}{r} 40 \\ \times\ 20 \\ \hline 800 \end{array}$ 52. $\begin{array}{r} 58 \\ \times\ 19 \\ \hline 522 \\ 580 \\ \hline 1102 \end{array}$ $\begin{array}{r} 60 \\ \times\ 20 \\ \hline 1200 \end{array}$

53. 2692 $\begin{array}{r} 700 \\ \times\ 4 \\ \hline 2800 \end{array}$ 54. 1716 $\begin{array}{r} 300 \\ \times\ 6 \\ \hline 1800 \end{array}$

55. 4308 $\begin{array}{r} 700 \\ \times\ 6 \\ \hline 4200 \end{array}$ 56. 2632 $\begin{array}{r} 300 \\ \times\ 8 \\ \hline 2400 \end{array}$

57. 135 58. 40 59. 192 60. 210
61. 42 62. 108 63. 32 x 18 = 576 ; 576
64. 26 x 3 = 78 ; 78 prizes were awarded to the students.
65. 15 x 24 = 360 ; 360 hot dogs were prepared.
66. 36 x 12 = 432 ; 432 buns were bought in all.
67. 16 x 48 = 768 ; 768 cups of soft drinks were in the boxes.
68. 2 x 118 = 236 ; May baked 236 cookies.
69. 236 x 10 = 2360 ; May got $23.60.

9 Dividing Multiples of 10, 100 or 1000

1. 8 ; 4 ; 400 2. 55 ; 11 ; 110 3. 36 ; 4 ; 40
4. 48 ; 6 ; 60 5. 6 ; 1 ; 100 6. 24 ; 6 ; 60

7. $\begin{array}{r} 50 \\ 9\overline{)450} \\ \underline{450} \end{array}$ 8. $\begin{array}{r} 300 \\ 4\overline{)1200} \\ \underline{1200} \end{array}$ 9. $\begin{array}{r} 10 \\ 5\overline{)50} \\ \underline{50} \end{array}$ 10. $\begin{array}{r} 700 \\ 8\overline{)5600} \\ \underline{5600} \end{array}$

11. $\begin{array}{r} 30 \\ 9\overline{)270} \\ \underline{270} \end{array}$ 12. $\begin{array}{r} 60 \\ 2\overline{)120} \\ \underline{120} \end{array}$ 13. $\begin{array}{r} 200 \\ 8\overline{)1600} \\ \underline{1600} \end{array}$ 14. $\begin{array}{r} 70 \\ 9\overline{)630} \\ \underline{630} \end{array}$

15. $\begin{array}{r} 20 \\ 2\overline{)40} \\ \underline{40} \end{array}$ 16. $\begin{array}{r} 600 \\ 6\overline{)3600} \\ \underline{3600} \end{array}$ 17. $\begin{array}{r} 20 \\ 7\overline{)140} \\ \underline{140} \end{array}$ 18. $\begin{array}{r} 3000 \\ 2\overline{)6000} \\ \underline{6000} \end{array}$

19. 300 20. 80 21. 30 22. 20
23. 800 24. 30 25. 40 26. 900
27. 50 28. 20 29. 100 30. 50
31. fishing
32. 60 ÷ 2 = 30 ; 30 $\begin{array}{r} 30 \\ 2\overline{)60} \\ \underline{60} \end{array}$
33. 320 ÷ 4 = 80 ; Mrs White needs 80 boxes to hold 320 muffins. $\begin{array}{r} 80 \\ 4\overline{)320} \\ \underline{320} \end{array}$
34. 180 ÷ 6 = 30 ; There are 30 groups. $\begin{array}{r} 30 \\ 6\overline{)180} \\ \underline{180} \end{array}$
35. 900 ÷ 3 = 300 ; There are 300 grams in each bag. $\begin{array}{r} 300 \\ 3\overline{)900} \\ \underline{900} \end{array}$
36. 2100 ÷ 7 = 300 ; There are 300 weeks in 2100 days. $\begin{array}{r} 300 \\ 7\overline{)2100} \\ \underline{2100} \end{array}$
37. 4500 ÷ 5 = 900 ; There are 900 stamps in each album. $\begin{array}{r} 900 \\ 5\overline{)4500} \\ \underline{4500} \end{array}$
38. 60 ÷ 6 ; 10 ; Mrs Smith can buy 10 bags of apples. $\begin{array}{r} 10 \\ 6\overline{)60} \\ \underline{60} \end{array}$

39. $\begin{array}{r} 10 \\ 8\overline{)80} \\ \underline{80} \end{array}$ 40. $\begin{array}{r} 200 \\ 3\overline{)600} \\ \underline{600} \end{array}$ 41. $\begin{array}{r} 1000 \\ 7\overline{)7000} \\ \underline{7000} \end{array}$ 42. $\begin{array}{r} 50 \\ 6\overline{)300} \\ \underline{300} \end{array}$

43. 500 ; 100 44. 2000 ; 500 45. 90 ; 30
46. 81 , 4 ; 80 , 4 ; 20 ; 20 47. 796 , 8 ; 800 , 8 ; 100 ; 100

Just for Fun

100

10 Dividing 2-Digit Numbers with No Remainders

1. $\begin{array}{r} 16 \\ 3\overline{)48} \\ \underline{3} \\ 18 \\ \underline{18} \end{array}$ 2. $\begin{array}{r} 32 \\ 2\overline{)64} \\ \underline{6} \\ 4 \\ \underline{4} \end{array}$ 3. $\begin{array}{r} 14 \\ 6\overline{)84} \\ \underline{6} \\ 24 \\ \underline{24} \end{array}$ 4. $\begin{array}{r} 15 \\ 5\overline{)75} \\ \underline{5} \\ 25 \\ \underline{25} \end{array}$

5. $\begin{array}{r} 18 \\ 4\overline{)72} \\ \underline{4} \\ 32 \\ \underline{32} \end{array}$ 6. $\begin{array}{r} 11 \\ 8\overline{)88} \\ \underline{8} \\ 8 \\ \underline{8} \end{array}$ 7. $\begin{array}{r} 23 \\ 3\overline{)69} \\ \underline{6} \\ 9 \\ \underline{9} \end{array}$ 8. $\begin{array}{r} 17 \\ 5\overline{)85} \\ \underline{5} \\ 35 \\ \underline{35} \end{array}$

9. 14 3)42 3 12 12	10. 13 6)78 6 18 18	11. 25 2)50 4 10 10	12. 24 4)96 8 16 16
13. 16 2)32 2 12 12	14. 12 6)72 6 12 12	15. 19 5)95 5 45 45	16. 12 7)84 7 14 14
17. 11 9)99 9 9 9	18. 12 8)96 8 16 16	19. 13 4)52 4 12 12	20. 21 3)63 6 3 3
21. 27 3)81 6 21 21	22. 16 5)80 5 30 30	23. 38 2)76 6 16 16	24. 19 4)76 4 36 36
25. 13 7)91 7 21 21	26. 15 6)90 6 30 30	27. 14 5)70 5 20 20	28. 19 2)38 2 18 18

29. 29	30. 37	31. 12	32. 17
33. 13	34. 13	35. 41	36. 19
37. 26	38. 14	39. 21	40. 14
41A. 11	B. 14	C. 17	D. 28

42. D ; C ; B ; A

43A. 15	B. 14	C. 36	D. 11

44. C ; A ; B ; D

45A. 29	B. 25	C. 17	D. 16

46. A ; B; C ; D

47A. 46	B. 11	C. 13	D. 28

48. A ; D ; C ; B
49. 70 ÷ 5 = 14 ; 14
50. 26 ÷ 2 = 13 ; Sally can buy 13 bags of chips with $26.
51. 39 ÷ 3 = 13 ; 1 kg of meat costs $13.
52. 96 ÷ 4 = 24 ; Each strip is 24 cm long.
53. 84 ÷ 7 = 12 ; There are 12 packets of candies.

Just for Fun

1. 38 2)76 6 16 16	2. 27 3)81 6 21 21	3. 15 6)90 6 30 30

11 Dividing 2-Digit Numbers with Remainders

1. 15R2 3)47 3 17 15 2	2. 12R3 4)51 4 11 8 3	3. 13R1 6)79 6 19 18 1
4. 18R1 2)37 2 17 16 1	5. 15R1 5)76 5 26 25 1	6 11R5 8)93 8 13 8 5

7. 11R5 6)71 6 11 6 5	8. 14R1 4)57 4 17 16 1	9. 16R1 2)33 2 13 12 1	10. 29R2 3)89 6 29 27 2
11. 12R4 5)64 5 14 10 4	12. 13R3 7)94 7 24 21 3	13. 14R1 6)85 6 25 24 1	14. 12R3 8)99 8 19 16 3
15. 38R1 2)77 6 17 16 1	16. 14R3 5)73 5 23 20 3	17. 13R3 6)81 6 21 18 3	18. 14R3 4)59 4 19 16 3

19. 14R2	20. 17R1	21. 14R3	22. 12R2
23. 13R1	24. 12R5	25. 24R1	26. 26R2
27. 37R1	28. 17R4	29. 11R3	30. 15R1
31. 11R4	32. 29R1		

33. 14R2 5)72 5 22 20 2	34. 16R3 4)67 4 27 24 3	35. 15R2 3)47 3 17 15 2	36. 27R1 2)55 4 15 14 1
37. 12R1 5)61 5 11 10 1	38. 12R3 7)87 7 17 14 3	39. 11R7 8)95 8 15 8 7	40. 12R1 6)73 6 13 12 1

41. 13R1	42. 23R2	43. 36R1	44. 12R4
45. 19R1	46. 17R3	47. 19R1	48. 11R5
49. 12R2	50. 14R4	51. 12R6	52. 13R2
53. 18R1	54. 16R2	55. radio car	

56. 89 ÷ 6 = 14R5 : 14 ; 5
57. 97 ÷ 7 = 13R6 ; There are 13 sandwiches in each bag. 6 sandwiches are left.
58. 47 ÷ 3 = 15R2 ; There are 15 glasses of water in each bucket. 2 glasses of water are left.
59. 29 ÷ 2 = 14R1 ;There are 14 students in each group. 1 student is left.

Just for Fun

12 ; 2

12 Dividing 3-Digit Numbers with No Remainders

1. 119 4)476 4 7 4 36 36	2. 171 3)513 3 21 21 3 3

3. 114	4. 243	5. 134	6. 76
7. 138	8. 174	9. 215	10. 133
11. 72	12. 93	13. 254	14. 63

15. 249 3)747 6 14 12 27 27	250 3)750 6 150 150	16. 139 5)695 5 19 15 45 45	140 5)700 5 200 200

17.
```
   99
8)792
  72
   72
   72
```
```
  100
8)800
  800
```

18.
```
  151
6)906
  6
  30
  30
    6
    6
```
```
  150
6)900
  6
  300
  300
```

19. 98 ; 700 , 7 ; 100
20. 163 ; 300 , 2 ; 150
21. 197 ; 800 , 4 ; 200
22. 183 ; 900 , 5 ; 180
23. 49 ; 300 , 6 ; 50
24. 52 ; 400 , 8 ; 50
25. 189 ; 600 , 3 ; 200
26. 99 ; 900 , 9 ; 100
27. B
28. A
29. A ; D
30. B ; D
31. B
32. D
33. A
34. C
35. 750 ÷ 5 = 150 ; 150
36. 648 ÷ 8 ; 81 ; Mrs White earned $81 each day.
37. 816 ÷ 6 = 136 ; Each child gets 136 g of peanuts.
38. 973 ÷ 7 = 139 ; May uses 139 beads to make 1 bracelet.
39. 528 ÷ 4 = 132 ; There are 132 blocks in each tower.

Just for Fun

1. A
2. C

13 Dividing 3-Digit Numbers with Remainders

1.
```
  124R5
6)749
  6
  14
  12
   29
   24
    5
```
2.
```
  141R3
4)567
  4
  16
  16
    7
    4
    3
```
3.
```
  129R2
3)389
  3
   8
   6
   29
   27
    2
```
4.
```
   94R1
9)847
  81
   37
   36
    1
```
5.
```
  121R5
8)973
  8
  17
  16
   13
    8
    5
```
6.
```
  317R1
2)635
  6
   3
   2
   15
   14
    1
```
7.
```
   75R2
7)527
  49
   37
   35
    2
```
8.
```
  183R4
5)919
  5
  41
  40
   19
   15
    4
```
9.
```
  136R1
3)409
  3
  10
   9
   19
   18
    1
```
10.
```
   93R3
7)654
  63
   24
   21
    3
```
11.
```
  131R3
6)789
  6
  18
  18
    9
    6
    3
```
12.
```
  271R1
2)543
  4
  14
  14
    3
    2
    1
```
13.
```
   68R1
9)613
  54
   73
   72
    1
```
14.
```
  284R2
3)854
  6
  25
  24
   14
   12
    2
```
15.
```
  236R1
4)945
  8
  14
  12
   25
   24
    1
```
16.
```
   88R2
8)706
  64
   66
   64
    2
```

17. 95R4
18. 113R4
19. 191R1
20. 113R4
21. 182R1
22. 56R3
23. 57R1
24. 156R2
25. 69R3
26. 257R1
27. 125R3
28. 46R8
29. 124R1
30. 259R1
31. 122R2
32. 121R2
33. 81R5
34. 99R5

35.
```
   95
5)479
  45
   29
   25
    4
```
```
  100
5)500
  500
```
36.
```
  129
6)778
  6
  17
  12
   58
   54
    4
```
```
  130
6)780
  6
  180
  180
```

37. 119R6 ; 960 , 8 ; 120
38. 115R4 ; 580 , 5 ; 116
39. 99R3 ; 700 , 7 ; 100
40. 99R7 ; 900 , 9 ; 100
41. 823
42. 473R1 ; 473 x 2 + 1 ; 947
43. 141R3 ; 141 x 4 + 3 ; 567
44. 387R1 ; 387 x 2 + 1 ; 775
45. 86R5 ; 86 x 7 + 5 ; 607
46. 165R4 ; 165 x 5 + 4 ; 829
47. 78R2 ; 78 x 8 + 2 ; 626
48. 748 ÷ 5 = 149R3 ; 149 ; 3
49. 429 ÷ 7 = 61R2 ; There are 61 cookies in each box. 2 cookies are left.
50. 260 ÷ 3 = 86R2 ; Each child gets 86 grams of golden raisins. 2 grams of golden raisins are left.
51. 369 ÷ 5 = 73R4 ; There are 73 baseball cards in each box. 4 baseball cards are left.
52. 462 ÷ 8 = 57R6 ; May can buy 57 boxes of candies. $6 is left.

Just for Fun

125

14 Zeros in the Quotient

1.
```
  104R1
7)729
  7
  2
  0
  29
  28
   1
```
2.
```
  206R2
4)826
  8
  2
  0
  26
  24
   2
```

3. 104
4. 107R3
5. 108R4
6. 108
7. 104R3
8. 104R1
9. 106R1
10. 206R1
11. 100R4
12. 107R3
13. 107
14. 102R5
15. 104R3
16. 103R2
17. ✗ ; 101 , 7 , 3 ; 710
18. ✓ ; 104 x 6 + 3 = 627
19. ✗ ; 106 x 5 + 4 = 534
20. ✓ ; 105 x 4 + 3 = 423
21. ✓ ; 108 x 9 + 4 = 976
22. ✗ ; 109 x 8 + 6 = 878
23. ✓ ; 208 x 3 + 2 = 626
24. 103 ; 103 x 7 = 721
25. 106R2 ; 106 x 5 + 2 = 532
26. 107R3 ; 107 x 4 + 3 = 431
27. 109R2 ; 109 x 6 + 2 = 656
28. 304R2 ; 304 x 3 + 2 = 914
29. 404R1 ; 404 x 2 + 1 = 809
30. 518 , 5 ; 103 , 3
31. 818 , 4 ; 204 , 2
32. 623 , 3 ; 207 , 2
33. 924 , 9 ; 102 ; 6
34. 746 , 7 ; 106 , 4
35. D
36. E
37. A
38. B
39. C
40. 632 ÷ 6 = 105R2 ; 105 ; 2
41. 869 ÷ 8 = 108R5 ; Mr Smith can buy 108 tapes. $5 is left.
42. 730 ÷ 7 = 104R2 ; Each strip is 104 cm long. 2 cm of ribbon is left.
43. 544 ÷ 5 = 108R4 ; She can make 108 cakes. 4 g of baking soda is left .
44. 829 ÷ 4 = 207R1 ; There are 207 packets. 1 battery is left.

Just for Fun

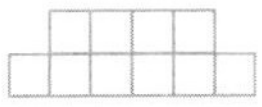
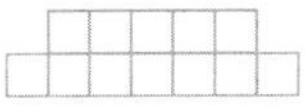

15 Dividing 4-Digit Numbers

1.
```
   520R2
9)4682
  45
   18
   18
    2
```
2.
```
  1254R1
3)3763
  3
   7
   6
   16
   15
    13
    12
     1
```
3.
```
  1493R2
5)7467
  5
  24
  20
   46
   45
    17
    15
     2
```
4.
```
  1401R3
6)8409
  6
  240
  240
    9
    6
    3
```
5.
```
   815R4
7)5709
  56
   10
    7
    39
    35
     4
```
6.
```
  1031R3
8)8251
  8
   25
   24
    11
     8
     3
```
7.
```
  1450R3
4)5803
  4
  18
  16
   20
   20
    3
```
8.
```
  1495R3
5)7478
  5
  24
  20
   47
   45
    28
    25
     3
```

9.
```
   1296R2
 7)9074
   7
   20
   14
    67
    63
     44
     42
      2
```

10.
```
   497R6
 8)3982
   32
    78
    72
     62
     56
      6
```

11. 698R1 12. 1374R4 13. 513R1 14. 972R5
15. 940R2 16. 1935R2 17. 565R4 18. 710
19. 2608R1 20. 584R6 21. 2188R1 22. 659R4
23. 286 24. 496R4 25. 1612R1 26. 2174R2
27. 900R6 28. 913R2 29. 670 30. 534R4
31. 1024R8 32. 1268R1 33. 1438R2 34. 120R5
35. 413 ; 3 36. 601 ; 4 37. 545 ; 4
38. 1162 ; 0 39. 2053 ; 3 40. 658 ; 1
41. 1090R2 42. 1056 43. 1154
44. 301R4 45. 2054 46. 1178
47. 986 48. 1459R1 49. 967R4
50. 968 51. stamps
52. 3265 ÷ 5 = 653 ; 653
53. 7560 ÷ 7 = 1080 ; He can go 1080 cm in 1 minute.
54. 8268 ÷ 8 = 1033R4 ; She can make 1033 crafts with 8268 strips of ribbon. 4 strips of ribbon are left.
55. 4286 ÷ 6 = 714R2 ; There are 714 boxes of doughnuts. 2 doughnuts are left.
56. 2086 ÷ 9 = 231R7 ; She can make 231 bracelets with 2086 beads. 7 beads are left.

Just for Fun

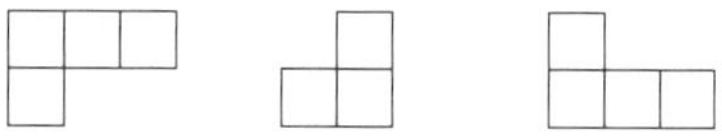

16 More Multiplying and Dividing

1.
```
     329
  x   46
    1974
   13160
   15134
```

2.
```
      57
  x   64
     228
    3420
    3648
```

3.
```
   164R1
 2)329
   2
   12
   12
     9
     8
     1
```

4.
```
   1256R4
 5)6284
   5
   12
   10
    28
    25
     34
     30
      4
```

5. 570 6. 1668 7. 476R2 8. 75R1
9. 889 10. 1068 11. 438R7 12. 2368
13. 1914 14. 105R4
15. A ; D 16. B ; D 17. A ; C
18. A ; D 19. B ; C 20. C ; D
21. A ; C 22. A ; D 23. B ; C
24. 16 x 26 = 416 ; 416
25. 200 ÷ 7 = 28R4 ; John can buy 28 basket of apples. $4 is left.
26. 8 x 128 = 1024 ; May buys 1024 candies.
27. 1024 ÷ 5 = 204R4 ; Each child gets 204 candies. 4 candies are left.
28. 882 ÷ 6 = 147 ; 147 pizzas were sold each day.
29. 147 x 4 = 588 ; Aunt Pam got $588 for selling pizzas each day.
30. 75 x 9 = 675 ; She needs 675 g of pepper to make 75 pizzas.
31. 6 , 325 ; 1950 ; 1950 , 4 ; 487R2 ; 487 ; 2
32. 484 ÷ 2 = 242 ; 7 x 242 = 1694 ; There are 1694 sheets of paper in 7 packs.
33. 36 x 48 = 1728 ; 1728 ÷ 7 = 246R6 ; Each student gets 246 stickers. 6 stickers are left.
34. 5910 ÷ 6 = 985 ; 9 x 985 = 8865 ; The total weight of 9 sacks of soil is 8865 grams.

Just for Fun

1. 9 2. 2

Final Review

1.
```
   15R1
 5)76
   5
   26
   25
    1
```

2.
```
   12R5
 7)89
   7
   19
   14
    5
```

3.
```
   17R1
 3)52
   3
   22
   21
    1
```

4.
```
   16R3
 4)67
   4
   27
   24
    3
```

5.
```
   31R7
 9)286
   27
    16
     9
     7
```

6.
```
   58
 3)174
   15
    24
    24
```

7.
```
   59R4
 8)476
   40
    76
    72
     4
```

8.
```
   54R1
 6)325
   30
    25
    24
     1
```

9. 317R1 10. 1034R3 11. 108R2 12. 1517R4
13. 452R8 14. 105R2 15. 467R6 16. 2102
17. 1633R1 18. 2071R1 19. 184 20. 120R8
21. 469R2 22. 231R1 23. ractice
24. 30R6 ; 30 , 9 , 6 ; 276
25. 258R4 ; 258 , 5 , 4 ; 1294
26. 816R2 ; 816 , 4 , 2 ; 3266
27. 117R6 ; 117 , 7 , 6 ; 825
28. 885R6 ; 885 , 8 , 6 ; 7086
29. 1047R1 ; 1047 , 6 , 1 ; 6283
30. 1924R2 ; 1924 , 3 , 2 ; 5774
31. 5076 32. 2628 33. 1192 34. 3815

35.
```
     28
  x  45
    140
   1120
   1260
```

36.
```
     37
  x  82
     74
   2960
   3034
```

37.
```
     66
  x  53
    198
   3300
   3498
```

38.
```
     21
  x  78
    168
   1470
   1638
```

39. 1152 40. 3112 41. 4284 42. 1156
43. 2226 44. 574 45. 1508 46. 2499
47. 117 , 8 ; 162 , 6 48. 26 , 1014 ; 1204 , 7
49. 87 , 609 ; 801 , 89 50. 9 , 4005 ; 4065 , 5

51.
```
      6 5
  x   3 9
    5 8 5
  1 9 5 0
  2 5 3 5
```

52.
```
      6 7
  x   2 3
    2 0 1
  1 3 4 0
  1 5 4 1
```

53.
```
      5 3
  x   4 6
    3 1 8
  2 1 2 0
  2 4 3 8
```

54.
```
    1 2 3 R 4
 7 )8 6 5
    7
    1 6
    1 4
      2 5
      2 1
        4
```

55.
```
    1 0 5 9 R 1
 4 )4 2 3 7
    4
      2 3
      2 0
        3 7
        3 6
          1
```

56.
```
    1 7 4 R 1
 3 )5 2 3
    3
    2 2
    2 1
      1 3
      1 2
        1
```

57. 4206 ÷ 8 = 525R6 ; 525 ; 6
58. 427 x 5 = 2135 ; Mr Smith gets $2135 from selling 427 magazines.
59. 826 ÷ 6 = 137R4 ; There are 137 flowers in each basket. 4 flowers are left.
60. 1995 ÷ 7 = 285 ; 1 bag of sugar weighs 285 grams.
61. 5 x 123 = 615 ; Ted buys 615 marbles.
62. 615 ÷ 6 = 102R3 ; There are 102 marbles in each bag. 3 marbles are left.
63. 6 , 275 = 1650 ; 1650 , 4 = 412R2 ; 412 ; 2
64. 826 ÷ 2 ; 413 ; 4 x 413 ; 1652 ; George has 1652 stamps.
65. 12 x 86 = 1032 ; 1032 ÷ 5 = 206R2 ; 206 students can get the pencils. 2 pencils are left.
66. 3640 ÷ 8 = 455 ; 7 x 455 = 3185 ; The total weight of 7 boxes of crackers is 3185 grams.
67. 56 ÷ 4 = 14 ; 2 x 14 = 28 ; It will take 28 hours to bake all the cakes.

1 Multiples

1. 9, 12, 15, 18, 21, 24
2. 18, 24
3. 15, 20, 25
4. 7, 14, 21, 28, 35
5. 8, 16, 24, 32, 40
6. 10, 20, 30, 40, 50
7. 11, 22, 33, 44, 55
8. 12, 24, 36, 48, 60
9. a. 6, 9, 12, 15, 18, 21, 24
   b. 8, 12, 16, 20, 24
   c. 12, 24
   d. 12
10. 8, 16, 24, 32
    8
11. 6, 12, 18, 24
    6
12. 24, 48, 72, 96
    24

Activity

1. 2; 7 or 7 ; 14
2. 14

2 Factors

1. 14
2. 7
3. 2
4. 1
5. 1, 2, 7, 14
6. 14, 7, 2, 1
7. 1, 2, 3, 6, 9, 18
8. 1, 2, 3, 4, 6, 8, 12, 24
9. 1, 2, 4, 5, 8, 10, 20, 40
10. 1, 2, 4, 7, 8, 14, 28, 56
11. 1, 2, 3, 4, 6, 8, 12, 24
12. 1, 2, 3, 5, 6, 10, 15, 30
13. 1, 2, 3, 6
14. 1, 2, 3, 6
15. 1, 2, 3, 4, 6, 12
16. 1, 2, 3, 6, 9, 18
17. 1, 2, 3
18. 1, 2, 4, 8, 16
19. 1, 2, 3, 4, 6, 8, 12, 24
20. 1, 2, 4, 8
21. 1, 2, 5, 10
22. 1, 2, 4, 8
23. 1, 2, 4, 5, 10, 20
24. 1, 2, 4, 7, 14, 28
25. 1, 2, 4
26. 4
27. 4
28. 1, 2, 3, 4, 6, 8, 12, 24
29. 1, 2, 3, 4, 6, 9, 12, 18, 36
30. 1, 2, 3, 4, 6, 12
31. 12
32. 1, 3, 5, 15
    15
33. 1, 2, 3, 6
    6
34. 1, 5, 25
    25
35. 1, 2, 4, 8
    8
36.
```
2 | 24  40
2 | 12  20
2 |  6  10
     3   5
```
2 x 2 x 2
8

37.
```
2 | 18  36
3 |  9  18
3 |  3   6
     1   2
```
2 x 3 x 3
18

38.
```
2 | 48  60
2 | 24  30
3 | 12  15
     4   5
```
2 x 2 x 3
12

Activity

3; 18; 19

3 Multiplication

1. 544, 544

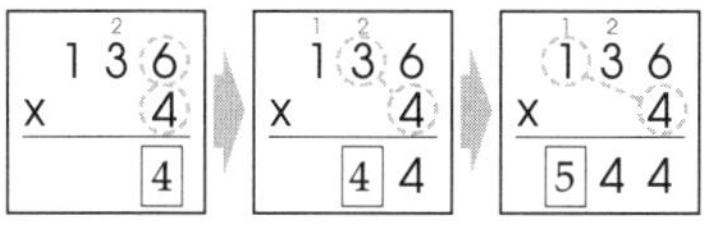

2. 717
3. 965
4. 828
5. 1184
6. a. 30 x 2
   60
   b. 12 x 5
   60
   60
7. 60, 60
8. 162, 162
9. 280, 280
10. 216
11. 230; 230
```
  23
x 10
 230
```
12. 16 x 20 = 320
    320
```
  16
x 20
 320
```
13. 1080
14. 1320
15. 900
16. 3010
17.

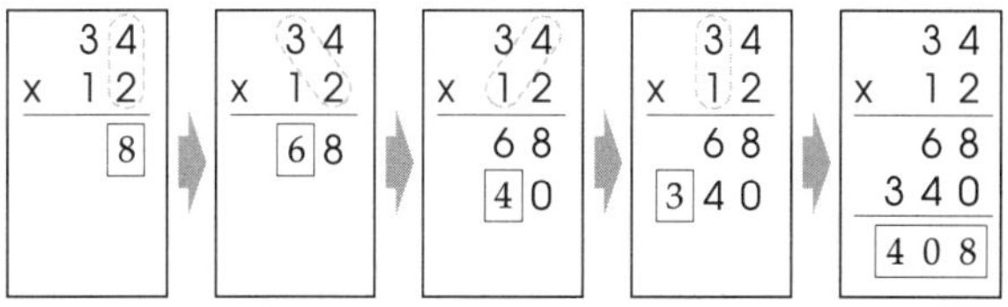

408; 408

18.
```
  15
x 37
 105
 450
 555
```
19.
```
  74
x 26
 444
1480
1924
```
20.
```
  48
x 19
 432
 480
 912
```
21.
```
  36
x 14
 144
 360
 504
```
22. 1363
23. 4558
24. 1426
25. 1650
26. 7680
27. 2958
28. 540
29. 1092
30. 1044; 1044
```
  87
x 12
 174
 870
1044
```
Estimate
```
  90
x 10
 900
```

31.
```
   27
 x 42
   54
 1080
 1134
```
Estimate
```
   30
 x 40
 1200
```

32.
```
   38
 x 25
  190
  760
  950
```
Estimate
```
   40
 x 30
 1200
```

33.
```
   16
 x 54
   64
  800
  864
```
Estimate
```
   20
 x 50
 1000
```

Activity

1. 520
2. 570
3. 210
4. 2030
(individual answer)

4 *Division*

1.
```
4)284  ⇒   7        ⇒   71
        4)284          4)284
                         28
                          4
                          4
```
71

2.
```
8)234  ⇒   2        ⇒   29 r 2
        8)234          8)234
          16             16
                          74
                          72
                           2
```
29; 2

3. 67 r 5
4. 83 r 6
5. 127 r 4
6. 280 r 1
7. 2 r 7
2; 7
```
     2 r 7
12)31
   24
    7
```
8. 5 r 3
5; 3
```
     5 r 3
19)98
   95
    3
```
9. 4 r 9
10. 4 r 4
11. 5 r 2
12. 5 r 1
13. 5 r 9
14. 3 r 3
15. 3 r 4
16. 2 r 11
17. 2 r 19
18. 4 r 8
19. 14; 14
```
      1        ⇒      14
10)140             10)140
   10                 10
    4                  40
                       40
```
20.
```
     18 r 15
20)375
   20
   175
   160
    15
```
21.
```
     28 r 3
15)423
   30
   123
   120
     3
```
22.
```
     19 r 8
16)312
   16
   152
   144
     8
```
23.
```
     39 r 10
17)673
   51
   163
   153
    10
```
24.
```
     21 r 5
23)488
   46
    28
    23
     5
```
25.
```
     21 r 5
24)509
   48
    29
    24
     5
```
26. 25 r 9
27. 18 r 5
28. 31 r 14
29. 17 r 26
30.
```
     26 r 0
15)390
   30
    90
    90
```
26 x 15 + 0
390

31.
```
     25 r 6
18)456
   36
    96
    90
     6
```
25 x 18 + 6
456

32.
```
     27 r 22
25)697
   50
   197
   175
    22
```
27 x 25 + 22
697

33.
```
     24 r 2
36)866
   72
   146
   144
     2
```
24 x 36 + 2
866

34. 16 r 13
35. 21 r 4
36. 15 r 10
37. 19 r 23
38. 132; 132
```
      132
26)3432
   26
    83
    78
     52
     52
```

39.
```
      173r2
27 | 4673
     27
     197
     189
      83
      81
       2
```

40.
```
      172r16
21 | 3628
     21
     152
     147
      58
      42
      16
```

41.
```
      83r37
39 | 3274
     312
      154
      117
       37
```

42.
```
      71r1
32 | 2273
     224
       33
       32
        1
```

43.
```
      258r6
31 | 8004
     62
     180
     155
      254
      248
        6
```

44.
```
      247r28
35 | 8673
     70
     167
     140
      273
      245
       28
```

45. 4682 ÷ 42 = 111 r 20
111; 20

46. 3068 ÷ 48 = 63 r 44
64

47. 1782 ÷ 68 = 26 r 14
27

Activity

1. 2
2. 36
3. 56
4. 263
5. 47
6. 0

5 *Direct Proportion*

1. 2 x 1 = 2
2 x 2 = 4
2 x 3 = 6
2 x 4 = 8
2 x 5 = 10
2. 12
3. 28
4. 10
5. Yes
6. 20, 35, 50, 60
7. 45
8. 20
9. 6, 12, 30, 48
10. 32, 56, 80, 96

Activity

C

6 *Fractions*

1. $\frac{3}{7}$, $\frac{4}{16}$
2. $\frac{9}{4}$, $\frac{15}{10}$
3. $4\frac{2}{3}$, $5\frac{6}{8}$
4. $1\frac{2}{7}$
5. $1\frac{1}{3}$
6. $2\frac{2}{5}$
7. $3\frac{1}{4}$
8. $\frac{7}{3}$
9. $\frac{25}{7}$
10. $\frac{13}{8}$
11. $\frac{21}{4}$
12. $\frac{29}{6}$
13. $\frac{22}{3}$
14. $\frac{4}{6} = \frac{8}{12}$
15. $\frac{2}{10} = \frac{3}{15}$
16. $\frac{6}{8} = \frac{15}{20}$
17. $\frac{21}{24} = \frac{35}{40}$
18. $\frac{2}{3}$
19. $\frac{4}{5}$
20. $\frac{4}{5}$
21. $\frac{7}{9}$
22. $\frac{4}{5}$
23. $\frac{1}{4}$
24. $\frac{3}{5}$
25. $\frac{1}{8}$
26. $\frac{3}{5}$
27. $\frac{1}{4}$
28. $\frac{1}{2}$
29. $\frac{2}{3}$
30. $1\frac{1}{8}$
31. $\frac{15}{10} = 1\frac{1}{2}$
32. $\frac{16}{12} = 1\frac{1}{3}$
33. $\frac{20}{16} = 1\frac{1}{4}$
34. $5\frac{5}{6}$
35. $1\frac{4}{9}$
36. $8\frac{1}{3}$
37. $2\frac{1}{6}$
38. $9\frac{3}{7}$
39. $6\frac{1}{3}$
40. 4
41. 6 ; 5
42. $3\frac{3}{5}$
43. $4\frac{2}{3}$
44. $2\frac{2}{5}$
45. $8\frac{1}{10}$

Activity

1. A
2. C
3. B

7 *Decimals (Addition and Subtraction)*

1. 0.5
2. 0.81
3. 0.8
4. 0.45
5. 0.4
6. 0.06
7. 1.08
8. 1.14
9. 0.97
10. 1.02
11. 1.14, 1.08, 1.02, 0.97
12. 35.213
13. 34.078
14. 34.005
15. 35.01
16. 35.213, 35.01, 34.078, 34.005
17. =
18. <
19. =
20. <
21. >
22. =
23. >
24. >
25. <
26.

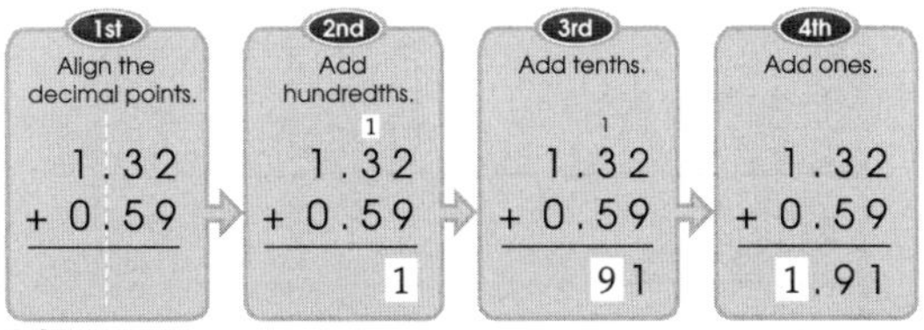

1.91

27.

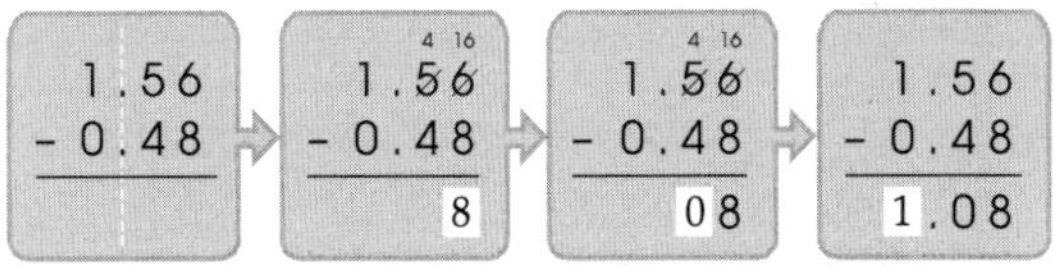

1.08

28. 4.61
29. 12.04
30. 7.27
31. 44.13
32. 1.37
33. 20.03
34. 21.26
35. 0.33
36. 2.36

```
   1.46
+  2.84
   4.30
-  1.94
   2.36
```

37. 2.85
$2 + 2 - 1 = 3$

38. 6.47
$2 + 6 - 1 = 7$

39. 13.61
$12 - 4 + 6 = 14$

40. 4.91
$15 - 6 - 4 = 5$

41. 14.66
$10 + 0 + 5 = 15$

42. 9.17
$13 - 8 + 4 = 9$

Activity

1. A
2. C
3. B

8 *Capacity*

1. 800
2. 400
3. 900
4. 400
5. $1000 - 400 = 600$
6. $1000 - 700 = 300$
7. $1000 - 500 = 500$
8. B
9. C

10.
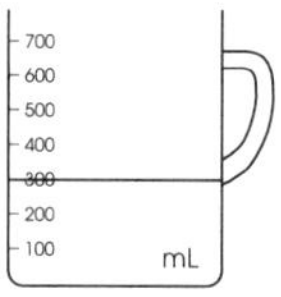

11.
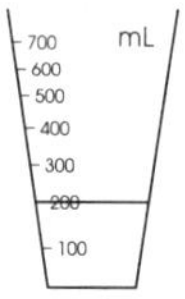

12.
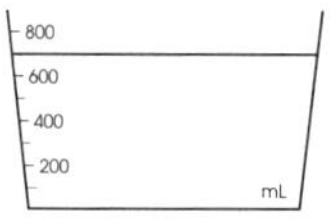

13. 8
14. 8
15. 16
16. 2000

Activity

C

9 *Solids*

1. Rectangular pyramid
2. Hexagonal prism
3. Triangular prism
4. Pentagonal pyramid

Solid	Number of faces	Number of vertices	Number of edges
5. Rectangular pyramid	5	5	8
6. Hexagonal pyramid	7	7	12
7. Triangular pyramid	4	4	6
8. Pentagonal prism	7	10	15
9. Triangular prism	5	6	9
10. Rectangular prism	6	8	12

11. A
12. E
13. C
14. D
15. B
16. F

17.
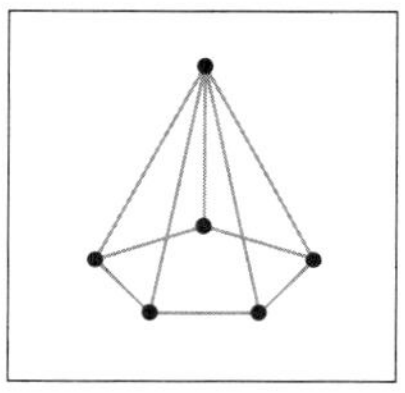

18.
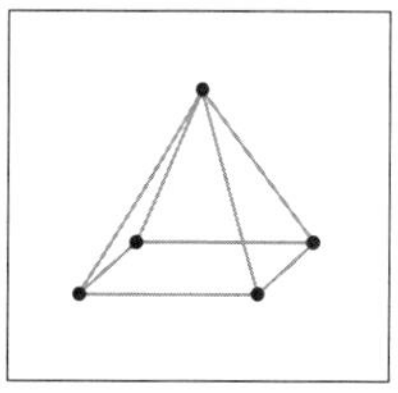

19.
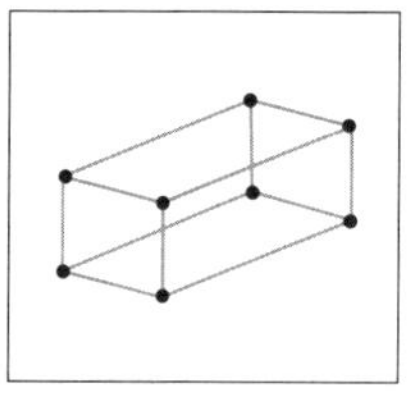

20.
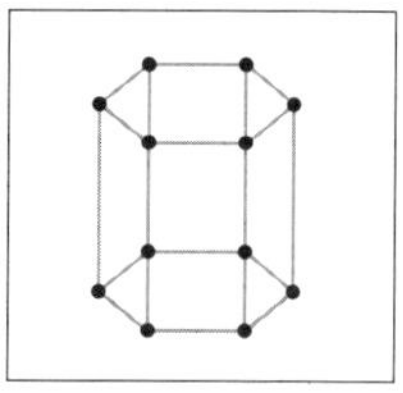

21. A
22. B
23. B
24. A

Activity

1. a. 40 b. 21
2. a. 48 b. 32

10 *Pictographs*

1. 70
2. 80
3. 100
4. 30
5. Sunday
6. 90
7. 380
8.

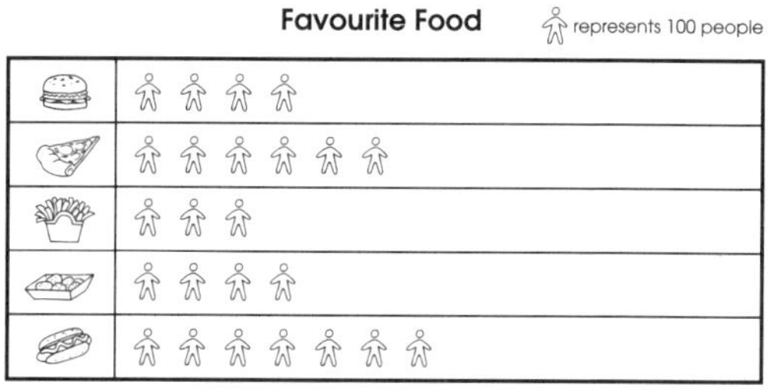

9. 5
10. 300
11. 2400

Activity

Jill
Nicky
Tim

Midway Test

1. 6, 9, 15, 18, 30
2. 15, 25, 30, 50, 60
3. 7
4. 75
5. 3
6. 5
7. 15
8. 20
9. 24
10. 1, 2, 5, 10
1, 2, 3, 4, 6, 12
2
11. 1, 2, 4, 8, 16
1, 2, 3, 4, 6, 8, 12, 16, 24, 48
16

12.

2	20	40
2	10	20
5	5	10
	1	2

20

13.

2	36	48
2	18	24
3	9	12
	3	4

12

14. 6.4, 5.8, 5.0, 4.9, 4.6, 3.9
15. 9.83, 8.65, 8.00, 7.24, 7.00, 6.69
16. 1.2
17. 2.56
18. 0.05
19. 6.205
20. 20.30

21. $$\begin{array}{r} 25.00 \\ -\ 20.30 \\ \hline \$\ 4.70 \end{array}$$

22. $$\begin{array}{r} 8.43 \\ +\ 9.99 \\ \hline \$18.42 \end{array}$$

23. $$\begin{array}{r} 20.00 \\ -\ 18.42 \\ \hline \$\ 1.58 \end{array}$$

24. $$\begin{array}{r} 4.05 \\ +\ 12.67 \\ \hline \$16.72 \end{array}$$

25. $$\begin{array}{r} 20.75 \\ -\ 16.72 \\ \hline \$\ 4.03 \end{array}$$

26. $$\begin{array}{r} 17 \\ \times\ 29 \\ \hline 153 \\ 340 \\ \hline 493 \end{array}$$

27. $$\begin{array}{r} 56 \\ \times\ 18 \\ \hline 448 \\ 560 \\ \hline 1008 \end{array}$$

28. $$\begin{array}{r} 23 \\ \times\ 36 \\ \hline 138 \\ 690 \\ \hline 828 \end{array}$$

29. 13 x 45 = 585
585

30. 23 x 15 = 345
345

31. $1\frac{5}{6}$

32. $1\frac{5}{8}$

33. $2\frac{2}{5}$

34. $\frac{16}{20}$

35. $\frac{3}{4}$

36. $\frac{3}{8}$

37. $\frac{6}{16} = \frac{3}{8}$

38. $\frac{6}{12} = \frac{1}{2}$

39. $9\frac{9}{15} = 9\frac{3}{5}$

40. $3\frac{3}{6} = 3\frac{1}{2}$

41. $11\frac{10}{18} = 11\frac{5}{9}$

42. $4\frac{10}{25} = 4\frac{2}{5}$

43. 2398 ÷ 4 = 599 r 2
600

$$\begin{array}{r} 599\text{r }2 \\ 4\overline{)2398} \\ 20 \\ \hline 39 \\ 36 \\ \hline 38 \\ 36 \\ \hline 2 \end{array}$$

44. 3846 ÷ 7 = 549 r 3
550

$$\begin{array}{r} 549\text{r }3 \\ 7\overline{)3846} \\ 35 \\ \hline 34 \\ 28 \\ \hline 66 \\ 63 \\ \hline 3 \end{array}$$

45. 7588 ÷ 38 = 199 r 26
200

$$\begin{array}{r} 199\text{r}26 \\ 38\overline{)7588} \\ 38 \\ \hline 378 \\ 342 \\ \hline 368 \\ 342 \\ \hline 26 \end{array}$$

46.

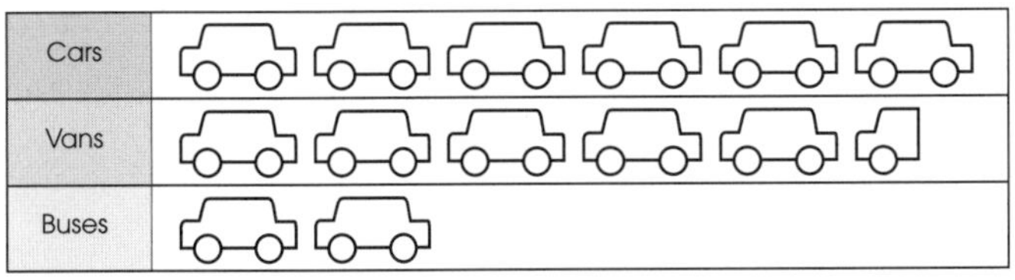

47. Cars
48. 400
49. 8
50. Triangular prism
51. Rectangular pyramid
52. Hexagonal prism
53. 2
54. 8
55. 4
56. 6
57. 8
58. 12
59. 6
60. 6
61. 12

11 *Brackets*

1. 25 + 9 = 34; 34
2. C
3. D
4. A
5. B
6. E
7. 19 + (9 + 4)
   19 + 13
   32; 32
8. 2 x (6 ÷ 3 + 9)
   22
9. (10 - 3) x 3 ÷ 7
   3
10. 45 - (30 - 12) ÷ 6
    42
11. (49 ÷ 7 + 1) x 4
    32

Activity

1. (4 - (4 - 4)) ÷ 4 = 1
2. 4 ÷ (4 - 4 ÷ 4 - 4 ÷ 4) = 2
3. (4 + 4 + 4) ÷ 4 = 3
4. 4 x (4 - 4) + 4 = 4

12 *More about Fractions*

1. <
2. >
3. <
4. >
5. >
6. >
7. $\frac{4}{10}$, $\frac{5}{10}$, $\frac{1}{2}$
8. $\frac{8}{14}$, $\frac{6}{14}$, $\frac{3}{7}$
9. $\frac{8}{24} + \frac{7}{24}$
   $\frac{15}{24} = \frac{5}{8}$
10. $\frac{17}{20} - \frac{12}{20}$
    $\frac{5}{20} = \frac{1}{4}$
11. $\frac{3}{40} + \frac{25}{40}$
    $\frac{28}{40} = \frac{7}{10}$
12. $\frac{10}{24} - \frac{1}{24}$
    $\frac{9}{24} = \frac{3}{8}$
13. $4\frac{6}{6}$
    $(4 - 2) + (\frac{6}{6} - \frac{5}{6})$
    $2\frac{1}{6}$
14. $3\frac{7}{7}$
    $(3 - 3) + (\frac{7}{7} - \frac{4}{7})$
    $\frac{3}{7}$

Activity

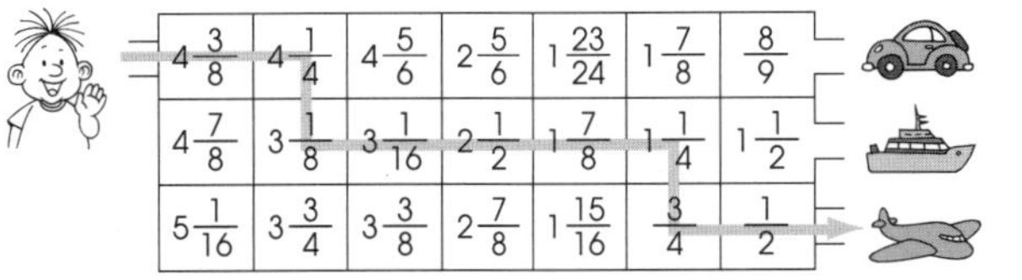

13 *Decimals (Multiplication and Division)*

1. 7.50
2. 8.72

```
  2.18
x    4
  8.72
```

3. 81.6
4. 46.2
5. 93.5
6. 86.60
7. 63.15
8. 94.44
9.

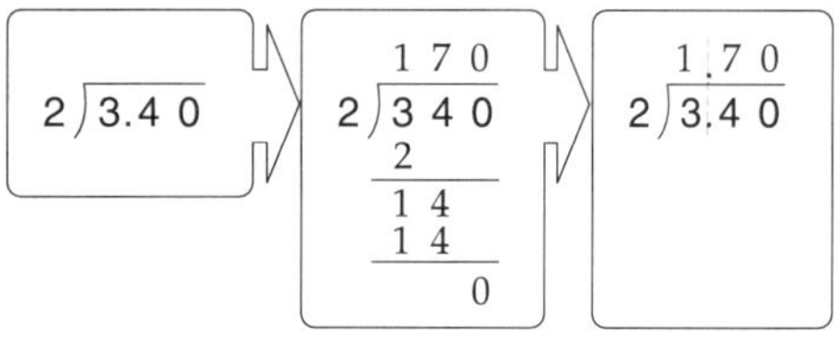

1.70

10.

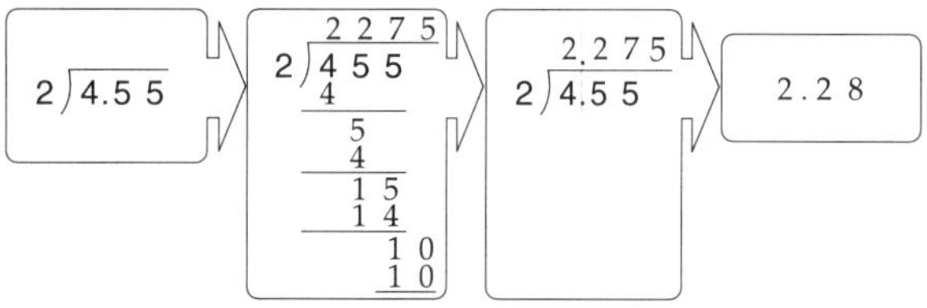

2.28

11. 6.82
12. 6.40
13. 2.59
14. 3.31
15. 4.57
16. 3.05
17.

```
    1.6
 5 ⟌8.0
    5
    3 0
    3 0
```

18.

```
     1.25
 4 ⟌5.00
    4
    1 0
      8
      20
      20
```

19.

```
     10.75
 4 ⟌43.00
    4
     3 0
     2 8
       2 0
       2 0
```

20.

```
      2.25
 12 ⟌27.00
     24
      3 0
      2 4
       60
       60
```

21.

```
     2.125
 8 ⟌17.000
    16
     1 0
       8
       20
       16
        40
        40
```

22. 3.99
    28 ÷ 7 = 4
23. 7.01
    56 ÷ 8 = 7
24. 3.02
    36 ÷ 12 = 3
25. 5.96
    66 ÷ 11 = 6
26. 4.95 + 1.25 = 6.2
    6.2
27. 0.66 + 2.4
    3.06
28. 12.48 - 3.78
    8.7
29. 15.63 - 4.86
    10.77
30. 15.89 + 20.24
    36.13

Activity

1. B
2. C

14 *Averages*

1. 49
2. 49; 7
3. 7
4. 4 + 5 + 3 + 1 + 0 + 2 + 5 + 4 = 24
5. 24 ÷ 8 = 3
6. 3
7. 3.4 + 1.8 + 7.3 + 6.4 + 2.4 + 2.9 + 2.4 = 26.6
8. 26.6 ÷ 7 = 3.8
9. 3.8
10. 20.38
11. 28.82
12. 20.54
13. 10.81

Activity

1. raised
2. lowered

15 *Algebraic Symbols*

1. 14
2. 13
3. 0
4. 1
5. 8
6. 81
7. 9
8. 4
9. y + 7
10. x - 4
11. k x 2
12. m ÷ 4
13. n x 6

Activity

C

16 *Quadrilaterals*

1. A, C
2. A, B, C, F
3. D
4. E
5. A, B

6 - 11.

	6	7	8	9	10	11
Rectangle		✓	✓		✓	
Parallelogram		✓	✓			
Square	✓	✓	✓		✓	
Rhombus	✓	✓	✓			
Kite						✓
Trapezoid				✓		

12. Parallelogram, Rectangle, Kite
13. Square, Parallelogram, Rhombus

Activity

6

17 *Area*

1. 18
2. 15
3. 16
4. Card A
5. 20
6. 12
7. 24
8. C
9. 10
10. 16
11. 15
12. 14
13. 19
14. 16
15. E
16. A
17. B, F
18. 12
19. 15
20. 13
21. 13

22.

	A	B	C	D	E
Length (cm)	6	8	8	5	1
Width (cm)	3	2	4	5	8
Area (cm^2)	18	16	32	25	8

23. 70
24. 2880
25. 420
26. 6
27. 64
28. 400

Activity

93

18 *Compound Bar Graphs*

1.

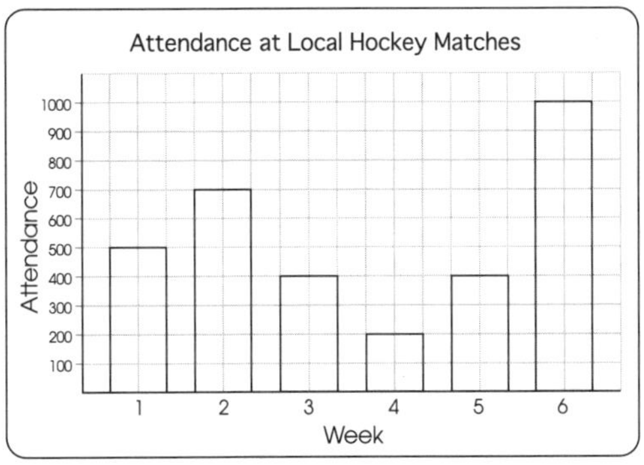

2. 6
3. 500
4. 6
5. 15
6. 16
7. 28
8. 6
9. 1, 8

Activity

4, 6
5, 2

19 *Money*

1. (Individual answer) $46.50
2. (Individual answer) $38.30
3. 5, 2.25
4. 10, 16.5
5. 5, 6.32
6. 15, 24.25
7. 20, 39.59

8. 		1	1	2	1	1	3
9. 		1	1	2			

10. 2.65
11. 26.62
12. 0.49
13. 3.53
14. 10.62

Activity

$4.39, $6.34, $9.27

20 *Coordinates*

1. 
2. 
3. (0, 2)
4. (4,1)
5. 

6 - 11.

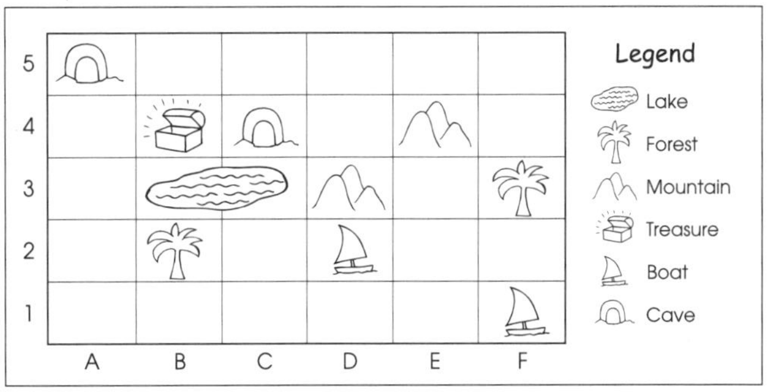

Activity

PIRATE

Final Test

1.

$ 4.99 × 5 = $ 24.95	$ 50.00 − $ 24.95 = $ 25.05

2.

$ 2.18 × 6 = $ 13.08	$ 20.00 − $ 13.08 = $ 6.92

3.

$ 3.29 × 7 = $ 23.03	$ 25.00 − $ 23.03 = $ 1.97

4.

$ 1.69 × 9 = $ 15.21	$ 50.00 − $ 15.21 = $ 34.79

5. 2.18 ÷ 2 = 1.09
   1.09
6. 3.29 ÷ 5 = 0.66
   0.66
7. 1.47
8. 7.75
9. 4.36
10. 13.75
11. 5.46
12. 15.2
13. 4.47
14. 52.5
15. 16
16. 38
17. 1.42
18. 34.96
19. >
20. <
21. =
22. =
23. <
24. >
25. 60 ÷ (6 x 5)
    2
26. (37 - 7) x 2
    60
27. 56 + 49 ÷ 7
    63
28. 56 ÷ 4
    14
29. $\frac{5}{12} + \frac{6}{12}$
    $\frac{11}{12}$
30. $\frac{10}{16} - \frac{7}{16}$
    $\frac{3}{16}$
31. $\frac{9}{25} + \frac{5}{25}$
    $\frac{14}{25}$
32. $\frac{11}{40} + \frac{15}{40}$
    $\frac{13}{20}$

33. $1\frac{2}{9} + 2\frac{3}{9}$

$3\frac{5}{9}$

34. $5\frac{10}{12} - 3\frac{1}{12}$

$2\frac{3}{4}$

35. $7\frac{9}{12} - 2\frac{5}{12}$

$5\frac{1}{3}$

36. $5\frac{8}{8} - 3\frac{5}{8}$

$2\frac{3}{8}$

37. $4\frac{9}{9} - 4\frac{8}{9}$

$\frac{1}{9}$

38. $2\frac{14}{20} + 5\frac{3}{20}$

$7\frac{17}{20}$

39. 4
40. 3
41. 6
42. 4
43. 8
44. 14
45. D, E
46. B, D, E, F
47. A
48. 72
49. 68
50. 23.4
51. 37.2
52. B
53. B
54. A
55. C
56. (2, 3); (5, 3)
57. (0,1)
58. Basketball court
59. Washroom
60. Snack bar
61. Fountain
62.

Week	1	2	3	4	5
Number of skiers	400	600	700	800	400
Number of Snowboarders	300	500	300	600	500

63. 4
64. 1 or 3
65. 5
66. 400

Unit 1

1. Clare has the most stickers. Two thousand seven hundred stickers.
2. Elaine has the fewest stickers. Nine hundred forty-five stickers.
3. No. of stickers : 2650 + 50 = 2700
   Clare has 50 stickers more than Doug.
4. No. of stickers : 2700 – 700 = 2000
   Emily has 700 stickers fewer than Clare.
5. No. of stickers : 2650 + 10 + 10 + 10 + 10 =2690
   He will have 2690 stickers.
6. No. of stickers : 945 – 100 – 100 – 100 = 645
   She will have 645 stickers.
7. Emily : 2000 $\xrightarrow{-100}$ 1900 $\xrightarrow{-100}$ 1800 $\xrightarrow{-100}$ 1700
   Megan : 1225 $\xrightarrow{+100}$ 1325 $\xrightarrow{+100}$ 1425 $\xrightarrow{+100}$ 1525
   Emily will have 1700 stickers; Megan will have 1525 stickers.
8. Gabe : 1245 $\xrightarrow{-5}$ 1240 $\xrightarrow{-5}$ 1235
   Megan : 1225 $\xrightarrow{+5}$ 1230 $\xrightarrow{+5}$ 1235
   It will take 2 weeks.
9. Doug : 2650 $\xrightarrow{+50}$ 2700 $\xrightarrow{+50}$ 2750 $\xrightarrow{+50}$ 2800 $\xrightarrow{+50}$ 2850
   Emily : 2000 $\xrightarrow{+10}$ 2010 $\xrightarrow{+10}$ 2020 $\xrightarrow{+10}$ 2030 $\xrightarrow{+10}$ 2040
   Doug will have 2850 stickers; Emily will have 2040 stickers.
10. No. of weeks :
    2000 $\xrightarrow{-400}$ 1600 $\xrightarrow{-400}$ 1200 $\xrightarrow{-400}$ 800 $\xrightarrow{-400}$ 400 $\xrightarrow{-400}$ 0
    It will take 5 weeks.

Challenge

No. of weeks	0	1	2	3	4	5
No. of stickers Penny has	30	36	42	48	54	60
No. of stickers Tanya has	35	40	45	50	55	60

It will take 5 weeks.

Unit 2

1. No. of marbles : 428 – 99 = 329
   He has about 300 marbles left.
2. No. of marbles : 214 + 183 = 397
   She has about 400 green and blue marbles altogether.
3. No. of marbles : 507 – 197 = 310
   She has about 300 marbles left .
4. No. of marbles : 89 + 280 = 369
   He has about 400 marbles altogether.
5. No. of marbles : 317 + 88 + 95 = 500
   He has 500 marbles.
6. Gabe and Jill have about 300 marbles in the end.
7. Distance travelled : 1425 + 876 = 2301 She travelled 2301 m.
8. Distance travelled : 328 + 829 = 1157 She travelled 1157 m.
9. Distance travelled : 515 + 372 + 686 = 1573
   She travelled 1573 m.
10. Distance travelled : 2301 + 1157 + 1573 = 5031
    She travelled 5031 m.
11. Difference : 1425 – 372 = 1053 She travelled 1053 m farther.
12. Difference : 686 – 328 = 358 She travelled 358 m farther.
13. Difference : 700 – 328 = 372
    She would have to travel 372 m farther.
14. Distance travelled : 829 + 288 = 1117 He travelled 1117 m.
15. Difference : 651 – 479 = 172 They collected 172 more cans.
16. Difference : 931 – 574 = 357 They collected 357 more cans.
17. No. of cans : 651 + 479 = 1130 They collected 1130 cans.
18. No. of cans : 394 + 503 = 897 They collected 897 cans.
19. No. of cans : 1823 + 795 = 2618 They collected 2618 cans.
20. No. of cans : 973 + 885 = 1858 They collected 1858 cans.
21. No. of cans : 574 + 931 = 1505 They collected 1505 cans.
22. C, D, E, A, B
23. Difference : 2618 – 897 = 1721
    Group C collected 1721 more cans than Group B.
24. Difference : 1505 – 1130 = 375
    Group E collected 375 more cans than Group A.
25. Difference : 1812 – 1567 = 245
    The difference in attendance was 245.
26. No. of people : 1812 + 1567 = 3379
    3379 people attended the two-day tournament.
27. No. of women : 1567 – 680 – 175 = 712
    There were 712 women.
28. Difference : 7812 – 6708 = 1104
    The difference in the ticket sales was 1104 dollars.

Challenge

1.

No. of blocks	1	10	100	1000
Weight (g)	100	1000	10000	100000

2. (10 blocks, 1000 g) ⟶ (20 blocks, 2000 g)
   There are 20 blocks.

Unit 3

1. No. of cobs of corn : 300 ÷ 5 = 60
   There are 60 cobs of corn.
2. No. of apples : 48 x 9 = 432 Gabe picks 432 apples.
3. No. of carrots : 163 x 3 = 489 Emily has 489 carrots.
4. No. of strawberries : 132 x 8 = 1056
   1056 strawberries are picked.
5. No. of apples : 135 x 6 = 810 Emily picks 810 apples.
6. No. of blueberries : 260 ÷ 4 = 65
   Each child would get 65 blueberries.
7. No. of apples : 328 ÷ 9 = 36...4 4 apples will be left over.
8. No. of carrots : 230 ÷ 8 = 28...6 6 carrots will not be tied up.
9. No. of tomatoes : 163 ÷ 6 = 27...1
   He picked 1 tomato from the last plant.
10. No. of cherries : 121 ÷ 5 = 24...1 1 cherry will be left over.
11. No. of peanuts : 207 ÷ 4 = 51...3
    3 peanuts will be left over.
12. No. of cherries : 320 ÷ 6 = 53...2
    2 cherries will be left over.
13. No. of onions : 315 ÷ 8 = 39...3 3 onions are left over.
14. No. of boxes : 124 ÷ 9 = 13...7 He needs 14 boxes.
15. No. of baskets : 156 ÷ 8 = 19...4 She needs 20 baskets.
16. No. of boxes : 215 ÷ 6 = 35...5 He needs 36 boxes.
17. No. of apples : 14 x 11 = 154 154 apples were picked.
18. No. of bags : 154 ÷ 7 = 22 22 bags are needed.
19. No. of strawberries : 45 x 13 = 585
    585 strawberries were picked.
20. No. of baskets : 585 ÷ 9 = 65 65 baskets are needed.
21. No. of peaches : 36 x 12 = 432 432 peaches were picked.
22. No. of students : 11 + 12 = 23
    No. of cherries : 36 x 23 = 828 828 cherries were picked.
23. No. of students : 13 + 12 = 25
    No. of blueberries : 48 x 25 = 1200
    1200 blueberries were picked.
24. No. of students : 11 + 13 = 24
    No. of raspberries : 85 x 24 = 2040
    2040 raspberries were picked.
25. Cost : 34 x 25 = 850 The total cost is 850¢ ($8.50).

26. No. of bags : 102 ÷ 4 = 25...2 25 bags can be bought.
27. Cost : 98 x 6 = 588 The cost is $588.00.
28. Cost : 34 x 5 = 170 (170< 173) Yes, it is.
29. Mass : 826 x 6 = 4956 The mass is 4956 grams.
30. Total cost : 100 – 37 = 63 Each bag costs : 63 ÷ 9 = 7
    Each bag costs $7.00.
31. Mass : 95 x 17 = 1615 The mass is 1615 grams.

Challenge

They earned : 38 x 4 = 152
No. of $5 bills : 152 ÷ 5 = 30...2
They were given 31 $5 bills., i.e. $155.
They would have to give back $3.00.

Unit 4

1. No. of marbles : 312 + 256 = 568
   There are 568 red or blue marbles.
2. No. of marbles : 250 ÷ 5 = 50
   Each person would get 50 green marbles.
3. No. of marbles : 113 x 6 = 678
   She will have 678 marbles.
4. No. of marbles : 446 – 176 = 270
   270 yellow marbles will be left.
5. No. of marbles : 224 ÷ 3 = 74...2
   Each bag will have 74 purple marbles.
   2 purple marbles will be left.
6. No. of marbles in 7 groups : 36 x 7 = 252
   Total no. of marbles : 252 + 4 = 256
   Emily took the jar of blue marbles.
7. No. of marbles in 4 shares : 62 x 4 = 248
   Total no. of marbles : 248 + 2 = 250
   Gabe took the jar of green marbles.
8. No. of marbles Gabe took : 65 x 6 = 390
   No. of marbles left : 446 – 390 = 56
   56 yellow marbles were left in the jar.
9. No. of marbles in 7 shares : 224 ÷ 7 = 32
   Each child got : 32 – 10 = 22 Each child got 22 marbles.
10. Total no. of marbles : 236 + 432 = 668
    No. of marbles in each share : 668 ÷ 4 = 167
    There were 167 marbles in each share.
11. No. of marbles : 300 – 30 = 270
    Each child got : 270 ÷ 5 = 54
    Each child got 54 white marbles.
12. No. of marbles in 8 bags : 56 x 8 = 448
    Total no. of marbles Emily had : 448 + 39 = 487
    Emily had 487 marbles.
13. No. of marbles in 6 bags : 72 x 6 = 432
    Total no. of marbles : 432 + 4 = 436
    Ray would have 436 marbles.
14. No. of marbles in 5 jars : 56 x 5 = 280
    No. of marbles in each jar : 280 ÷ 4 = 70
    There would be 70 marbles in each jar.
15. Difference : 3260 – 910 = 2350 The difference is 2350.
16. Difference : 5620 – 4700 = 920 The difference is 920.
17. Total score : 470 x 6 = 2820 His score would be 2820.
18. Ray's score : 2820 < 3260 No, he can't.
19. Total score : 830 x 7 = 5810 Her total score would be 5810.
20. Jane's score : 5810 > 5620 Yes, she can.
21. Total score : 63 x 15 = 945 Her total score would be 945.
22. No. of points : 972 ÷ 9 = 108 She got 108 points in 1 min.
23. No. of cherries : 234 ÷ 6 = 39 Each bird ate 39 cherries.
24. No. of birds : 32 x 6 = 192 There were 192 birds.
25. No. of birds : 233 + 69 = 302 There were 302 birds.
26. No. of cherries : 134 x 8 = 1072 They ate 1072 cherries.
27. No. of cherries : 108 + 156 = 264 It ate 264 cherries.
28. No. of cherries : 333 ÷ 9 = 37 It ate 37 cherries.
29. No. of cherries : 763 – 319 = 444
    There would be 444 cherries left over.
30. No. of cherries : 872 – 427 = 445
    There were 445 good cherries.

Challenge

Capacity of 6 bags of milk : 2 x 6 = 12
Milk 4 cats drink in a week : 1 x 4 = 4 Milk left : 12 – 4 = 8
No, it is not correct. Emily should have 8 L of milk left.

Unit 5

1. Total score : 1230 + 758 + 1080 + 980 = 4048
   Average : 4048 ÷ 4 = 1012
   Emily's average score is 1012.
2. Total score : 866 + 1008 + 982 + 520 = 3376
   Average : 3376 ÷ 4 = 844
   Joe's average score is 844.
3. Total score : 790 + 562 + 1682 + 858 = 3892
   Average : 3892 ÷ 4 = 973
   Peter's average score is 973.
4. Difference : 1012 – 844 = 168
   The difference is 168.
5. Difference : 1012 – 973 = 39
   The difference is 39.
6. Difference : 973 – 844 = 129
   The difference is 129.
7. Total : 200 x 4 = 800; no. of marbles in 4 jars is 800.
   Gabe's jars are A, B, C and D.
8. Total : 300 + 125 + 175 + 200 + 400 = 1200
   Average : 1200 ÷ 5 = 240
   The average number of marbles in each jar would be 240.
9. Total : 90 x 4 = 360; total amount in 4 piggy banks is 360¢.
   Wayne's piggy banks are B, C, D and E.
10. Total : 55 + 60 + 80 + 70 + 150 = 415
    Average : 415 ÷ 5 = 83
    The average amount in each piggy bank would be 83¢.

Challenge

1. Total score : 76 + 92 + 80 + 72 = 320
   Average : 320 ÷ 4 = 80 Her average score is 80.
2. Total score : 76 + 92 + 80 + 72 + 0 = 320
   Average : 320 ÷ 5 = 64 Her average score would be 64.

Unit 6

1. No. of classmates : 4 + 2 + 1 + 3 + 2 = 12
   Emily asked 12 classmates.
2. $\frac{4}{12}$ of her classmates prefer apples.
3. $\frac{1}{12}$ of her classmates prefer bananas.
4. $\frac{5}{12}$ of her classmates prefer oranges or grapes.
5. 10 students do not like oranges.
   $\frac{10}{12}$ of her classmates do not like oranges.
6. 8 classmates do not like bananas or grapes.
   $\frac{8}{12}$ of her classmates do not like bananas or grapes.
7. 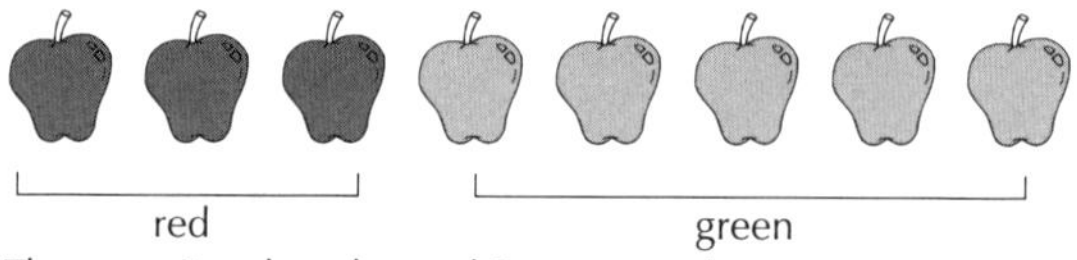

   There are 3 red apples and 5 green apples.
   $\frac{5}{8}$ of the apples are green.

8. 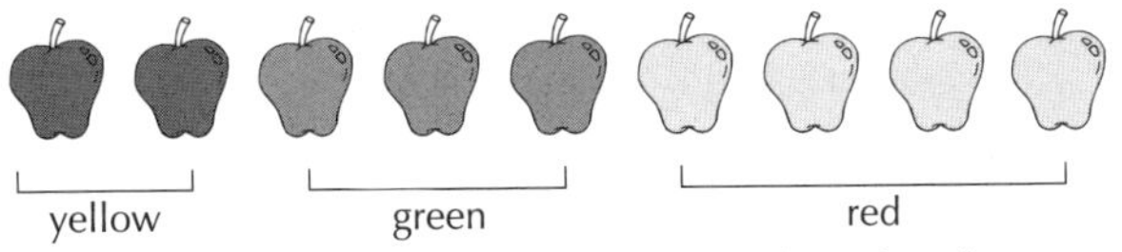

There are 2 yellow apples, 3 green apples and 4 red apples.

$\frac{4}{9}$ of the apples are red.

9. 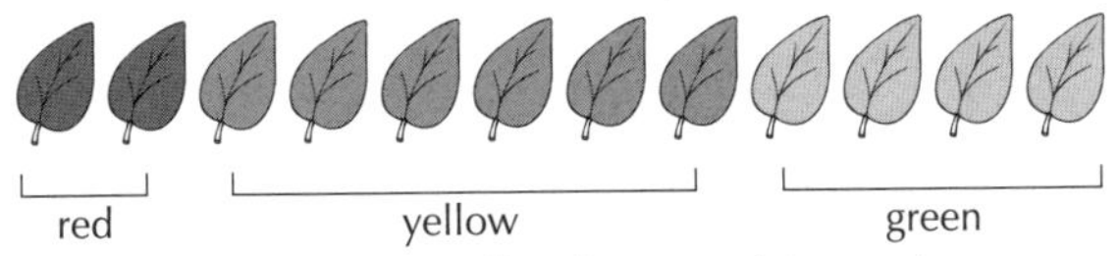

There are 2 red leaves, 6 yellow leaves and 4 green leaves.

$\frac{4}{12}$ of the leaves are green.

10. 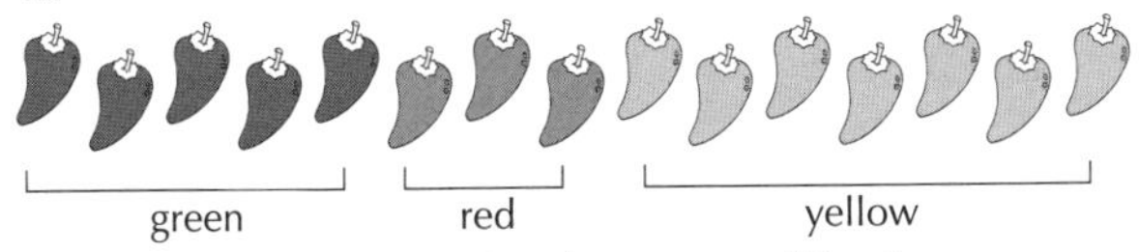

There are 5 green peppers, 3 red peppers and 7 yellow peppers.

$\frac{7}{15}$ of the peppers are yellow.

11. No. of slices eaten : 5 + 6 = 11
    11 slices were eaten.
12. $\frac{11}{24}$ of the Hawaiian pizza was eaten.
13. No. of slices eaten : 6 + 8 = 14
    $\frac{14}{24}$ of the pepporoni pizza was eaten.
14. No. of slices left over : 24 – 14 = 10
    $\frac{10}{24}$ of the pepperoni pizza was left over.
15. No. of slices : 24 + 24 = 48
    There were 48 slices of pizzas in all.
16. She ate 2 slices of pizzas in all.
17. Emily ate $\frac{2}{48}$ of the pizzas.
18. No. of slices : 1 + 2 = 3
    Michael ate $\frac{3}{48}$ of the pizzas.
19. No. of slices eaten : 5 + 6 + 6 + 8 = 25
    $\frac{25}{48}$ of the pizzas were eaten.
20. $2\frac{2}{8}$
21. $3\frac{2}{6}$
22. $2\frac{5}{8}$
23. $1\frac{3}{4}$
24. $3\frac{5}{6}$
25. Uncle Bob has more pizzas.
    $2\frac{5}{8}$ is greater than $2\frac{2}{8}$.
26. Uncle Tim has more pizzas.
    $3\frac{5}{6}$ is greater than $3\frac{2}{6}$.

Challenge

They are correct because $\frac{1}{2}$, $\frac{2}{4}$ and $\frac{4}{8}$ are equivalent fractions.

Midway Review

1. No. of apples : 24 x 36 = 864
   There were 864 apples in all.
2. No. of apples : 864 ÷ 3 = 288
   There were 288 apples in each group.
3. No. of apples : 39 x 5 = 195
   They sold 195 apples in all.
4. No. of apples : 38 x 6 = 228
   They sold 228 apples in all.
5. No. of apples Emily's group sold : 195 + 30 = 225
   No. of apples Doug's group sold : 228
   225 < 228
   No, she was wrong.
6. No. of apples : 252 ÷ 6 = 42
   Each child sold 42 apples.
7. Difference : 252 – 195 = 57
   Gabe's group sold 57 more apples than Emily's group.
8. No. of apples : 252 + 195 = 447
   They sold 447 apples in all.
9. 252 > 228 > 195 Gabe's group sold the most apples.
10. No. of apples : 252 + 228 + 195 = 675
    They sold 675 apples in all.
11. Average : 675 ÷ 3 = 225
    On average each group sold 225 apples.
12.

5	6	6
288	288	288
195	228	252
93	60	36
39	38	42

13. No. of apples left over : 93 + 60 + 36 = 189
    189 apples were left over in all.
14. $\frac{17}{40}$ of the apples sold were green.
15. No. of apples that were not green : 38 – 20 = 18
    $\frac{18}{38}$ of the apples Doug sold were not green.
16. Difference : 81 – 54 = 27
    Gabe's group collected $27.00 more than Emily's group.
17. Total amount : 54 + 63 + 81 = 198
    They collected $198.00 in all.
18. Average : 198 ÷ 3 = 66
    On average each group collected $66.00.
19. Container D holds the greatest amount.
    It holds one thousand two hundred sixty-four grams.
20. Total amount : 384 + 632 = 1016
    The total amount is 1016 g.
21. Difference : 1264 – 772 = 492
    D holds 492 g more than B.
22. Difference : 1264 – 952 = 312
    Container C holds 952 g less than D.
23. Try (A, C) : 384 + 312 = 696 ✗
    Try (A, E) : 384 + 460 = 844 ✗
    Try (C, E) : 312 + 460 = 772 ✓
    Containers C and E hold about the same amount as B.
24. Amount in D : 1264 ÷ 2 = 632
    Container F holds about half the amount in D.
25. Amount of lemonade mix in 1 container : 936 ÷ 3 = 312
    It was container C.
26. Try (A, B) : 384 + 772 = 1156 ✗
    Try (A, D) : 384 + 1264 = 1648 ✓
    They were containers A and D.
27. Total amount : 384 x 8 = 3072
    There were 3072 g of lemonade mix altogether.
28. A
29. C
30. D
31. B
32. B
33. A
34. C

Unit 7

1. Robert
2. Raymond was the last to finish the race.

3.

	Name
1st	Robert
2nd	Winston
3rd	George
4th	Ricky
5th	Raymond

4. He would be the third to finish the race.
5. He would be the fifth to finish the race.
6. Gabe is taller than Jason.
7. Emily is shorter than Sally.
8. Judy is shorter than Nicky but taller than Sally.
9. Jason is taller than Nicky but shorter than Gabe.
10. Gabe, Jason, Nicky, Judy, Sally, Emily
11. There are 2 children with a height above 1.23 m.
12. There are 2 children with a height below 1.10 m.
13. Yes, 1.2 is equal to 1.20 because the last zero after a decimal can be omitted.
14. No, 1.80 is different from 1.08.
    1.80 is near 2 while 1.08 is near 1.
15. C
16. F
17. E
18. D
19. A
20. B
21. Containers B, C, D and F have a capacity greater than 1.5 L.
22. Containers A, E and F have a capacity smaller than 2.15 L.
23. Containers C, D and F have a capacity greater than 1.5 L but smaller than 3.15 L.
24. Lisa, 10.6 min.
25. John, 10.8 min.
26. Albert, 11.2 min.
27. Peter, 15.8 min.
28. Sue, 20.4 min.
29. Larry, 21.4 min.
30. Jack, 22.6 min.

Challenge

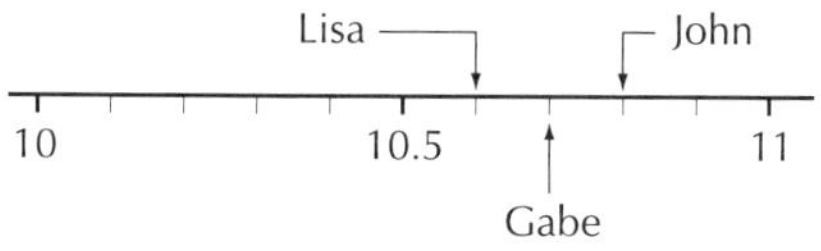

His time would be 10.7 min.

Unit 8

1. Time taken : 1.5 + 3.7 = 5.2; 5.2
2. Time taken : 1.3 + 2.5 = 3.8
   She practised for 3.8 hours.
3. Difference : 2.5 – 1.3 = 1.2
   She practised for 1.2 hours longer.
4. Total time : 1.45 + 1.37 + 1.61 = 4.43
   Her total time is 4.43 minutes.
5. Difference : 1.45 – 1.37 = 0.08
   The difference is 0.08 minute.
6. Best time : 1.62 – 0.4 = 1.22
   Her new best time is 1.22 minutes.
7. Judy's time : 80.1 – 6.3 = 73.8
   It was 73.8 seconds.
8. Distance : 1.68 + 1.07 = 2.75
   She swam 2.75 km in all.
9. Difference : 3.8 – 2.95 = 0.85
   She can swim 0.85 km farther than her friend.
10. Difference : 80.3 – 74.2 = 6.1
    She lost the race by 6.1 seconds.
11. Time taken : 89.7 – 42.9 = 46.8
    He took 46.8 seconds to swim the 2nd lap.
12. Time taken : 4.05 – 1.23 – 1.45 = 1.37
    She took 1.37 minutes to swim the 3rd lap.
13. Distance : 1.88 – 1.25 = 0.63
    The distance is 0.63 km.
14. Distance : 8.67 – 4.45 = 4.22
    The distance is 4.22 km.
15. Peterston to Ashmorly : 4.45 – 2.59 = 1.86
    Shelby to Peterston : 6.48 – 4.45 = 2.03
    Ashmorly is closer to Peterston.
16. Shelby to Peterston : 6.48 – 4.45 = 2.03
    Jacob to Shelby : 8.67 – 6.48 = 2.19
    Peterston is closer to Shelby.
17. Ashmorly to Jonesville : 2.59 – 1.88 = 0.71
    Peterston to Ashmorly : 4.45 – 2.59 = 1.86
    The distance from Jonesville to the nearest station is 0.71 km.
18. Distance travelled : 1.25 + 1.25 = 2.50
    She travels 2.5 km a day.
19. Distance : 1.25 + 3.2 = 4.45
    She arrived at Peterston.
20. Distance : 4.45 – 2.57 = 1.88
    She arrived at Jonesville.
21. Distance : 1.88 – 1.25 = 0.63
    Jonesville and Littleton are closest to each other.
22. Fares : 1.86 + 1.86 + 0.95 = 4.67
    Their fares would be $4.67.
23. Difference : 4.67 – 3.19 = 1.48
    He would need $1.48 more.
24. Difference : 1.86 – 1.28 = 0.58
    He needs to pay $0.58 more.
25. Fares : 1.86 + 1.86 + 0.95 + 0.95 + 0.95 = 6.57
    Money saved : 6.57 – 5.80 = 0.77
    They would save $0.77.
26. Fares : 0.95 + 0.95 + 0.95 = 2.85
    Their fares would be $2.85.

Challenge

Uncle Sam should buy 1 senior ticket, 3 adult tickets and 1 child ticket. Fares : 0.95 + 1.86 + 1.86 + 1.86 + 0.95 = 7.48
Uncle Sam should pay $7.48.

Unit 9

1. D
2. Bag C weighs 0.7 kg.
3. Bag I weighs 0.1 kg.
4. Bag H weighs ten-tenths of a kilogram.
5. Bag J weighs nine-tenths of a kilogram.
6. Bag A weighs four-tenths of a kilogram.
7.

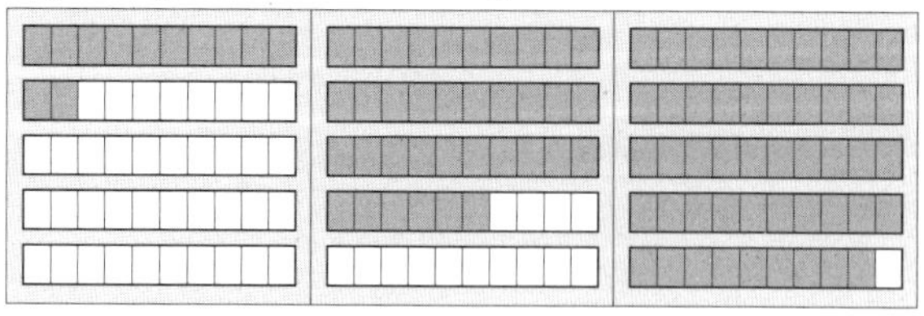

8. ($1.2 = 1\frac{2}{10}$); She sold $1\frac{2}{10}$ boxes of cookies.
9. ($3.6 = 3\frac{6}{10}$); He sold $3\frac{6}{10}$ boxes of cookies.
10. ($4.9 = 4\frac{9}{10}$); He sold $4\frac{9}{10}$ boxes of cookies.
11. Cookies that are not chocolate flavour : 1 – 0.3 = 0.7, ($0.7 = \frac{7}{10}$);
    $\frac{7}{10}$ of a box of cookies is not chocolate flavour.
12. ($\frac{4}{5} = 0.8$); 0.8 of her allowance was saved.
13. ($\frac{3}{4} = 0.75$); 0.75 of his pie was eaten.
14. ($\frac{12}{25} = 0.48$); He drank 0.48 of a glass of water.
15. ($\frac{13}{20} = 0.65$); She spent 0.65 of a lesson on classwork.

16. ($\frac{9}{12}$ = 0.75); 0.75 of a box of eggs was eaten.
17. ($\frac{32}{50}$ = 0.64); 0.64 of a box of chocolates is left over.
18. ($\frac{16}{20}$ = 0.8); 0.8 of a bag of buns was eaten.
19. ($\frac{3}{15}$ = 0.2); 0.2 of a box of cupcakes is left over.
20. One and three-tenths
21. One-tenths
22. One and five-tenths
23. Seven-tenths
24. Two-tenths
25. One and four-tenths
26. One and eight-tenths

Challenge

1. $\frac{17}{20}$ = 0.85, 0.85 > 0.68
   Emily has more chocolates.
2. $1\frac{1}{5}$ = 1.20, 1.20 < 1.25
   Elaine has more pencils.

Unit 10

1. 10, 15, 20, 25, 30; 35¢
2. 4, 6, 8, 10, 12
   He collected 14 stickers in the 7th week.
3. 9, 11, 13 , 15, 17
   He bought 21 marbles in the 8th week.
4. 3, 5, 8, 12, 17, 23
   She would see 23 birds on Saturday.
5. 80, 70, 60, 50, 40
   She had 30 pencils after 7 weeks.
6. 8, 12, 16, 20, 24
   8 nickels weigh 32 grams.
7. 10, 15, 21
   28 blocks are needed for 7 layers.
8. 20, 25, 30, 35, 40
   He took 165 seconds to complete the race.
9. a.
   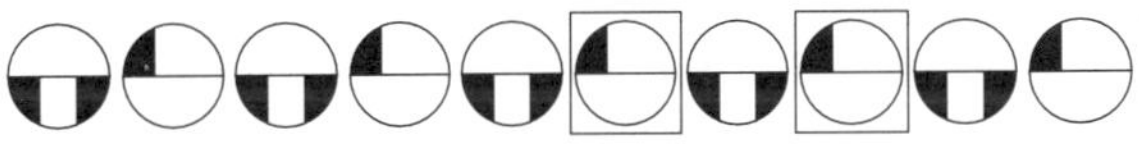
   b. size; shape
10. a.

   b. All the figures have the same pattern and orientation.
11. a.
   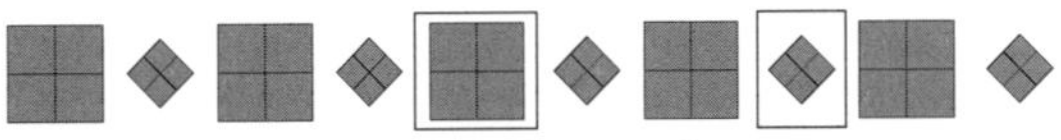
   b. All the figures have the same shape and pattern.
12. a.

   b. All the figures have the same shape and pattern.
13. a.
   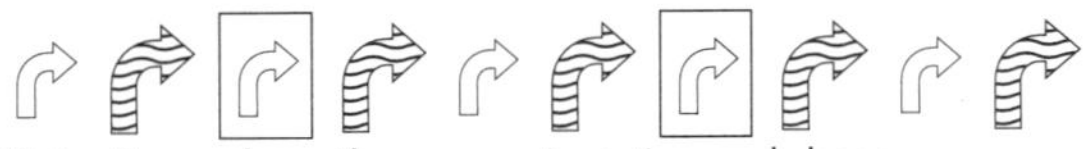
   b. All the figures have the same orientation and shape.
14. Sept. 7, Sept. 10, Sept. 13
15. The 8th time that she walks her dog in Sept. is on Sept. 22.
16. Sept. 9, Sept. 16, Sept. 23, Sept. 30
17. The first time that she plays basketball in Oct. is on Oct. 7.

Challenge

	Mon	Tue	Wed	Thu
No. of candies bought	10	12	14	16
No. of candies eaten	3	6	9	12

She would buy 16 candies and eat 12 on Thursday.

Unit 11

1. 15 – ? = 9
   Emily hid 6 marbles.
   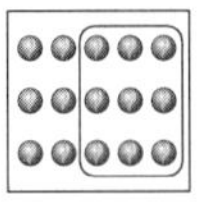
2. 20 – ? = 12
   Gabe hid 8 marbles.
   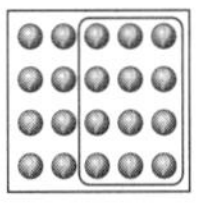
3. 9 + ? = 12
   Emily had 3 marbles.
   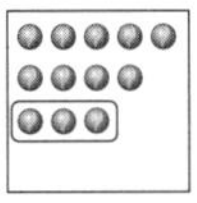
4. 12 + ? = 18
   Gabe had 6 marbles.
   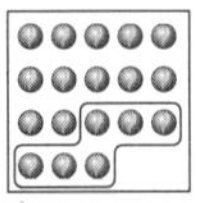
5. 9 + ? = 15
   Gabe needs 6 pencils.
6. 20 – ? = 15
   Emily gave 5 pencils to Gabe.
7. ? – 6 = 8
   Gabe had 14 candies to start with.
8. ? + 8 = 21
   David had 13 candies to start with.
9. 27 – ? = 19
   Emily ate 8 candies.
10. 16 + ? = 45
    The cost of a pencil is 29¢.
11. 16 – ? = 5
    The cost of a candy is 11¢.
12. 50 – ? = 21
    A candy costs 29¢.
13. ? – 67 = 8
    He paid 75¢.
14. ? – 12 = 29
    He had 41 candies to start with.
15. ? + 5 = 63
    David has 58 stickers.
16. ? – 39 = 36
    Gabe has 75¢.
17. 3 + 4 + 8 = 15
    The sum is 15.
18. 12 – 9 = 3
    The difference is 3.
19. 15 + 3 + 9 + 4 = 31
    The sum is 31.
20. 15 – 8 = 7
    It is 7 more.
21. 12 + 8 – 15 = 5
    It is 5 more.
22. 3 + 15 – 12 = 6
    It is 6 more.
23. 4 + ? = 3 + 9, 4 + ? = 12
    The number is 8.
24. 8 + ? = 4 + 9, 8 + ? = 13
    The number is 5.
25. 9 – ? = 3 + 4, 9 – ? = 7
    The number is 2.
26. 128; 29
27. 125; 32
28. 133; 29
29. 135; 31
30. 125.5; 31

Challenge

No. of chocolates before Reston shared with Jane : 4 x 2 = 8
Reston's share before his friends each gave him 1 chocolate :
8 – 5 = 3
No. of chocolates in the box : 3 x 6 = 18
Reston had 18 chocolates at the beginning.

Final Review

1. There are 12 blocks, 3 having a letter A.
   $\frac{3}{12}$ of the blocks have a letter A.
2. ($\frac{3}{12}$ = 0.25); Twenty-five hundredths of the blocks have a letter A.
3. Height : 1.5 x 3 = 4.5
   The tower will be 4.5 cm tall.
4. There are 6 blocks with B and C.
   She uses $\frac{6}{12}$ of the blocks from the first tower.
5. Height : 1.5 x 6 = 9
   It is 9 cm tall.
6.

No. of towers	1	2	3	4	5	6	7
No. of blocks	7	14	21	28	35	42	49

7.

No. of towers	7	8	9	10	11
No. of blocks	49	56	63	70	77

He needs 77 blocks.

8.

No. of stacked-up towers	1	2	3	4	5	6	7
Height of new tower (cm)	10.5	21	31.5	42.0	52.5	63.0	73.5

9.

No. of stacked-up towers	7	8	9
Height of new tower (cm)	73.5	84.0	94.5

He needs 9 7-block towers.

10. Suggested answer : No. It will fall easily.
11. Weight : 14 x 65 = 910
    It will weigh 910 grams.
12. No. of blocks : 952 ÷ 4 = 238
    Each child will get 238 blocks.
13. ($\frac{4}{5}$ = 0.8); 0.8 of a bag of blocks is red.
14. Time taken : 2.45 + 3.16 = 5.61
    She took 5.61 minutes to build the two towers.
15. Difference : 3.16 – 2.45 = 0.71
    She needed 0.71 minutes more to build the second tower than the first one.
16. No. of blocks left : 1500 – 623 = 877
    877 blocks were left.
17.

No. of piles	1	2	3	4
No. of blocks	200	400	600	800

18. She got 4 piles in maximum.
19. No. of blocks left : 877 – 800 = 77
    77 blocks were left.
20. No. of blocks : 375 x 3 = 1125
    He needed 1125 blocks.
21. No. of blocks left : 1500 – 1125 = 375
    Yes. He had enough blocks.
22. James used more blocks because $\frac{7}{15}$ is greater than $\frac{4}{15}$.
23. $\frac{4}{10} > \frac{3}{10} > \frac{2}{10} > \frac{1}{10}$
    Green, yellow, red, blue
24. No. of blocks left : 25 – 7 = 18
    $\frac{18}{25}$ of the blocks were left.
25. Height of a 32-block tower = height of 2 16-block towers

No. of 16-block towers	1	2
Height (m)	0.16	0.32

It will be 0.32 m tall.

26.

No. of 16-block towers	1	2	3	4
Height (m)	0.16	0.32	0.48	0.64

4 16-block towers are needed.

27. 6, 8, 10
28. 3, 4, 5
29. 15, 20, 25
30. 9, 12, 15
31. 22, 33, 44, 55
32.

No. of blocks	5	6	7	8
Total no. of stickers	55	66	77	88

There would be 8 blocks with stickers.

33. No. of stickers : 11 x 9 = 99
    She would need 99 stickers.
34. 1 + ? = 7
    She would need 6 more stickers.
35. They are the same in size and shape.
36. Total amount : 15 x 11 = 165
    She will pay 165¢ ($1.65) for the stickers on 1 block.
37. Total amount : 165 x 3 = 495
    She will pay 495¢ ($4.95) for the stickers on 3 blocks.
38. C
39. C
40. D
41. B
42. A
43. B
44. C

RISING majestically from Egypt's Giza plateau is one of the most breathtaking sights on earth: three tremendous pyramids of stone, their monolithic angles standing in stark contrast to the modern jumble of nearby Cairo. Though deprived of the limestone casings that once made them brilliantly radiant in the sun, the pyramids and their smaller satellites at Giza still present an awesome vision. They were built over four thousand years ago to house the remains of kings who hoped to reign in the afterlife. And they are the most recognizable icons of ancient engineering in the world.

The greatest of the three, built for the pharaoh Khufu and known as the Great Pyramid, was the tallest building in the world until well into the Middle Ages. By almost any standard, it remains—after forty-five centuries—an architectural marvel. Some 2,300,000 blocks of stone were used to build Khufu's colossal tomb, ranging anywhere from fifteen tons to a couple of tons in weight. Its four sides slope upward at an angle of 51°50', meeting at a point 481 feet high. Perhaps most stunning of all, the Great Pyramid, like its companions, is very nearly perfect in its cardinality, deviating imperceptibly from true north.

More wonders lie within. If the ancient Egyptians built on a grand scale, they also built with ingenious sophistication. The pyramid—called *Akhet Khufu* or "Horizon of Khufu," by its builders—houses a suite of spaces whose precision and tolerances inspire awe even today. The Grand Gallery, reached by an ascending chamber, features a magnificently corbeled arch that culminates twenty-six feet above the floor with a ceiling made of titanic stone slabs. It gives onto an antechamber and, ultimately, onto the King's Chamber itself, within which Khufu's mummy was laid in its granite sarcophagus. This room was protected from the crushing weight of the pyramid above by a series of stress-relieving chambers topped by a cantilevered roof, one of the most brilliant architectural accomplishments in the whole structure.

In its heyday, during the third millennium BC, the Horizon of Khufu was the centerpiece of its own elegant, carefully laid-out mortuary complex. Surrounding the Great Pyramid itself was an enclosure made of limestone, twenty-six feet high, on the east wall of which stood a mortuary temple—the terminus of a long causeway that served as the sole means of entering the complex. Nearby, four diminutive pyramids stood at the foot of their immense master: a series of three tombs built for queens of Khufu's era and, just behind them, an even smaller "satellite pyramid," whose purpose remains a matter of conjecture. Low-lying mastabas—the tombs of family and nobility—spread out in rows from the queens' pyramids.

Previous page: Open papyrus campaniform capital from the Temple of Karnak.

Unit 1

1. cm 2. dm 3. km 4. m 5. mm
6. 1 cm = 10 mm ⟶ 15 cm = 150 mm 150 mm
7. 1dm = 10 cm ⟶ 3 dm = 30 cm It is 30 cm wide.
8. 10 cm = 1 dm ⟶ 80 cm = 8 dm It is 8 dm high.
9. 10 mm = 1 cm ⟶ 70 mm = 7 cm It is 7 cm long.
10. 1 km = 1000 m It is 1000 m across.
11. 1 cm = 10 mm ⟶ 135 cm = 1350 mm He is 1350 mm tall.
12. 1 m = 10 dm ⟶ 12 m = 120 dm It is 120 dm away from her.
13. 100 mm = 10 cm = 1 dm ⟶ 200 mm = 20 cm = 2dm
    It is 2 dm tall.
14. Red house : 8 m = 80 dm Yellow house : 750 cm = 75 dm
    Difference : 80 – 75 = 5 The red house is 5 dm taller.
15. 10 dm = 1 m ⟶ 300 dm = 30 m Height : 120 + 30 = 150
    It is 150 m above ground.
16. White dog : 120 m = 12000 cm Black dog : 1300 dm = 13000 cm
    Difference : 13000 – 12000 = 1000
    The black dog runs 1000 cm farther.
17. 1000 m = 1 km ⟶ 3000 m = 3 km Length : 15 – 3 = 12
    The shorter trail is 12 km.
18. 10 mm = 1 cm ⟶ 20 mm = 2 cm Length : 15 + 2 = 17
    It is 17 cm long.

Challenge

Length of each sheet of paper in cm : 112 ÷ 4 = 28
Length of 75 sheets of paper in cm : 28 x 75 = 2100
2100 cm = 210 dm = 21 m
The line will be 2100 cm or 210 dm or 21 m long.

Unit 2

1. Aug 28 (noon) – Aug 31 (noon): 3 days Aug 31 (noon) – Sep 22 (noon): 22 days Total no. of days : 3 + 22 = 25 25
2. Time taken : 7 h 28 min – 2 h 10 min = 5 h 18 min
   The flight took 5 h and 18 min.
3. (1 h = 60 min; $\frac{1}{4}$ h = 15 min) Time taken : 60 + 15 = 75
   They stayed in the park for 75 minutes.
4. Time : 7 h 45 min + 20 min + 75 min = 9 h 20 min
   They returned home at 9:20 a.m.
5. ($\frac{3}{4}$h = 45 min) Time taken : 45 x 7 = 315
   She needed 315 minutes in a week.
6. Time taken : 7 h 10 min – 7 h 0 min = 10 min
   Irene gets dressed 10 minutes after she wakes up.
7. Time : 7 h 0 min + 6 min = 7 h 6 min
   She gets out of bed at 7:06 a.m.
8. Time taken : 8 h 35 min – 8 h 0 min = 35 min
   She spends 35 minutes on the school bus.
9. Time : 8 h 30 min + 35 min = 9 h 5 min (9:05 a.m.)
   Yes, she will be 5 minutes late.
10. Time taken : 10 h 0 min – 9 h 35 min = 25 min
    Her French class takes 25 minutes.
11. Time : 8 h 0 min – 8 min = 7 h 52 min
    She leaves home at 7:52 a.m.

Challenge

Time for lunch : 10 h 0 min + 1 h 45 min = 11 h 45 min
Duration : 11 h 45 min – 7 h 30 min = 4 h 15 min
She has 4 h 15 min between breakfast and lunch.

Unit 3

1. No. of dollars : 1 No. of cents : 25 + 10 x 2 = 45
   Total cost : 1 + 0.45 = 1.45 'Jumping In and Out'
2. No. of dollars : 5 x 2 = 10 No. of cents : 25 + 10 x 2 = 45
   Total cost : 10 + 0.45 = 10.45 He ordered 'Bugs, Bees & Beetles'.
3. No. of dollars : 5 + 2 = 7 No. of cents : 10 x 5 = 50
   Total cost : 7 + 0.5 = 7.5 He ordered 'It's Raining Fish'.
4. No. of dollars : 2 x 2 = 4 No. of cents : 25 x 3 + 10 x 2 + 1 x 4 = 99
   Total cost : 4 + 0.99 = 4.99 She ordered 'The Purple Monster'.
5. No. of dollars : 10 + 2 + 1 = 13 No. of cents : 5 x 4 = 20
   Total cost : 13 + 0.2 = 13.2 He ordered 'How To... Hair Pins'.
6. No. of dollars : 2 x 2 + 1 = 5 No. of cents : 25
   Total cost : 5 + 0.25 = 5.25 She ordered 'Sam, Not Again!'.
7. No. of dollars : 10 + 1 x 3 = 13 No. of cents : 25 x 3 + 10 + 1 x 2 = 87
   Total cost : 13 + 0.87 = 13.87
   His order was 'Stamp Collecting Manual'.
8. No. of dollars : 5 x 2 + 2 = 12 No. of cents : 10 x 3 + 5 + 1= 36
   Total cost : 12 + 0.36 = 12.36 His order was 'How Fast is Fast?'.

	$20	$10	$5	$2	$1	25¢	10¢	5¢	1¢
9.	1					1		1	4
10.		1	1	1	1		1	1	2
11.		1		1		2	2		3
12.			1	1	1	1	2		3
13.		1			1	1	1		1
14.	1	1		1		1	1	1	
15.	2				1	2	2		

16. Change : 10 – 5.73 = 4.27
    $4.27 = 2 twoonies + 1 quarter + 2 pennies
    The change was $4.27 (2 twoonies, 1 quarter, 2 pennies).
17. Change : 15 – 11.35 = 3.65
    $3.65 = 1 twoonie + 1 loonie + 2 quarters + 1 dime + 1 nickel
    The change was $3.65 (1 twoonie, 1 loonie, 2 quarters, 1 dime, 1 nickel).
18. Change : 20 – 18.43 = 1.57
    $1.57 = 1 loonie + 2 quarters + 1 nickel + 2 pennies
    The change was $1.57 (1 loonie, 2 quarters, 1 nickel, 2 pennies).
19. Change : 23 – 22.14 = 0.86
    $0.86 = 3 quarters + 1 dime + 1 penny
    The change was $0.86 (3 quarters, 1 dime, 1 penny).
20. Change : 30 – 21.15 = 8.85
    $8.85 = 1 $5 bill + 1 twoonie + 1 loonie + 3 quarters + 1 dime
    The change was $8.85 (1 $5 bill, 1 twoonie, 1 loonie, 3 quarters, 1 dime).
21. Change : 20 – 12.88 = 7.12
    $7.12 = 1 $5 bill + 1 twoonie + 1 dime + 2 pennies
    The change was $7.12 (1 $5 bill, 1 twoonie, 1 dime, 2 pennies).
22. Change : 10 – 4.71 = 5.29
    $5.29 = 1 $5 bill + 1 quarter + 4 pennies
    The change was $5.29 (1 $5 bill, 1 quarter, 4 pennies).
23. Change : 15 – 13.82 = 1.18
    $1.18 = 1 loonie + 1 dime + 1 nickel + 3 pennies
    The change was $1.18 (1 loonie, 1 dime, 1 nickel, 3 pennies).
24. Cost : 1.47 + 1.47 = 2.94 He paid $2.94.
25. Cost : 3.99 + 1.25 = 5.24 She paid $5.24.
26. Cost : 2.75 + 3.99 + 4.16 = 10.9 She paid $10.90.
27. Cost : 2.6 + 2.6 + 2.6 = 7.8 She paid $7.80.
28. Cost : 3.74 + 4.19 + 0.81 = 8.74 He paid $8.74.
29. Cost : 21.32 + 2.6 = 23.92 He paid $23.92.
30. Amount given : 5.72 + 3.69 + 2.15 + 4.3 + 0.14 = 16
    He gave the cashier $16.00.

Challenge

Cost of 1 poster : 2.25 Cost of 10 posters : 2.25 x 10 = 22.5
Cost of 11 posters : 22.5 + 2.25 = 24.75
Cost of 12 posters : 24.75 + 2.25 = 27 (27 > 25)
Jennie can buy 11 posters.

Unit 4

1. Perimeter : 3 + 1 + 1 + 2 + 1 + 2 + 1 + 1 = 12   12 cm
2. Perimeter : 2 + 2 + 2 + 2 + 2 + 2 = 12   Its perimeter is 12 cm.
3. Perimeter : 5 + 4 + 3 = 12   Its perimeter is 12 cm.
4. Perimeter : 2.5 + 2 + 3 + 2 + 2.5 = 12   Its perimeter is 12 cm.
5. Perimeter : 1 + 5 + 1 + 5 + 1 + 2 + 2 = 17   Its perimeter is 17 cm.
6. Perimeter : 2 + 1.5 + 2 + 1.5 + 2 + 3.5 + 6 + 3.5 = 22
   Its perimeter is 22 cm.
7. Perimeter : 30 + 20 + 30 + 20 = 100   Its perimeter is 100 cm.
8. Perimeter : 60 + 60 + 60 + 60 = 240   Its perimeter is 240 cm.
9. Perimeter : 36 + 36 + 24 = 96   Its perimeter is 96 cm.
10. Perimeter : 8 + 6 + 8 + 6 = 28   The perimeter is 28 m.
11. Perimeter : 3 + 1.2 + 3 + 1.2 = 8.4   The perimeter is 8.4 m.
12. Perimeter in dm : 9 + 16 + 9 + 16 = 50
    10 dm = 1 m ⟶ 50 dm = 5 m   The perimeter is 5 m.
13. Length : 350 ÷ 5 = 70   The length of each side is 70 cm.
14.
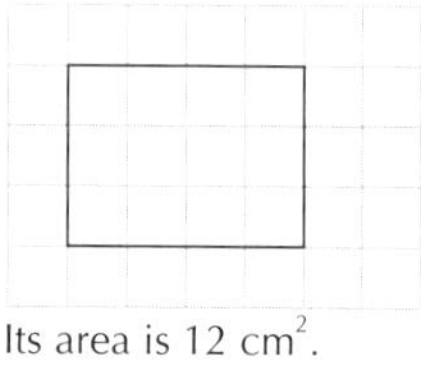
Its area is 12 cm^2.
15.
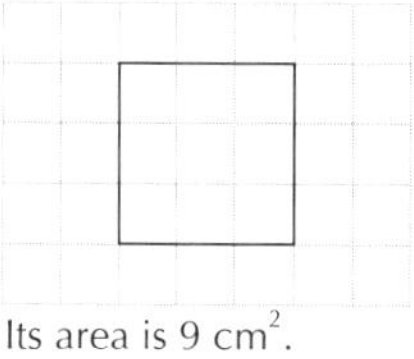
Its area is 9 cm^2.
16.
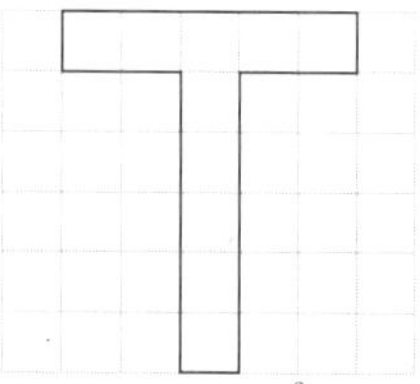
Its area is 10 cm^2.
17.
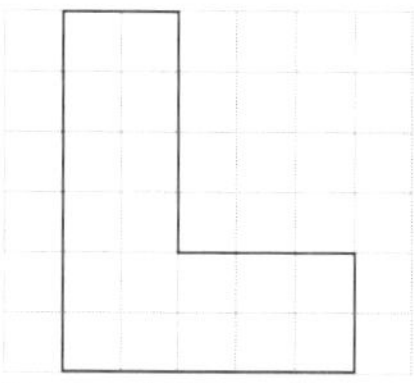
Its area is 18 cm^2.
18. Magnets C and D have the same perimeter of 22 cm, but the area of magnet D is 8 cm^2 larger than that of magnet C.
19.
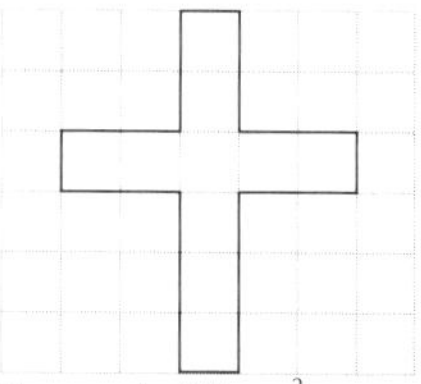
Its area is 10 cm^2.
20.
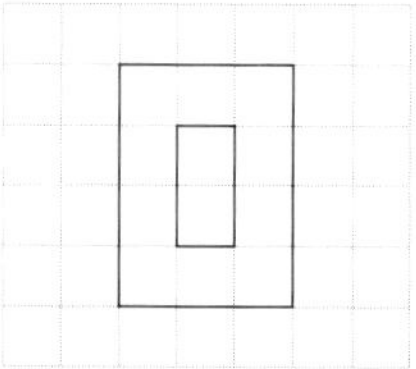
Its area is 10 cm^2.
21. Magnets E and F have the same area of 10 cm^2, but the perimeter of magnet E is 2 cm longer than that of magnet F.
22. There are 13 completely covered squares and 8 mostly covered squares.   Total area : 13 + 8 = 21   The area is about 21 cm^2.
23. There are 13 completely covered squares and 10 mostly covered squares.   Total area : 13 + 10 = 23   The area is about 23 cm^2.
24. There are 10 completely covered squares and 8 mostly covered squares.   Total area : 10 + 8 = 18   The area is about 18 cm^2.
25. There are 4 completely coverd squares and 14 mostly covered squares.   Total area : 4 + 14 = 18   The area is about 18 cm^2.
26. a. Area : 2 x 1 = 2   The area is 2 m^2.
    b. Space left : 12 – 2 = 10   10 m^2 of space is left.
27. Length of fencing : (4 + 4 + 3 + 3) – 12 = 2
    2 m more fencing is needed.
28. Difference : (4 x 3) – (5 x 2) = 2   There will be a difference of 2 m^2 in area.
29. a–b
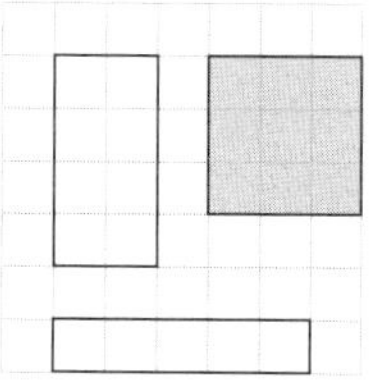

    c. Irene got the biggest area by making a square with the 12-m fence.

Challenge

Suggested answer:

Length (m)	Width (m)	Perimeter (m)
20	10	60 ✗
16	8	48 ✗
14	7	42 ✓

The length is 14 m and the width is 7 m.

Unit 5

1. mL   2. L   3. kg   4. m^3 5. g   6. cm^3 7. mL
8. There are 4 layers of 12 blocks.   Volume : 1 x 12 x 4 = 48
   The volume is 48 cm^3.
9. There are 1 layer of 25 blocks, 1 layer of 9 blocks and 1 layer of 1 block.   Volume : 1 x 25 + 1 x 9 + 1 x 1 = 35   The volume is 35 cm^3.
10. There are 4 layers of 12 blocks and 4 layers of 4 blocks.
    Volume : 1 x 12 x 4 + 1 x 4 x 4 = 64   The volume is 64 cm^3.
11. There are 1 layer of 9 blocks, 1 layer of 4 blocks and 1 layer of 1 block.   Volume : 1 x 9 +1 x 4 + 1 x 1 = 14   The volume is 14 cm^3.
12. (1 L = 1000 mL) Capacity : 1000 ÷ 4 = 250
    The capacity of each glass is 250 mL.
13. Capacity : 250 x 20 = 5000   (5000 mL = 5 L)
    The capacity of the bucket is 5 L.
14. Capacity : 250 ÷ 5 = 50   The capacity of each egg cup is 50 mL.
15. (250 mL = 0.25 L)   Capacity : 5 + 0.25 x 10 = 7.5
    The capacity is 7.5 L.
16. Capacity : 1 ÷ 2 = 0.5   The capacity is 0.5 L (500 mL).
17. (1 L = 1000 mL)   Capacity : 1000 ÷ 5 = 200
    The capacity is 200 mL.
18. 1 glass holds 250 mL of water ; a tub holds 250 L of water.
    No. of glasses of water needed : (250 x 1000) ÷ 250 = 1000
    1000 glasses of water are needed.
19. Mass (four 21-g bags) : 21 x 4 = 84 (84 > 80)
    Four 21-g bags would give her more cookies.
20. Mass (3 little bags) : 43 x 3 = 129 (129 < 150)
    One big bag would give him more candies.
21. Mass (sixteen 50-g packets) : 50 x 16 = 800
    Mass (five 165-g packets) : 165 x 5 = 825 (825 > 800)
    Five 165-g packets have more potato chips.
22. Mass : 1 x 2 = 2   The mass is 2 kg.
23. Mass : 2 x 3 = 6   The mass is 6 kg.
24. Mass : 6 x 2 = 12   The mass is 12 kg.
25. Mass : 12 x 4 = 48   The mass is 48 kg.
26. No. of rabbits : 48 ÷ 1 = 48   48 rabbits would be needed.
27. No. of rabbits : (2 x 2 + 6) ÷ 1 = 10   10 rabbits would be needed.
28. No. of dogs : 48 ÷ 6 = 8   8 dogs would be needed.
29. No. of cats : 48 ÷ 2 = 24   24 cats would be needed.
30. Mass of the cats : 48 – 6 x 6 = 12   No. of cats : 12 ÷ 2 = 6
    6 cats must be added.
31. Mass (6 cats) : 2 x 6 = 12   Mass (1 pig) : 12
    Both sides will weigh the same.
32. Mass (1 calf) : 48   Mass (6 dogs and 4 cats) : 6 x 6 + 2 x 4 = 44
    (44 ≠ 48)   No, it is impossible because a calf is heavier than 6 dogs and 4 cats together.

Challenge

Suggested answer:

Ben's mass (kg)	Tim's mass (kg)	John's mass (kg)
30	24	54 ✗
29	23	52 ✗
28	22	50 ✓

The mass of Tim is 22 kg.

Unit 6

1. a. They have 4 right angles and their opposite sides are equal.
   b. 3 shapes are not quadrilaterals because they do not have 4 straight sides.

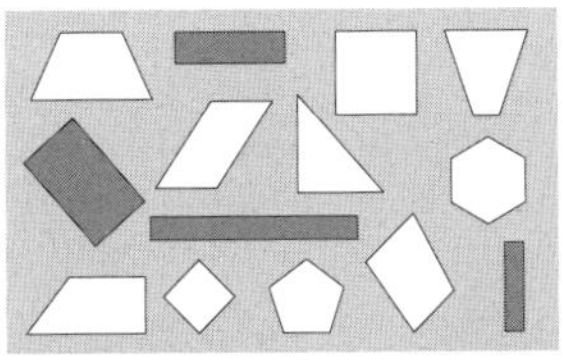

2. No, it is not. It has 5 sides but one of its sides is not straight.

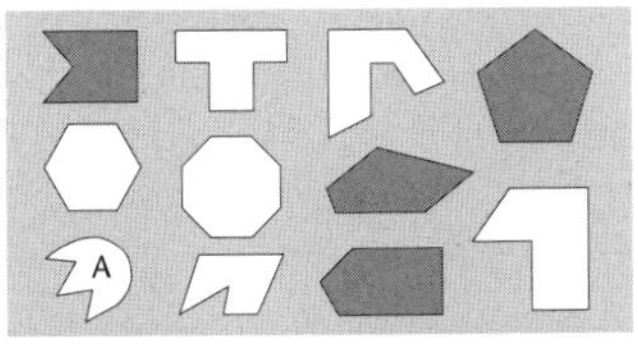

3. They have 6 straight sides.

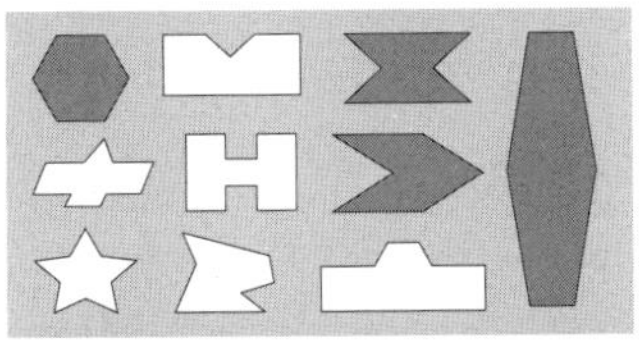

4. Both a rhombus and a parallelogram have 2 pairs of parallel lines with no right angles. A rhombus has 4 equal sides and a parallelogram has opposite sides equal.

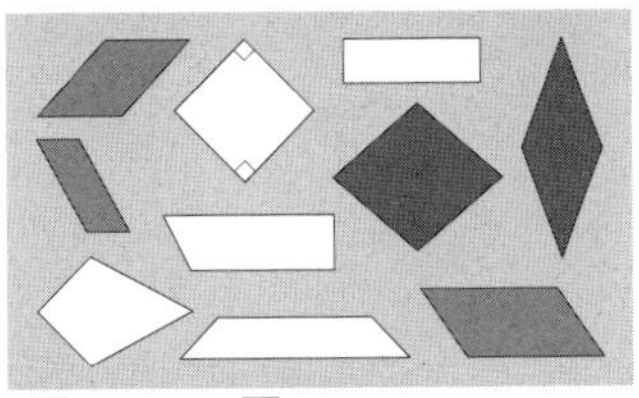

blue brown

5. It is a rectangle.
6. It is a rhombus.
7. It is a pentagon.
8. It is a regular hexagon.
9. They are triangles.
10. It is a square.
11. It is a parallelogram.
12. It is a regular octagon.
13. It is a prism.
14. It is a pyramid.
15. It is a cube.
16. It looks like a cone.
17. It is a cylinder.
18. It is a sphere.
19. It is a triangular prism.
20. It is a tetrahedron.
21.

Number of faces	Number of curved surfaces	Number of straight edges	Number of vertices
2	1	0	0
6	0	12	8
6	0	12	8
0	1	0	0
1	1	0	1
5	0	8	5
5	0	9	6
4	0	6	4

Challenge

It is a triangular prism. It is a hexagonal pyramid.

Midway Review

1.

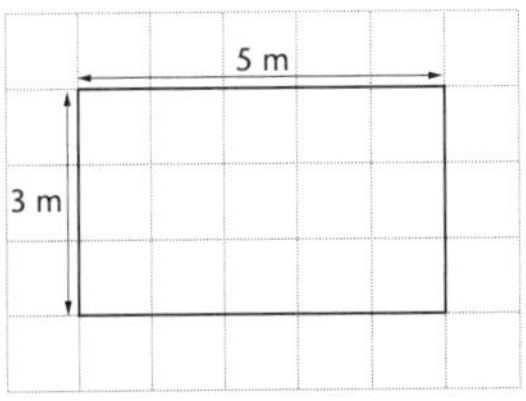

2. Cost : 80 ÷ 5 = 16
   It costs $16.00 for 1 m.
3. Total cost : 16 x 16 = 256
   The total cost is $256.00.
4. Cost : 40 x 15 = 600
   (600¢ = $6) He pays $6.00.
5. Cost : 35 x 6 = 210
   He pays $210.00.
6. Time : 9 h 45 min + 4 h + 25 min + 25 min = 14 h 35 min
   He finished at 2:35 p.m.
7. There are 3 rows of 5 squares. Area : 5 x 3 = 15
   The area of the flower bed is 15 m^2.
8. Area : 4 x 4 = 16 (16 > 15) The flower bed is bigger if it is a 4-m square.
9. No. of flowers : 12 x 15 = 180 There will be 180 flowers.
10. Cost : 8.89 + 1.33 = 10.22 He will pay $10.22.
11. Change : 10.25 – 10.22 = 0.03 The change was $0.03 or 3¢.
12. Volume (A) : 1000 x 15 = 15000 Volume (B) : 1000 x 13 = 13000
    Volume (C) : 1000 x 14 = 14000
    Pile A is 15 000 cm^3; Pile B is 13 000 cm^3, and Pile C is 14 000 cm^3.
13. No. of bricks : 15 + 13 + 14 = 42 No. of layers : 42 ÷ 4 = 10...2
    They will be 10 layers with 2 bricks left over.
14. Height : 10 x 10 = 100 (100 cm = 1 m)
    The height of the brick tower will be 1 m.
15. Volume : 1000 x 10 x 4 = 40000 The volume will be 40 000 cm^3.
16. AA shop offers a better deal. In the other shop, 10 bricks cost 500¢ ($5.00), which is $0.50 more.
17. No. of slabs : 10 x 9 = 90 He should buy 90 slabs.
18. Total cost : 90 x 3 + 25.5 = 295.5 He will pay $295.50.
19. Change : 50 – 37.28 = 12.72
    (1 $10 bill + 1 twoonie + 2 quarters + 2 dimes + 2 pennies)
    He receives 1 $10 bill, 1 twoonie, 2 quarters, 2 dimes and 2 pennies.
20. A is a cylinder; B is a triangular prism; C is a rectangular prism and D is a rectangular pyramid.
21.

Label	No. of completely covered squares	No. of mostly covered squares	Area (cm^2)
TT Biscuits	22	16	38
BB Chocolates	8	6	14

The label of TT Biscuits and BB Chocolates are about 38 cm^2 and 14 cm^2 respectively.

22. Capacity : 400 x 5 = 2000 1000 mL = 1 L ⟶ 2000 mL = 2 L
    The jug can hold 2 L of juice.
23. Mass : 25 x 80 = 2000 1000 g = 1 kg ⟶ 2000 g = 2 kg
    The total weight is 2 kg.
24. Time : 1 h 38 min + 25 min = 2 h 3 min
    All the ice cubes would melt at 2:03 p.m.
25. B
26. D
27. C
28. B
29. A
30. D
31. B
32. A

Unit 7

1. T = 90° O = 40° B = 55° F = 80°
   S = 120° F = 35° L = 60° A = 30°
2. Right angle = 90° Angle S (120°) is greater than a right angle.
3. Angle on a straight line is 180°
   Suggested answer:
   Angle T + Angle O + Angle B = 90° + 40° + 55° = 185° ✗
   Angle T + Angle L + Angle A = 90° + 60° + 30° = 180° ✓
   The sum of angles T, L and A is 180°.
4. B L A S T O F F
5.

6.

7.

8.

Challenge

The hands will next be at 90° when it is 3:30 (30 minutes to 4).

Unit 8

1. translation
2. They used reflection.
3. They used translation.
4. They used rotation.
5. They used reflection.
6. They used rotation.
7. 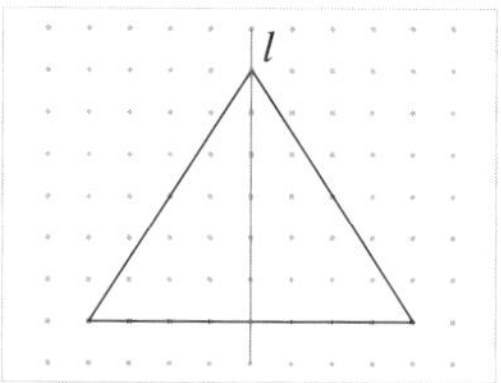

8. 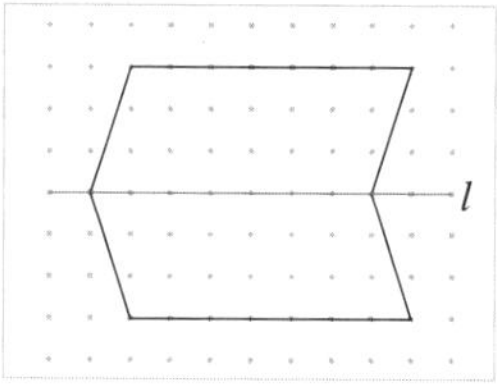

9. 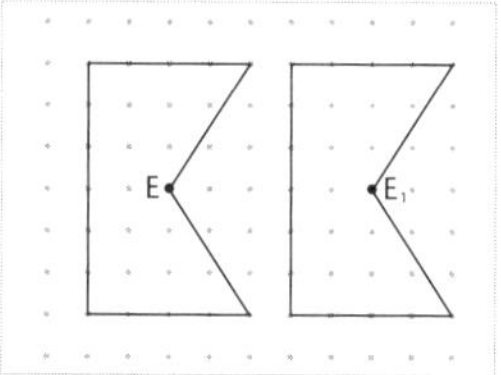

10. 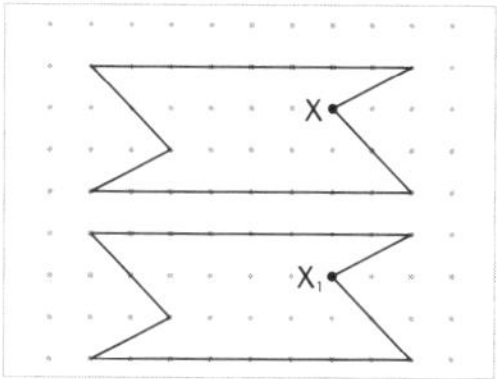

11. Irene used rotation ($\frac{1}{2}$ turn clockwise or counterclockwise) to make the image of the shape.
12. The shape is slid 5 units horizontally.
13. Yes, the shapes and their images are congruent.
14. Rotation is used to form the pattern.
15. The card has $\frac{1}{4}$ turn counterclockwise each time.
16. The next card is the same as the 2nd card  .
17. Cards 3, 7, 11, 15 and 19 would look like  .
    5 cards would look like  .
18. The 13th card would look like  .
19. The pattern repeats every 4 cards. To repeat 6 times, I would need 24 (6 x 4) cards.
20.  would be in the pattern.
21. No, the transformation would be $\frac{1}{2}$ turn clockwise or counterclockwise.
22. Cards, 1, 3, 5, 7 and 9 would be left behind.
    5 cards would be in the pattern.
23. 
24. 
25. C has the most lines of symmetry.
26. 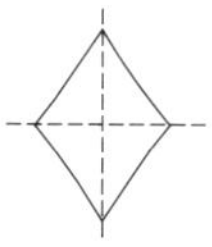
    It has 2 lines of symmetry.
27. 
    It has 1 line of symmetry.
28. A square has more lines of symmetry. It has 4 lines of symmetry and a diamond has only 2.
29. The square will become 2 rectangles. Alan could draw 2 lines of symmetry on each half.
30. The square will become 2 triangles. Alan could draw 1 line of symmetry on each half.
31. 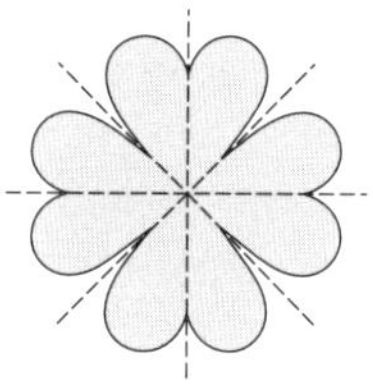

Challenge

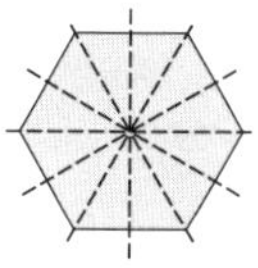
Hexagon

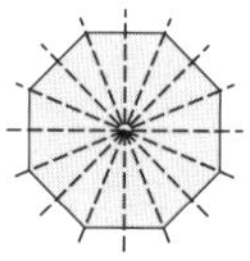
Octagon

A hexagon has 6 lines of symmetry and an octagon has 8. A decagon would have 10 lines of symmetry.

Unit 9

1. 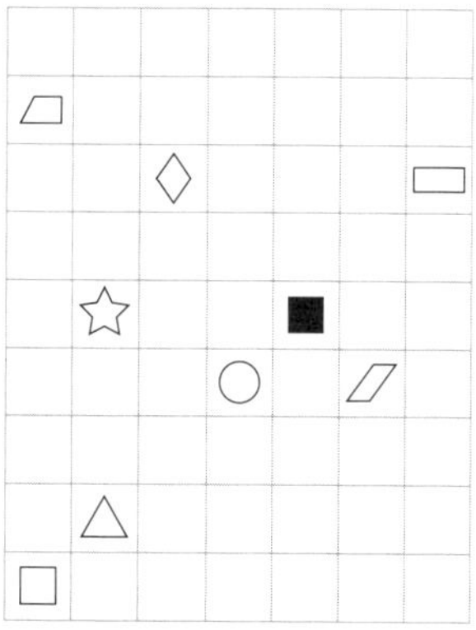
2.  is at F4 and  is at B5.
3. Rows : 1 to 9 = 9 Columns : A to G = 7
   There are 9 rows and 7 columns on the grid.
4. The ordered pairs of all the  are (1, 3), (1, 5), (2, 1) and (5, 2).
5. The ordered pairs of all the  are (2, 4), (3, 2), (3, 3), (6, 1) and (6, 5).
6. The ordered pairs of all the  are (1,1), (4, 2), (5, 4) and (6, 3).
7. Point : 1 + 3 + 2 = 6 Her score is 6.
8. Point : 3 + 1 = 4 His score is 4.
9. Irene is the winner.

10 and 11.

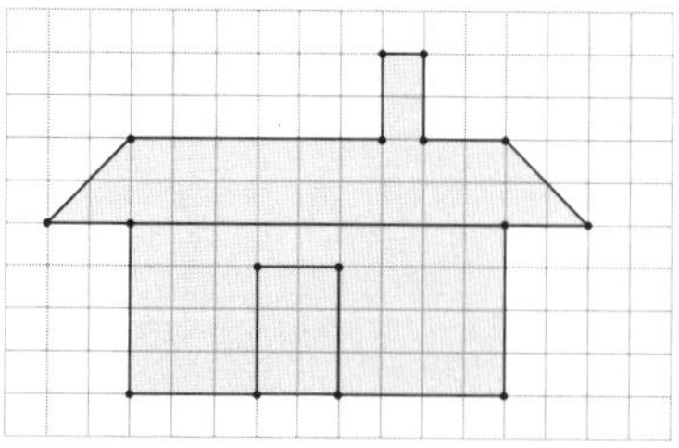

12. I have drawn a house.
13. The picture occupies 58 whole squares and 4 half-squares.
    Area : 58 + 4 ÷ 2 = 60 The area of the picture is 60 cm².
14. The ordered pairs are (9, 2), (9, 4), (11, 4) and (11, 2).
15. The ordered pairs are A (3, 4), B (0, 1) and C (6, 1).
16. They are (3, 5) and (3, 0).

17. 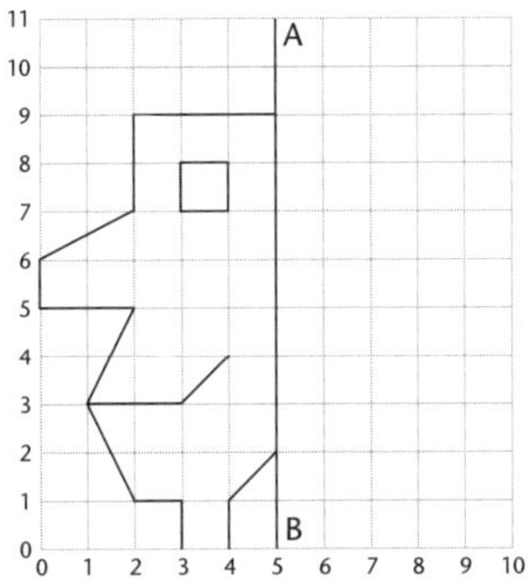

18. a. The 4 ordered pairs are (3, 7), (3, 8), (4, 8) and (4, 7).
    b. The 2 ordered pairs (2, 9) and (5, 9) show the top of the head.
    c. The 3 ordered pairs (1, 3), (3, 3) and (4, 4) show the mouth.
    d. The 4 ordered pairs (2, 7), (0, 6), (0, 5) and (2, 5) are used to make the nose.

Challenge

1. The 4 ordered pairs (6, 8), (4, 7), (4, 6) and (6, 6) would make the nose.
2. The 4 ordered pairs (6, 7), (6, 8), (7, 8) and (7, 7) would make the eye.

Unit 10

1. Likely 2. Unlikely 3. Unlikely
4. Unlikely 5. Likely
6. A die has 6 faces of different numbers.
   There are 6 possible outcomes.
7. There is only a 2 on a die. The probability is 1 out of 6.
8. There is only a 6 on a die. The probability is 1 out of 6.
9. 1, 2 and 3 are less than 4. The probability is 3 out of 6 (1 out of 2).
10. There is a 1 and a 2 on a die.
    The probability is 2 out of 6 (1 out of 3).
11. There are 3 even numbers on a die.
    The probability is 3 out of 6 (1 out of 2).
12. There are 5 numbers (1, 2, 4, 5, 6). The probability is 5 out of 6.
13. a. The probability of rolling a 2 or a 6 is 1 out of 6.
       They are equally probable.
    b. Probability of rolling a 4 : 1 out of 6.
       Probability of rolling a number less than 4 : 3 out of 6
       Rolling a 4 is less probable.
    c. Two numbers (5 and 6) are larger than 4.
       Probability of rolling a number larger than 4 : 2 out of 6
       Rolling a number less than 4 is more probable.
    d. There are no numbers larger than 6 on a die. It is not probable.
    e. Probability of rolling a 1 : 1 out of 6 It is not probable.
14. One quarter of the spinner is .
    The probability is 1 out of 4.
15. One quarter of the spinner is .
    The probability is 1 out of 4.
16. One quarter of the spinner is .
    The probability is 1 out of 4.
17. Half of the spinner is .
    The probability is 1 out of 2.
18. One-twelfth of the spinner is .
    The probability is 1 out of 12.
19. I should use spinner B. I have more chances to get .
20. I should use spinner B. I have fewer chances to get .
21. I should use spinner A. I have more chances to get .
22. Yellow ; R, Y Blue ; B, B Yellow ; B, Y
23. There are 4 possible outcomes.
24. The probability is 1 out of 4.
25. No, he is not correct. The probability of picking 2 blue balls is the same as the others.
26. The probability is 0 because there is only 1 red ball.
27. No, it would not be equally likely. It has a fewer chance to pick the red ball.

Challenge

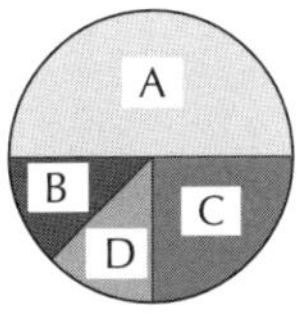

Unit 11

1. 111 people were surveyed.
2. Alan surveyed 52 people. Irene surveyed 59 people.
   Difference : 59 – 52 = 7 Irene surveyed 7 more people.
3.

Month	No. of People
Jan	卌 卌
Feb	卌 卌
Mar	卌 ////
Apr	卌 卌 //
May	卌 ///
Jun	卌 卌
Jul	卌 卌 ////
Aug	卌 卌
Sep	卌 卌 /
Oct	卌 //
Nov	//
Dec	卌 ///

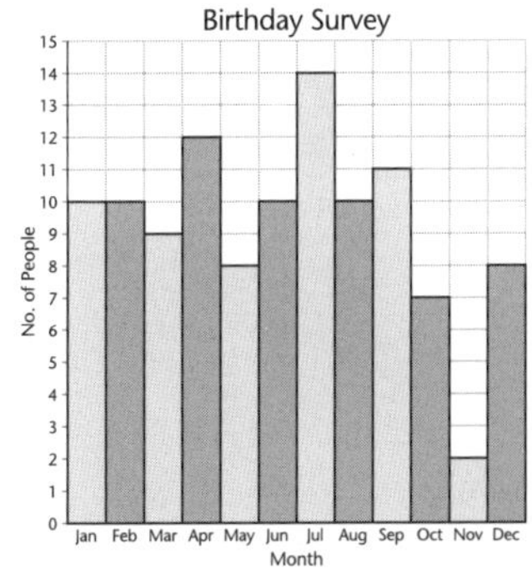

4. The title is 'Birthday Survey'. 5. The label is 'Month'.
6. The label is 'No. of People'.
7. November had the fewest birthdays.
8. July had the most birthdays.
9. Difference : 14 – 2 = 12 The difference is 12.
10. 7 months had 10 or more birthdays.
11. No, I can't. 12. No, it doesn't.
13.

No. of Birthday Parties
卌 卌 卌 卌 卌 卌 卌 卌 卌 卌 卌 卌
卌 卌 卌 卌 卌 卌 卌 卌 卌
卌 卌 卌 卌 卌 卌 卌 卌 卌 卌 卌 卌 卌 卌 卌 卌
卌 卌 卌 卌 卌 卌 卌 卌 卌 卌 卌
卌 卌 卌 卌 卌 卌 卌 卌 卌 卌 卌 卌 卌 卌
卌 卌 卌 卌 卌 卌 卌 卌 卌 卌 卌 卌 卌 卌 卌 卌 卌 卌

14. 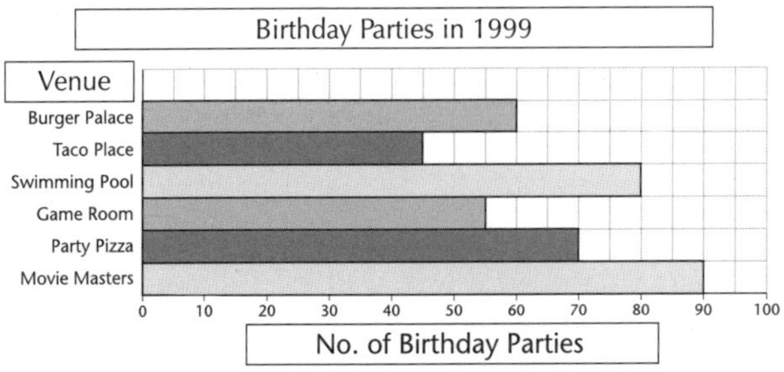

15. Taco Place held the fewest birthday parties.
16. Movie Masters held the most birthday parties.
17. Difference : 55 – 45 = 10 10 more birthday parties were held in Game Room than in Taco Place.
18. No. of birthday parties : 60 + 45 + 80 + 55 + 70 + 90 = 400
    There were 400 birthday parties altogether.

19.

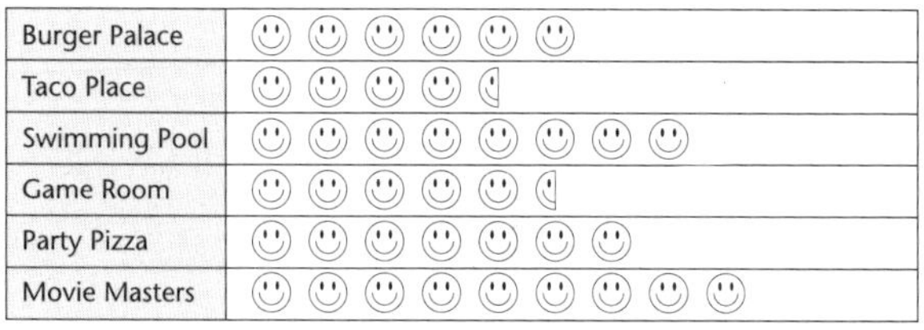

20. The best way is to use a half happy face.
21. No. of people : 60 + 45 + 70 = 175
    175 people chose to have their party at a restaurant.
22. No. of people : 55 + 90 = 145
    145 people preferred to have their party at an activity centre.
23. Fraction : $\frac{80}{400} = \frac{80 \div 80}{400 \div 80} = \frac{1}{5}$
    $\frac{1}{5}$ of the parties took place at the Swimming Pool.

Challenge

1. Yes, they do. On the bar graph, the income of D is 4 times of that of A; C is 3 times of A, and B is 2 times of A. The sectors on the circle graph are of the same proportion as the bars on the bar graph.
2. It represents the total weekly income of the 4 people.

Final Review

1, 2 and 4.

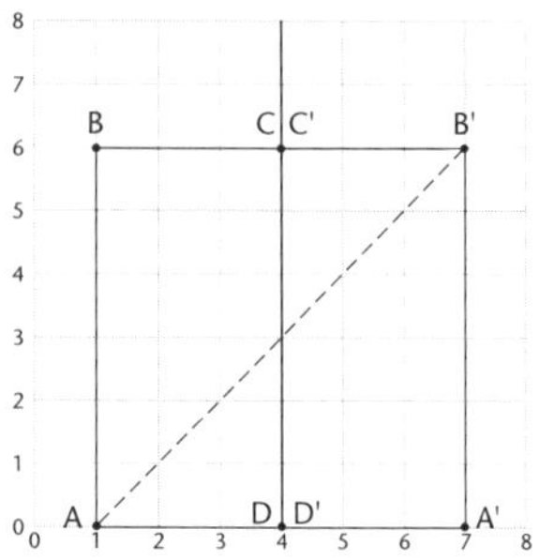

3. I have drawn a rectangle.
5. The ordered pairs are A'(7, 0), B'(7, 6), C'(4, 6) and D'(4, 0).
6. Area : 6 x 3 = 18
   The area of the shape is 18 cm^2.
7. Perimeter : 6 + 3 + 6 + 3 = 18
   The perimeter of the shape is 18 cm.
8. The image is a flipped image. If it is a slid image, the image C', B', A' and D' should be read as B', C', D' and A'.
9. The triangle occupies 15 whole squares and 6 half-squares.
   Area of the triangle : 15 + (6 ÷ 2) = 18
   The shape itself and the triangle are the same in area.
10. X is a parallelogram ; Q is a triangle ; Y is a rectangle ; T is a square
11.

	X	Q	Y	T
Perimeter (cm)	12	8.5	11	10

X, Y, T, Q

12. (1 kg = 1000 g) One set : 2 x 4 = 8 No. of sets : 1000 ÷ 8 = 125
    125 sets of these shapes would be needed to weigh 1 kg.
13. She would use shapes Y and T.
    She would use 4 Ys and 2 Ts.
14. She would use shapes Q and T.
    She would use 4 Qs and 1 T.
15.

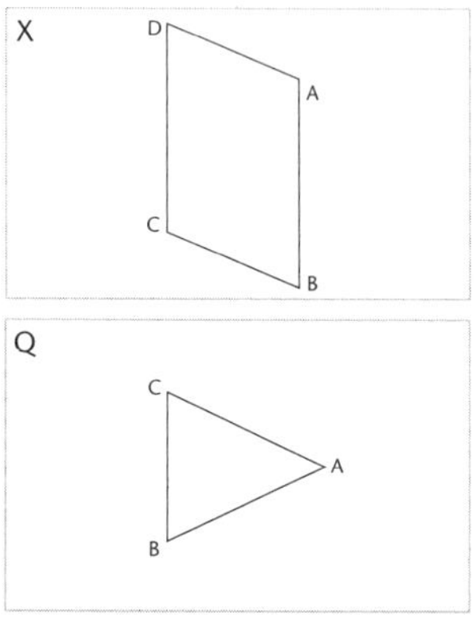

16.

Tally
////
///
/
/
//
//

17. No. of die rolls : 24 + 18 + 21 + 16 + 22 + 22 = 123
    123 die rolls were made.
18. 1 was rolled most often.
19. 4 was rolled least often.
20. Difference : 24 – 21 = 3
    There were 3 more rolls.
21. Volume : 500 x 8 = 4000
    The volume is 4000 cm^3.
22. 1000 mL = 1 L ⟶ 1000 cm^3 = 1 L ⟶ 4000 cm^3 = 4 L
    Its capacity is 4 L.
23. Time taken : 123 x 10 = 1230
    They took 1230 seconds (20.5 minutes).
24. Time : 11 h 04 min + 21 min = 11 h 25 min
    They would finish at 11:25 a.m.
25.

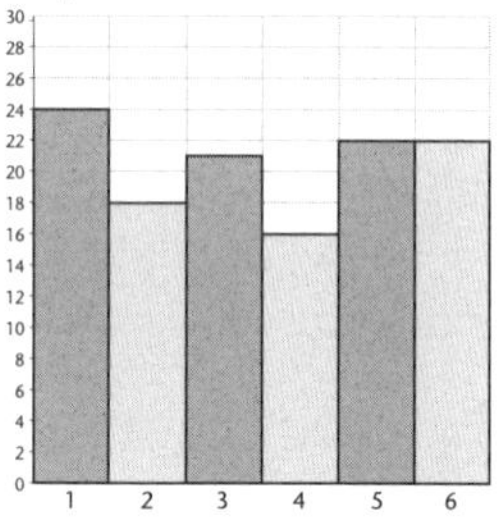

26. They would expect the probability of rolling each number to be 1 out of 6.
27. The probability of spinning each number is the same (1 out of 6) because the spinner is divided evenly into 6 parts.
28. The probability is 1 out of 6.
29. 2 numbers (5 and 6) are greater than 4.
    The probability is 2 out of 6 (1 out of 3).
30. 3 numbers (1, 2 and 3) are less than 4.
    The probability is 3 out of 6 (1 out of 2).
31.

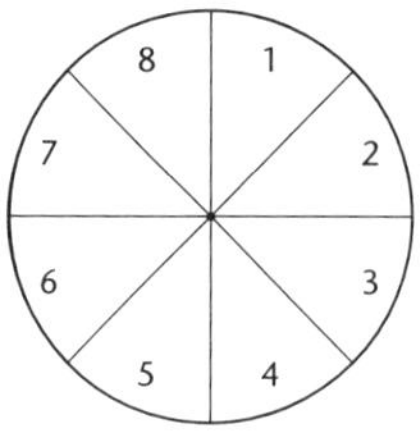

32. Angle : 360° ÷ 6 = 60°
    Each angle is 60°.
33. Angle : 360° ÷ 8 = 45°
    Each angle is 45°.
34. It can either be a cone or a cylinder.

35. D 36. B 37. A 38. C
39. B 40. D 41. B 42. C
43. A